The Sinner's Sanctuary

The Sinner's Sanctuary
Gospel Freedom from Death, Condemnation, and the Law

Hugh Binning

Edited by
David Searle

Introduced by
Sinclair B. Ferguson

Soli Deo Gloria Publications
An imprint of Reformation Heritage Books
Grand Rapids, Michigan

The Sinner's Sanctuary
© 2025 by Soli Deo Gloria

All rights reserved. No part of this book may be used or reproduced in any manner whatsoever without written permission except in the case of brief quotations embodied in critical articles and reviews. Direct your requests to the publisher at the following addresses:

Soli Deo Gloria Publications
An imprint of Reformation Heritage Books
3070 29th St. SE
Grand Rapids, MI 49512
616-977-0889
orders@heritagebooks.org
www.heritagebooks.org

Printed in the United States of America
25 26 27 28 29 30/10 9 8 7 6 5 4 3 2 1

Library of Congress Cataloging-in-Publication Data

Names: Binning, Hugh, 1627-1653, author. | Searle, David C., editor.
Title: The sinner's sanctuary : gospel freedom from death, condemnation, and the law / Hugh Binning ; edited by David Searle ; introduced by Sinclair B. Ferguson.
Description: Grand Rapids, Michigan : Soli Deo Gloria Publications, an imprint of Reformation Heritage Books, [2025] | Includes bibliographical references. | Summary: "A series of forty sermons on Romans 8:1-15"—Provided by publisher.
Identifiers: LCCN 2024061008 (print) | LCCN 2024061009 (ebook) | ISBN 9798886860214 (hardcover) | ISBN 9798886860221 (epub)
Subjects: LCSH: Bible. Romans, VIII, 1-15—Sermons. | Sermons, English—17th century.
Classification: LCC BS2665.54 .B56 2025 (print) | LCC BS2665.54 (ebook) | DDC 227/.106—dc23/eng/20250220
LC record available at https://lccn.loc.gov/2024061008
LC ebook record available at https://lccn.loc.gov/2024061009

For Neil
a brother in Christ for sixty years

CONTENTS

Hugh Binning, Preacher of *The Sinner's Sanctuary*   xi

1. The Day of Complete Redemption (Romans 8:1)   1
2. The City of Refuge (Romans 8:1)   21
3. The Marks of the Justified Believers (Romans 8:1)   31
4. The Walk of the New Man in Christ (Romans 8:1)   47
5. The Principles and Motivation of Spiritual Walking
    (Romans 8:1)   61
6. No Walking in the Spirit—No Fruit of the Spirit
    (Romans 8:1)   73
7. True Freedom in Christ (Romans 8:2)   84
8. Strive Earnestly for True Freedom in Christ
    (Romans 8:2)   94
9. Salvation for Sinners Accomplished (Romans 8:2)   104
10. The Only Remedy for Sinners (Romans 8:3)   113
11. The Fountain of Sweetest Consolation (Romans 8:3)   124
12. The Mystery of the Incarnation (Romans 8:3)   135
13. Sin Fully and Finally Dealt With (Romans 8:3)   147
14. In Christ Justice and Mercy Embrace (Romans 8:4)   156
15. The Relationship between Justification
    and Sanctification (Romans 8:4)   164
16. The Spirit Versus the Flesh (Romans 8:4–5)   172
17. The Desires of the Flesh Are against the Spirit
    (Romans 8:5)   185

18. The Great Difference between Flesh and Spirit
    (Romans 8:5–6) 197
19. The Way of Death and the Way of Life
    (Romans 8:6) 206
20. The Vile Ugliness of Enmity against God
    and the Bitter Fruit of Rebellion
    against Him (Romans 8:7) 219
21. The Implacable Enmity of the Carnal Mind
    against God (Romans 8:7–8)................... 232
22. No Other Way—In Christ Alone (Romans 8:8) 245
23. The Vivid Contrast between Those in the Spirit
    and Those in the Flesh (Romans 8:9) 253
24. The Holy Spirit Dwells in Genuine Believers
    (Romans 8:9) 262
25. Our Union with Christ through the Indwelling Spirit
    (Romans 8:9) 272
26. Love Unites Christ with the Soul That Is Cleansed
    (Romans 8:10) 281
27. The Truth about Death without Christ
    (Romans 8:10) 289
28. Christ Has Removed the Sting from Death
    (Romans 8:10) 297
29. Death's Terrors Outside of Christ Contrasted with
    Death's Joys for Those in Christ (Romans 8:10) 304
30. The Blessed Hope (Romans 8:11) 311
31. The Twofold Resurrection (Romans 8:11) 318
32. The Believer's Unlimited Eternal Debt of Love
    (Romans 8:12) 326
33. The Threefold Cord and Our Souls on the
    Weighing Scales (Romans 8:12–13) 334
34. Choose This Day Whom You Will Serve
    (Romans 8:13) 341
35. Mortification Restores Human Dignity
    (Romans 8:13–14) 348
36. The Spirit of Adoption, Part I (Romans 8:14–15) 355

37. The Unspeakable Privilege of Adoption
   (Romans 8:14–15) 362
38. The Spirit of Adoption, Part II (Romans 8:15) 369
39. What a Man Is on His Knees before God in Prayer,
   That He Is and That Alone (Romans 8:15) 376
40. Toward Understanding the Precious Privilege
   of Prayer (Romans 8:15) 383

HUGH BINNING,
Preacher of *The Sinner's Sanctuary*
Sinclair B. Ferguson

The Sinner's Sanctuary consists of a series of forty sermons on Romans 8:1–15. They were preached by Hugh Binning, minister in Govan, now part of Glasgow, on the south bank of the River Clyde in the west of Scotland. They are representative of his all-too-brief ministry from 1650 until his death in 1653 at the age of twenty-six. He was, by any measure, a remarkable minister. But today he is largely forgotten. Indeed, it is unlikely that many people (even in his native land of Scotland) would be able to place him in the long story of the kirk. We owe a debt to David Searle, the editor of this volume, for bringing Binning's ministry back to life for us in this twenty-first-century garb.

The Seventeenth Century

Hugh Binning lived during one of the most complex periods of Scottish church history, but he did not live long. He belongs, therefore, to that long-admired group of ministers who appear to us to have been cut short too early, and yet, under God, have made an impact that lingers long after their death.

The details of Binning's life can be quickly related. He was born in 1627 on his father John's estate at Dalvenan, near Kirkmichael in Ayrshire. His mother, Margaret, was a McKail, and Hugh McKail, the Covenanter martyr of 1666, was a nephew. At age thirteen, Hugh (or Hew) matriculated at the University of Glasgow, and following graduation began the study of theology with a view to the ministry. His studies were interrupted when, although only eighteen, he was elected to the post of regent in philosophy. He clearly had a measure of Calvin's genius for both memory and intellectual penetration.[1] In addition to his teaching responsibilities, he continued his theological studies and was ordained to the pastoral charge of Govan some four years later. Judging by his literary remains, of which *The Sinner's Sanctuary* represents less than a quarter, he served the people of Govan and beyond with great diligence in the brief time they were privileged to have his ministry. He died of consumption (pulmonary tuberculosis) in 1653 in his twenty-sixth year.

Binning lived in tumultuous times. It will be remembered that, following the death of Elizabeth I in 1603, the throne of England had passed from the Tudor dynasty to the Stuarts in the person of James VI of Scotland, who also became James I of England. While the crowns were thus united, the two parliaments remained independent for a further century (they were eventually united in 1707). James was deeply committed to the divine right of kings and to maintaining that right, as Elizabeth I had done, by controlling the episcopate and through them the whole church. But the underlying tensions between king and parliament that simmered during his reign erupted under his son, Charles I, and eventually led to the outbreak of the civil wars between 1642 and 1651. While these were *English* wars, they also involved the Scots. Charles's execution in January 1649 led to the establishment of a republic in England and the ensuing protectorate of Oliver Cromwell. Meanwhile, the loyal Scots proclaimed his son, Charles II, king and celebrated his coronation at Scone in Perthshire in January 1651. Two unhappy conflicts followed.

---

1. John Howie comments, "The abstruse depths of philosophy, which are the torture of a slow genius and a weak capacity, he dived into without any pain or trouble; so that, by his ready apprehension of things, he was able to do more in one hour than some others could do in many days by hard study and close application." John Howie, *The Scots Worthies*, rev. ed. (W. H. Carslaw, 1870; repr., Edinburgh: Banner of Truth Trust, 1995), 208.

Conflicts

First, a combination of Scottish support for the Stuart monarchy and his own fear of Presbyterianism establishing itself in England led Oliver Cromwell to invade and occupy Scotland. Against substantially greater numbers, his disciplined New Model Army routed the Scots at the Battle of Dunbar (1650). During his residence, Cromwell visited Glasgow, accompanied by his chaplains Joseph Caryl (who had served as one of the divines of the Westminster Assembly) and the younger but even greater figure of John Owen. A long-lived but undocumented recollection credits Hugh Binning with defending Presbyterian church order over against Congregationalism in discussions with the Independents (i.e., separatists) Caryl and Owen. After asking the name of the young man who had performed so impressively and receiving the answer "Hew Binning" (which in a West Scotland accent may well have sounded more like "Shugh Bunning"), Cromwell is reputed to have replied, "He hath bound well"—and then, placing his hand on the sword at his thigh, added, "But this will loose all again!" The story, while lacking contemporaneous documentation, is by no means impossible.

It is by no means easy for twenty-first-century Christians to appreciate how important church unity was to mid-seventeenth-century Presbyterians or why they feared congregationalism so much. Throughout the sixteenth and seventeenth centuries, a major element in the Roman Catholic Church's criticism of the Reformed churches was that one division—namely, from Rome—would inevitably produce the domino effect of uncontrollable further division. Scottish Presbyterians saw the development of Independency as a threat to unity and a fulfillment of this prophecy. They therefore regarded with deep suspicion the presence in the New Model Army of the more radical voices of Quakers, Mechanic Preachers, Ranters, and the like. For the Scots, in addition to the principle that biblical church order was presbyterian, the country's adoption of the 1638 National Covenant and the 1643 Solemn League and Covenant (between the nations) meant maintaining them was a primary, God-honoring duty. Cromwell, for his part, with his twin fears of monarchy and Presbyterianism, seems to have placed more stock in the events of providence. Thus, while he was conscious that fellow believers would lose their lives in military conflict, he read his stunning victories as evidence that God was on the side of both his strategy and his army. Hence his (in)famous letter to the general assembly of the Church of Scotland, "I beseech you, in the bowels of Christ, think it possible you may be mistaken."[2]

A second conflict emerged within the context of these external tensions. In accepting the throne in Scotland upon his father's death, Charles II professed loyalty to the Scottish covenants—a profession the church accepted. But leading Scottish ministers read his profession differently and formed essentially two parties within the kirk—"Resolutioners" (who were sympathetic to the king), and Protesters (who mistrusted him). In October 1650, the Protesters presented the kirk's general assembly with a protest against the haste with which Charles's promise had been accepted and against the willingness of the kirk to "promise… power to the king before he had evidenced any change of his principles." They further stated that "the continuing of that power in his hand was sinful till that change should appear." In the following years, they took a step further and refused to acknowledge the authority of any general assembly in which the "plurality" was "corrupt."

The tragedy inherent in the situation was the way it divided men who had been comrades in arms. Robert Baillie stood with the Resolutioners while Samuel Rutherford and George Gillespie, his fellow commissioners at the Westminster Assembly, were among the most resolute Protesters. And with the latter stood Hugh Binning. In the aftermath, Rutherford's friend David

---

2. "Life of David Dickson," in *Select Practical Writings of David Dickson* (Edinburgh: Free Church of Scotland, 1845), xlvii. Written on August 3, 1650, from Musselburgh on the outskirts of Edinburgh.

Dickson (a Resolutioner and the author of the first commentary on the Westminster Confession of Faith), acknowledged that he and his brethren had been too naive in their trust in Charles II.[3]

Although Hugh Binning was younger than other leading figures in the debates, he nevertheless played a significant part in them. But inevitably his relationship with some of his older brethren was strained, as was also true of his younger contemporary Andrew Gray.[4] And perhaps an element that added to the strain was Binning's preaching style. This leads us to the main theme of this introduction to *The Sinner's Sanctuary*.

Preaching Style

Preaching styles have varied over the years. The dominant style in any era has usually been shaped by two factors. The first is the influence of preachers to whom ministerial students listen and whom they regard as models to be followed. The second is the influence of rhetorical theories and styles—*tempora mutantur, nos et mutamur in illis* (times change, and we change with them). While the first influence is much more evident than the second, the latter nevertheless exerts a powerful, if unrecognized, influence.

In the case of Hugh Binning and of Andrew Gray (their names were coupled together in the minds of their critics), even a superficial comparison of their sermons with the standard

---

3. An insight into the strength of feeling on both sides can be found in a letter written in 1657 by the Resolutioner James Sharp in which he gives an account of a confrontation between himself and George Gillespie that took place in the presence of Oliver Cromwell, John Owen, Thomas Manton, and others in London. See William Stephen, ed., *A Register of the Consultations of the Ministers of Edinburgh and Some Other Brethren of the Ministry*, vol. 1, 1652–1657 (Edinburgh: Scottish History Society, 1921), 348–69. Sharp later became archbishop of St. Andrews and was murdered at Magus Moor in 1679.

4. Shortly after turning twenty, Andrew Gray (1633–1656) was installed as minister of the Outer High Kirk (meeting in Glasgow Cathedral) in 1653. Visitors to Glasgow Cathedral today can still see the evidence of an Outer and an Inner Church—a pulpit still stands in the outer section as well as one in the inner section of the building.

preaching style of their day reveals a striking, and apparently quite self-conscious, change.[5]

This difference was expressed in a decidedly negative way by both Robert Baillie (1602–1662) and David Dickson (1583–1663), two leading ministers in the west of Scotland and, at one time, joint holders of the chair of divinity in the University of Glasgow. Historians are indebted to the loquacious Baillie for the eyewitness accounts (not to mention scuttlebutt) he left us in his *Letters and Journals* (including correspondence from the Westminster Assembly at which he was one of the Scots commissioners). Baillie was less than sympathetic to Binning, not only because he, Baillie, was a Resolutioner while Binning adopted the view of the Protesters, but because, as an older man, he clearly did not appreciate the younger man plowing his own furrow when it came to homiletical style. In a letter to his cousin William Spang in July 1654 he wrote of Binning and of Andrew Gray,

> He hes the new guyse [style] of preaching, which Mr Hew Binning and Mr Robert Leighton began, contemning [despising] the ordinarie way of exponing [expounding] and dividing a text, of raising doctrines and uses; bot runs on in a discourse on some common head, in a high, romancing, unscriptural style, tickling the ear for the present, and moving the affections in some, bot leaving, as he confesses, little or nought to the memorie and understanding. This we must misken [be ignorant of, here probably in the sense of ignore], for we cannot help it.[6]

---

5. A comparison of Binning's sermons on Romans 8:3–4 (below, 113–86) with, for example, those of Thomas Jacomb, makes this immediately evident. See Jacomb, *Romans Eight: Verses One to Four* (Edinburgh: Banner of Truth Trust, 1996), 160–373.

6. Robert Baillie, *Letters and Journals of Robert Baillie*, ed. David Laing (Edinburgh: Robert Ogle, 1841–42), 3:258–59. The letter is dated July 19, 1654. I have maintained the original spelling but altered the medial *s* to the modern style. Twentieth-century writers in this period have taken a better view of Binning. Commenting on his preaching, Professor G. D. Henderson wrote, "He deserves to be remembered as one of the first rank of Scotland's preachers.... Every page contains something that is well said and worth saying." G.D. Henderson, *Religious*

This despite the fact that Gray's colleague in the Inner High Kirk, the great James Durham, once said that Binning's preaching "could make men's hair stand on end."[7] David Dickson's critique was similar, but with an even stronger sting in the tail. Tricks of rhetoric, Dickson allegedly commented, did not save many souls.[8]

It is a serious question whether either Baillie or Dickson actually sat under the ministry of Binning with the kind of frequency that would enable them to give a balanced assessment of his preaching. Their comments probably contain elements of truth (with respect to the description) but also elements of prejudice (with respect to the critique). And perhaps the latter was exacerbated by the differences between Binning and themselves on the issues that troubled the church at large. Nevertheless, they give us a useful entry point into reflecting on Hugh Binning the preacher and, therefore, on what to expect as we begin to read his sermons on Romans chapter eight.

For admirers of Binning, it would be the find of the decade were a journal penned by him to be unearthed in an as-yet-uncatalogued box of manuscripts somewhere in one of the great libraries of Scotland—especially if it contained his reflections on preaching. Nevertheless, in the absence of such a discovery, it is clear that even prior to his preaching ministry he had given careful thought to basic questions of understanding and communication. As regent in philosophy, he had already established a reputation for deconstructing the approach and dense

---

Life in XVII Century Scotland (London: Cambridge University Press, 1937), 216. Likewise, Principal John Macleod commends the way he paid "special attention to the vesture of [his] thought. A thinker like Binning had thoughts that it was worth a man's while to clothe in worthy words." John Macleod, *Scottish Theology*, 3rd ed. (1943; repr., Edinburgh: Banner of Truth Trust, 2015), 95.

7. Robert Wodrow, *Analecta, Or Materials for a History of Remarkable Providences Mostly Relating to Scotch Ministers and Christians*, ed. M. Leishman (Edinburgh: Maitland Club, 1842–43), 3:54.

8. William G. Blaikie, *The Preachers of Scotland* (Edinburgh: T&T Clark, 1888), 134. Blaikie provides no documentation, but the relationship between Baillie and Dickson lends credibility to the criticism.

vocabulary of the older scholastic methodology and simplifying the approach to philosophical issues. This move on his part is undoubtedly reflected in his preaching. Baillie referred to the traditional style of preaching as exposition and division—analyzing doctrines and then proceeding to various aspects and dimensions of their application. His colleagues at the Westminster Assembly advocated this approach as "found by experience to be very much blessed of God, and very helpful for the people's understandings and memories."[9] But they had not regarded it as fixed according to the law of the Medes and Persians, and acknowledged, "This method is not prescribed as necessary for every man, or upon every text."[10] One has the impression Robert Baillie was less flexible.

It may be helpful to set this view of the Westminster divines (including Baillie) in a broader context. Perhaps Baillie might have been more sympathetic had Gray, Leighton, and Binning been older men. Even Robert Leighton (1611–1684), whom he associates with Binning and Gray, was a decade younger.[11] Older men often find it irksome when younger men (perhaps assumed

---

9. The Directory for Public Worship (1645), "Of the Preaching of the Word."
10. Directory, "Of the Preaching of the Word."
11. Robert Leighton seems to have been viewed as the fountain of the new style of preaching and was regularly associated in that context with both Hugh Binning and Andrew Gray. It is perhaps significant in the light of the following comments on Peter Ramus that Leighton did not seem to have a particularly high view of the beneficial effects of the study of Aristotle. In the seventh of his series of *Exhortations to the Candidates for the Master of Arts in the University of Edinburgh*, he told them, "To speak the truth, the philosophy which prevails in the schools, is of a vain, airy nature, and more apt to inspire the mind with pride rather than to improve it." Robert Leighton, *The Whole Works of Robert Leighton, D.D.* (New York: Robert Carter and Brothers, 1859), 719. Leighton later became Bishop of Dunblane and then Archbishop of Glasgow. His works include a still-famous exposition of 1 Peter. Perhaps significantly, the plaque commemorating him in St. Giles Cathedral, Edinburgh, bears the words, "Blessed are the peacemakers for they shall be called children of God" (Matt. 5:9). Seventeenth-century Scotland was not an easy time or place in which to be a man of irenic spirit, not least for one willing to accept the office of bishop, even if he viewed the role as that of pastor and preacher.

therefore to be *immature*) buck long-accepted patterns. But those patterns were not quite so long accepted in the Reformed churches as might be assumed from listening to Robert Baillie's critique.

Reformed Preaching

A glance at the sermons preached by John Calvin during his long ministry in Geneva reveals a different pattern of preaching from the formula of the Westminster divines (and doubtless illustrates the wisdom of *not* establishing it as required for all). Certainly, Calvin's sermons contain biblical doctrine and are rich in application, but they are by no means shaped according to the Westminster formula. Understandably so, since at the height of his powers Calvin was preaching every weekday and twice on the Lord's Day. And he characteristically employed the *lectio continua* method, working his way systematically, day after day, through whole books of the Bible, only occasionally peaching on what would later be called an "ordinary."[12] Calvin was burdened with many additional responsibilities—serving as professor of Old Testament and lecturing each week, sustaining a massive correspondence, sitting on Thursdays with other members of the Consistory listening to the pastoral flotsam and jetsam of Geneva, participating in the meetings of local ministers on Fridays, writing commentaries and various treatises, and revising his *Institutes*. In addition, his health was far from robust. While it must have been exhilarating for parishioners to wait only twenty-three hours for the next sermon, from a practical point of view, this placed massive demands on Calvin's time, so preaching *lectio continua* was essential to sustaining such an intense program of biblical exposition. Yet, there was a beautiful simplicity in his homiletical approach, and he certainly never transgressed the later warning of the Westminster divines that a preacher ought

---

12. A text or passage to which the preacher would return in successive sermons in an extended exposition of its doctrine and uses.

"not always to prosecute every doctrine which lies in his text."[13] Nor did he burden his hearers with multiple divisions.

What, then, explains the transition to the method that Baillie regarded as normative? While we do not have access to Binning's personal thought processes, we are able to trace at least one major influence on this standard method in preaching. It lies in the work of the French humanist scholar Pierre de La Ramée (Peter Ramus, 1517–1572).

Peter Ramus

Born a Roman Catholic, Ramus became a Calvinist and was killed in the St. Bartholomew's Day Massacre in Paris in 1572. A creative thinker (inter alia, he suggested the abolition of university tuition fees), Ramus was critical of Aristotle, particularly his logic. His position inevitably set him on a collision course with the authorities since Aristotle's work had been almost canonized through the acceptance and use of the theology of Thomas Aquinas. Ramus sought to replace Aristotelian complexity with what he saw as a method of greater simplicity—influenced (so it seems to the present writer) by his great interest in the connected disciplines of logic and mathematics. For Ramus, then, a key to both understanding and communication in any discipline was the *organization* of the subject matter by the teacher so that it could be more readily understood and more clearly communicated. At its best, the method enabled a teacher or communicator, in this case the preacher, to state his theme or topic and then divide it—that is, analyze it stage by stage to lay bare its significance.[14]

To the extent that this new method became influential and began to permeate much (but by no means all) university teaching, its impact was felt most by men whose ultimate goal

---

13. Directory, "Of the Preaching of the Word."

14. An indication of how far Ramus's influence spread in Europe is seen in the life of one of his pupils, Andrew Melville, who was a major influence in the development of the Reformed churches in Scotland. Thomas M'Crie, *The Life of Andrew Melville*, 2nd ed. (Edinburgh: William Blackwood, 1824), 23–24.

was communication—teaching large numbers of people through the regular exposition of Scripture. And so, the development of the so-called Plain Style of preaching, which focused on understanding and application rather than on literary eloquence and aesthetic effect, found the Ramist approach a helpful handmaid. This is not to say that preachers were self-consciously Ramists, any more than most preachers today reflect to any great extent on the source and nature of the influences that lie behind the way they preach. But such influences are always present. They are as present today, even if often unnoticed, just as much as the Ramist influence was present in evangelical preaching from the late sixteenth through the seventeenth centuries. We would be naive to assume contemporary methods of preaching simply employ the method sempiternal.

Seventeenth-Century Preaching

The role of Peter Ramus in the development of Puritan preaching should not be misinterpreted as though what was preached was Ramism rather than Scripture. This was certainly emphasized in the most famous book on preaching to emerge within the English Puritan movement—namely, *The Arte of Prophecying* by William Perkins (1558–1602).[15] Indeed, Perkins's lesser-known contemporary, Richard Bernard (1568–1642), argued that the method was in fact itself biblical. In his pastoral manual, *The Faithful Shepherd*, he specifically argued from 1 Corinthians 11:23–34 that this pattern of preaching was already evident in the ministry of the apostle Paul. We can enumerate his argument as follows:[16]

---

15. The original publication was written in Latin by Perkins in 1592 and was therefore addressed primarily, if not exclusively, to preachers rather than to their hearers. It was posthumously published in English in 1606.

16. As summarized in Richard Bernard, "Dedicatory Letter," in *The Faithfull Shepherd, Wholly in a Manner transposed, and made anew, and very much inlarged, both with precepts and examples, to further young Divines in the study of Divinitie* (London: printed by Arnold Hatfield for John Bill, 1621).

1. vv. 23–25: The text, drawn from Matthew 26:26–28
2. v. 26: The scope of the exposition
3. v. 27: The doctrine
4. v. 28: The use of the doctrine
5. v. 29: The reason that reinforces the doctrine
6. vv. 30–31: The application
7. v. 32: The answer to an objection
8. vv. 33–34: The exhortation and summary repetition of what was reprehended, and its remedy

Even a cursory glance at the section on preaching in the Directory for Public Worship reveals the extent to which this perspective became almost de rigueur.[17] Whether or not Binning had read Richard Bernard, he was certainly very familiar with the Directory. But he clearly felt this method was not one he should adopt. In fact, he explicitly (and boldly) spells out his concerns about the standard practice at the beginning of sermon 23 in *The Sinner's Sanctuary* (on Romans 8:9):

> Paul speaks of a right dividing of the word of truth (2 Tim. ii:15.): not that ordinary way of cutting it all in parcels, and dismembering it, by manifold divisions, which I judge makes it lose much of its virtue [i.e., power, force], which consists in union, though some have pleasure in it, and think it profitable; yet I do not see that this was the apostolic way, that either

---

17. The Inner High Kirk and the Outer High Kirk in Glasgow constituted two sections of the same building. By contrast with Andrew Gray's preaching, that of James Durham, Gray's next-door neighbor in the Inner High Kirk, very clearly illustrated the Westminster method. At the end of his expositions of the letters to the churches in Revelation 2:1–3:22 he includes an excursus on preaching, arguing that these two chapters exemplify the preaching of Christ to the churches and therefore provide preachers with significant indications of the nature of true preaching. See James Durham, *A Commentarie upon the Book of the Revelation* (Glasgow: Robert Sanderson, 1680), 223–29. Parallels abound between what Durham says in this essay and the section, "Of the Preaching of the Word," in The Directory for the Public Worship of God (1645)—a document in which the Scots Commissioners to the Westminster Assembly were heavily involved. See Baillie, *Letters and Journals*, 2:117, 131, 148.

they preached it themselves, or recommended it to others; but rather he means, the real distribution of the food of souls unto their various conditions, as it is the duty of a steward to be both faithful and wise in that, to give every one their own portion....[18]

Perhaps Binning felt that while exegesis of Scripture is a work possible for a person of any age, detailed pastoral application that extends a sermon to an hour or longer is probably beyond the capacity of someone comparatively recently out of his teens; indeed, it could be inappropriate and therefore unwise. How Binning's preaching might have developed had he lived longer is a matter of some speculation. Robert Wodrow—who believed his ministry would have been more profitable to his congregation if he had followed the common method—records that at the end of his life, Binning himself reached the same conclusion:

> He followed much Mr Leighton's way of preaching, which made him less useful to the common people of Govan. Mr R. Muir of Kilbride told me, that Mr Ralf Rodger told him, that Mr Binning, at his death, did very much regrate [regret] him his taking such a way of preaching; and said, if he had lived, he was fully resolved to have followed that way of preaching, by doctrine, reasons, and uses, which he declared he was then pleased with.[19]

Hugh Binning's Preaching

We have only edited versions of the sermon manuscripts Binning left behind, without any indication of the extent to which they were pruned for publication by his original editors. Nor do we know the extent to which he may have elaborated on his written text in the pulpit. Given the preaching traditions among

---

18. Hugh Binning, *The Works of Hugh Binning*, ed. M. Leishman, 4th ed. (Edinburgh: A. Fullerton and Co., 1858), 213–14.

19. Wodrow, *Analecta*, 3:40. Wodrow also records that Ralf Roger remembered Binning saying that "his manner of preaching was matter of griefe to him." *Analecta*, 3:438.

Scottish evangelicals in this period, it is highly unlikely that he took his manuscript into the pulpit with him, and so the time taken to communicate the material contained in the written text and the time taken to preach the sermon was almost certainly not identical. The sermons as written in *The Sinner's Sanctuary* would typically not have taken more than half an hour to preach.

But it is not only form, or for that matter length with its corresponding impact on detailed content, that marks out Binning's sermons. His typical approach is different and much more varied than the standard method. He sounds much more topical than exegetical, and indeed he is. And so, by and large, his introductions can begin at some distance from the details of the specific text. Rather than beginning by unfolding its words, he employs the main theme and gradually leads the hearer toward the truth of the text. Binning is not so much an *exegetical* preacher as he is a *thematic* expositor.

From all accounts, Binning had already reflected on these rhetorical and methodological issues as a teacher of philosophy. And granted that lecturing and preaching are different communication genres, it is very often the case that a person's general approach in one genre comes to expression in the way he communicates in the other. In my own view, this is very evident in Binning's sermons. It would, however, be a false move on our part if we assumed from the critique of Baillie and Dickson that his sermons are lacking in order or in application.[20] He did not throw out the baby with the bathwater, as it were. There is order and development, and there is no lack of application. What is different is the route by which he draws his hearers into the central motif on which he wants to focus attention, placing less demand on the memory of the hearer.

---

20. The same is true of the sermons of Andrew Gray who appears to have been an exceedingly popular preacher, more so than the learned James Durham, his neighbor in the Inner High Kirk (Glasgow Cathedral). There was apparently sufficient free space in the Inner High Kirk for Durham to find himself preaching to the *overflow* from the Outer High Kirk where Andrew Gray occupied the pulpit.

That is not to say that his sermons are popular in the sense of being light or superficial. Binning's preaching makes its own demands on the listener. It is possible to detect the philosopher in Hugh Binning, leading us gently to reflect with him on his great theme. And it is possible that the impetus here was not only his predilection for conceptual thinking; it may also have been an evangelistic tactic designed to interest the hearer and to stimulate thought. If so, Binning would be neither the first nor the last preacher to depart from the Ramist method. Richard Bernard might be able to trace it in 1 Corinthians 11, but not *everywhere* in Paul, nor in the preaching of the One whom the common people heard so gladly.

Yet, it is important to stress that Binning does seek to expound and apply God's Word. Sermon 10, the first of four sermons on Romans 8:3, provides a random sample that illustrates (1) the difference in Binning's preaching, (2) the way he holds up his theme and draws the hearer in, while at the same time (3) he expounds the text and (4) is sensitive to the importance of application. He begins by holding up God's sending of Christ into the world the way a jeweler might hold up a diamond to the light. He then points us to three of its facets before he reaches his peroration: the reason Christ was sent, what He accomplished, and what the effect of this is in our lives.

David Dickson was surely inappropriately critical in saying that Binning's and Gray's "tricks of rhetoric" would not save souls. After all, the traditional method was a form of rhetoric. As we can see in sermon 10, Binning was not lacking in expressing the importance of coming to faith in Christ:

> This, then, I leave upon your consciences, beseeching you to lay to heart the impossibility you are encompassed with on both hands; justice requiring a ransom, and you have none, and justice requiring new obedience again, and you can give none; old debts urging you, and new duty pressing you, and ye alike disabled for both; that so finding yourselves thus environed with indigency and impossibility within, you may be

constrained to flee out of yourselves unto him that is both able and willing. This is not a superficial business, as you make it. It is not a matter of fancy, or memory, or expression, as most make it. Believe me, it is a serious business, a soul-work, such an exercise of spirit as useth to be when the soul is between despair and hope. Impossibility within, driving a soul out of itself, and possibility, yea, certainty of help without, even in Christ, drawing a soul in to him. Thus is the closure made, which is the foundation of our happiness.[21]

Influence and Lessons

Did Binning contribute to a transformation in Scottish preaching? That question would be a worthy research project for a doctoral student to pursue. As we have noted, preachers tend to be shaped by the preaching they hear and by the training they receive, directly or indirectly, from their teachers. There is doubtless a thesaurus of Scottish homiletical material from the two hundred years after Binning on which such a study could be based. And given the fact that Binning's various works were reprinted over the years, it might be possible to trace his influence. But whether by immediate influence or simply by rerouting the stream a little, Binning's preaching does exhibit some characteristics that emerge in the later tradition of Scottish preaching. And there are certainly lessons (or perhaps uses) that can be gleaned from reflecting on his preaching.

Perhaps our first reflection should be to moderate the impact of Baillie's comment that Binning's preaching was of a "high, romancing, unscriptural style, tickling the ear for the present, and moving the affections in some."[22] To a modern reader, this conveys the impression of preaching that was both superficial and overly emotional. But as becomes clear when reading Binning, he did not make the mistake of seeking to bypass the intellect in order directly to appeal to and affect the emotions. If

---

21. See below, page 123.
22. Baillie, *Letters and Journals*, 3:258–59.

indeed he shared Jonathan Edwards's desire that his preaching should touch and raise the affections of his hearers, he also held with Edwards that the preacher does not address the affections directly as though he could circumvent the mind.[23] Rather, the reality of the truth communicated to the mind will in turn have a corresponding impact and influence on the affections commensurate with the nature of the truth communicated. And certainly the solemnity of Binning's closing words in sermon 10 (quoted above) should be adequate to dismiss any thought that he was merely a tickler of ears. In fact, he meets C. S. Lewis's communication test: we should not tell those to whom we communicate (either in speaking or in writing) *how they should feel* about something. Rather, we should describe and expound that something *so that they will thus feel* about it.[24]

Second, a distinction can be made between preaching that seems to carry with it the atmosphere of the workshop and preaching that has the atmosphere of the showroom. He does not overload his preaching by taking us down the diamond mine, as it were, to demonstrate to us how its detailed workings produce precious stones. He takes us straight to the jeweler's shop to show and sell us the ring. He does not burden us with details of how he came to understand the text in the way he does, or by detailing the technicalities of interpreting it. He holds up the finished product, the ring, so that we can admire and purchase it.

Third, Binning's preaching still requires careful attention and thought—he was, at that time, a preacher who taught philosophy until recently. His approach to preaching deliberately avoids the kind of intensity of information and multiplicity of divisions that can give hearers too little breathing space for

---

23. Jonathan Edwards, *Some Thoughts on the New England Revival* (Boston, 1743; repr., Edinburgh: Banner of Truth Trust, 2005), 115–17.
24. C. S. Lewis, *Letters to Children*, ed. L. W. Dorsett and M. L. Mead (London: William Collins, 1985), 63–64.

meditation, reflection, and personal application. Perhaps Binning had learned something here from his master. The Lord Jesus Himself told the apostles that He had many things still to teach them, "but you cannot bear them now" (John 16:12). It is the Spirit, not the preacher, who is the ultimate teacher. He takes what is Christ's and shows it to us (John 16:14). Good preaching allows Him space to work in the minds and hearts of its hearers.

If we fast-forward through the following centuries, we can find examples of how the novel characteristics of Binning's preaching reappeared in different form. If speculation is permitted in assessing historical figures, then my own suspicion is that even if Wodrow's testimony to Binning's volte-face in relation to the older method is accurate, Binning's employment of it, had he lived, would have been less rigorous than it had become in the hands of some. So, for example, in the eighteenth century, we see Thomas Boston employ less intensity of division and subdivision—although the general form remains. And in the nineteenth century, it seems to have been relatively common in Thomas Chalmers's sermons, in distinction from the lecture, to approach the text from a thematic distance, drawing the hearer in to the theme or burden of the text. And while in Robert Murray M'Cheyne there is a more immediate focus on the text, the form of the sermon has a much greater simplicity than was suggested by the Westminster divines. There is a studied lack of heaviness, and a spirit of inviting hearers to admire the ring rather than descend into the mine to discover how the precious jewel was excavated. In him, Binning has at least one young and notable successor.[25]

Finally, Binning's preaching also demonstrates a basic principle that is well illustrated in the history of Scottish preaching: individuality. Preachers need to grow in the gifts of personality

---

25. Interestingly, at the beginning of his ministry, Robert M'Cheyne also tended to eschew divisions, but came to recognize their usefulness in helping hearers to follow the development of the sermon.

and ministry God has given them, and, no matter how much they may admire them, not pretend to possess the gifts others have. Only in this way will they be fully themselves. The cloning process that is sometimes created in schools and training programs is usually a hindrance to this aspect of preaching. Baillie tended toward a one-size-fits-all methodology, which tends to produce a level of competence, but in that context a young preacher may never get beyond the sameness that such fixed methods of approach tend to produce.

We know from Robert Baillie's own testimony that as professor of divinity in Glasgow he taught a class which covered the section on preaching in the Directory for Public Worship.[26] No doubt he would have preferred that Hugh Binning had sat under his instruction. But had Binning preached as Baillie would have preferred, he would have been a young David wearing Saul's homiletical armor. Perhaps rather daringly, the young philosopher-pastor preferred the stones and sling he knew he could employ effectively, rather than a method that would have denied who he really was and the specific way he was wired with the gifts of Christ. Clearly Binning was developing his views on preaching—natural enough since he was still in his twenties— but it would be idle to speculate about his development had he lived.

Thus, while Richard Bernard might claim that the standard method was to be found in Scripture, the truth of the matter was, and still is, that Ezekiel could never have preached Isaiah's sermons, nor Paul the sermons of the apostle John, and vice versa. The Scriptures are rich in illustrations of Phillips Brooks's famous definition of preaching as modes of communication. Moreover, it seems certain that the Lord Jesus, the preacher par excellence, had more than one mode of communication; so it would be erroneous to make a single mode the permanent

---

26. Robert Baillie to David Dickson, March 8, 1651, Baillie, *Letters and Journals*, 3:131.

model. Presumably, Robert Baillie could not have preached the sermons of Hugh Binning with ease, and the reverse is almost certainly true—a principle that Richard Bernard himself could have illustrated from Scripture.

There was a day when books of sermons sold and passed through several editions. That is rarely true today. It is also true that *reading* a sermon is different from being present in person when it was preached. Today, however, we are not restricted to written versions of what we have not heard in person—we are able to hear and see preaching at any hour of the day or night. But Hugh Binning's sermons come from another era than ours; his style of preaching is different from the sermons most contemporary Christians hear. But when we travel to a foreign country and see it through the eyes of its citizens, we then return home to discover that we now also view our own country in a different light. So too, it can prove to be an illuminating and even life-redirecting experience to make the reading journey to another place and another time. It is, no doubt, the editor's and publisher's joint desire that this will be true for readers of Hugh Binning's *The Sinner's Sanctuary*.

So, thanks to David Searle's devoted labors in giving a modern hue to Hugh Binning's seventeenth-century Scottish accent and vocabulary, in these pages you can be transported back in time and perhaps far away in space to the south banks of the River Clyde, to find yourself among the citizens of Govan coming to hear their remarkable young parish minister. The grace and power of his sermons belie his youthfulness. Perhaps not all who came could follow in detail what their minister was teaching them, but his sense of the wonder of the gospel and of the privileges of the Christian life would surely have touched them deeply. And they still communicate to us that there is no greater privilege in all the world than being a Christian. So, the original publishers of *The Sinner's Sanctuary* were surely right to tell its first readers—however quaintly they may seem to us to have expressed it—

If worthiness of matter—as the curious carved stones of the temple were to the disciples—be amiable to thine eyes, and nervous sentences, solid observations, with a kind of insinuating, yet harmless behaviour, be taking with thy spirit, here they are also. And acquainting thyself with them, either as the sinner or the saint (which thine own conscience shall best inform thee of), there shall be virtue found to proceed from them, either for thy soul's refining from the dross of this corrupt age, or to a diligent heed-taking to preserve thyself pure from the pollutions which are in the world through lust, to be more and more pure against the day and coming of Christ our Saviour.[27]

And still today, although at a distance of three hundred fifty years, read thoughtfully and meditated on quietly, Binning's sermons can reproduce the same experience.

---

27. From the original Preface to *The Sinner's Sanctuary*, reprinted in *The Works of Hugh Binning* (Grand Rapids: Reformation Heritage Books, 2021), 118.

SERMON 1

The Day of Complete Redemption

There is therefore now no condemnation to them which are in Christ Jesus, who walk not after the flesh, but after the Spirit.
—ROMANS 8:1

The Threefold Evils Which Afflict Us

There are three things which concur to make man miserable—sin, condemnation, and affliction. Everyone may observe that "man is born to trouble, as the sparks fly upward" and that his days here are few and evil. He "is made to possess months of vanity and wearisome nights are appointed" for him (Job 5:7; 7:3). He is "of few days and full of trouble" (Job 14:1). Heathens have written many meditations on the misery of man's life, and in this have outstripped most Christians. We count among our miseries only some afflictions and troubles, such as poverty, sickness, reproach, banishment, and the like.

The heathen have numbered even the natural necessities of humanity among our miseries—to be continually turned around in a circle of eating, drinking, and sleeping. What burden should it be to an immortal spirit constantly to tread round on that wheel! While Christians make more of the body than the soul,[1] the heathen have accounted this body a burden to the soul. They

---

1. He means that Scripture teaches that our bodies are to be cleansed and rendered fit to be temples of the living God (e.g., see 2 Cor. 6:14–7:1).

place among the greatest miseries of men prosperity, honor, pleasure, and such things upon which men pour out their souls. For they see them as vanity and vexation in themselves, both in the enjoying and losing of them. But alas, they have not known the fountain of all this misery, which is sin and its final accomplishment, namely, condemnation. They thought trouble came out of the ground and dust, either by a natural necessity or by chance. However, the Word of God uncovers to us both the ground of our misery and its end.

The Grounds of Human Miseries

Its ground and beginning were man's defection from God and so walking according to the flesh. It has been from this corrupt fountain that all the calamities and streams of miseries in the world have flowed. It has not only extended itself to all humanity but even to the whole creation, subjecting it to futility (Rom. 8:20). "O man," said the Lord to Adam, "not only shall you eat your food in pain, but the ground is cursed because of you, and you who were created immortal, will return to the dust which you have magnified above your soul" (Gen. 3:17–19).

The end of man's defection is the outcome of the beginning, in that the beginning had all the evil of sin in it, and now the end has all the evil of punishment in it. These streams of this life's wretched state flow into an infinite, boundless, and bottomless ocean of eternal wrath. If you live according to the flesh you shall die, for "to set the mind on the flesh is death" (Rom. 8:6), and this means not only death here, but eternal death after this. The miseries then of this present life are not a proportionate punishment of sin: they are but a guarantee given of that massive debt which is to be paid on the final day of reckoning—that is, condemnation—for they "shall be punished with everlasting destruction from the presence of the Lord, and from the glory of his power" (2 Thess. 1:9).

The Remedy for Human Misery
Now, as the law exposes the perfect misery of mankind, so the gospel has brought to light a perfect remedy of all this misery. Jesus Christ was manifested to take away sin, and therefore His name is "Jesus, for he will save his people from their sins" (Matt. 1:21). This is the Lamb of God who takes away the sins of the world. Judgment was by one unto condemnation of all, but now there is "no condemnation to them which are in Christ Jesus" (Rom. 8:1).

Thus two evils are removed, which indeed have all evil in them. First, He takes away the curse of the law, made upon all who are under it; second, by His Holy Spirit He takes away the sin against the law. He has a twofold virtue, for He "came by water and blood" (1 John 5:6–7)—by blood to cleanse away the guilt of sin, and by water to purify us from sin itself.

However, in the meantime there are many afflictions and miseries common to all humanity that come upon us. You may ask, "Why are not these removed by Christ?" I say, the evil of them is taken away, though they themselves remain. Death is not taken away, but the sting of death is removed. Although death, afflictions, and all miseries are overcome by Jesus Christ, so they have become His instruments in order that we might benefit by them. The evil in them is God's wrath and our sinfulness, but these are now removed by Jesus Christ.

Though Sin Remains in Us It No Longer Has Dominion
They would be removed completely if it were not for our good that they remain because "all things work together for good to them that love God" (Rom. 8:28). So then we have a most complete deliverance in extent, but not in degree. Sin remains in us but not in dominion and power. Wrath is sometimes kindled because of our sin, but it cannot ever increase to everlasting burnings. Afflictions and miseries may change their name and be called "discipline" and "trials," and as such they are good and

not evil. Nevertheless, Christ has reserved for us until another day our full and perfect deliverance which is therefore called the day of complete redemption, when all sin, wrath, and misery shall have an end and be swallowed up through our "adoption, to wit, the redemption of our body" (Rom. 8:23). This is the sum of the gospel, and this is the substance of this chapter.

Our Consolation in Christ Jesus

The threefold consolation answerable to our threefold evils is that there is "no condemnation to those who are in Christ Jesus." Here in our text is a blessed message to condemned, lost sinners who have that sentence within their breasts. This was the purpose of Christ's coming and dying, that He might deliver us from sin as well as from death, and so that the righteousness of the law might be fulfilled in us. This is why He has given the Holy Spirit, and dwells in us by the Spirit, to quicken us who are "dead in trespasses and sins" (Eph. 2:1).

Oh, what consolation will this be to souls who look upon the body of death within them as the greatest misery and groan with Paul, "O wretched man that I am! Who shall deliver me from the body of this death?" (Rom. 7:24)! This cry arises from Romans 7:17: "Now then it is no more I that do it, but sin that dwelleth in me." But because there are many grounds of heaviness and sadness in this world, the gospel opposes them. It bestows upon us the expectation we have of that blessed hope to come, of which we are so sure that nothing can rob us of it. In the meantime, "the Spirit also helpeth our infirmities" and "all things work together for good to them that love God" (8:26, 28).

From all this the believer in Jesus Christ has grounds of triumph and boasting before the perfect victory, even as Paul does in the name of believers, from verse 31 to the end. Upon these considerations, he who cried out not long before, "O wretched man that I am! Who shall deliver me from the body of this death?" now cries out, "Who shall condemn me?" The distressed wrestler has become a victorious champion; the defeated soldier has become more than conqueror. Oh, that your hearts could be persuaded to hearken to this joyful sound and to embrace Jesus Christ for grace and salvation! How quickly would a song of triumph in Christ swallow up all your present complaints and lamentations!

The Threefold Lament
All the complaints among men may be reduced to one or other of these three—I hear the most part bemoaning themselves thus: either (1) "Alas, for the afflictions and unhappiness of this life, this evil world!" or else (2) "Alas for poverty, for contempt, for sickness! Oh! miserable man that I am, who will take this disease away?" or else (3) "Who will show me any good thing?"—any temporal good? (Ps. 4:6). But if you knew and considered your final end on the last day, you would cry out more and you would refuse to be comforted even if these three causes of complaint were removed.

But I hear some bemoaning themselves more sadly because they have heard the law and the sentence of condemnation that is coming upon them. The law has entered and "killed" them. "Oh! What shall I do to be saved?" they cry. "Who will deliver me from the wrath to come?" And, "What are all present afflictions and miseries compared to eternity?"

Though Christ Forgives, Sin Is Still Present in Us
Yet there is one lamentation beyond all these. It is when the soul finds the sentence of absolution in Jesus Christ, but his eyes are then opened to see that body of death and sin within himself, and that he is a man whose sin is totally diffused throughout every part of his being. Then that soul bemoans itself with Paul, "O wretched man that I am! Who shall deliver me from the body of this death?" (Rom. 7:24). He cries, "I am delivered from the condemnation of the law, but what comfort is it, as long as sin remains so powerful in me? Nay, this makes me often doubt

my deliverance from wrath and the curse, seeing sin itself is not taken away."

Now, if you could be persuaded to hearken to Jesus Christ and embrace this gospel, oh what abundant consolation you will have! What a perfect answer to all your complaints! They would be swallowed up in such a triumph as Paul's are here: "I thank God through Jesus Christ our Lord" (Rom. 7:25). Embracing the gospel would uncover for you a perfect remedy of sin and misery, that you should complain no more, or at least, not as they complain who have no hope. You shall never have a remedy of your earthly miseries unless you anticipate them by beginning with what is eternal. "Seek ye first the kingdom of God… and all these things shall be added unto you" (Matt. 6:33). But first, seek to flee from the wrath to come and you shall escape it, for when the evil of time is concluded, all your afflictions shall be removed. So first remove the greatest complaints of sin and condemnation, and then how easy is it to endure all the lamentations of this life, and even to rejoice in the midst of them!

Three Truths about the Christian

We have in this verse three things of great importance to consider: first, a great and precious privilege; second, the true nature of the child of God; third, the special property of a believer.

The first, this great and precious privilege which is implied in our text, is one of the greatest in the world because for our souls it is of eternal consequence. Second, we learn that the essence of the believer's nature is that it is of God because he is in Jesus Christ; this new nature is implanted in him by faith. Third, his distinguishing property is serenity and is consistent with the privilege of his godly nature; consequently, the believer does not live as the worldly man lives, according to his base flesh, but he lives according to the Spirit.

These three qualities of the child of God are mutually consistent with each other for they comprise a harmonious unity and are constantly in perfect step with one another. That rich privilege together with the sweet property of godliness share a common center with the man who is in Jesus Christ, and who lives according to the Spirit. Further, whoever enters into Christ and abides in Him encounters and participates in both justification and sanctification; these two are to be found nowhere else, other than present together in the life of the believer.

If you knew the nature of a Christian, you would fall in love with these properties for themselves, but if these will not allure you, consider also the incomparable privilege the believer has beyond all others that you may fall in love with the nature of the Christian. Let concern for yourselves and your own well-being draw you into Jesus Christ, that you may walk even as He walked. For I assure you, once you are truly in Christ, you would love the Christian's very nature and daily conduct, not only for the absolution from your sins and the salvation that accompanies it, but for its own sweetness and excellency beyond all other.

Like the people of Samaria, you would not simply believe on account of the woman's testimony, which points to our own necessity and misery, but you would believe in Jesus Christ and walk according to the Spirit for the testimony these graces have in your consciences (John 4:42). You would no more be allured by only these three privileges to embrace Christianity, but you would think Christianity itself to be the greatest privilege, a reward unto itself. "Godliness is great gain in itself,"[2] even if it did not have such sweet consequences.

All Are under the Sentence of Condemnation

That you may know this privilege, consider the condition of all men through their fallen state. Paul expresses it thus: "As by one man sin entered into the world, and death by sin…judgment came upon all men to condemnation…and so death passed upon all men, for that all have sinned" (Rom. 5:12, 18). See then how all are under a sentence of condemnation by one act of trespass!

---

2. Pietas ipsa sibi merces est.

This sentence is the curse of the law, "For as many as are of the works of the law are under the curse: for it is written, Cursed is every one that continueth not in all things which are written in the book of the law to do them" (Gal. 3:10).

If you knew the consequences of this curse, you would indeed think it a privilege to be delivered from it. Sin is of an infinite deserving because against an infinite God it is an offense of an infinite magnitude, and therefore the curse upon the sinner involves eternal punishment. Oh what weight is in the apostle's words, ye "shall be punished with everlasting destruction, from the presence of the Lord and the glory of his power" (2 Thess. 1:9). If it was truly understood, it would weigh down upon a man's soul, filling it with fearful sorrow to the point of death.

Banishment from the Heavenly Kingdom
This condemnation includes both "condemnation and punishment, knowing the penalty of condemnation,"[3] and both are infinite in themselves and eternal in their continuance. What an unpleasant and bitter life would one lead, being born to inherit a kingdom and yet losing it by being banished from it? But no heart can conceive what an incomparable loss it would be to suffer banishment forever from a heavenly kingdom.

In God's favor is life, and in His presence are rivers of pleasures forevermore. When your petty penny losses[4] greatly afflict your spirits, how much more would the apprehension of so great an impending loss do to you? Would it not be like a death to you, even worse than death, to be separated from this life and eternally banished from the presence of His glory? If there should be no more punishment but this only; if the wicked were to endure forever on earth; and the godly, whom they despised and mocked, were translated to heaven, what torment would it be to your souls to think upon that blessedness which the godly

---

3. Damnum et pœnam, pœnam damni sensus.
4. *penny losses*: trivial financial losses.

enjoy above and how foolishly you have been deprived of it for something of no value? What would a rich man's advantages and gains be to him when he considers what an infinite loser he is—how he has sold a kingdom for a dunghill?

The Banishment Is for All Eternity
Now if there was any hope that after some years his banishment from heaven might end, his misery might be assuaged, but there is not one single drop of such consolation. He is eternally banished from that glorious life in the presence of God, which those enjoy whom he despised. Or consider the case of a man who has been shut up all his lifetime in a pit, knowing that he would never see the light ever again, would not this be torment enough to him? But then imagine intense pain being added to his perpetual darkness, so that he is incessantly tormented within by a gnawing worm, as well as fire added to his agony. What then? His passions that so greedily sought satisfaction are now in equal measure sensible to feeling the pain of his torment.

And when there is no end to his anguish, for it is eternal—alas, whose heart can comprehend such suffering? In this life there is some comfort in knowing that bodily afflictions will end in death, for physical pain destroys itself when it destroys the body. But when there is an immortal soul for pain to feed upon, what then? At length even the body shall live on in the sense that physical death will not completely destroy it, but it shall be subjected to an everlasting destruction in a "living death."

This is the sentence that is declared against us all in the Word of God, and not one jot of His word shall fall to the ground: heaven and earth may fail sooner. Would you not consider it to be an irrevocable decree if every nation on earth, along with all the angels above, convened to condemn a man to death and pass the death penalty upon him? Nay, but this word that is daily spoken to you, which passes this sentence upon you all, is even more certain; indeed, this sentence of death must be executed, unless you are under that blessed exception made here and elsewhere in the gospel: "There is therefore now no condemnation to them which are in Christ Jesus" (Rom. 8:1).

It Is the Eternal God with Whom We Have To Do

I beseech you, consider what it is to have such a judge condemning you. Would not any of you be afraid if you were under the sentence of a king? If that judgment were upon your head, who of you would be in contented peace and quietness? Would you not flee from the anger of a king, whose wrath is like the roaring of a lion? But here upon your heads is the sentence of the King over all kings and nations. I ask those to whom this death sentence applies, "Who would not fear thee, O King of all nations?" (Jer. 10:7). For the One with whom you have to do is not a great man who has strength to destroy your body; nor is it someone who is determined to kill you. This would indeed be a matter of immense concern.

Rather is it the great and eternal Jehovah who lifts up His hand to heaven and swears He lives forever, He it is who is against you. It is He who has all power over your body and soul and has no alternative but to exercise His omnipotence toward you. He is able to kill both soul and body and cast you into hell. On account of the just penalty of your sin He will not spare you but will pour out upon you all the curses in this Book.

You would have no peace of mind if you were declared a rebel by the king and parliament; but alas, that is a small thing. They can only reach your body. But neither can they always do that because you may flee from them. But whither can you flee from God? You cannot escape from His dominions, for the earth and sea are His, and everything in them. Men may not always be able to track you down, and so they can have no guarantee of finding you. But darkness cannot hide you from the Lord of all. He may delay for a long time because, whenever He pleases, He can overtake and find you.

I beseech you, then, to consider this. It is of eternal consequence for your soul. What profit is it for a man to gain the world, if he then loses his soul? If the gainer be lost, what then is gained? This is of eternal consequence! What are many thousands of years compared to this? You may try to look beyond all these things and might comfort yourselves in some forlorn hope, but you cannot see into your eternal destiny. There is still far more ahead of us than what is now past; nay, in truth there is nothing past—life has only just begun.

Christ Could Scarcely Bear the Weight of the Divine Wrath

Oh, that you would consider this curse of God that is upon us all! What effects had the curse upon Christ when He bore it? It made His soul heavy unto death: it was a cup that He could scarcely drink. He who fashioned and sustains the frame of this world was almost near to succumbing under the weight of this wrath. It made Him sweat blood in the garden. He that could do all things and speak all things was reduced to tears. "Saying, Father, if thou be willing, remove this cup from me."

When this condemnation was so terrible to Him, the Mighty One upon whom all help was laid, what shall this be to you? No man's sorrow was ever like His, nor pain ever like His, even if all the scattered torments on earth were joined together in one. But because He was God, He overcame and came out through it. But what do you think shall be the condition of those who shall endure that same torment—and not for three days, or three years, or even some thousands of years, but beyond imagining—for all eternity?

None of Us Can Bear the Weight of the Divine Wrath

I beseech you solemnly to consider this condemnation which awaits you; do not ignore it. Do you think you can endure what Christ endured? Do you think you can bear the weight of wrath according to God's power and justice? And yet the judgment of this condemnation is come upon all men. But alas! Who fears Him according to His wrath? Who knows the power of His anger? You may sleep secure, as if all this belonged to the past and does not apply to you. We declare unto you in the Lord's name that this condemnation is yet awaiting you because you have not rightly examined yourselves. It is preached to you that you may flee from it. But if you yourselves will not admit your guilt and condemnation, the righteous Judge must condemn you.

The Immense Privilege of God's Mercy

Now, since it is true that this condemnatory sentence is passed on all men, what a privilege must it be to be delivered from it and to have that sentence repealed by a new act of God's mercy and favor? David proclaims him a blessed man whose sins are forgiven and covered; and, indeed, blessed are those who escape that pit of eternal misery. Because there is no human entitlement to a heavenly inheritance and kingdom or to be delivered from that wrath to come upon the children of disobedience, this is an infinitely greater felicity than the enjoyment of all earthly delights.

There Is No Price We Can Pay for Our Souls

"What shall a man give in exchange for his soul?" (Matt. 16:26). "Skin for skin, yea, all that a man hath will he give for his life" (Job 2:4). The riches, advantages, and pleasures that men spend their labor for, all these will they part with in order to escape with their lives. The covetous man will cast his coffers overboard rather than lose his life; the sensuous man will suffer pain and torment in cutting off a limb rather than die. But if men knew their souls and the immortality and eternity that awaits them, for their souls they would not only give skin for skin and all that they have but their lives also. You would choose to die a thousand deaths in order to escape this eternal death.

You may ask, "What shall a man give in exchange for his soul?" Indeed, what would he give, and what does he have to give? We cherish any privilege that we have, and two things cause us to value it. First, the necessity of it and second, the preciousness of it; these two are important here. Is it not a necessity to live and have a being? Everyone must think so since they will give all they have to redeem themselves. All other things are incidental to them, for their lives are their dearest possession; therefore, they will surrender everything rather than themselves.

But I ask this: What is more necessary than simply to be alive? Surely it is to be safe eternally. To escape the divine condemnation is far more important than anything else. And the truth of this will be seen on the last day when men shall cry for hills and mountains to fall on them and save them from the wrath of the Lamb (Rev. 6:16). Men will choose rather to forfeit their lives than to fall under that wrath. Oh, how acceptable would a man's nonexistence be to him on that great day of wrath! Who shall be able to stand when kings and princes, slaves and free, great and small, shall cry out for mountains to grind them into powder rather than to hear that sentence of condemnation? And yet their cries shall not be answered.

The Final Judgment Day

O blessed are all those that trust in Him when "his wrath is kindled but a little" (Ps. 2:12). You toil and vex yourselves and spend your time worrying about your body and life, but as precious as they are to you now, you would gladly exchange them one day for immunity from God's wrath and curse. How will that man think his lines are fallen in pleasant places—how will he despise the glory of earthly kingdoms, even if all were united in one—who considers in his heart how all kings, tongues, and nations must stand before the judgment seat of God? There will the books of His divine law be opened by which to judge them, as also the books of their consciences to verify His accusation and precipitate their own sentence.

Then, in the open view of all the sons of Adam and the angels, all secrets shall be brought out and their accusation read as large as their lifetime. And as many curses shall be pronounced against everyone as there will be revealed breaches of the law of God, of which they are found guilty. Then all those who have been condemned will seek to hide in dark corners, and they will cry for mountains to fall upon them. But alas, there can be no hiding place from His presence.

What do you think the man who will stand before God and is absolved in judgment by Jesus Christ will think within himself, notwithstanding his provocations more than many of those who have been condemned? What will a king then think of his crown and dominions when he reflects on them? What will the poor, persecuted Christian then think of all the glory and perfection of this world when he looks back upon it? Oh know, poor, foolish men, what madness it is to barter your souls for trifles! You run the greatest hazard of all for a fleeting moment's satisfaction. You will repent of this folly too late and will become wise to judge yourselves fools, only to find that there is no longer any opportunity to repent of your sin.

This solemn warning is both necessary and exceedingly valuable. The truth is that your souls at present are kept captive under that sentence of everlasting imprisonment; you are all prisoners, though you do not realize it. What will you give in ransom for your souls? Your sins and iniquities have sold you to the righteous Judge of all the earth as malefactors, and He has passed the sentence of your perpetual imprisonment under Satan's custody in hell.

The Price of a Soul Is Infinitely Costly
Now what will you give to redeem your souls from that pit? How few know the worth of their souls! And so they offer to God some of their riches in exchange for their souls. Do not some of you think that you have made satisfaction for your sins by paying a civil penalty to the judge? Many others think their own tears and sorrow for their sin may be a suitable price to avoid justice, at least if their penitence is joined with the promise of amendment at some time in the future. And so men consider their sins are pardoned, and their souls redeemed.

But alas, the redemption of the soul is infinitely costly, for the soul lives forever. All your substance would be utterly spurned if you were to offer it. A few of you might give all your possessions for your souls! And yet though you give it, it will not suffice even though you pay up to your last farthing. Nor will your sorrow and reformation complete the sum, no, nor even begin it. "For though thou wash thee with nitre, and take thee much soap, yet thine iniquity is marked before me, saith the Lord God" (Jer. 2:22). The condemnation would still stand against you.

Imagine that the whole world convenes to settle this matter of finding a ransom for mankind. Suppose all the treasures of monarchs, the mines and depths of the earth, the coffers of rich men—all of these—were searched; nay, let the earth, the sea, the heavens, and sun and moon be added to achieve the very highest possible value. Even more, add on all the merits of angels above and men below, all their good actions and sufferings, yet the final sum of all those additions would not pay the least farthing of this debt. The earth would say, "I am unable to pay the ransom price" and the heavens above would give the same answer. Angels and men might say, "We have heard about this infinitely costly ransom price, but how to raise it is hidden from all living creatures."

Christ Has Paid the Ransom Price
Where then is this redemption from the curse? Where shall a ransom be found? Indeed, God has found it; it is with Him. He has given His Son as the ransom for many, and His blood is more precious than souls, or than any gold and silver. Is not this then a great privilege, that if all the kingdoms of the world were sold at the highest price, yet they could not provide the ransom? What a jewel is this! What a pearl!

Whoever of you have escaped this wrath, consider the greatness of your privilege. Oh, consider the dignity that has been bestowed upon you, that you may engage your hearts to Him, to become His, and His wholly! For "ye are bought with a price" and therefore are no longer your own (1 Cor. 6:20). Christ has given Himself for you and was made a curse to redeem you from the curse. Oh, how you should live as privileged men, as redeemed people!

Ponder on the Hope of Deliverance

I beseech you to gather up your thoughts and consider and ponder on this sentence that is passed against every one of us. There is now hope of delivery from it if you will take it to heart. But if you will still continue in the ways of sin and refuse to repent, be sure of this: you are but multiplying those curses, weaving into bonds the many cords of your iniquities, to bind you in everlasting chains. You are but digging a pit for your souls, you who sweat in your sins and continue in them and will not embrace this ransom offered.

The key and lock of that pit is eternal despair. Oh, consider how quickly your pleasures and gains will end, and spare some of your thoughts from present things to contemplate eternity, and that thread that you are spinning out for ever and ever. Consider the infinite length of the years of the Ancient of Days, who has no beginning of days nor end of time! Be mindful now of this, lest you are reduced to misery for as long as God is blessed, and that is forever.

The Unspeakable Privilege of Being "in Christ"

Everyone would love to have more privileges than others, but there is one that carries a soul far away from this world, and that is the believer in Jesus Christ. For those who believe are said to be "in Christ," engrafted into Him by faith, as living members of that body of which Christ is the head. Christ Jesus is the head of His body, the church, and as its head He communicates life to all its members, for He is "the fulness of him that filleth all in all." There is a mighty working power in the Head, which diffuses itself throughout the members (Eph. 1:19, 22–23). There are many expressions of union between Christ and believers. There is no natural union between men, but this spiritual union of Christ with believers binds us together in Christ.

The foundation and the building have a common dependence in the cornerstone, for in him the walls are joined together. It is Christ Jesus who is the foundation and "the chief cornerstone, in whom the whole building being fitted together, grows into an holy temple in the Lord" (Eph. 2:20–21). The head and members of a body are united, and so it is with Christ and believers; they "grow into him in all things" (Eph. 4:15). Parents and children have the closest of bonds; so it is with Christ Jesus and the everlasting Father, for He shows to the Father the children who He has given Him. We are His brothers, and He is not ashamed to call us so; moreover, we are one flesh with Him.

There is a marriage between Christ and the church which is the great meditation of the Song of Solomon. He is the vine tree, and we are branches grafted into Him. Nay, this union is so intimate that it is mutual; "I in them and they in me," says Christ who dwells in us by faith, enabling us to believe in Him and love Him (cf. John 15:5). We dwell in Christ by that same faith and love. Christ Jesus is our "house," as it were, for from Him we get all our "furniture" for living. He is also our storehouse and treasure, our place of strength and pleasure; further, He is our city of refuge with its strong tower and a pleasant river to refresh us. But we are also His habitation where He dwells by His Spirit; we are His workhouse, where He fashions all His curious pieces of the new creation, forming it for the day of His espousals, the great day of redemption.

Reflect on What We Once Were

This gives us to understand what we once were. We may stand here and reflect upon our former condition and find reasons for both delight and sorrow. We were once without Christ in the world, and therefore "having no hope and without God in the world" (Eph. 2:12). How I wish it was engraved on men's hearts that they are born out of Christ Jesus, that they are wild olives growing up from the stock of degenerate Adam. He was once planted a noble vine, but how quickly turned he into a corrupt plant; instead of grapes, he brought forth wild grapes that were sour!

We all come from a wild olive tree which is "contrary to nature" (Rom. 11:24). It grows outside the garden of God in the barren wilderness; it is no use for anything for it only brings forth fruit unto death and needs to be cut down and cast into the fire. It is a tree which the Lord has cursed: "cursed is the ground because of you…thorns and thistles it shall bring forth for you" (Gen. 3:17). This was the fatal sentence pronounced on Adam.

The Worthless "Fruit" of the Godless

Oh that you would know your condition by nature, how all your good inclinations, dispositions, and education cannot make your stock or your fruit good! "Israel is an empty vine, he brings forth fruit only for himself" (Hos. 10:1); this is our name. Nay, but many delude themselves into thinking that they do bring forth good fruit. Have not the godless spread forth their branches, and brought forth many pleasant fruits of temporal patience, sobriety, magnanimity, prudence, and such like? Do not some cultured men do many acts of civility profitable to others? Do not many pray and read the Scriptures from their youth up? Yes, indeed, these are fruits of a sort, but for all that, such a man is an empty vine, for he brings forth fruit only for himself; and so, as in the original, he is a vine whose fruit is worthless for he does not fear the Lord (Hos. 10:1–3).

All these fruits are but for himself and from himself; he does not direct them to God's glory, but only to his own praise or advantage, to make them his ornament. He is unaware of his own futility in seeking all his adornment and life from the wrong source. What were all these fair blossoms and fruits of the heathen nations? Indeed, they were more worthy and far better than those we see now among the multitude of professing Christians, for theirs are but shining sins.[5]

What is all your praying and fasting, but for yourselves? The Lord asked the people, "Did ye at all fast unto me, even to me?" (Zech. 7:5). No, they did it for themselves, as do many among us today. Herein is the wildness and degeneracy of your natures. Either you bring forth very bitter fruits, such as intemperance, avarice, contention, swearing, and the like, or else you produce fruits that have nothing but a fair skin, like apples of Sodom that are beautiful on the tree but when handled turn to ashes; so none of your fruits are either from God or for God.

The Self-Deception of the Unregenerate Heart

I think everyone entertains this secret persuasion in his heart: although our nature may be weak, yet it is not wicked; it may be helped with education, care, and diligence, and improved upon until it pleases God and benefits others. Who is persuaded in heart that he is an enemy to God, and cannot be subject to God's law? Who actually believes that his heart is desperately wicked? Is it common for a person to believe that? Ah, but it is indeed deceitful above all things, and its deceit is uncovered when it seeks to persuade you that you do have a good heart in God's sight. Will not profane men, whose hands are defiled, maintain the uprightness of their hearts?

They say, "No one is born good but will become so."[6] I beseech you, consider that you were born out of Christ Jesus. Yet you imagine that you are born and educated as Christians and that you have the name "Christian" from infancy, for you have been baptized. But I ask about this claim: Water baptism does not engraft you into Jesus Christ. Nay, it declares this to you, that by nature you are far off from Jesus, and wholly defiled and that all your thoughts are only evil.

---

5. *Splendida peccata.*
6. *Nemo nascitur bonus sed fit.*

The Concluding Appeal

Now, I beseech you, how did it come about that you have been changed? Or has there even been a change? Is not the greater part of our natures "the old man"? Are any of you truly new creatures? Those who are in Christ are new creatures (2 Cor. 5:17). Just now you have Adam's nature which you were born with. You bear the image of the earthly, and do you not still bear it, who are still earth-bound? Do you think that in your fallen state you can inherit the kingdom of God? Can you pass over from a state of condemnation to a state of life with no longer any condemnation, without there being a radical change?

No, you cannot! The flesh and blood with which you were born cannot inherit the incorruptible. You must be engrafted into the second Adam and bear His image before you can say that you are partakers of His blessings (1 Cor. 15:47–49). Now I must challenge your consciences: How many of you have been changed? Are not most of you just the same as you have been from your childhood? Do not be deceived; you are still strangers from the promises of God and without this hope in the world.

SERMON 2

The City of Refuge

There is therefore now no condemnation to them which are in Christ Jesus.
—ROMANS 8:1

Fallen Sinners Must Have a Mediator

All the promises of Scripture are yea and amen in Christ Jesus (2 Cor. 1:20). For all of them are fulfilled in Him and from Him they are imparted to us. When man was still in his unfallen state he was spontaneously with God and in God without the need of a Mediator. But our falling away from God has left us without God and the distance is so great, as Abraham tells the rich man, that neither can those above go down to him, nor he below come up to them. There is a gulf of separation between God and us, for a great chasm has been fixed, therefore there can be no meeting (Luke 16:26). And so we who are without God are without hope in the world (Eph. 2:12). There can no longer be access to God as before the fall.

The Tree of Life is compassed about with "a flaming sword which turned every way" (Gen. 3:24). God has become a consuming fire to us so that none can come near these everlasting burnings, much less dwell with them (Isa. 33:14). Because there can be no meeting, God has worked out the only way how sinners may draw near to Him and not be consumed. He will meet with us in Jesus Christ, that living temple, and this is His trysting place. It was necessary for Him to be a Mediator, to make a bridge over that gulf of separation, so that we could come to God. This is why Christ took upon Himself human nature, to become the new and living way; His flesh is the curtain through which we may pass (Heb. 10:20). God was in Christ, therefore, reconciling the world to Himself (2 Cor. 5:19).

Salvation Is in the Sun of Righteousness

All the light of consolation and salvation that is from God is embodied in this Sun of Righteousness. All the streams of grace and mercy run through the channel of His well-beloved Son. It follows, then, that God is not to be found outside of Jesus Christ, for whoever is without Christ in this world is without God. It is because "God was in Christ reconciling the world to himself" (2 Cor. 5:19) that "there is therefore now no condemnation to them that are in Christ" (Rom. 8:1). Nevertheless, out of Christ God condemns the world, therefore His condemnation is upon all who are not in Christ.

The City of Refuge

When all the descendants of Adam were declared rebels because of his and their own rebellion the Lord appointed a city of refuge, that whoever is pursued by the avenger of blood may enter for protection and safety.[1] Outside the city is the sword of the avenger, justice reigning throughout all the world. However, justice may not enter this city to seize and drag out anyone to face condemnation. Therefore, those who flee to the city for refuge may lay hold upon the hope set before them in Jesus Christ. Although naked justice may pursue them to the gates of this city and condemnation follow hard after them right until the very moment before they enter in, neither the condemnation nor justice may follow them through the gates into the city. Those who have fled for refuge there are safe.

---

1. The laws regarding the six cities of refuge are recorded in Num. 35:9–29.

The Dire Danger of Failing to Enter the City of Refuge
Therefore, what a miserable state those souls are in who, still in their fallen natures, are wandering in the open fields outside the walls of the city of refuge! How many foolish men apprehend no danger, but cavort about beyond the city's gates, but will not enter in! Alas, the avenger of blood shall fall upon you before you know it, and if that avenger finds you outside the city, woe to you! All your prayers and entreaties will not prevail. Justice is blind and deaf; it cannot deal partially or show respect of persons, nor can it hear your supplications. It is strange that men are absorbed with so many petty inconsequential things and continue to neglect to find out the meaning of being in Jesus Christ, on whom their salvation entirely depends.

Faith in Jesus Christ is the soul's flight into the city of refuge. Now no one flees until they realize that they are in danger or see that they are being pursued. The danger threatening them is that they are perishing under eternal condemnation. The pursuer is the law of God and His righteous justice; these have a flaming sword in their hand, which is the curse of God and His sentence of condemnation. For God erects a tribunal in His word, whereby He judges men.

Conscience Condemns the Sinner
God causes the law to enter into the consciences of those toward whom He has a purpose of goodwill so that their awareness of their offenses might abound. He sends out some messenger of affliction or conviction, bringing them before His judgment seat to hear their accusation read to them. There the soul stands trembling as his conscience witnesses and acknowledges all of which the word justly accuses him. The sinner's mouth is stopped for he can have no excuses regarding the accusations. Then the judge pronounces the sentence upon the guilty person, "Cursed is every one that continueth not in all things which are written in the book of the law to do them" (Gal. 3:10)!

The condemned soul cries, "Guilty, O Lord, guilty! I do indeed deserve the curse. Oh, what shall I do to be saved?" Then the stricken soul looks to the right and to the left, seeking some refuge, but there is none. Whither shall he flee? He looks within himself and sees nothing there. Meanwhile the accusing, witnessing conscience becomes his tormentor. A fire is kindled within his soul, which feeds upon the fuel of innumerable sins.

Now the soul is almost overwhelmed, and searches for any place to which he can flee from himself and from that burning wrath. Then, behold! the Lord shows him a city of refuge near at hand, where there is no condemnation, even Christ Jesus, who Himself has borne the curse that He might redeem us from it. The vision of peace is here, and there the soul flees from itself and from justice, into that discovered righteousness of Christ. Thus the more that the offense abounded, now the more has grace superabounded (Rom. 5:20), so that there is no longer any condemnation of him.

The Two Tribunals: Justice and Mercy

I beseech you to consider this, and let it be written on the table of your hearts. There are two tribunals upon which God sits, one out of Christ Jesus and another in Christ Jesus. There is a throne of justice, where no sentence passes other than naked unmixed justice, without any disposition of mercy and before this throne all men must appear. You know of the covenant of works God once made with us: "If ye do these things thou shalt live, if not, thou shalt die the death" (cf. Lev. 18:5; Gen. 2:17). According to this we must all be judged, that justice suffer no prejudice or bias. Therefore seated upon this judgment throne God speaks out of His law the language of Mount Sinai, as He reads to us our charge; and because all the world is guilty, therefore the sentence of death is passed upon all.

Now, whoever comes before this tribunal to be judged, know that it is a subordinate court, for there is another, higher court of mercy and judgment where both justice and mercy meet together. Though mercy is predominant, justice and judgment are its foundation, but it is mercy and truth that come before the Judge's face; these two also come nearest to sinners to give them access to God. And to this you may appeal from that tribunal of justice. "If you, O Lord, should mark iniquities, O Lord, who could stand? But there is forgiveness with you, that you may be feared" (Ps. 130:3–4).

Christ Is Enthroned in the Higher Tribunal
Whoever comes to this higher court, there Christ Jesus sits on His throne to absolve him from that sentence. You may wonder what impartiality is in this and ask, "Is this not prejudicial toward justice, and will it not be an abomination to the Lord to justify the wicked and ungodly sinner?" I answer that there is no injustice here because Jesus Christ has paid the price for us and was made a curse for our sins that we might be the righteousness of God in Him. Therefore it is in justice that God can forgive sins and release that sinner from the condemnation of the law who flees into Jesus Christ.

You may rightly answer, "I will take this for God's last word. I now hear that all final judgment is committed to the Son that He may give life to whom He will. He calls me, therefore to Him will I go for He has the words of eternal life. When He justifies who then shall condemn me?"

The Awesome Judgment for Those Outside the City of Refuge

Now, those who are unwilling to arraign themselves before the tribunal of God's justice, who will not acknowledge their guilt until their mouths are stopped, and who thus do not hear their sentence of condemnation read and admit their culpability, they cannot come to Jesus Christ to be absolved, for He justifies only those who are self-condemned as lost sinners. So, your day is surely coming when you must answer to divine justice.

The tribunal of mercy shall be removed, and Christ shall sit upon a throne of pure justice, to judge those who have not judged themselves. Alas, I pity you, most of you, for your great loss! At present you live in apparent peace and quietness outside the gates of the city of refuge. We declare unto you in the Lord's name, you are under the curse of God! Will you continue in your false security, as you shut out the evil day from your minds? Oh, rather trouble your peace for a season and reflect upon your sins! Enter into judgment with yourselves until you see nothing in your hearts but perdition. Yet, there does not need to be any hazard, because salvation is being brought near in the gospel. Nevertheless, if you will not take time so much as to judge yourselves, then you shall be judged when there is no Mediator to plead for you, and none to whom you can appeal.

Condemned Sinners May Come to God through Christ
But those who take the sentence of condemnation upon themselves and acknowledge the righteousness of the Lord's curse upon them, in Christ's name we invite you all to come draw near to Jesus Christ. There is no condemnation to those who are in Him. If you stand arguing and raising various questions regarding so urgent a matter, you wrong your own souls and dishonor the Lord. Therefore, be absolutely assured that God is in Christ reconciling the world to Himself. This is why you, a condemned sinner, may come to God in Christ.

If you ask for some guarantee, we urge that there should be no such questioning when you are dealing with an issue of eternal consequences. If a man was starving outside a city's walls and he was told that there was plenty within, would he not be a fool to enter into discussions about the kind of food that was freely available? Would he not strive to enter the city? Surely this is sufficient for you to abandon all your objections when you are in such dire extremities and like to bring destruction upon yourself!

"Wherefore he is able also to save them to the uttermost that come unto God by him" (Heb. 7:25). What more do you need? Let there be then a closure between "absolute necessity" and "sufficient ability" to save. Will you continue to stand disputing outside the city's gates when the avenger of blood is hovering above your head? If you will continue to insist on more answers to your questions about believing, then I can only tell you all that I know is in the Word of God for the grounds of faith.

First, you do acknowledge your piteous condition and need; that, you admit, is your complaint. Second, you cannot deny that Christ has mercy and sufficient grace in Himself; as the apostle has said, "He is able to save to the uttermost." To these two grounds for faith I add a third, namely, that He is also willing to save both you and whoever else is willing to be saved by Him; indeed, He is more willing than you are.

Sinners Are Commanded to Believe on Christ
If you still question this, I desire you to consider the whole tenor of the gospel. How many invitations there are! How many persuasions! How many promises to those who come! Yea, how many peremptory commands to believe on Him! More—how many solemn warnings against you if you will not come to Him to have life! Has He given Himself for the sins of the world, and will He not be willing that sinners partake of the free forgiveness He was at so much pains[2] to purchase?

Do you think that Christ will be content that His death should be in vain? And, indeed, it would be in vain if He did not welcome the worst sinners. Yea, it would be in vain if He did not draw such sinners to Him and make them willing to come. Besides this, He has promised so absolutely, freely, and fully that there should be no imaginable exception to His assurance that "him that cometh to me, I will in no wise cast out" (John 6:37).

Therefore why do you imagine there may be an exception when Christ has not made one? Why do you sin against your own souls? "Ah," you say, "if I was in Christ, all would be well!" and, "If only He would welcome such a sinner as me!" Christ answers you in express terms, "The Spirit and the bride say,

---

2. *pains*: exertion, striving, or taking great trouble for some purpose.

Come.... Whosoever will, let him take the water of life freely" (Rev. 22:17).

Christ Is Willing to Save
You declare your willingness in so speaking, and He declares His willingness in so promising. Nay, your looking toward Him from far off is a fruit of His willingness. Yet He assures us, "Ye have not chosen me, but I have chosen you," and loved you first. If you still will not believe this, hearken to His command, for He commands that you believe on the Son: "And this is his commandment, That we should believe on the name of his Son Jesus Christ" (1 John 3:23). What further warrant do you need to do whatever He commands? Therefore, why do you continue to question this? Is not this His command? And is it not even more authoritative, because it is a new command and His final command? And since God bestows on us the honor of uniting us with His Son that we may have life, oh, who should have the effrontery to continue to question His willingness?

I do not know of any other grounds than these. Indeed, I think if any come to Christ—or attempt to come—on other grounds, he does not come rightly. Even if the most holy man attempts to come not as an ungodly sinner, nor on account of his own extreme necessity and Christ's sufficiency, he will never be able to come to Jesus Christ.

The Arrogant Folly of Many
There is a foolishness among some which, if it were not so common, I would not mention it as it is so ridiculous. "How can I come to Christ," they say, "when I am so unclean and guilty and there is nothing but condemnation in me? If I were such and such, then I would come to Him." Alas, I cannot imagine anything more absurd or contrary to common sense and reason! If you were "such and such," as you appear to fancy a desire to be, you would not ever come to Christ because you would not need Him. The very thing which you claim as a reason why you

should not come, is the great reason urgently pressed upon you in the gospel why you should come.

What madness is this? "I am so unclean," you say, "so I will not come to the fountain to wash." Why was the fountain opened, but for sin and uncleanness? And the more uncleanness, the greater the need; and the greater the need, the more reason to come. Necessity is a great compunction, and that compunction is all the warrant we need: I am pursued by the law, I have condemnation within me, and nothing but condemnation.

Well then, come to Christ Jesus, the city of refuge, where there is no condemnation. Why else was this city appointed, but for this end? I beseech you, everyone who uses these specious arguments, even taking a kind of delight in them, to know what they entail and how they wrong your own souls. More, realize how they dishonor Christ, and God the Father. Nay, acknowledge how foolish and ridiculous they are. If it was not on account of your confusion, they would not even deserve an answer, rather a rebuke or silence.

I have seen people take delight in moving objections against the truth, yea, and earnestly studying how to object to any answers given them from the truth. Alas! You who engage in such folly are interfering with God's Word to your own hurt; you are going in a direction which will never lead you into any comfort, but will keep your soul from reaching any certainty, being like a wave tossed hither and thither! If you do not believe, but continue to dispute, you shall never find firm assurance.

Believers Must Study to Know How Great Their Salvation Is

Before I conclude, I would speak a word to those who have believed and have fled for refuge to Christ. Oh, it concerns you most of all to study to understand this condemnation from which you have been delivered, that you may be thankful and may keep secure within this city. I say, there is no one in the world who ought to have more deep and earnest meditation on the curse and wrath of God, than you who have been delivered from them through Christ. Why? So that you may know how great a salvation you have received, how great a condemnation you have escaped, and must from now on live each day as those who have been bought with a price.

Your regeneration by the Holy Spirit makes you not your own, but Christ's because He has given you that new beginning. Indeed, your redemption should make you twice more His and no longer your own because, when your former condition was worse than could ever be imagined, He created you anew all over again. So you are twice His: first He transformed you by His Word, having bought you with a price, the costly price of His own blood.

Again, keeping this curse always in your view, with the sight and application of it for the atonement of your sins, will make much of the working in you of Christ. Oh, how often will you flee into that city! I think they are the greatest enemies of Jesus Christ and His grace, who say a believer has no more use of the law. I do not know who can use the law if the believer cannot use it. Neither do I know who can embrace its purpose and fulfillment in Christ, but the one who is in Christ. For certainly the believer does not only have the use of the Lord's commands as a rule of obedience, but also as a reminder of the curse, not to bring him again into the law's bondage, no, no, but to make him see always the continual necessity of Jesus Christ, that he may make his dwelling in Him, there always to abide.

SERMON 3

The Marks of the Justified Believers

Who walk not after the flesh, but after the Spirit.
—ROMANS 8:1

It is difficult to determine which of these two blessings is the greatest privilege of a Christian, either that he is delivered from condemnation, or that he is enabled to walk according to the Spirit, having been made a new creature. In other words, do we owe more to Christ for our justification or for our sanctification? For He is made both to us. However, it is more necessary to conjoin them together than to compare them with each other. Neither is more necessary than the other, either to be delivered from wrath or to walk according to the Spirit.

Restatement of the Doctrine of Justification

I think those who have escaped from condemnation will now have the great stream and current of their affections and endeavors toward sanctification, not so that they may be accepted before God but because they have already been accepted by Him. The text does not say that there is nothing condemnable in those that are in Christ, rather that there is no condemnation upon them. There is, indeed, a body of death and law of sin within their natures which are defiled with original pollution; there are also many streams flowing from their fallen natures which the sprinkling of the blood of Christ in justification does not take away.

Any who say there is no sin in them are liars, and the truth is not in them (1 John 1:8). But herein is the grace and mercy of God in Jesus Christ: the curse wherein is the sin has been removed, and so has the condemnation. And thus the soul's justification is parallel to Christ's condemnation.

There was in Christ nothing deserving condemnation, no sin, no guile in His mouth; yet condemnation was laid upon Him, because He took the place of sinners. Our iniquities were laid *upon* Him, but not *in* Him. He who knew no sin was made a curse for us, that in Him we might be made the righteousness of God (2 Cor. 5:21; Gal. 3:13). So then, the soul that flees into Jesus Christ's righteousness, although that soul deserves condemnation, is no longer condemned because Christ's righteousness is laid upon it and He has taken away the curse. Guilty sinners are absolved because the innocent Son of God was condemned. The curse was applied to Him who had no sin, only was *made* sin, or had sin *laid upon* Him. Therefore, the sentence of absolution from the curse is applied to those who themselves have no righteousness but are made the righteousness of God by free and gracious imputation.

First Error: Justification Removes All Sin in Those Justified

I am emphasizing this because there have been many unhelpful and unsound opinions expressed in this careless generation. For example, it has been argued that there is no sin in the justified because justification had entirely removed it; when a man is justified it is as if he had never had any sin at all. No, the condemnation of Jesus Christ did not blot out His own innocence and holiness; it was only the divine justice that considered Him a transgressor, who in Himself remained the holy and spotless Lamb of God. Similarly, the sinner's justification before God does not eradicate or blot out the corruption and defilement of his nature, but only erases our names out of the roll of

His debtors. Justice having been satisfied in our cautioner,[1] we are therefore now counted as righteous before God.

Those Justified Must Continue to Be Displeased with Themselves
There is another reason why I am emphasizing this. It is so that you may loathe and abhor yourselves—yes, you who have been made clean by the blood of Jesus Christ—as if you had never been cleansed. Because God no longer regards your sins as debts, so much the more ought you to remember them with shame. Indeed, you should be amazed that they have been pardoned. When we grasp that now God looks favorably on us, it is common for us to look upon ourselves with complacency. Yet I do not think that anyone can thoughtfully consider the grace of God in Jesus Christ to them without loathing themselves even more.

But I commonly find that superficial and careless thoughts of God's pardon produce shallow conceits of themselves in men's hearts. I find this true even in God's children; our self-abhorrence dissipates when peace and favor are spoken to us. Therefore I beseech all who believe there is no condemnation for them, to reflect on how much there remains in them that deserves condemnation; everything in us all is deserving of it. Let this grace of God in blotting out our transgressions beget in us self-loathing and self-abhorrence. The more you believe that He is pleased with you, the more displeased you must be with yourselves, because it is not you with whom He is pleased but His own well-beloved Son.

The day of redemption is coming, when there shall be no condemnation, and no longer anything incurable or sinful either. In heaven you shall be forever clean and spotless but, while you are here on earth, you must never forget the truth about yourselves that you are loathsome and full of abominations. Because the Lord is pacified toward you, says Ezekiel, "remember and be confounded because of your shame, when I atone for you and for all that you have done" (16:63; see also 20:43–44; 36:26–32).

---

1. *cautioner*: one who becomes security for another, a representative, a substitute.

Second Error: Becoming Dead to Any Sense of Sin

There is a new and extraordinary mortification now advocated by many whose highest advancement consists in not feeling, knowing, or confessing sin but in being dead to any sense or conviction of it. Alas, where are our reforming times gone? Is not this the spirit of antichrist? This is no godly mortification, rather is it a crucifying of repentance and holiness. Indeed, it is putting to death the new man for it is a quickening of the lusts of the old man and amounts to living to sin. This is a part of that new (but falsely so-called) gospel that is being preached by some, which, if an angel should bring it from heaven, we ought not to believe. "For no one can lay a foundation other than that which is laid, which is Jesus Christ," already "built on the foundation of the apostles and prophets" (1 Cor. 3:11; Eph. 2:20). Lord, give the Spirit to understand these mysteries already revealed, but save us from such new false "discoveries" and "illumination." That which we have already received is able to make us perfect to salvation.

Almost everyone is now claiming the right to this privilege of Christians of being pardoned and absolved from condemnation, without any examination of the claim. In the meantime, not only do their iniquities testify against them but their continuance in transgressions causes the godly to say that "there is no fear of God before their eyes" (Rom. 3:18). Therefore, the apostle describes those who are in Jesus Christ to be such as walk "not after the flesh, but after the Spirit." His intention is to guard against the presumptuous fancy of those who continue to live in their sins and claim to hope for heaven, and so to stir up every justified soul to a new way of living, now they are in Jesus Christ.

I would make two points regarding this. First, that the Scripture gives marks and characteristics of justified and reconciled persons, by which they may be known both to themselves and others. Second, that the Christian, having been delivered from condemnation, has a new manner of living for he is a new creature in Christ.

Obedience Is a Mark of Those Who Are Justified

It might seem a strange thing that this first point should be questioned by this generation (as if such a clear and important truth could pass without scrutiny), when the very tenor of the Scripture makes so much of it. I wonder how anyone who reads this chapter, or the epistles of James and John, could have any doubts about it? "And hereby do we know that we have come to know him, if we keep his commandments" (1 John 2:3).

Is not the evidence of our state and condition that our daily living conforms to the will of God? What divine truth can we be sure of if this is uncertain? The beloved disciple, who knew how to preach Christ, asserts it in express terms, "I write these things to you who believe in the name of the Son of God, that you may know that you have eternal life" (1 John 5:13). This was the whole great purpose of that evangelic and divine epistle.

I find that Antinomians[2] compound this question so that they may have the more advantage in their darkness. The question is not concerning the grounds of a man's believing in Christ but concerns our assurance, on the one hand, and the substance of what we believe, on the other hand. It is a great mistake when Christians confuse these two. It makes Christians very unreasonable in their doubts and practice. Therefore, let us have this in the forefront of our thinking: faith, in its first and pure action, is more the adherence and cleaving of a lost soul to Christ than the evidence of his blessing in Him, or of Christ's everlasting love.

The Spirit's Seal Brings Assurance

You all are aware that it is one thing to know something, but something else to reflect upon it, and realize that you love it. John wrote to believers, that they might know they did believe, and so

---

2. An Antinomian is one who takes the principle of salvation by faith and divine grace to the point of asserting that the saved are not bound to follow the moral law contained in the Ten Commandments.

believe even more. These things then are both separable and the second follows the first: "In whom also after that you believed you were sealed" (Eph. 1:13). The persuasion of God's love and our interest in Christ is the Spirit's seal set upon the soul.

There is a mutual sealing here. The soul, by believing and trusting in Jesus Christ, "sets his seal to this, that God is true," as John says (3:33). When God speaks in His law, the soul receives that testimony of His justice and holiness and, by condemning itself, subscribes to the justice and righteousness of the sentence. And when Christ speaks in the gospel the soul, by approving and consenting with all its heart to the offer, seals that doctrine of free salvation; therefore, that soul now assents to the way of salvation in Christ and the truth of His promises. And thus is the truth of God and Christ sealed by the soul's believing. Then the Spirit of Jesus Christ afterward, when He pleases, illuminates and shines upon the soul and uncovers to him those things that are freely given, and witnesses to the conscience of the believer that he is a son of God. Thus the Spirit seals the believer and gives His testimony to His truth.

Now if we speak of the first, that is, of believing in Christ to salvation, the only ground of which I know is that which applies to all sinners and is offered in the gospel to all. I speak, on the one hand, of our sin, misery, and utter destitution; and, on the other hand, of Christ's invitation to all to come and receive His full and perfect salvation. No one should seek anything from within himself upon which to build his coming to Christ. Though it is true that no one can come to the Savior until he is convinced of his sin and miserable state, yet neither should anyone offer their convictions as a warrant to come to Christ for salvation. Those who are in earnest about this question, "How shall I be saved?" should not spend time in reflecting on and examining themselves until they find something promising in themselves.

Rather from discovering their sinful, miserable condition they should turn straightaway to the grace and mercy of Christ, without delaying to search for something in themselves to warrant their coming to Him. There should be nothing before the inward eye of the soul other than sin, misery, and absolute necessity, compared with the superabundant grace and righteousness there is in Christ. Thus our only hope is in Christ alone, as we receive Him as offered freely "without money and without price" (Isa. 55:1).

No One Can Be Saved through the Preparatory Work of the Law

I know it is not possible for a soul to receive Christ until there has been some preparatory convicting work of the law to uncover sin and that person's miserable condition. However, to assume that in exchange for the awareness of sin Christ is ready to accept that as the price for His free water and wine is to mix in together Christ and the law. No one should be encouraged to think they are accepted by Christ because they have been convicted of their sin. And for souls to seek the preparatory work of the law in order to find satisfaction therein, without considering the promise of the gospel, is nothing less than to attempt to establish their own righteousness, while remaining ignorant of the righteousness of Christ.

This is why many corrupt the simplicity of the gospel by their rigid exactions of law's preparatory work, thus making them either conditions or restrictions of gospel commands and promises, such as Christ's invitation, "Come unto me, all ye that labour and are heavy laden" (Matt. 11:28). Hence they seem to exclude persons not so qualified from having a warrant to believe. Alas, this is a great mistake in the use of such words. Certainly, these gospel promises are not deliberately given to exclude any who will come, for "whosoever will, let him take the water of life freely" (Rev. 22:17). Rather, such invitations are given to encourage weary and broken souls who consider themselves to be the only persons excluded, by showing them the nature of true faith, in that, before a soul can come to Christ, he must be totally a soul beaten out of itself (cf. Ps. 51:17).

Therefore, I conclude, it is foolish conceit in many Christians to object against believing by using such ridiculous arguments as these: If I were as such and such a person, or if I did love God, or if I had these fruits of the Spirit, or if I walked according to the Spirit—then I might believe. Alas, how directly opposite is this to the terms of the gospel! I say that if you place your hope in any such arguments, and on that basis come to Jesus Christ, then you do not truly come, for you are seeking to establish your own righteousness.

An Awareness of Our Sin Must Persuade Us of the Necessity of Christ
Does any saint, though ever so holy, consider himself to be under such absurd notions of grace when he comes to Christ to be justified? No indeed! But, knowing himself to be ungodly, rather must he deny all that even though God has declared him righteous. Furthermore, it is both unreasonable and incongruous to seek the fruits before the tree has been planted, or to refuse to plant the tree until you can see its fruits. Also, it is contrary to the free and merciful doctrine of the gospel for anyone to seek any goodness in himself when he is but full of sin before he applies to Jesus Christ.

I repeat, there must be some sense of his sin, otherwise he has not rightly discovered sin, but he should not be at pains to find within himself that sense of sin in order to make it a motive for faith in Christ. He ought to go straight toward Christ, and not pause or turn back to seek first some merit in himself. He must indeed examine himself, but not to find himself to be a pious, humble sinner who has some moral grounds for believing. Rather must his self-examination find himself to be a lost perishing sinner, void of all grace and goodness, so that he may find the absolute necessity of Jesus Christ. In this way I think the many disagreements about a soul's true condition preparatory to believing may be reconciled.

Faith Will Be Known through Its Purifying Work in Our Hearts

Now if the question be, as indeed it is, about the grounds of our assurance and knowledge of our own faith, certainly it is as clear as the noonday that as the good tree is known by its fruits and the fire by its heat, so the indwelling of faith in the heart is known by its purifying of the heart and its working by love. A cleansed heart makes us new creatures, so that we and others may know the difference. This does not imply any impairment to the free grace of Christ, nor any attempt to establish our own righteousness. Indeed, believers are so afraid to attempt to establish their own righteousness that they will claim no holiness at all, and rather abandon any pretense of it for fear of relying upon it, for that would be a remedy worse than the disease. This is because holiness is not a ground of our acceptance before God, but only a naked evidence of our believing in Christ and being accepted by God.

We must understand that believing in Christ and being accepted before God have a necessary connection together in the Scriptures, and that the former is more obvious and easier to be discerned than the latter. I am certain that the Lamb's Book of Life is a great mystery, and similarly that every man's regeneration and transformation shall be just as mysterious and hidden as the veiled and secret decrees of God's election. Nonetheless, the Spirit may choose to reveal both the one and the other.

Would commending Christ's grace be at all derogatory to Him when a soul looks upon itself, beautified with his comeliness and adorned with his graces, and yet, because that soul loathes itself, it knows it must ascribe all the honor and praise to Him? Surely not! Would it not be more injury to the fountain and fullness of grace in Christ not to see and contemplate those blessed streams, nor to behold the grace flowing out of this fountain, thus acknowledging from whence they derive?

A Warning against Turning Grace into a Carnal Liberty

I think some Christians, when they become aware of the graces within themselves, may be tempted to idolize them, making them, as it were, mediators. But surely it is no remedy to counter that evil by abandoning all sight and knowledge of the graces freely given us from God. Shall we not speak of the freeness of God's gratuitous grace, because human corruption can turn grace into carnal liberty and wantonness? If these graces are now in us, I am sure it is no virtue to be ignorant of them, for that would be rather a weakness and darkness. It must then be the light and grace of God to know them, and therefore to rejoice in our assurance of faith. For that assurance is neither a forced, ungrounded persuasion, nor merely a strong fancy, devoid of any evidence for it.

There can be no doubt that the apostle's counsel is for us to make our calling and election sure (2 Peter 1:10). How may anyone venture to look into those secrets of the Lamb's Book of Life and read their name there? Undoubtedly His secrets do not belong to us, for they are concealed in an inaccessible light, that will only confound and darken us more. Therefore, those who would be certain of their election, according to the Scriptures, must read the transcript and copy of the book of life, which is written in the hearts and souls of God's elect.

The Seal of the Believer's Election

The thoughts of God are written in His works upon men's spirits. His election has this seal upon it: "The Lord knoweth them that are his," and who can break open this seal (2 Tim. 2:19)? "For who hath known the mind of the Lord?" (Rom. 11:34). No one can, until the Lord by His Spirit transcribes His thoughts in some lineaments and drafts of His own image on those who are new creations; then it may be known they are the epistle of Christ, not written with ink and paper, "but with the Spirit of the living God, not in tables of stone, but in fleshy tablets of the heart" (2 Cor. 3:3). Christ writes His everlasting thoughts of love and goodwill to us in this letter to the Corinthians, and lest we think this extols the creature and abases Christ, the apostle adds in verse 5, "Not that we are sufficient of ourselves to think anything as of ourselves; but our sufficiency is of God."

Seeing His grace in ourselves does not prejudice the grace of God, unless we see it as independent of the fountain, and fail to recognize its true source. No, we must acknowledge that we ourselves have nothing in which we can glory. It is not safe to look straight at the sun; because it is too dazzling for our weak eyes, it is wise not to do that. The best way to look at the sun is through water; then we are better able to see it.

The Spirit's Order Is First to Go Down That We May Go Up

Both God's everlasting love and redemption through Jesus Christ are too glorious to gaze upon with the eyes of flesh; they will dazzle and even blind the spirits of men with their transcendent brightness. Therefore, we must look on the beams of this "sun," as they are palely reflected in our hearts; this is how we may behold the conformity of our souls unto His will, wrought by His Spirit. Then we shall know something of the thoughts of God toward us. If men at the first flight should ascend so high as to be persuaded of God's eternal love and in particular Christ's purchase of them, they will do no more than scorch their waxen wings and melt them, until they fall down into a pit of desperation from that false heaven of their ungrounded persuasion.

The scriptural order is first to go down in order that you may go up. First go down in yourselves and make your calling sure, and then you may rise up to God and make your election sure. You must come by this divinely intended parabola; there is no passing upward by a direct line and getting straight through, unless by the immediate revelation of the Spirit, which is by no means the ordinary route; so let no one lay claim to having taken it.

An Abnormal and Rare Inner Testimony of Grace

I acknowledge that there are occasions when the Spirit may intimate to someone God's thoughts toward his soul and its own miserable state and condition, by an immediate overpowering testimony that silences all doubts and objections and needs no other work or mark to make plain its sincerity and reality. That light of the Spirit shall be apparent in its own light, and so it needs no other witness. The Spirit of God sometimes may speak to a soul, "Son, be of good comfort, thy sins are forgiven thee." Such a beam may break into the soul like an arrow from heaven, without reference to any work of the Spirit upon the heart or word of Scripture as a means to apply it. But this is abnormal and most unusual.

The Normal Testimony Is When Our Consciences Bear Witness
The ordinary testimony of the Spirit is certainly conjoined with the testimony of our own consciences whereby we cry "Abba Father! The Spirit itself beareth witness with our spirit, that we are children of God" (Rom. 8:16). And our consciences bear witness to the work of the Spirit in us, which the Spirit knows to be according to the Word of God. The Spirit makes known to us things that are freely given; but He works by comparing spiritual things with spiritual (1 Cor. 2:10, 13). The fruit and special work of the Holy Ghost in us is the *medium*, and the Spirit's light irradiates and shines upon it and enables the heart to see these truths clearly. For though we be the children of light, yet our light is clouded by so much darkness, as there must be a supervenient[3] and accessory light of the Spirit to disclose and unveil the Spirit's light to us.

The Relevance and Application of This Teaching
Now what is the relevance of all this for us? I fear that there are many ungrounded persuasions among us and that many are

---

3. *supervenient*: something that overtakes or comes over.

building on a sandy foundation. There may even be strong opinions that all is well with those who hold such persuasions, without any examination of their souls or manner of living according to the Word of God; certainly, when the tempest blows, this persuasion cannot stand (Matt. 7:24–27). For example, some teach that no one should question whether they believe or not, but that at present they believe. I think none can believe too suddenly; faith is always in season. It is never too late for faith and repentance.[4] It is certainly never late in respect of the promise, nor is it too early in respect of a man's spiritual condition.

Nevertheless, I cannot think anyone can believe until the Spirit has convinced them of their unbelief. Therefore, I think that most people are nearer faith in Jesus Christ when they know that they lack faith. Nay, it is a part of faith, that is, believing God's Word and affirming that He is true, for a man to take issue with his unbelief and his natural inability—indeed, to begin to loathe them. Consider those who did not believe in Christ because they had such high regard for the opinions of others, and so plotted to kill Him: I think they would have done well to have taken heed to Christ's challenge. For if men must take issue with their sin, they ought to search and identify their sin that they may uncover it, to have it dealt with.

Antinomian Error

Because Antinomians make unbelief the only sin in the world, I wonder how it is that they cannot endure unbelief being exposed and admitted. It seems they do not think it so heinous a sin. It is doubtless true that no one should deliberately abstain from believing in Christ until he first inquires whether he has ever believed or not; but whatever his past has been, he must then put his faith in Jesus Christ, and so flee to Him as a lost sinner and a saving Mediator. But to argue (as do the Antinomians) that everyone will straightaway be convinced that God has loved him

---

4. Nunquam sera est fides nec pænitentia.

and Christ has redeemed him is the futile hope of the hypocrite; such a persuasion is like a spider's web which, when leaned upon, shall immediately give way. That man's expectation shall perish; he has kindled sparks of his own and ignited a wildfire; because he does not walk in the true light of the word he must lie down in sorrow.

The Peril of Self-Deception

Many of you already deceive yourselves and no one can persuade you otherwise, such is the strength of that delusion and fantasy. It is the great part of the heart's deceitfulness to flatter itself in its own eyes, making a man think well of himself and his heart's condition. I beseech you, do not venture your soul's salvation on such groundless opinions; never to question the matter is to leave it always uncertain. If you would judge yourselves according to the Scriptures, many of you have the marks and characters of those who are outside the city of refuge and therefore will have their part in the lake of fire. Will there be no condemnation for you who have never condemned yourselves? Certainly, the more you are averse to condemning yourselves, the closer you are to the lake of fire.

You are not all in Christ, "for they are not all Israel, which are of Israel" (Rom. 9:6). Many (nay, the majority of you) are only Christians in name; you have no real union with Christ, or principle of life from Him. The love you have for yourselves makes you easily believe well of yourselves. Know this, that self-love can blind the eyes, and cause you to imagine that God loves you also. Nay, everyone too easily assumes that what he desires to be is a reality. Therefore, I beseech you, consider if you have any firm grounds for your hopes and confidences, for those whose confidence is in themselves will find such confidence has been in vain.

"You Believe in God, Believe Also in Me"

It would be no disadvantage to you to have your hopes shaken so that instead of a vain presumption you may have the true anchor of hope, "a hope which entereth into that within the veil" (Heb. 6:19). I think one thing that keeps men far from the kingdom of God is that they are not aware that they do not believe in Him. We would make much progress with you by the Word, if we could persuade you that you do not believe, nor have believed from the womb. We could then say to you, as Christ said to His disciples, "Ye believe in God, believe also in me" (John 14:1). It is as if He had said, "You have accepted that it is God the judge and lawgiver who is pronouncing a curse on you, and a verdict that you have hearts that are desperately wicked; now, believe also in Me, the Redeemer. You have believed God in the law, in that you have judged yourselves to be under sin and wrath; now, believe Me in the gospel that brings a ransom from wrath and a remedy for sin."

It is this very unbelief that is the origin of the world's perdition—unbelief in the law. First, you do not consider you are under its condemnation. Second, you do not believe that you have not yet fled to Jesus Christ for refuge. It is these two failures to believe that keep souls in a deep sleep, until final judgment awakens them.

But unto every one of you, I would give this direction: Do not let examination of what you are hinder you from your chief duty and Christ's chief commandment—to believe in Him. I know that many Christians are confused as to what is most important, so they are always wavering because they are more taken up with what concerns comfort and joy rather than that which is Christ's greatest honor and glory. I say that the weightiest matter of the gospel is to consider its precious promises, to believe the excellency and power of Jesus Christ, to love Him in your souls, and to delight in Him; this is the sum and substance of the gospel.

The new and great commandment of the gospel is to face each day knowing His fullness, and to endeavor to understand more of your own inward waywardness and thus even more of His infinite grace. To obey this is the first and most essential part of a Christian's daily walk. Second, knowing that you do believe and have discerned your interest in Christ will be a matter of assurance but of secondary concern. Therefore, I say, whenever you find you are not clear about this second concern, you should be always exercised in the first. For it is Christ's fullness and grace to which we are first called, and if the Lord's people were more exercised in the consideration and belief of the fundamental truths and promises of the gospel, I do not doubt but that the light of these would in due time clear up their concerns over secondary issues. "These ought ye to have done, and not to leave the other undone" (Matt. 23:23). It is still safest to lay to one side secondary issues when they are causing you concern, because to be taken up with them may deflect you from your primary duty, and of course this is Satan's intention. It is better, if you have such concerns, at present to hold fast to Christ's promises in the gospel and to abide in Him, until these secondary matters resolve themselves.

SERMON 4

The Walk of the New Man in Christ

Who walk not after the flesh, but after the Spirit.
—ROMANS 8:1

Christ is made to us of God both righteousness and sanctification; and therefore, those who are in Christ do not only escape condemnation, but they walk according to the Spirit, and not according to the flesh. These two are the sum of the gospel. There is not a greater argument to holy living than this: there is no condemnation for you, neither is there a greater evidence of a soul having escaped condemnation, than walking according to the Spirit. We have spoken a little in general of the evidence that may be had of a person's state from his manner of living and the Spirit's working within him. I am now going to speak of the conjunction of these two, and the influence which that privilege has on this duty, and something of the nature of this description of those "who walk not after the flesh, but after the Spirit."

Humanity's Corruption by Sin

In the creation man was composed of soul and body. There was a right order of subordination of these, suitable to their nature. In his soul he reached angels above, but in his body he was like the beasts below. His body, i.e., his flesh, was a servant to the soul in that it was directed and guided according to the desires and motives of the soul. Now sin has entered, all the beauty of the erstwhile creation has been defaced, including man who is now misplaced. Indeed, sin has driven him out from that due line of subordination to God his Maker, for he would have been equal to God. Thus this beautiful order in mankind has been corrupted, for it has been turned upside down, as it were, completely contrary to its original creation. This corruption has made the servants to ride on horses and the prince to walk on foot.

This is the just punishment of our first sin. Adam's soul was placed by creation under the sole command of its Creator, above all the creatures and his own senses; but in one sin, he proudly exalted himself above God, and lamentably subjected himself below his senses by hearkening to their persuasion. He saw it was good and tasted it, and it was sweet and so he ate of it. What a strange way was this! To be like God, he made himself unlike himself, more like the miserable beasts.

The Soul Has Become a Bondslave of the Flesh

Now, I say, this is the deserved punishment of man. His soul that was a free prince is made a bondslave to the lusts of his flesh; flesh has gotten the throne and keeps it, and lords it over the whole man. Therefore, now the whole unregenerate man is called flesh, as if he had no immortal spirit: "That which is born of the flesh is flesh" (John 3:6); and here in Romans 8:8 is a description of natural men that they "are in the flesh" because flesh is the predominant part that has captivated men's reason and will. However, it is not only the grosser corruptions in a man that have their use and seat in his flesh and body and are referred to under that name. But the whole nature of man is now but flesh, for example, that which is most excellent in him, his soul and spirit, his light and understanding and the most refined principles of his conversation and conduct.

Nay, not only such natural gifts and illuminations, but even the light of the gospel and the law of God, that in some way enter his soul, change their nature and name; all but darkness and flesh in him, because the flesh has dominion over all that. The clouds and vapors that arise from the flesh cover all these with a mist and obscure them. The corruptions of the soul are most strengthened and given fullest expression here. Sin is become co-natural to the flesh, and so by the flesh a man is ensnared and subjected to sin.

Christ includes all our prerogatives and endowments under this: "Born not of blood, nor of the will of the flesh" (John 1:13) and "flesh and blood hath not revealed it unto you" (Matt. 16:17). Even all the outward aspects of religion and all the common privileges of Christians may be so comprehended. "What shall we say then that Abraham our father, as pertaining to the flesh hath found?" (Rom. 4:1, cf. Phil. 3:3). This imports so much—that all those outward privileges, illuminations, and reformations may so far coexist and unite with the corruption of man's nature as to have one name with it. These are not able to conquer our flesh, rather our flesh subdues them all, and makes the outward aspects of religion serve itself, till a stronger than it comes, even the Spirit, to subdue it and cast it out of the house. This then is how the image of God in man has been defaced; nay, the very image and nature of man, as man, is despoiled. Sin has marred and disordered that image.

The New Man in Christ

When this second creation or regeneration comes the creature is made new and formed again by the powerful Spirit of Jesus Christ. The change made is that flesh is put off the throne as a usurper; the spirit and soul of a man is seated on a throne above it, but placed according to its proper order, that is, under a holy and spiritual law of God. And thus Jesus Christ is the repairer of the breaches, and restorer of the ancient paths in which to dwell.

Now the soul has a new rule instituted governing it, and new principles by which to act. He whose course of living was after the corrupt dictates and commands of his fleshly affections and was of no higher strain than his own sparks of nature and the borrowed light that would direct him, now he has a new rule established, that is, the Spirit speaks in the Word to him, pointing out to him the way. And there is a new principle, that Spirit leading him in all truth and quickening him to walk in it.

This is the soul's perfect liberty, to be delivered from being under the dominion of sin and lusts. Thus it is that the Son makes a man free indeed by the free Spirit. The Son Himself was made a servant that we might be made free, no more bondservants of sin in the lusts thereof, for when the Spirit of the Lord comes, there is liberty. There the spirit and reasonable soul of a man is elevated into its first native dignity; there the base flesh is dethroned and made to serve the spirit and soul in a man. Christ is indeed the greatest friend of men, as they are men. Sin made us beasts, but Christ makes us men.

The Truth Is Incarcerated in the Unregenerate

Unbelievers are unreasonable men, αλογος, brutish—yes, in a manner, beasts. This is the common designation of man in Scripture. Faith makes a man reasonable for it imparts the saving and sanctified use of reason. It is a shame for any man to be a slave to his lusts and passions for it imposes the character of a beast upon him. Those who are led by senses and affections are degenerated from human nature; all such are out of Christ. Sin and flesh reign in them and the principles of light and reason within are captivated, incarcerated within a corner of their minds. Those in this state see the generally received truths among men, that God is; that He is holy, just, and good; that heaven and hell really exist. But acknowledging these received truths is altogether ineffectual and has no influence on men's living, no more than if they were unknown, even because the truth is detained in unrighteousness. The corruptions of men's flesh are so rank that they overgrow all these seeds of truth and choke it as the thorns did the seed in Matthew 13:7.

Do Not Be Still Entangled in That Yoke of Bondage!

For you who are called and are in Jesus Christ, oh, know to what you are called! It is to a liberty and privilege indeed. You are no more debtors to the flesh, for Christ has loosed that obligation of servitude to it. Therefore, let it be a shame to you who are Christians to live any longer in such darkness, and to be still entangled in that yoke of bondage! "He that rules his spirit" is greater than the mighty, "than he that taketh a city" (Prov. 16:32). Thus we are called to be more than conquerors. Those who conquer the world remain as slaves to their own lusts; but let it be far from you to continue in that state. You ought to conquer yourselves, which is more than conquering the world.

It is not only unbecoming for a Christian to be led with passions and lusts, it is also below us if we are now no longer through sin below the beasts. Therefore, I beseech you to aspire to the liberty Christ has obtained for you and hold it fast. Be not fashioned any more according to those former lusts. Know that you are the men you were created to be and that you have reasonable and immortal spirits in you. Why should you then walk as beasts? "Understand, ye brutish among the people: and ye fools, when will ye be wise?" (Ps. 94:8).

Partakers of the Divine Nature

But I say more. You who are Christians, know that this is more than to be human; it is to be a divine man in that you are partakers of the divine nature and must live accordingly. Christians are called to a new manner of living that is a fruit coming from the root of faith, whereby they are implanted in Christ. You see these agree well together. Those who are in Christ do not "walk after the flesh but after the Spirit." Walking after the flesh is the common way of life of the world, who are without God and without Christ, but Christ gives no latitude to such a walk. This is a new nature to be in Christ, and therefore this new nature must have a new way of living, it must "walk after the Spirit."

Some Are in the Visible Church but Not in Christ Jesus

While we consider the conversations[1] of the most part of men, they may be a commentary to expound this part of the words, what it is to "walk after the flesh." As the apostle says, "The works of the flesh are manifest" (Gal. 5:19), and indeed they are because they are written in great letters on the outside of many in the visible church, in order that whoever passes by may read them. Do, but also read that catalog given by Paul (vv. 19–21), and then come and see them in congregations. It is not so uncertain and subtle a matter to know that many are yet outside the boundary of Christ Jesus, that is, outside the walls of the city of refuge. You may see their mark on their brow. Is not drunkenness, which is so frequent, a palpable evidence of this? Did not Paul write of their "envy, reviling, wrath, strife, seditions, fornications, and such like"? Oh, do not deceive yourselves! There is no room in Jesus Christ for such impurities and impieties. There is no toleration of sin within His city and kingdom. Sinners are indeed pardoned, yea, received and accepted, drunkards, unclean persons, and those like them; none are excluded from entering Christ's city, but they must renounce these lusts, if they would stay here. Christ will not keep both, for He must either cast out the sin or the sinner if he will not part with his sin.

I beseech you, know which it is that you walk after—the flesh or the Spirit. If the flesh is your leader, whither will it lead you? Oh, it is sad to think of it: it will lead you to perdition, for "If ye live after the flesh, ye shall die" (v. 13). You think the flesh is your great friend, so you do all you can to satisfy and please it, and, oh how pleasant is the satisfaction of your flesh to you! You think it is freedom to follow it and consider being restrained to be bonds and chains. But, oh! know and consider that the flesh will lead you away from the kingdom's guidance to which you once committed yourself; nay, it will lead you to bypass heaven, for "they which do such things will not inherit

---

1. *conversations*: lifestyle or manner of living.

the kingdom of God" (Gal. 5:21). It is a blind guide, corruption, and humor,[2] having no eyes, nor any discernment of that pit of eternal misery. Those who follow the flesh choose the way that is best paved and trodden, the path that is easiest and along which most choose to walk; yet certainly it will lead you straight into this pit of darkness.

An Appeal to Those Who Are Still Carnal

Therefore, turn off this way and from following your blind lusts. Rather suffer your lusts to be crucified. Be avenged on them for both of your eyes that they have put out, and for their treacherous dealings with you in leading you along the highway to destruction. Come into Jesus Christ and you shall get a new guide for the way, the Spirit who shall lead you into all truth and to that blessed eternal life. Christ is the way along which you must walk, and He is the life into which we must enter at the end of our journey, and the truth according to which we must walk. Now He has given His Spirit, the Counselor, to be our leader along this way, according to His rule and pattern for that life. In a word, the Spirit shall lead you on the straight path to Christ. You shall begin in Him, and end in Him. He shall lead you from grace to glory. The Spirit who came down from heaven shall lead you back to heaven. All your walk in this life must be within the compass of Christ. Outside of Him there is no way to heaven.

But we must not comprehend this as meaning that only men's more gross abominations constituted "walking after the flesh." For though even these will draw a great number from being truly in Christ Jesus, the scope of "walking after the flesh" must be further enlarged to include the motives and affections

---

2. Humorism was a system of medicine, adopted by ancient Greek and Roman physicians and philosophers, detailing the makeup and workings of the human body. According to the theory of the four humors, the substances that make up the human body are black bile, yellow bile, blood, and phlegm.

of the unrenewed spirit, and those common principles according to which men live each day. And therefore the apostle names many things among the works of the flesh and faculties of the old man (see Col. 3:7–8; Gal. 5:19–21), some of which—such as anger, wrath, covetousness—I doubt whether many will take much account of for they are so common; but they still issue from natural sinful passions.

What man is there among us in whom some of these do not stir? Many of your hearts and eyes are given to covetousness, and your souls bow down toward them just as your physical bodies do; indeed, your souls are in servitude to them far more than your bodies are. Are not the hearts of men so fixed upon this world, that they cannot rise above to a treasure in heaven? Therefore, although your vocations may be lawful, yet all your daily strenuous endeavors have this seal of the flesh stamped on them, and before God are nothing less than "walking according to the flesh."

How All-Pervading and Insidious Are the Works of the Flesh!

We see how rank the corruptions of men are, anger domineering in them, often leading them captive. And this they consider but a light matter, yet it is not so in Scripture. How often is it branded as folly by the wise man! And this folly is the natural fleshly corruption with which men are born, and in so many it rises up to the elevation of malice and hatred of others. Then it is imprinted with the image of the devil rather than of mere human infirmity. Even if we suppose a man is not much given to any of these, nevertheless what a spirit of pride and self-love is in him! It is even in those who hoist the lowliest sail and steer for the humblest port. It also includes those who are affable and agreeable, and others who seem most courteous toward inferiors and equals. Yet, alas, this evil is ever deeply engraved on men's spirits.

If they could but watch over their hearts and observe all its secret reflections and the comparisons it makes, together with all the desires of applause and favor from others, all the surmises and angry stirrings of spirit upon any suggestion of disrespect, then they would uncover their diabolic pride! This sin of pride is more native to us and inbred, for it is our mother-sin that brought us down from our original excellence and innocence. This weed grows both upon a glass window and upon a dunghill; it lodges in palaces and cottages. Nay, it will spring and grow out of a pretended humility and lowly bearing. In a word, common to all men are our ambitious designs and insatiable appetite for worldly things, our overweening conceit and love for ourselves, the inner stirrings of our lusts, our disregard for any rule over unlawful objects gained unlawfully—all men pursue these. Everyone has some predominant passion or idol that absorbs him most. Some are finer and more subtle than others, some have their pleasures and gains without, others their own gifts and parts within, but both are alike odious before God, for both are gross sinful flesh and corruption before Him.

Two Common Errors
There are two errors among men concerning the spiritual walk regarding which our text speaks. One is the doctrine some hold in these days and the other is the practical error of many of us.

The First is Separating the Spirit from the Word
Regarding the first, many are claiming to have some new and high discoveries as to Christ and the Spirit; they have fallen upon the most refined and spiritualized flesh instead of the true Spirit. They separate the Spirit from the Word, and reckon the Word and Law of God, which was a lamp to David's feet, to be among the fleshly rudiments of the world. But, as Isaiah says, if they speak not "according to the law and to the testimony, it is because there is no light in them" (8:20). Thus their new light is but an old darkness, that could not endure even the dimmer light of the Old Testament prophets. If those in error do not speak according to the Word, it is because there is no Spirit in them. Is it not the Spirit, the Counselor, whom Christ promised to send

both to the apostles and to all who should believe in His name through their Word? For that Spirit was a Spirit of truth who would lead into all truth. And lest men should foist their own fancies and imaginations on the Spirit of God, Christ added, "he shall bring all things to your remembrance," those things that Christ had spoken, and we have written here (John 14:26).

In Colossians 3, when he reproves the works of the flesh and declares they had put them off, the holy apostle commends the believers, in opposition to these false teachers of whom we are speaking, to "let the word of Christ dwell in you richly in all wisdom, teaching one another in psalms and spiritual songs, with grace in your hearts to the Lord" (v. 16). Here the Spirit is not casting out the Word but bringing it in plentifully and sweetly agreeing with it. The Spirit that Christ sent did not put men above ordinances but above corruptions and the body of death in them. It is a poor and easy victory to subdue grace and ordinances—every slave of the devil does that. As men and angels fell from their own dignity by aspiring higher, so I fear those that will not be content with the estate of Christ and His apostles, but would fain soar up in a higher strain of spirit, thereby trampling on the apostolic ministration as fleshly and carnal—I fear they fall from Jesus Christ, and come into greater condemnation.

It is true indeed that "the letter killeth" (2 Cor. 3:6), that is, the covenant of works preaches but condemnation to men, whereas the Spirit of the gospel gives life. Nay, if the gospel is separated from the Spirit of life in Jesus, it becomes a savor of death to souls. Shall we therefore separate the Spirit from the gospel and the Word because the Word alone cannot bring us life? David knew how to reconcile this: "Quicken thou me according to thy Word," and "thy Spirit is good, lead me into the land of uprightness, quicken me, O Lord" (Pss. 119:25; 143:10–11). The Word was his rule, and the Spirit applied his soul to the rule. Thus we see that Word holds out the present pattern to which we should be conformed.

Now if the Word stands alone, a man may look all his days on it, and yet not be changed; however, when the Spirit is within him, the Word transforms and changes his soul to more and more conformity to that pattern as he meditates upon it. If a man shall shut his eyes on the pattern, he cannot know what he is, and what he ought to be. If he looks only on the Spirit's work within, and makes that his rule, he has only an imperfect rule and an incomplete copy. And yet this is the highest attainment of those who aspire to "new light." They have forsaken the Word as their rule, and instead have replaced it by another law within them, that is, what is already written on their hearts, which is in substance this, as they suppose: "I am bound to do no more than I have already power to do; I am not to endeavor more holiness than I have already."

In their own apprehension, these men are indeed perfect here but do not know it is only in part; they believe in part, and obey in part, because they have progressed no further than the length of their own law and rule, their rule being of no perfection. This was not so with Paul who, forgetting what he had already attained, followed on to what was before him, and continued to reach forward (Phil. 3:12). Let not us, my brethren, believe every spirit, and everything that comes out under the name of doctrine; Christ has forewarned us. Rather pray for more of that Spirit which may quicken the Word to us and quicken us to obey the Word. There must be a mutual enlivening of both Word and Spirit. The Word must be the ministration of life by the Spirit of Jesus, who can use it as a sword to divide the soul and spirit; and we must be quickened to the obedience of the truth in the Word.

The Word is the incorruptible seed; but it cannot of itself bring us to birth, or be a principle of new life within us, unless the living Spirit comes into our hearts. Therefore, know that the Word is your pattern and rule and that the Spirit is your leader and helper, whose virtue and power must conform you to that rule (1 Peter 1:12, 23). Thus we see that Peter joins these two— the purification and cleansing of the soul, which Christ attributes to the Word: "Now ye are clean through the word which I have spoken unto you" (John 15:3). Peter attributes the Word's enlivening power to the Spirit working according to the pattern of truth. It is true that the Spirit of God needs no pattern to look to; yet we must have it and carefully observe it, else we know not the Spirit of truth from a lie and delusion. We can only try the spirits by this rule; yet it is by steadfastly looking on this glorious pattern in the Word, along with the example of Christ Jesus's life, that we are conformed unto Christ, as by the Lord (2 Cor. 3:13). Certainly living which is conformed to the imaginations of a man's own heart rather than the blessed will of God revealed in His Word must be carnal. Can such living please God, when a man will not so much as hearken to what is God's will and pleasure? As other heresies, so especially this is a work of the flesh.

The Second Error Concerns Conduct That Outwardly Appears to Be Blameless

Now there is another principle among many of us. Some regard being separated from the gross pollutions of the world as spiritual "walking," that is, to have the outward appearance of being blameless before men. This is the notion which the multitude fancies. Do not be deceived! You may pass the censure of all men, and be without reproach among them, and yet still be but walkers *after the flesh*. It is not what you are in the sight of the world that can prove you to be spiritual men, though in fact it may prove many of you to be carnal. What you are outwardly may well demonstrate that many of you walk after the flesh. If you will not believe this, I ask you if you think drunkenness is walking in the Spirit? Do you think you are following the Spirit of God in uncleanness? Is it not that Holy Spirit who purges us from all filthiness?

Consider your daily walk and see that you are not so much as conformed to the letter of the Word in anything, you who do not care to read and meditate upon the Scriptures. Is this walking after the Spirit of truth? If drunkenness, railing, contention, wrath, envy, covetousness, and such like, be the Spirit's way, then I confess many of you do walk after the Spirit; but if these are manifestly works of the flesh, and manifestly your way of living, then why do you dream that you are Christians?

But suppose that you could not be charged with any of these outward things; suppose that you have a form of religion and godliness, yet I say, all that is visible before men cannot prove that you are living spiritually. Remember it is the Spirit you must walk after. Now, what shall be the chief agent here? Surely not the body—what fellowship can your body have with him that is a Spirit? The body, indeed, may worship that eternal Spirit, being enabled by the Spirit; but I say, on its own that can never prove you to be Christians. We must then lay aside a number of those who only profess but have no other ground of confidence except such things as may be seen of men.

If these men would enter into their hearts, how many vain thoughts would they find lodging there? Oh, how little of God is truly there! God is almost absent in all their thoughts. They give him a morning and evening salutation, but there is no more of him throughout the rest of the day. And is this walking after the Spirit, which bespeaks a constancy? And what part of a man can be neglected most, but his spirit? The body is distracted with other necessary things, yet we might always ignore our souls before God.

Now, how should a man obey that command—"pray always"? It is impossible that he should do nothing else but pray in an expressly formal way. But the soul's walking with God, between times of prayer, should compensate for that. And thus prayer is continued, though not formally in itself, but in meditation on God. Such meditation has in it the seed of all worship, and is in effect prayer and thanksgiving, amid all our duties.

Concluding Challenge

Let us then consider this, whether our bodies are more exercised in religion than our souls: more, are they not the chief agents in our living? How many impertinencies, roving thoughts, and wandering imaginations do we have throughout the day? The most part of our conversation, if it is not profane yet is vanity, that is, unprofitable in the world. It neither advantages us spiritually nor glorifies God. It is almost to no purpose; and this is enough to make it all fleshly living. As for our thoughts, how do they go unlimited and unrestrained? Are they like a wild ass, traversing her ways, and gadding about, fixed on nothing—at least not on God? Nay, are they fixed on anything but God? If it is to be spiritual service, should it not carry the seal of our spirit and affection on it? We are like so many shadows walking, as pictures and statues of Christians, without that genuine soul and life which ought to reside in the temper and disposition of the spirit and soul toward God.

SERMON 5

The Principles and Motivation of Spiritual Walking

Who walk not after the flesh, but after the Spirit.
—ROMANS 8:1

It is no wonder that we cannot speak anything to purpose of this subject and that you do not bear its fruit, because it is indeed a mystery to our judgments and a great stranger to our practice. Because there is so little of the Spirit, both in those who teach and those who come to be taught, we can only speak of it as something obscure and unknown. Thus we cannot enable you to conceive of it in the living notion of it as it is. Only we may say in general that it is certainly a something divine, and quite alien to our common or even our religious walk. We only know the least of it, for we have such little experience of it. But this much we should recognize—it is something to which we have not yet attained. Although it is beyond us, yet we are called to aspire to it. How it should stir up in our spirits a holy fire of ambition to partake of such a thing when we hear it is attainable! Nay, even more so when Christ calls us to Himself, that we may thus walk with Him!

I would have Christians who are men of great projects and resolutions, who are of high and unlimited desires, not satisfied with their attainments. Men who are still aspiring unto more of God, more conformity to His will, more walking after the Spirit, more separation from the course of this world. And this is indeed to be of a divine spirit. The divine nature is present, as it were, in a state of violent conflict, for in this fallen world it is out of its own element. Now, it is known by this: it is still moving upward, taking no rest in this world and its standards and gradations, but is resolved upon a continual motion toward its proper center—God, His holiness, and His Spirit.

The Nature of Spiritual Walking

We desire to speak a word of these three. First, the nature of the spiritual walking. Next, its connection and union with that blessed state of non-condemnation. Third, of its order and how it flows from a man's being implanted in Christ Jesus. These three are latent in the words, "Who walk not after the flesh, but after the Spirit."

First, the Spiritual Rule of Walking

This spiritual walking is according to a *spiritual rule*, from *spiritual principles*, for *spiritual ends*. These three being established aright, the walk is ever the living of a Christian within their compass. It is according to the Word as the holy rule; it is from the faith and love of Jesus Christ as the predominant principles. Nay, the Spirit of Jesus, living in the heart by faith, and dwelling in it by love, is as the first wheel of this motion, the "first moved."[1] And as it begins in the spirit, so it ends there, in the glory of Jesus Christ, and our heavenly Father. Consider this then: it is not a lawless or irregular walk, it is according to the spiritual rule, and the rule is perfect, and it is a motion toward perfection, not a rest in what is now attained.

The course of this world is the way and rule of the children of disobedience (Eph. 2:2). There is a spirit indeed that works in

---

1. The concept of *primum mobile* (first moved) was introduced by Ptolemy to account for the apparent daily motion of the heavens around the earth. In classical, medieval, and Renaissance astronomy, the Primum Mobile was the outermost moving sphere in the geocentric model of the universe. Here it has the meaning of the First Cause.

them, and a rule it works by. The spirit is that evil spirit, contrary to the Holy Spirit of God, and you may know what spirit it is that is at work by the way it leads men into a broad way, pathed and trodden in by many travelers. It is the king's high street, the common way along which most people walk just as their neighbors and others do. But that king is the prince of this world, Satan, who blinds the eyes of many, that they may not see the pit of misery before them, toward which the pathway is leading them.

Believers Must Exhibit a Divine Singularity
A Christian must have a kind of singularity, not in opinion but rather in practice, to be more holy and to walk more abstracted and separate from the dregs of the world's pollution. This must be a divine singularity. Indeed, those who are separate from the godly in their outlook ought seriously to examine themselves; they have every reason to be more suspicious of themselves when they offend against the generation of the just. But if those who are suspicious of themselves intend to be different from the majority, nay, even to differ from the multitude of professing believers in their desire and practice of holy humility and their spiritual walk, I think this is commendable though not the usual pathway most follow. Men may rightly aspire to as great a difference as possible from the conversations and practice of others, as long as their purpose is more conformity to the Word of God, the rule of all practice.

The law is spiritual and "holy," says Paul, "but I am carnal" (Rom. 7:12, 14). Therefore, spiritual walking is to see its excellent spiritual rule before our eyes, so that we who are carnal may be transformed and changed into more likeness to that holy and spiritual law. If a man has an imperfect rule of his own fancy and devising before his eyes, he will never be satisfied with his attainments, but, with Paul, will forget them in such a way as to reach forward still to what lies before him. Because so much length would always be before us that would swallow up all our advancement, this would maintain our progress along the way, making it constant.

Comparisons with Others Are Retrograde Motions
A man should never say, "Master, let us make tabernacles, it is good for us to be here" (cf. Mark 9:5). No, indeed, the dwelling place and resting must be seen to be above. As long as a man has so much of his journey still to accomplish, he must not sit down in his advancement, nor compare himself with others, nor exalt himself above others. Why? Because there is still a far greater distance between him and his spiritual rule than between himself and the slowest walker. This made Paul more sensible of a body of death (Rom. 7:24), than lower[2] Christians tend to be. Reflections on our attainments and comparisons with others, which are so often the work of our spirit, not the Holy Spirit, are a retrograde motion; they do not lead us forward but to misspend our time; they cause us to return whence we have come, whereas we ought to go straight forward.

I beseech you, Christians, consider what you are doing if you would prove yourselves so indeed. I know not how you can evidence it better than by honoring and esteeming His Word and commandments, exceeding large and precious as they are, for there is no end to their perfection. The Word is much undervalued in the opinion of many; alas, it is as little cared for in the practice of most. There is certainly little of God there where His Word is not magnified and honored. There can only be darkness on that pathway where this candle, which was a lamp to David's feet, shines not.

Some promise to us liberty, but they themselves are the servants of corruption, for it is no liberty to be above all law and rule. It was innocent Adam's liberty to be conformed to a holy and just command, nay, this was his beauty. This Spirit indeed gives liberty where He is, but His liberty is from our sins and

---

2. That is, less mature.

corruptions; His is not a liberty to indulge them. It loosens a man from the chains of his own corrupt lusts, freeing him to walk in the way of His commandments. The Spirit enlarges the prisoner's heart and then he runs, not at random, but along the way of His commands (Ps. 119:32). It was our bondage to be as wild asses, traversing our ways, to be gadding abroad, constantly changing our pathways. Now, here is the Spirit's liberty to bring us into His way, the way that is unchanging.

The Second Principle: The Word Must Guide Our Walking

Let us then learn this second principle—the Word must be the rule of your walking both common and religious. Never think that spiritual walking is restricted to religion or to some solemn duties. Remember, it is a walk, a continuous thing without interruption. Therefore, your whole manner of living ought to be like so many steps progressing forward to heaven. Your spiritual walk should not begin only when you come to pray or read or hear, as with so many. They are on a quite different pathway and element when they step out of their everyday callings into religious ordinances. But Christians, your walk should be continued as you eat and drink, even in your sleeping and acting in your daily vocation. Therefore, when you come to pray or read, you must be but stepping forward along the way, out of one darker, obscurer path, into a more beaten way. Remember, the Word can make us perfect to salvation.

There is a principle in the hearts of folks which is vented[3] now by many, and consequently the Word does not reach their particular carriages[4] and conversations in civil matters. These men appear to be out with the sphere and compass of the Word, while they commonly cast up to ministers, "Meddle with the word and

---

3. *vented*: to air a negative or insulting opinion.
4. *carriages*: ways of conduct or behavior.

spiritual things and not with our matters."[5] Truly I think, if we separate these from the Word, we may quickly separate all religion from such actions, and if such actions and administration are out with the court of the Word, they are also out with the court of conscience—conscience, religion, and the Word being commensurable.[6] Therefore I beseech every one of you, take the Word for the ruling of your callings and conversations among men. Extend it to all your actions, that in all these you may act as Christians as well as men. It is certainly on account of the licentiousness of the spirits of men, that they cannot endure the application of the Word to their particular actions and behavior.

Thus we see this spiritual walk proceeds from spiritual principles. It is certain, the Spirit of Jesus Christ is He in whom "we live, and move, and have our being" spiritually (Acts 17:28). Without Him we can do nothing. And therefore Christians ought to walk with such a subordination to and dependence on Him as if they were mere instruments, and patients under his hand. Though I think in regard to endeavored activity they should diligently bestir themselves, as if they acted independently of the Spirit; I mean that they ought to bestir themselves in their denial of themselves and in their dependence on the Spirit, thus each one ought to act as if he did not act at all but the Spirit only acted in him. This is the divinity of Paul[7] when he says, "I laboured more abundantly than they all: yet not I, but the grace of God which was with me.... I live; yet not I, but Christ liveth in me" (1 Cor. 15:10; Gal. 2:20).

Oh, how difficult is it to reconcile these two in the practice of Christians which yet cannot really be, except they be together! It is certainly one of the great mysteries of Christianity, to draw our strength and activity from another, to look upon ourselves

---

5. The reference could possibly be to some of Cromwell's English soldiers billeted in Glasgow who were objecting to ministers commenting on their conduct of affairs of state.

6. *commensurable*: measurable by the same standard.

7. Binning means, "This is the divinely empowered energy of Paul."

and our actions as if they can do nothing—they are empty vines, and that notwithstanding all infused and acquired principles. Whatever we ought to do in judging and discerning of our condition, yet I am sure that Christians, in the exercise and practice of godliness, should look upon themselves as void of any principle in and of themselves either to do or think.

It is not that we are sufficient of ourselves. The proficient and growing Christian should look no more on his own inclinations and habits than if he had none. He should consider himself to be ungodly, in whom no spiritual fruit can grow; he should see himself even as one who cannot pray as he is in himself. But alas, we come to our religious duties in the confidence of our qualifications for them. We act more confidently in them because we have become accustomed to them, and so we make grace and religion a kind of art and discipline, in which our usage and experience has made us experts.

Learn to Fix Your Gaze upon Christ's Grace and the Spirit's Enabling

Learn now this one thing, which would be instead of many rules and doctrines to us: to shut out of your eyes the consideration of what you are by gifts, or grace, or experience. Do not dwell upon such considerations, rather fix your eyes on the grace of Jesus Christ, and upon the power and virtue of the Holy Spirit, which is given by promise. Then, when the way is all the easier to you, both by delight and custom, yet you may find it according to your natural principles as insuperable as at the beginning and may still cry out, "Draw me, and I will run after You, lead me, and I will walk with You." Do not measure the call into duties by the strength you find in yourself but look unto Him who strengthens us with all-might.

Now, the Spirit works in us by subordinate spiritual principles, as believing in Christ and loving of him as our Lord and Savior, and these two acts drive on a soul sweetly in the way of obedience. Fear, where not mixed in its actions with faith and love, is a spirit of bondage, but the Christian ought to walk according to the spirit of adoption which cries, "Abba, Father." Yet how many Christians, in a servile and slavish manner, are more driven to their duty by terrors and chastisements than by love! There is an experience of liberty in Christian walking when there is no restraint upon the spirit by this slavish fear. This, I say, is not beseeming[8] those that are in Christ Jesus. You ought to have the Spirit of your Father for your leader and guide.

The Sweetness of Christ's Love

Oh how sweet, also how certain and necessary, would be this walking in the Spirit! The love of Christ would be an inward principle of progress and would make our spiritual actions as easy and pleasant as natural growth. Fear is a violent principle like the impulse of a stone thrown upward; as long as that visible impression remains it moves but still slower and slower, until at length it disappears. But if you believed in Christ and your hearts were engaged to love Him, oh how would it be a pleasant and natural thing to walk in His way, as a stone goes downward!

Consider your principles, that guide you to the matters and duties of religion. Many men there be, in whom there appears no difference in their work to those who behold them; but oh how wide a difference God discerns in them! Engines and artifice may make dead and lifeless things move and walk as orderly as things that have life. But spiritual principles make a huge difference in that the one is moved from without, the other from within itself. Most of us act as irrational and brute beasts in religion: nay, we walk as inanimate and senseless creatures. It is one or some other consideration outside of ourselves that motivates us—custom, censure, education, and such like.

Ah, these are the principles of our religion! How many would have neither religion nor any form of it if they were not among such company! Therefore, we see many who change

---

8. *beseeming*: becoming or fitting.

their principles according to the company they are in, as some fish changes its skin, according to the color of those nearest to it. How many desire to do many things but they do not dare because of punishment and censure; for that same reason they dare not leave other things undone! In a word, the majority of us are such as would walk in no path of godliness, if it were not the custom of the time and fear of men that constrained us.

Third, the Spiritual Ends of Spiritual Walking
But, my brethren, let it not be so among you, you who are in Christ Jesus. Let this be predominant in your hearts to constrain you not to live to yourselves but unto God, even this, that you believe Christ has died for sinners, that they might live from sin (2 Cor. 5:14–15). And from this let your hearts be inflamed with His love, that it may carry you on a sweet and blessed necessity to walk in all well-pleasing to him. Let the consideration of His love lay on you a constraint, but a constraint of willingness, to live to Him who has thus loved you. But as the principle is spiritual, so must the end be. And I think these two complete the mystery of the practice of Christianity: to act from another principle unto another end, even as, likewise, these two make up the mystery of iniquity in our hearts when we act from within ourselves for ourselves.

Every man naturally makes a god of himself and is his own Alpha and Omega, the beginning of his actions and the end of them; but this pertains only to God. The fall has cut off the subordination of the soul to God in its actions, so that it cannot now derive all from that blessed fountain of all-being and well-being. Consequently, this channel of reference of all our actions to God has stopped in that they do not tend unto Him, as they are not derived from Him; thus they again revert unto a man's self. There is one point of self that makes it our aim and design, to which possibly many do not take heed.

This is why habitually we act and walk in Christian duties for our salvation, in order to obtain life eternal as our chief and only end. Yet this is for an inferior end because we ought not to walk mainly *for* life, but *to* life. We should not walk according to the command only because it is given from heaven, but we should walk in its way because the command's end is heaven. Our spiritual walking can never purchase for us a right to the least of His mercies. When we have done all, this should be our soul's language, "We are unprofitable servants" (Luke 17:10); our righteousness does not reach as high as heaven. What gain is it to the Almighty that you are righteous? Yet for the most part, we regard our walking as if it is a hire for the reward.

But this is the covenant of works: doing something to earn life is naturally imprinted in our hearts. Though we cannot ever attain it, but we try to gain it by what we do; though we cannot walk unto all well-pleasing, nevertheless we attempt to walk in order to pacify God. Self-righteousness is men's great idol, which, when all other baser and grosser idols are down, they still seek to establish. But, Christians, observe this evil within yourselves and allow this mystery of godliness to be wrought in you—the abasing of yourselves, the denial of yourselves.

Christ's Love for Us Is the Great Purpose of Obedience

In respect of diligence and earnestness—doing, walking, running—I would have you engaged in it as thoroughly as if you were to be saved by it alone. Nevertheless, you must deny all that and no more consider it or lean upon it than if you ought to do nothing, or indeed have done nothing. But your ends should be much more divine and high, as your nature is; they should be to glorify God in your mortal bodies, since you are His, and bought with a price. Oh how ought you not to think of yourselves as your own! The great purpose of your obedience should be a declaration of your sense of His love, and of your obligation to Him. You ought to walk in His way because you have escaped condemnation, and have been saved by Him, and not only that you may be saved.

It is to the glory of our heavenly Father and the honor of the Redeemer for Christians to walk as Christ walked, and to follow His footsteps. This commends the grace of Jesus Christ exceedingly. Therefore, to walk unto all well-pleasing cannot but be the choice and delight of believing souls. It is to have His glory as their great design to aim at, who for our salvation laid aside His glory, and embraced shame and reproach. We used to walk in obedience to God in order to pacify God for our disobedience. But let Christians abhor such a thought. Christ's blood alone must pacify, but the walking of His children in His well-beloved Son pleases God. When He is once pacified for sin, when He once accepts your persons, your performances are His delight. Now this should be the great scope of a soul, that all its powers should be fixed on this—to please Him and live to Him.

Now these three being established, we must conceive that the chief agent and party[9] in this walking must be spiritual; therefore, our mortal bodies are not capable of instigating or pursuing this walk after the Spirit. Outward ordinances are but the shell wherein the kernel must be enclosed. All our walking that is visible to men is but like a painted or graven image or statue that has no breath or life in it unless the Spirit activate and quicken it. I say not only the Spirit of God, but the spirit and soul in man; for the Spirit's immediate and divine operations are upon such an appropriate subject as the immortal soul. Verily, there is a spirit in man, and the inspiration of the Almighty gives him understanding.

Nonetheless, we must not abolish the outward form, that is, the human body, because it does have something of divinity in it, even the stamp of God's authority. Therefore, I fear that those who are obsessed solely with ordinances are monstrous[10] Christians. A man is composed of both spirit and body, acted upon, and quickened by that Spirit. Without either of these he is not

---

9. *party*: someone concerned with or participating in an action.
10. *monstrous*: outrageous or scandalous.

a complete man. So I say, he is not a Christian who does not worship God in both spirit and truth (John 4:23); nor is it religion that excludes either the inward soul-communion with God, or the outward ordinance and appointment of God. But alas, this may be our malady: we come and worship God, drawing nigh with our bodies, but our hearts are far removed. Here is the death of the worship of many—their souls are separated from their bodies.

These are but pictures and images of Christians. We have mouths and faces of saints: but oh how little of divine affection or of soul-desires breathes within us! We are those who, by resting in a form, deny the power of godliness, and this is the great sin of this generation. The essentials, the vital spirits of Christianity, are exhausted, and some dry bones, like an anatomy or corpse of a Christian, remain behind. I beseech you, gather your spirits to this spiritual walking: they only can follow the Spirit. Your bodies are earthly and ungainly, and the way is all upward to the holy hill. Look inwardly and measure yourselves. Outward appearance is no just measure. Retire within your souls, and engage them in this exercise, and enter them to this motion, and your spirits will sweetly and surely act upon your bodies and mortality, in all matters of godliness.

SERMON 6

No Walking in the Spirit— No Fruit of the Spirit

Who walk not after the flesh, but after the Spirit.
—ROMANS 8:1

The Vital Relationship between Justification and Sanctification

It is one of the greatest mysteries in a Christian's practice to join together the two doctrines which the gospel has conjoined: justification and sanctification; the gospel places them in their due order.[1] There is much miscarrying[2] of both of these, when they are either separated or misplaced. But the truth is, they can only be rightly understood when they are in their right order. Yet often it happens that in men's apprehensions and endeavors they are joined.

This, then, is the right understanding of a living, believing Christian: he joins the study of holiness with the exercise of faith in Christ for remission of sin and the imputation of Christ's righteousness; but not only does he join them together, he also

---

1. Early on in Sermon 5 Binning had stated: "We desire to speak a word of these three. First, the nature of the spiritual walking. Next, its connection and union with that blessed state of non-condemnation. And third, of its order and how it flows from a man's being implanted in Christ Jesus. These three are latent in the words, 'Who walk not after the flesh, but after the Spirit.'" In that fifth sermon he dealt only with "The Nature of Spiritual Walking." Now he comes to his second point of "its connection and union with that blessed state of non-condemnation."

2. *miscarrying*: wrong understanding.

does so to derive his understanding from this uniting of them. There is both a union between these and an order established in Scripture.

Holiness Neglected by Many
The majority of those who profess the gospel are of two sorts; they either separate holiness from imputed righteousness, or else disjoin Christ's righteousness from holiness. I do not say that anyone who truly seeks to be covered with the righteousness of Jesus Christ, and to have his sins freely pardoned, will not also study to walk before God in all well-pleasing. But the truth is that many do claim and profess to seek salvation and forgiveness in Christ's blood, and always have the mercy of God and merits of Christ on their lips, who yet make it clear by their conversation that they do not so much as desire or intend to seek after holiness.

I do not speak of those who are Antinomians in profession, but of a great multitude in the visible church who are really more Antinomians in practice than most of our professed Antinomians. They hear all about free grace and free redemption in Jesus Christ, of the tender and enduring mercies in God, and this they take for the whole gospel. Then presently, depending upon the notion of mercy and grace, they conclude for themselves, not only immunity and freedom from all the threats of the Word and from hell, but likewise they adopt secretly in their own hearts a liberty to sin so much the more securely.

The door of mercy cast open in the gospel and the free access to Christ manifested therein, through the corruption that is within us has proven to be the very occasion of many giving indulgence to their lusts and of delaying reformation and genuine turning to God. You all profess that you seek to be justified and saved by Jesus Christ; yea, you persuade yourselves that through Christ you have escaped condemnation. Now then, conjoin that profession and persuasion with your daily walk, and oh how contrary you may find them to one another! "Your faith is vain," for "ye are yet in your sins" (1 Cor. 15:17). The grace of God that has appeared to some has effectually taught them to deny ungodliness and worldly lusts, and to live righteous, sober and godly lives (Titus 2:11–12). But if we may surmise your teaching by your daily walk, it seems the notion of grace and the gospel that has formed itself in your minds has taught you another doctrine—to avow ungodliness and follow worldly lusts.

The Vanity of Trusting in Good Works
Is there so much as even a shadow of this spiritual walking in many? I confess, it is natural for every man to seek his own righteousness, and it is the arm of God that must cause men to bow and submit to Christ's imputed righteousness. Yet the majority of men seem to be so far from seeking any righteousness that they are rather seeking the fulfillment of their own carnal lusts, working wickedness with greed, not caring how little they have to put confidence into. And yet it is certain that however much a man attains to some form of religion or civil honesty, he is ready to put his trust in it, and to lean the weight of his soul upon it. But because seeking heaven by doing and working is natural to you all, I wonder that you do not attempt more. How can you satisfy your consciences in the expectation of heaven, when you take so little pains in religion, and are so loose and profane in your whole manner of living? I wonder, seeing you have it naturally engraved in your hearts to establish your own righteousness, that you do not labor to have more of it with which to fill your eyes.

But again, on the other hand, there are some who have a form of religion and labor to be of a blameless life among men, and who try their best to persuade themselves they are seeking holiness and walking spiritually. But alas, you may find it but a painted appearance of religion that is an abomination in the sight of God; because for them it is the entire ground of their acceptation before God. If ever this question was moved in some of you, "What shall I do to be saved?" you have already condescended on such a walk—your painted appearance of religion—for the answer. It is natural to all, even those who have least appearance of godliness, to seek heaven by doing God's will. Those who have no more to speak of than their baptism, or receiving the Lord's Supper, or attending well the solemn assemblies, will ground their hope of salvation on these things. How much more will civil and honest men, commonly so-called, who pray and read, and profess godliness—how much more, I say, will they establish that to which they strive as the ground of their confidence before God!

Our Imperfect Righteousness Cannot Save Us
Now, this is generally an unknown malaise that destroys the world, and yet few are convinced of it, namely, how hard it is to be driven out of ourselves in order to seek life in another. Oh that you would understand how, in a manner, it is the crucifying of a man's self thus to deny himself: that is, to have a sort of righteousness[3] but not to trust in it. Who is he that cannot endure to look upon himself for moral vileness? Alas, men flatter themselves in their own eyes, and look with a more favorable eye on their own actions than they ought! Who is he that abhors himself even for abominable works? But who shall be found to abhor himself for his most religious and best actions? Who casts these out of his sight as unclean and menstruous things (Isa. 64:6)? Therefore, I say, though thy righteousness is equal to or exceeds any Pharisee's righteousness, you cannot enter into heaven (Matt. 5:20).

The Only Garment of Beauty is Christ's Righteousness
The poor publican, who was a vile and profane sinner, yet had a righteousness exceeding the Pharisees' (Luke 18:9–14). Though he had none of his own, yet he had a righteousness without blemish, of Christ's purchasing, having by faith fled to the mercy

---

3. Binning is most probably referring to what Calvin describes as the believer's imperfect righteousness in *Institutes of the Christian Religion*, 3.14.9, 18. See also Robert Bruce's Sermons on Hebrews 11, *Preaching Without Fear or Favour* (Fearn, Ross-shire: Christian Focus Publications, 2019), 529–32.

of God, in and through a Mediator. It is not more doing, more praying, more exact walking, that can make you more righteous in God's accounts; none of these can earn absolution from law-condemnation, any more than they can for the most profane and wretched sinner. Nevertheless, the more base and vile you are in your own eyes, the more you will hide your best doings from your own eyes. For as you look on your uncleanness and betake yourself to Christ and to His unspotted and perfect righteousness, the more honorable and precious you are in His eyes. Therefore, God is said to dwell in the hearts of the humble and contrite, not for the worth of their humility and repentance, no, no, but for the pleasure He has in His well-beloved Son's righteousness. That is the only beautiful garment in the eye of a humbled soul that sees nothing desirable in itself.

Therefore, I long that this conjunction which is made in the gospel, was also engraved in your hearts and on your practices, so that you would seek after holiness, without which no man shall see God. Seek to be perfect in the fear of God, but not as though you were thereby to be justified. Seek it with that diligence and earnest study as if you were to be saved by it yet seek it as if it was to be denied in spite of your diligence. How sweet a conjunction would this be in the Christian's practice, to walk and run after the prize as if his walking did actually obtain it, and yet to look upon his walking as if it were worth nothing at all. Your diligence and seriousness in godliness should be upon the growing hand,[4] as if all that you do would save you; yet you ought to deny all that, and look to the righteousness of Another, as if nothing were done at all by you.

The Union of Justification and Sanctification Must Be Stamped on Our Hearts

See how Paul unites these in his daily practice, "I count all as loss and dung that I may win Christ, and be found in him, not

---

4. *upon the growing hand*: increasing.

having mine own righteousness, and yet I press toward the mark, and follow after" perfection, as having attained nothing yet (Phil. 3:8, 9, 12, 14). One of these two is the origin of much stumbling and wandering in our Christian way. Either there is no necessity and constraint laid upon the souls of many to walk in all well-pleasing, and to perfect holiness in the fear of God—indeed we look on it with indifference as to be determined according to the measure of what we receive from God; or else we look on it as something not at all urgent. We think that it is meant for ministers or for more eminent professors of the faith.

This is why there arises much carnal liberty in many who walk outside the boundary of Christian liberty; it is because of an indifference in their spirit that gives that latitude to those walking along the Christian pathway. Or else there is not that following of holiness in such a way as is consistent with the establishing of Christ's righteousness—I mean there is no self-denial in their actions. We think and behave as if we were sufficient in and of ourselves and walk as if we were thereby justified; we commend ourselves to God in our own consciences, whenever we can impose the filthy rags of well-doing upon the testimony of our consciences. But by this means the Lord is provoked. Because we do not honor the Son, the Father counts Himself despised, and the Spirit is grieved and tempted to depart and to leave us to our own vain imaginations, until the idol which we have established falls down and our understanding returns to us.

As it would be of great moment to the peace of Christians and increase in holiness to have that union of justification and sanctification stamped on their hearts, so especially to have the evangelic method and order of these impressed on their consciences would exceedingly conduce[5] to both their quickening and comforting. As there is nothing that either so deadens, darkens, or saddens the spirits of the godly as darkness in this particular, the ignorance of—and failure to understand—the method and order of that

---

5. *conduce*: lead or contribute to.

well-ordered covenant must certainly be very prejudicial to the life and consolation tendered by the gospel.

Godly Living Flows from an Inner Principle of Life
This spiritual walking flows from the believer's state of non-condemnation in Christ. Once he is in Jesus Christ, thereafter he walks after the Spirit of Christ. You may make engines to cause a dead statue to walk, but it cannot walk of itself till it has a principle of life in it. Walking is one of the operations of life that flows from some inward principle, and so in the same way this spiritual walk and progress of a Christian in his course is the proper operation of the new nature of which he is a partaker in Christ Jesus. You know it is impossible that, where there is no life and no principle within, there can be any true and genuine movement that puts the creature into motion. Although, I concede, a man may by art and some external impulse so fashion a piece of timber or stone that it may appear to you to be walking like a living creature. Nevertheless, it is not possible that any of the sons of Adam, who are by nature dead in sins, can walk spiritually, before they have been united to Jesus Christ by believing in Him for righteousness and salvation.

Feigned Spiritual Walking
There may be a similar feigned walking of carnal unregenerate men, as may deceive all the senses and judgments of beholders. The unregenerate may be acting from base external principles in matters of religion, so that a beholder shall perceive no difference between them and others in whom Christ lives and walks. But before God it is nothing else but an artificial walk, a painted and lifeless business, because the Spirit that raised up Christ is not stirring in them. They are not living members of that Head that quickens all, nor have they been driven out of their own righteousness to Christ and into the city of refuge. Their principles are no higher than walking in order to obtain salvation and acceptance of God in a legal way; they are walking to

pacify Him, or to please men and their own consciences; they are walking for gain or credit, or advantage in the way; or else they are walking according to custom or having been schooled in this way.

These are not living principles. But when once a soul has embraced Christ Jesus, the Lord becomes in a manner a soul to actuate and quicken that soul. He animates it, and moves it in God's ways, according to the covenant of grace: "I will put my Spirit within you and cause you to walk in my statutes" (Ezek. 36:27). There is first a quickening, and then follows walking. "You who were dead in trespasses and sins… hath he quickened together with Christ" (Eph. 2:1, 5); then the promise through Ezekiel follows in due order, "I will cause you to walk in my statutes." Christ comes into the heart to dwell, and then He walks within it, "I will dwell in them and walk in them" (2 Cor. 6:16).

Christ Walks in Believers
And what does it mean that Christ will walk in believers? It is nothing else but Christ by His Spirit enabling them to walk in His way. Even when we are renewed and quickened there is so little in us to make this spiritual action our greatest desire, so that we look on ourselves, not so much as workers with Him, but as being enacted by Him. We should look on our souls and bodies as fashioned of clay that cannot move, but only as they are moved by Him as their soul and life. According to the scriptural dialect, this means that Christians are nothing else but Christ living and walking in them.

This is the truth which Christ, when He is to go out of the world, introduced to His disciples in John 15:1—He is the vine, and we are the branches. The branch must be first united to the tree, and grafted into the tree, ere it brings forth fruit. Without the tree it withers. So must a soul be first engrafted into Jesus Christ, implanted in Him by faith in His death and sufferings, before it can grow up into the similitude of His resurrection, or "walk in newness of life," as Paul says in Romans 6:4; "Without me ye can do nothing" (John 15:5). You must first be one with Him, by believing in Him and receiving Him as a complete Savior, and then the sap and virtue of the tree flows into the dead branch and shooting forth it blossoms and bears fruit.

Now, if this doctrine of Christ and His apostles was duly pondered and believed, oh what a change would it make in the lives and spirits of Christians! This is the order established in the gospel, and it is an order suitable both to His grace and our necessity (as all that is in it speaks forth of an excellent contriver[6]). But when we go about to establish our souls in some other method, it is impossible for us not to weary and vex our souls in vain. How else can we choose but to torment ourselves and become involved even more in vanity? Our methods and ways are just contrary to Christ's.

No Walking in the Spirit—No fruit of the Spirit
When we have not closed[7] entirely with Christ Himself, we perplex our souls how to find the fruits of the Spirit of Christ and how to walk after the Spirit. We trouble ourselves to find the living evidences of a spiritual life before we have laid hold on Christ, who is the life of our souls. This is turned into an objection by many and it keeps them from believing in Christ, all because they do not find that spiritual life stirring in them. How cross[8] is this to the declared mind of Christ in the gospel! Such an attitude cannot but darken a man's spirit more and dry up the influences of the Spirit of God, because it keeps you from the fountain of all consolation. You may disquiet your souls by persisting in this, but you shall never make any progress this way. Without Him "ye can do nothing" (John 15:5), and yet, because you are empty-handed and because you have nothing to offer, you will not come to Him.

---

6. *contriver*: an inventor or person who devises something.
7. *closed*: having come close together or made an agreement.
8. *cross*: troubling or contrary.

It is strange how little reason is in this, if your eyes were but opened. You refuse or else delay to abide in the vine till you bring forth fruit, yet you cannot bring forth fruit until you be in the vine. You attempt to walk, yet you will not have the life by which you must walk. Paul lived indeed, but what a life! "The life that I live is by the faith of the Son of God." Faith in Christ transported him out of himself to Christ, or received Christ into his soul, and Christ in the soul was the life of his soul (Gal. 2:20). Your walking is like a dead man attempting to go. Will one expect figs of thorns, or grapes of thistles?

I beseech you, know what wrong you are doing to yourselves and to Christ. You wrong yourselves, because you stand in the way of your need of mercy; thus you stand aback from your life, from Him who is "the way, the truth, and the life" (John 14:6). You desire to walk in the way, but no man can walk in this way by his own strength. Christ must quicken you to walk in Himself. You must get life in Him, and not bring it with you. You are in a vain expectation of fruits from yourselves—they will never see the sun. When you have wearied yourselves in such a vain pursuit, you must at length come and begin here. Until you do, you are wronging Christ's grace and mercy.

We Can Only Stand before God in His Son's Clothing

This order is suited on purpose for our desperate condition, and yet you presume to reject it, and seek another. To your skillful and tender Physician you offer an order which will undo you. I beseech you, know the origin of your miseries, doubts, barrenness, and darkness. Here it is: you are still perplexing yourselves about grace and duties and fixing your sights on these. Consequently, you neglect Christ as your righteousness, He who died, is risen again, and is now sitting at God's right hand for us. You must first close with Him, as ungodly men. Though you considered you were godly, you must shut your eyes on any such thing, and lay your dead and benumbed hearts upon the living Jesus. Answer all your challenges with His absolution, and stand before God, in His Son's clothing. Put His garment immediately over your nakedness and vileness, and we may persuade you it shall yield you abundant consolation and life. Because He lives, you shall live, and walk.

Oh, if only you were more frequent and serious in the consideration of His excellent majesty, of His beautiful and lovely qualifications as the Mediator for sinners and His precious promises which are all "yea and amen," confirmed in Him! And if you were less in the vain and unprofitable debates of self-interest and such like, I am persuaded then you would be more fruitful Christians. This is not as the business of a holiday, to be done at your first coming to Christ, and no more. No, it must run alongside all your life. The aged, experienced Christian must still come along as an ungodly sinner to a blessed and living Savior and have no other ground of glory or confidence before God, but Christ Jesus crucified.

SERMON 7

True Freedom in Christ

For the law of the Spirit of life in Christ Jesus hath made me free from the law of sin and death. —ROMANS 8:2

You know there are two principal things in the preceding verse. First there is the privilege of a Christian, and second there is the property or character of a Christian. The first is that he is one that never enters into condemnation: "He that believeth shall not perish" (John 3:15). And second, he is one who walks not after the flesh (though he be in the flesh), but in a more elevated way above men, after the guiding and leading of the Holy Spirit of God.

Two Questions
Now there may be objections arising in many consciences—how can these things be? First, have not all sinned, and come short of the glory of God, and so the whole world has become guilty before God? Is not every man lying under a sentence of death? "Cursed is every one that continueth not in all things…" (Gal. 3:10). How then can he escape condemnation? Second, you speak of walking after the Spirit as proper to the Christian whose walk is not carnal. Who is he that does not often step aside out of the way, and follow the conduct and counsel of flesh and blood? Is not sin dwelling here in our mortal bodies? Then who can say, "My heart or way is clean"?

You may object, therefore, that both this privilege and this property of a Christian seem to be but big words, but no real thing. And indeed I confess the multitude of men have no other opinion but to regard them as fancied imaginary things. Few believe the report of the gospel concerning the salvation of elect ones, and few understand what this spiritual walking is. Many conceive it is not a thing that pertains to men, all of whom are led about with passions and affections; they rather think that it pertains to angels or spirits who are perfected.

The Answers Are in Verse 2

However, we have in the words of verse 2 an answer to satisfy both objections. The apostle grants something implicitly, and it is this. Yes, it is true indeed, Christians are under a twofold law, captives and bondmen to these—a law of sin in their members, bringing them in subjection to the lusts of the flesh. Sin has a powerful dominion and tyranny over every man by nature; it has a sort of light and power over him. Likewise, everyone was under a law of death, the law of God cursing him and sentencing him to condemnation because of sin. These two—the law of sin and the law of God—were joint conquerors of all mankind. But, says the apostle, there is deliverance from this bondage. Freedom is obtained for believers by Jesus Christ, and so "there is no condemnation to them which are in Christ," and so they do not walk after the leading and direction of that law of sin within them, but after the guidance of our blessed tutor—the Spirit of God.

How Can We Be "Free from the Law of Sin and Death"?

You ask how this comes to pass, that is, by what authority or law or power is this release and freedom obtained? Here it is: "by the law of the Spirit of life, which is in Christ." Christ is not an invader or unjust conqueror; He has fair law for what He does, even against those laws which detain unbelievers in bondage. There is a higher and later law on His side, and He has power and strength to accomplish His design. He opposes law unto law, and life unto death, and spirit unto flesh. That is, He has a law of the Spirit opposing a law of sin and flesh, and a law of life opposing a law of death. In a word, the gospel or covenant of grace opposes the law or covenant of works. The powerful and living Spirit of grace that wrought mightily in Him is set forth against the power of sin and Satan in us and against us. The gospel gives Him right and title to conquer, and the covenant of grace equips Him for the work; and by these two are believers in Jesus Christ made freemen, who were formerly bondmen.

That which we would gather from these words, "the law of sin and death," is the common lot of all men by nature, namely, to be under the power of sin and sentence of death. Whereas the special exemption of believers in Christ is first their immunity to it, second their deliverance from it, and third the true ground and cause of this deliverance from that bondage. These three are contained in the words of verse 2 and form a purpose indeed of a high nature and importance for us all. Our life and death are wrapped up in this. You may hear many things more gladly, but if you only realized it, none so profitable. Therefore, let us gather our spirits to the consideration of these particulars.

The Bondage of the Laws of Sin and Death

As to the first, all men are under the bondage of a twofold law—the law of sin within them, and the law of death without them. Man was created righteous, but, says the wise man, he "sought out many inventions" (Eccl. 7:29). A sad invention indeed! He found out misery and slavery to himself, who was made free and happy. His freedom and happiness were to be in subjection to his Maker, under the just and holy commands of his Lord, who had given him breath and being. It was no captivity or restraint to be compassed about with the hedges of the Lord's holy law, no more than it is a restraint on a man's liberty to have his way hedged in, where he may safely walk, that he may keep himself within it, protected from pits and snares on every hand.

But, alas—if we may say "alas" when we have such a redemption in Jesus Christ—Adam was not content with that happiness, but seeking after more liberty, he sold himself into the hands of strange lords, first sin and then death. "Other lords besides thee, O Lord our God, have had dominion over us" (Isa. 26:13). This is too true in this sense: Adam seeking to be as the Lord Himself, lost his own lordship and dominion over all the works of God's hands, and so he became a servant to the basest and most abominable of all, even that which is most hateful to the Lord—to sin and death. And this is the condition into which we are now born.

Consider it, I pray you. We are now born captives and slaves, the most noble, the most ingenuous, and the most free of us all. Paul speaks of it as a privilege to be born free, that is, to be free in man's commonwealth. It is counted a dignity to be a free citizen or burgess of a town. Liberty is the great claim of people nowadays; and indeed, it is the great advantage of a people to enjoy that mother and womb privilege and right. But alas, what is all this to be freeborn in a civil society? It is but the state of a man among men. It reaches no further than the outward man, his life or estate.

True Freedom Pertains to the Soul, Not to the Body

But here is a matter of far greater moment[1]: do you know what state your souls are in? Your souls are of incomparably more worth than your bodies, as much as eternity surpasses this inch of time, or immortality exceeds mortality. Your souls are yourselves, indeed; your bodies are but your house or tabernacle you lodge in for a season. Now then, I beseech you, ask whether you be born free or not. If your souls be slaves, you are slaves indeed; for so the evangelist changes these. Matthew writes, "What is a man profited, if he loses his own soul?" (16:26). And Luke asks,

---

1. *moment*: importance, weight, consequence.

what has he gained, "if he lose himself?" (9:25). Therefore, you are not free indeed except your souls be free.

What is it, I pray you, to enjoy freedom among men? I ask you, what are you before God, whether bond or free? This is the business[2] indeed. The Pharisees pleaded a claim to the liberty and privilege of being Abraham's sons and children and thought they might hence conclude they were God's children. But our Lord Jesus uncovers this mistake, when He tells them of a freedom and liberty that He came to proclaim to men, to purchase for them, and bestow on them. They stumbled at this doctrine. They said, "What are you talking to us about when you speak of making us free? We were never in bondage, because we be Abraham's children" (cf. John 8:33).

Membership of a Church Does Not Free Us from Our Bondage
This is even the response of our hearts when we are told that we are born heirs of wrath, and slaves of sin and Satan. Here is the secret whispering of hearts: "We are Abraham's children; we were never in bondage to any. We are baptized Christians; we have a church state with its privileges and liberties, not only as subjects of the state, but as members in the church. So why do you say that we are bondmen?" I would wish you were all free indeed, but that cannot be till you know your bondage. Consider then, I beseech you, that you may be free subjects in a state, and free members in a church, and yet in bondage, under the law of sin and death. This was the Jews' mistake: it was the ground of their presumption and occasioned their stumbling at this stone of salvation laid in Zion.

You think you have church privileges, and therefore what more do we need? Be not deceived, you are servants of sin, and therefore not free. There are two sorts or rather two ranks of persons in God's house—sons and slaves. The son abides in the house for ever, the slave but for a time (John 8:35). When the

---

2. *business*: concern.

time expires, he must go out, or be cast out. The church is God's house, but many are in it that will not dwell in it. Many have the outward liberties of this house, but yet have no interest in the special mercies and loving-kindness proper to children. The time will come, that the most part of the visible church, who are baptized, have eaten with Him at His table and had a kind of friendship with Him here, shall be cast out as bondmen; Isaac only shall be kept within, the child of the promise.

The Inner Sanctuary of God—The Assembly of the "Firstborn"

The house we are talking about has an inward sanctuary. But there are also some outer porches to which many have access, who have never entered the inward sanctuary, the secret of the Lord; so they shall not dwell in the house above. It is not so much our concern as to who shall enter the holy hill, but who shall stand and dwell there. The day of judgment will be a great day of excommunication. Oh, how many thousands will be then cut off from the church of the living God, and delivered over to Satan, because they were really under his power, while they were church members and Abraham's sons!

Let me tell you, then, that all of us were once in this state of bondage of which Christ speaks: he that "committeth sin is the servant of sin…and the servant abideth not in the house for ever" (John 8:34–35). So that I am afraid, many of us who are in the visible church and stand in this congregation shall not have liberty to stand in the assembly of the firstborn, when all the sons are gathered in one to the new Jerusalem. Sin has a right over us, and it has a power over us, and therefore it is called a law of sin. There is a kind of authority that it has over us, by virtue of God's justice, and our own voluntary consent. The Lord in His righteousness has given over all the posterity of Adam, for his sin, which he sinned as a common person representing us—He has given us all over to the power of a body of death within us. Since man did choose to depart from his Lord, He has justly delivered him into the hands of a strange lord to have dominion over him.

The Justice of God's Holy Righteousness— "God Gave Them Up"

The transmitting to all men of such an original pollution is an act of glorious justice. As He in justice gives men over to the lusts of their own hearts now for following of these lusts contrary to His will, so was it, at first, "by one man's disobedience many were made sinners" (Rom. 5:12), and, in God's holy righteousness, sin entered into the world with the permission of God to subdue and conquer the world to itself, because man would not be subject to God. But as there is the justice of God in it, so there is a voluntary choice and election, which gives sin a power over us. We choose a strange lord, and he lords it over us. We say to our lusts, come you and rule over us. We submit our reason, our conscience, and all, to the guidance and leading of our blind affections and passions. We choose our bondage for liberty. And thus sin has a kind of law over us, by our own consent.

It exercises a jurisdiction; and when once it is installed with us and clothed with its power, it is not so easy again to put it out of that throne. There is a conspiring, so to speak, of these two, to wield the jurisdiction and the authority of sin over us. God gives us over to iniquity and to unrighteousness, thus we yield ourselves over to it (Rom. 6:16, 19). We yield our members to iniquity as its servants. A little pleasure or commodity is the bait that ensnares us to this. We give up ourselves and join ourselves to our idols, and God ratifies it, in a manner, and passes such a sentence: "Let him alone," he says, "go ye, serve ye everyone his idols" (Hos. 4:17ff.; Ezek. 20:39). In effect he says, "Since you would not serve me, be doing—go serve your lusts, look and see if they be better masters than I; look what wages they will give you."

Now, let us again consider what power sin has, being thus clothed with a sort of authority. Oh but it is mighty and works mightily in men! It reigns in our mortal bodies (Rom. 6:12).

Here is the throne of sin established in the lusts and affections of the body, and from hence it emits laws and statutes, and sends out commands to the soul and to the whole man. Man chose at first to hearken to the counsel of his senses, that said it was pleasant and good to eat of the forbidden fruit; but that counsel is now turned into a command. Sin has gotten a scepter there, to rule over the spirit which was born a free prince. Sin has conquered all our strength, or we have given up unto it all our strength. Any truth that is in the conscience, any knowledge of God, or religion, all this is incarcerated, detained in a prison of unrighteous affections.

"Who Will Deliver Me from This Body of Death?"
Sin has many strongholds and bulwarks in our flesh, and by these sin commands the whole spirit and soul in man, leading captive every thought to the obedience of the flesh. You know how strong it was in holy Paul (Rom. 7:21–24). What a mighty battle and wrestling he had, and how near he was to fainting and giving over. How then must it have an absolute and sovereign full dominion over men in their natures! There being by nature no contrary principle within to debate with it, it rules without much restraint. There may be many convictions of conscience and sparkles of light against sin, but these are quickly extinguished and buried. Nay, all these principles of light and knowledge in the conscience do oftentimes strengthen sin, as some things are confirmed, not weakened, by opposition. Unequal and faint opposition strengthens the adversary as cold, encompassing springs makes them hotter.

So it is here. Sin takes occasion by the command to work "all manner of concupiscence" (Rom. 7:8). Without the law, sin is in a manner dead; but when any adversary appears, when our lusts and humors are crossed, then they unite their strength against any such opposition, and bring forth more sinful sin. The knowledge and conscience that many have serve nothing but to make their sins greater; they exasperate and embitter their spirits and lusts against God. "Art thou come hither to torment us before the time?" (Matt. 8:29). It is a devilish disposition that is in us all; we cannot endure the light because our deeds are evil.

Satan's Kingdom Is Very Spacious
Let us but consider these particulars, and we shall know the power and dominion of sin. First, consider the extent of its dominion, both in regard of all men, and all in every man. I say "all men" for there is none of us exempted from it: the most noble, and the most base. Sin is the catholic king, the universal king, or rather Satan, who is the prince of this world, and by this law of sin he rules the world which is even the contradiction of the law of God. Who of you believes this, that Satan's kingdom is so spacious that it is even over the most part of the visible church? This is the emperor of the world.

The Turk[3] vainly arrogates this title to himself, but the devil is the real ruler, and we have God's own testimony for it. All kings, all nobles, all princes, all people, rich and poor, high and low, are once subjects of this prince, ruled by this black law of sin. Oh, know your condition, whose servants you are! Think not within yourselves, "we have Abraham for our father," we are baptized Christians. No, know that all of us are once the children of Satan and do his works, fulfilling his will.

The Law of Sin Embraces Every Faculty of the Soul

Moreover, all that is in us is subject to this law of sin—all the faculties of the soul. The understanding is under the power of darkness, the affections are under the power of corruption, the mind is blinded, and the heart is hardened, the soul is alienated from God, who is its life. All the members and powers of a man are yielded up as instruments of unrighteousness, every one of them to execute that wicked law, and fulfill the lusts of the flesh. This dominion is over all a man's actions, even those that are in

---

3. *Turk*: a Muslim or followers of the teachings of Muhammad.

best account and esteem among men. Your honest, upright dealing with men, your most religious performances to God, they are more conformed to the law of sin, than to the law of God. "This nation, and the work of their hands, and that which they offer, is unclean" (Hag. 2:14). All your works, even your good works, are infected with this pollution. Sin has defiled your persons and they defile all your actions—the infection is mutual. These actions again defile your persons still more: Unto the impure all things are impure, "even their mind and conscience is defiled" (Titus 1:15). Do what you can, you who are in nature cannot please God; it is but obedience to the law of sin that is in you.

Only the Spirit of Jesus Christ Can Bring Victory
But second, consider the intensity and force of His power, how mighty it is in working against all oppositions whatsoever, unless it be overcome by almighty power. Nothing but all-might can conquer this power. The spirit that works in men by nature is of such activity and efficacy that it drives men on furiously, as if they were possessed, to their own ruin. How much has it of a man's consent! And so it drives him strongly and irresistibly. Much will, desire, and greediness will make corruption run like a river over all its banks set in the way thereof—whether counsel, persuasion, law, heaven, hell—yet men's corruption must be over all these. Preaching, threatening, convictions of conscience, are but as flaxen ropes to bind a Samson. Sin within easily breaks them. In a word, no created power is of sufficient virtue to bind the strong man; it must be One mightier than he, and that is the Spirit of Jesus Christ.

Do you not see men daily drawn after their lusts, as beasts, following their senses as violently as a horse rushes to the battle? If there be any gain or advantage to oil the wheels of affection, Oh how men run headlong! There is no crying will hold them back. In sum, sin is become all one with us; it is incorporated into men, and become one with their affections, and so sin commands all.

SERMON 8

Strive Earnestly for True Freedom in Christ

For the law of the Spirit of life in Christ Jesus hath made me free from the law of sin and death.
—ROMANS 8:2

Whereabout the thoughts and discourses of men now run is either freedom and liberty, or else bondage and slavery.[1] All men are afraid to lose their liberties and be made servants to strangers. For indeed liberty, whether national or personal, even in civil respects, is a great mercy and privilege. But alas, men know not, neither do they consider, what is the ground and reason of such changes, and from what fountain it flows, that a nation, for a long time free from a foreign yoke, should now be made to submit their necks unto it.

Many wonder how it is that our nation, unconquered in the days of ignorance and darkness, should now be conquered in the days of the gospel; and there want not many ungodly spirits who will rather impute the fault to the reformation of religion, than take it to themselves. There are many secret heart-jealousies among us, that Christ is a hard master and cannot be served.

---

1. The subjection of the Scots to English rule under Oliver Cromwell has occasioned much of the imagery of this sermon. During the Interregnum, Scotland was kept under the military occupation of an English army under General Monck. The period of Cromwell's domination over Scotland is sometimes termed the "Usurpation."

But would you know the true origin of our apparent and threatened bondage? Come and see; come and consider something expressed in these words of my text.

Spiritual Bondage, Not Civil Bondage, Should Be Our Concern

All your thoughts are busied about civil liberty; but you do not consider that you are in bondage while you are free, and that to worse masters than you feared. We are under a law of sin and death that has the dominion and sway in all men's affections and daily living; and when the glorious liberty of the sons of God is offered to us in the gospel, when the Son has come to make us free, we love our own chains and will not suffer them to be loosed. Thus it is that a nation that has despised such a gracious offer of peace and freedom in Jesus Christ is robbed and spoiled of peace and freedom.

When this law of the Spirit of life in Christ is published and proclaimed openly to congregations, to judicatories and to persons, yet few do regard it. The generality is in bondage to a contrary law of sin, and this they serve in the lusts thereof. Yea—which most of all aggravates and heightens the offense— even after we have all of us professed a subjection to the law of God and to Jesus Christ, the King and Lawgiver, we are in an extraordinary way engaged to the Lord, by many oaths and covenants, to be His people.[2] We did consent that *He* should

---

2. In the sixteenth century Scotland, like the rest of Europe, was rocked by the Reformation. Early in the century Protestant ideas had spread through Scotland and gradually took hold until the Reformation in 1560. Three years earlier in 1557 a group of Scottish nobles met and signed a *covenant* to uphold Protestant teachings. In the seventeenth century, the Solemn League and Covenant was an agreement between the English and Scots by which the Scots agreed to support the English Parliamentarians in their disputes with the royalists and both countries pledged to work for a civil and religious union of England, Scotland, and Ireland under a Presbyterian parliamentary system; it was accepted by the Church of Scotland on August 17, 1643. However, the context makes it clear that the mention of the word *covenant* is an obvious extrapolation of the word so

be our King and that we should be ruled in our profession and practice by His Word and will, as the fundamental laws of this His kingdom; we did solemnly renounce all strange lords that had tyrannized over us, and did swear against them, never to yield willing obedience to them; namely, the lusts of the world, ignorance of God, unbelief, and disobedience.

We Have Rebelled against Our True Lord and Prince
Now you may know what has become of all this work. The generality of all ranks has rebelled against that Lord and Prince, and withdrawn from His allegiance, and revolted unto the same lusts and ways—these same courses against which we had, both by our profession of Christianity as well as by our solemn oaths, engaged ourselves. And so men have voluntarily and heartily subjected themselves unto the laws of sin and desires of the flesh. Hence is the beginning of our ruin. Because we would not serve our own God and Lord in our own land, therefore are so many led away captive to serve strangers in another land, therefore we are like to be captives in our own land. Because we refused homage to our God, and obeyed strange lords within, therefore are we given up to the lust of strangers without.

I would have you thinking, and that seriously, how there are worse masters you serve than those you most hate, and how there is a worse bondage, whereof you are insensible, than those you fear most. You fear strangers, but your greatest evil is within you. You might retire within and behold worse masters and more pernicious and mortal enemies to your well-being. This is how it is with all men by nature, indeed with all men according to their nature—sin ruling and in command of them, lording it over them. Thus they willingly follow after its commands, and so are oppressed and broken in judgment.

---

well-known at that time by every Scot, for Binning is also referring to the personal *covenant* every Kirk member has solemnly made to follow and obey Jesus Christ as Lord and King.

Men Are Slaves to Various Lusts and Vices

If you could but rightly look upon other men, you might see that those who are servants of divers lusts are not their own men, so to speak; they do not have command of themselves. Consider a man who is given to drunkenness and see what a slave he is! Whither does his lust not drive him? Though he bind himself with resolutions and vows, yet he cannot hold himself to them. Shame before men, loss of estate, decay of health, temporal, nay, eternal, punishment, all these things together cannot keep him, whenever he has opportunity, from fulfilling the desires of that lust. Or consider a man given to covetousness, how he serves that idol! How he forgets himself to be but a man, or to have a rational soul within him, so devoted he is to his idol!

Thus it is with every man by nature. There may be many petty little gods that he worships upon occasion, but every unrenewed man has some particular thing predominant in him, to which he has sworn obedience and devotion. Even men most civilized, most removed from the more gross outward pollutions—nevertheless their hearts within are but temples full of idols, to the love and service of which they are devoted. Some of the fundamental laws of Satan's kingdom rule in every natural man, either the lust of the eyes, or the lust of the flesh, or the pride of life (1 John 2:16). Every man sacrifices to one of these his credit and honor, or his pleasure, or his profit. Self, in whatever way it may be refined and subtilized[3] in some, yet at best is but an enemy to God. Therefore, outside that sphere of self a man cannot act upon righteous principles, till a higher Spirit enters which is spoken of here in our text.

Spiritual Bondage Robs Us of Our Peace, Both Personal and National

Oh, that you would take it as bondage to be under this woeful necessity of satisfying and fulfilling the desires of your flesh

---

3. *subtilized*: cleverly styled or made less noticeable.

and mind (Eph. 2:2). Because many count this bondage as liberty and freedom, they look upon the laws of the Spirit of life as cords and bonds and consider how to cast them off and cut them asunder. But consider what a wretched life you have with your imperious lusts. The truth is, sin for the most part is its own punishment. I am sure you have more labor and toil in fulfilling the lusts of sin than you might have in serving God. Men's lusts are never at rest, they are continually summoning them to service, for they are ever driving and dragging men headlong, hurrying them to and fro so that they cannot enjoy repose.

What is the cause of all the disquiet, disorder, confusion, trouble, and wars in the world? From whence do contentions arise? "Come they not hence," says James 4:1, "even of your lusts that war in your members?" It is these that trouble the world, and these are the troublers of Israel's peace. These take away inward peace, domestic peace, and national peace. These lusts, covetousness, ambition, pride, passion, self-love, and such like, by the ears set nation against nation, men against men, people against people. These multiply enterprises beyond necessity, these multiply cares without profit, and so bring forth vexation and torment.

It Is Easier to Serve the Lord Than to Serve Our Lusts
If a man had his lusts subdued, and his affections composed unto moderation and sobriety, oh what a multitude of noisome and hurtful cares should he then be freed from! What a sweet calmness should possess that spirit! Will you be persuaded of this, beloved in the Lord, that it is easier to serve the Lord than to serve your lusts? And that they cost you more labor, disquiet, perplexity, and sorrow than the Lord's service will? Will you not be so persuaded that you may weary of such masters, and groan to be freed from being under such a law of sin?

Serving the Law of Sin Makes Us Subject to the Law of Death
But if that will not suffice to persuade you, then consider in the next room if you are determined to serve a law of sin, you must

be subject to a law of death. If you will not be persuaded to quit the service of sin, then tell me, "What think you of your wages?" "The wages of sin is death" (Rom. 6:23)—that you may certainly expect. "And can you look and long for such wages?" God has joined these together by a perpetual ordinance. They came into the world together: "sin entered…and death by sin" and they have gone hand in hand together since (Rom. 5:12). And think you to dissolve what God hath joined?

Sin Is a Merciless Taskmaster
Before you go farther and obey sin more, think, I pray you, what it can give you. What does it give you for the present other than much pain, toil, and vexation, instead of promised pleasure and satisfaction? Sin does with all men in the same way as the devil does with some of his sworn vassals and servants. They have a poor wretched life with him. They are wearied and troubled as they strive to satisfy all his unreasonable and imperious commands. He loads them with base service, and they are still kept in expectation of some great reward; but for the present, they have nothing but misery and trouble. At length he becomes the executioner and perpetual tormentor of those whom he made to serve him. Such a master is sin and such wages you may expect.

Death Imports Destruction
Before you go on or engage further, consider what your expectation is—death! Because we are under a law of bodily death, therefore we are mortal. Our house is like a ruinous lodge, that drops through, and one day or other it must fall. Sin has brought in the seeds of corruption into men's nature, which dissolve it, else it had been immortal. But there is a worse death after this, a living death, in respect of which simple death would rather be chosen. Men will rather live very miserably than die. Nature has an aversion to it—"skin for skin, yea, and all that a man hath will he give for his life" (Job 2:4). Death imports a destruction of

being, which everything naturally seeks to preserve. But oh what a dreadful life is it, worse than death, when men will choose death rather than life! Oh how terrible will it be to hear that word, "to the mountains, Fall on us, and to the hills, Cover us" (Luke 23:30).

What these words of Christ envisage is newly risen men, their bodies and souls meeting again after a long separation—and this for their mutual entertainment one to another: the body wishing it were still in the dust of death, and the soul desiring it might never again be in the body! Surely if we had sufficient grace as to believe and tremble at this, before we be forced to experience it, there would be some hope. If we could persuade ourselves once of this, that the ways of sin, all of them—how pleasant, how profitable whatsoever gain they bring in, whatsoever satisfaction they seem to give—are nothing else but "the ways of death" that go down into the chambers of hell (Prov. 14:12; 16:25).

The Ways of Sin Deceive Us
Consider also that they will delude and deceive us, and so in the end destroy us. If we might once believe this with our heart, there would be some hope that we would break off from them, and choose the untrodden paths of godliness, which are pleasantness and peace. However, this is the condition of all men, once to be under sin, and under a sentence of death for sin. It is the unbelief of this and a false conceit of freedom that securely and certainly destroys the world, by keeping souls from Jesus Christ, the Prince of Life.

There Is a Freedom and Deliverance

But there is a deliverance, and that is the thing expressed in the words. There is freedom attainable from both unbelief and a false conceit of freedom. And I think that the very hearing of the possibility of such a freedom (redemption from sin and misery)—yea, and that some are actually delivered—might stir up in our hearts some holy ambition and earnest desire after such a state. Oh, might it awaken our hearts to pursue it! But this is the woefulness of a natural condition, that a soul under the power of sin can neither help itself nor rightly desire help from another, because the will is also in bondage. This makes it a very desperate and remediless business to any human expectation, because such a soul is well pleased with its own fetters and loves its own prison, and so can neither long for freedom, nor welcome the Son who is come to make free.

Nevertheless, there is a freedom and deliverance; and if you ask who those are who are partakers in it, the text declares it to you: it is those who are in Jesus Christ and who walk according to the Spirit of Christ. All those, and those only, who, when they find themselves "dead in trespasses and sins" and under the power and dominion of sin, and likewise under the sentence of death and condemnation (Eph. 2:1), begin to lift up their heads upon the hope of a Savior. They then as poor prisoners begin to look unto their Redeemer, for their eyes and looks are strong entreaties. Instead of making many requests, they are constrained to an entire renunciation of their former ways and prevailing lusts, and they give up themselves, in testimony of their sense of his unspeakable favor of redemption, to be wholly Christ's and not their own.

Those Who Have Been Delivered Await Complete Redemption

There are some souls who are now free from the dominion of sin and from the danger of death, who were once led about with divers lusts along with many others, who walked after the course of this world, and fulfilled the desires of the flesh. Along with others they were once children of wrath, but now they are quickened in Christ Jesus and have abandoned their former ways. They have another rule, another way, other principles. Their study is now to please God and grow in holiness. The ways they delighted in, in former times, are now loathsome. They know the filthy puddle from which they drank greedily is now their chief grief and burden, that so much of that old man must still be carried about with them; this is expressed in many groans from them as it was with Paul, "O wretched men that I am! who shall deliver me?" (Rom. 7:24). Such souls are, in a manner, so to speak, half redeemed, who being made sensible of their bondage, groan and pant for a Redeemer. The day of their complete redemption is at hand.

The Testimony of Those Who Have Been Freed

All of you are witnesses that there are some thus freed, but they are signs and wonders indeed to the world. Their kinsmen, acquaintances, friends, and neighbors wonder what is become of them. They think it strange they no longer walk and run into that same excess of riot along with them. But whosoever you are that have escaped from the slavery of sin, you now wonder at the world that runs so madly on toward their own destruction. You think it strange that you once ran so long with them, and that they will not now run with you in these pleasant ways.

Strive Earnestly for Deliverance

Do you think it strange that you run so slowly, when so great a prize is to be obtained—an immortal and never-fading crown? If mortifying and crucifying the lusts of the flesh and if dying to the world and to yourself seem very hard and unpleasant to you, if it be as the plucking out of your eyes or cutting off of your hand, know then that corruption is still much alive and has power in you (Matt. 18:8–9). But remember, that if you can have but so much grace and resolution as to kill and crucify these lusts, without foolish and hurtful pity, if you can attain that victory over yourself you shall never be a loser. You will not repent of it afterward. To die to ourselves and the world, to slay sin within us—O that makes way to a life hidden from the world, one hour of which is better than many ages in sinful pleasure!

Therefore quicken yourself often with this thought, that there is a true life after such a death, and that you cannot pass into it, except by the valley of the death of your lusts. Remember, that you are only killing your enemies, who embrace you in order to strangle you. Thus stir up yourself with this consideration that the life of sin will be your death. Better to enter heaven without these lusts, than go to hell with them.

SERMON 9

Salvation for Sinners Accomplished

> *For the law of the Spirit of life in Christ Jesus hath made me free from the law of sin and death.* —ROMANS 8:2

What is it that makes the deliverance of men from the tyranny of sin and death most difficult and utterly impossible to nature? It is that sinners have given up themselves to it, as if it were true liberty; thus consequently the will and affections of men are conquered, and sin has its imperial throne seated within them. Alien conquerors invade men against their will, and so they rule against their will. They retain men in subjection by fear and not by love. And so whenever any occasion offers, they are glad to cast off the yoke of unwilling obedience. For sin has first conquered men's judgment by blinding it—putting out the eye of the understanding—and then invading the affections of men, drawing them over to its side. In this way the tyranny of sin keeps all in a most willing obedience.

Now, what hopes then are there of deliverance, when the prisoner accounts his bondage liberty and his prison a palace? What expectation of freedom can there be when all that is within us conspires to upholding that tyrannous dominion of sin, against all that would cast off its usurpation as if those who would deliver them were mortal enemies?

The Sinner's Inability
Yet there is a deliverance possible, but such as would not have entered into the heart of man to imagine. It is here expressed in our text: "the law of the Spirit of life in Christ Jesus has made me free from the law of sin and death." This declares how and by what means we may be made free. Not indeed by any power within us, nor by any created power outside of us. Sin is stronger than all these, because its imperial seat is within, far beyond the reach of all created power. There may be some means used by men, to beat it out from the outworks of the outward man, to chase it out of the external members; some means to restrain sin from such gross out-breakings; but there is none can lay siege to the soul within, or storm the understanding and will, where it has its principal residence.[1]

It is inaccessible and impregnable by any human power. No entreaties or persuasions, no terrors or threatening, can prevail. It can neither be stormed by violence, nor undermined by skill, because it is within the spirit of the mind. Naught can be achieved until at length some other spirit stronger than our spirit comes, that is, until the Spirit of life, which is in Christ, comes and binds the strong man, and so makes the poor soul free. You heard that we were under a law of death, and under the power of sin. Now there is another law, answering this law, with a power to overcome this power.

The Sinner's Only Hope
You may indeed ask by what law or authority can a sinner, who

---

1. The imagery employed in the second half of this paragraph and on into the opening sentences of the next paragraph is that of a fortified castle under siege from an assailant endeavoring to unseat the tyrant who is firmly ensconced within the castle's inner Keep; though the assailant manages to penetrate the outer walls (the "outworks"), thus restraining the tyrant from some of his sallies forth from the "outworks," the assailant's forces are powerless to breach the impregnable walls of the Keep, where the tyrant is able to hold out undefeated and secure. Binning's imagery then mutates into an allusion to Christ's metaphor in Matt. 12:29 of the strong man's house.

is bound over by God's justice unto death and condemnation, be released? Is there any law above God's law, and the sentence of His justice? The apostle answers that there is a law above it, a law after it—*the law of the Spirit of life.* Jesus Christ opposes law to law: the law of life to the law of death, the gospel to the law, the second covenant to the first. Thus it is then, Jesus Christ the eternal Son of God, full of grace and truth, did come in man's stead. He came when the law and sentence of death was passed upon all mankind, and there was no expectation from the terms of the first covenant that there should be any dispensation or mitigation of its rigor. He obtained this, that the sins and punishment of so many as God had chosen unto life might be laid upon Himself.

And so He took part of our flesh for this end that He might be made a curse for us, and so redeem us from the curse. Thus, having satisfied justice and fulfilled the sentence of death by suffering death, "Him hath God exalted with his right hand to be a Prince and a Savior," and the head of all things (Acts 5:31). In compensation of this great and weighty work given Him by His Father, all judgment is committed to Him, and so He sends out and proclaims another law in Zion; that law delivers a different sentence, one of life and absolution to all and upon all them that shall believe in His name.

Thus you see the law of death has been abrogated by a new law of life, because our Lord and Savior who suffered under the law of death has brought in a life-giving law. So that it appears now to be true what was said at first, *there is no condemnation to them that are in Christ*—there is no law, no justice against them.

But How Can a Dead Soul Stir, Rise, and Walk?

But then another difficulty, as great as the former, is in the way. Though such a law with its sentence of life and absolution be pronounced in Christ's name in the gospel, nevertheless, we are dead in sins and trespasses. We neither know nor feel our misery, nor are we able to come to a Redeemer. As there was a law of death above our heads so there is a law of sin within our hearts, which rules and commands us; and there is neither will nor ability to escape from under it.

It is true, life and freedom are indeed preached in Christ to all that come to Him for life. To all who renounce sin's dominion remission of sin is preached. But here is the greatest difficulty: how can a dead soul stir, rise, and walk, and how can a willing captive, who is a slave to sin, renounce it when he has neither the ability to will or to do? Indeed, of what avail is this life and freedom, if all has been purchased for us, if eternal life and forgiveness of sins have been brought near us, and all the business has been done to our consent, and this only was lacking? If these had been the terms, "I have purchased life for you, now rise and embrace it of yourselves," truly it would have been an unsuccessful business. Christ would then have lost all that was given Him, if the moment and weight of our salvation had been hung upon our acceptation.

The Spirit of Life Can Quicken Dead Sinners

Therefore, provision has been made for this also, that there should be a power to overcome this contrary power within us, a spirit of life in Christ to quicken dead sinners, to raise them up and draw them to Him. And so the second Adam has this prerogative beyond the first, that He is not only a living soul in Himself, but a quickening Spirit to all that are given to Him by the Father (1 Cor. 15:45). So then, as Christ Jesus has law and right on His side to free us from death, He also has virtue and power in Him to accomplish our deliverance from sin. As He has fair law to loosen the chains of condemnation and to repeal the sentence passed against us, without prejudice to God's justice, having fully satisfied the same in our name, so He has sufficient power given Him to loosen the fetters of sin from off us.

Even when He has paid the price and satisfied the Father, so that justice can crave nothing, yet He had one adversary still to deal with. For Satan has sinners bound with the cords of their own lusts in a prison of darkness and unbelief. Jesus Christ therefore comes out to conquer this enemy also, in order to redeem His elect ones from that unjust usurpation of sin and by His strong hand to bring them out of the prison. Therefore, He is one who is mighty and able to save to the uttermost; He has the might to do it, as well as the right to it.

Consider, then, my beloved, these two things, which are the breasts of our consolation and the foundation of our hope. We are once lost and utterly undone, both in regard of God's justice and our own utter inability to help ourselves, which is strengthened by our unwillingness, and thus made a more desperate business. But now God has provided a suitable remedy: He has "laid help upon one that is mighty," indeed, who has almighty power (Ps. 89:19). For Christ by His power has first conflicted with the punishment of our sins and with His Father's righteous wrath, and, having overcome, discharged and satisfied that wrath, has purchased His right to us, so that He could give salvation to whom He will. He conquered and by His power obtained this supreme authority of life and death.

Applying the Remedy to Sinners
Now, having this authority established in His person, the next work is to apply this purchase, indeed, in actuality to confer this life. And therefore He has almighty power to raise up dead sinners, to create us again to good works, and to redeem us from the tyranny of sin and Satan, whose slaves we are. He has the *Spirit of life*, which He communicates to His seed; He breathes it into those souls that He died for and dispossesses that powerful corruption that dwells in us. Hence it comes to pass that they walk after the Spirit, though they be in the flesh; because the powerful Spirit of Christ has entered and taken possession of their spirits (Isa. 59:20–21).

Therefore, let us not be discouraged in our apprehensions of Christ. When we look on our ruinous and desperate estate, let us not conclude that it is past hope, and past His help too. We do proclaim, in the name of Jesus Christ, that there is no sinner, howsoever justly under a sentence of death and damnation, but they may in Him find a relaxation from that sentence, and that without the impairing of God's justice. And this is a marvelous ground of comfort that may establish our souls (1 John 1:9), even this, that law and justice is upon Christ's side, and there can be nothing to accuse or plead against a sinner who employs Him for his advocate (1 John 2:1). But know this also, that you are not delivered from death that you may live under sin; nay, you are redeemed from death that you may be freed from the law of sin. But that must be done by His almighty Spirit, for it cannot be done otherwise.

The Deliverance from Our Inner Corruption

I know not which of these is matter of greatest comfort—that there is in Christ a redemption from the wrath of God and hell, or that there is also a redemption from sin and corruption which dwells within us. But sure I am, both of them will be most sweet and comfortable to a believer; without both, Christ would not be a complete Redeemer, nor we completely redeemed. Neither would a believing soul, in whom there is any measure of this new law and divine life, be satisfied without both of them.

A Partial Gospel

Many are miserably deluded in their apprehensions of the gospel. They take it up as if it were only a proclamation of freedom from misery, death, and damnation, and so the majority catch at nothing else in it; from thence they take liberty to walk after their former lusts and courses. This is the woeful practical use that the generality of hearers make of the free intimation of pardon, and forgiveness of sin, and deliverance from wrath. They admit some general notion of that but stop there and examine not what further there is in the gospel.

Thus you will see the slaves of sin professing a kind of hope of freedom from death. I speak of the servants and vassals of corruption, who walk after the course of this world. They fulfill the lusts and desires of their mind and flesh yet fancy a freedom and immunity from condemnation. They are men living in sin yet thinking of escaping wrath. Such dreams could not be entertained in their minds if they did but drink in all the truth and opened both their ears to the gospel!

If our spirits were not narrow and limited, we would not exclude the one-half of the gospel, that is, our redemption from sin. There is too much of this, even among the children of God—a strange narrowness of spirit, which admits not the whole and entire truth. It falls out often that when we think of deliverance from death and wrath, we forget in the meantime its end and purpose, which is that we may be freed from sin, and serve the living God without fear. And if at any time we consider and busy our thoughts about freedom from the law of sin and victory over corruption, such is the scantiness of room and capacity in our spirits, that we lose the remembrance of deliverance from death and condemnation in Christ Jesus. Thus we are tossed between two extremes—the quicksands of presumption and wantonness, and the rocks of unbelief and despair or discouragement. Both of these do kill the Christian's life and make all to fade and wither.

Correcting the Misunderstanding of the Gospel
Here is the way, the only way, to preserve the soul in good ease: first, we must keep continually in our sight that we are redeemed from death and misery in Christ and second, in order that we may be redeemed from that sin that dwells in us, we should not serve ourselves or continue in our sins. Both of these are purchased by Jesus Christ and accomplished by His power—the one in His own person, the other by His Spirit within us. This is how I would have you correcting your misapprehensions of the gospel. Do not so much look on victory and freedom from sin as a duty and task, though we be infinitely bound to it; rather, see it as a privilege and dignity conferred upon us by Christ.

Look not upon it, I say, merely as your duty as many do; by this means they are discouraged by the sight of their own infirmity and weakness, as being too weak for such a strong party. Rather look upon it as the one-half, and the greater half, of the benefit conferred by Christ's death; indeed, regard it as the greater half of the redemption which the Redeemer by His office is bound to accomplish. He will redeem Israel from all his iniquities, for "with him is plenteous redemption" (Ps. 130:7–8). This is the plenty, the sufficiency of it, that He redeems not only from misery, but also from iniquity, indeed from all iniquities.

Groaning Inwardly as We Wait Eagerly for Our Adoption

I would not desire a believer's soul to be in a better posture here away[2] than this, to be looking upon sin indwelling as his bondage and redemption from it as his freedom. Nor would I desire the believer to account himself in so far free, as the free Spirit of Christ enters and writes that free law of love and obedience in his heart, thus blotting out these base characters of the law of sin. Rather it would be a better frame of mind to be groaning for the redemption of the soul (Rom. 8:23). For why does a believer groan for the redemption of the body, if not because he shall then be freed wholly from both the law of sin and from its presence? I know not a greater argument for a gracious heart, to subdue his corruption and strive for freedom from the law of sin, than the freedom obtained from the law of death. Nor is there any clearer argument and evidence of a soul delivered from death than to strive for the freedom of the spirit from the law of sin. These jointly help one another.

The prospect of freedom from death will raise up a Christian's heart to aspire to a freedom and liberty from sin; again, freedom from sin will witness and evidence that such a one is delivered from death. When freedom from death is an inducement to seek after freedom from sin, freedom from sin being a

---

2. That is, in this world.

declaration of freedom from death, then all is well. Indeed, thus it will be in some measure with every soul that is quickened by this new law of the Spirit of life, for it is the entry of this that expels its contrary, the law of sin. And indeed the law must enter into the soul along with the command and the promise, so that the affections of the soul may thereby be enlivened (the soul being changed into the likeness or similitude of that mold), otherwise merely having it in a book, or in one's memory and understanding, will never make him the richer or freer.

The Law of Love Now in the Believer's Heart

Christians look to the pattern of the law, and the word of the gospel within it. But they must be changed into its image, by beholding it, and so they become a living law to themselves. The Spirit writes these precepts and practices of Christ's, in which He commands imitation, upon the fleshly tables of the heart (Jer. 31:31–34). And now the law is not a rod above their heads, as above a slave, but it is turned into a law of love within their hearts and has something like a natural instinct in it.

Waiting upon God

All that men can do, either to themselves or others, will not purchase the least measure of freedom from their predominant corruptions, nor can it deliver you from your sins, till this free Spirit who blows where He pleases shall come. It is our part to hoist up the sails and wait for the wind, to use what means we can to wait on Him in His way and order.[3] But all will be in vain, till this stronger One comes and casts out the strong man, till this arbitrary and free wind blows from heaven, and fills the sails.

---

3. Binning is probably referring his hearers to the study of God's Word, prayer, and the sacrament of the Lord's Supper, as well as to regular worship with other believers.

SERMON 10

The Only Remedy for Sinners

For what the law could not do, in that it was weak through the flesh, God sending his own Son in the likeness of sinful flesh, and for sin, condemned sin in the flesh.
—ROMANS 8:3

The Mystery of the Incarnation

The greatest design that ever God had in the world is certainly the sending of His own Son into the world. And it must needs have been some great business that drew so excellent and glorious a person out of heaven. The plot and contrivance of the world was a profound piece of wisdom and goodness, the making of men after God's image was done by a high and glorious counsel. "Let us make man after our image" (Gen. 1:26). There was something special in this expression, importing some peculiar excellency in the work itself, or some special depth of design about it. But what think you of this consultation—let one of us be made man, after man's image and likeness?[1] That must be a strange piece of wisdom and grace. "Great is the mystery of godliness: God was manifest in the flesh" (1 Tim. 3:16).

No wonder that Paul cried out, as one swallowed up with this mystery! Indeed, it must be some odd matter beyond all

---

1. Perhaps unexpectedly, Binning is extrapolating from the statement of the creation of homo sapiens to the incarnation.

that is in the creation, wherein there are many mysteries, able to swallow up any understanding, but that in which they were first formed. This must be the chief of the works of God, the rarest piece of them all—God to become man. Yea, the Creator of all to come in the likeness of a creature—he by whom all things were created (John 1:3), and yet to come in the likeness of the most wretched of all—in the likeness of sinful flesh. Strange, that we do not dwell more, in our thoughts and affections, on this subject. Either we do not believe it or if we did, we could not but be ravished with admiration at it.

John, the beloved disciple who was often nearest unto Christ, dwelled most upon this, and made it the subject of his preaching: "That which was from the beginning, which we have heard, which we have seen with our eyes, and our hands have handled" (1 John 1:1). He speaks of that mystery as if he were embracing Jesus Christ in his arms, and holding Him out to others, saying, "Come and see." This divine mystery is the subject of these words we have just read, but the mystery is somewhat unfolded and opened up to you in them, yet in a manner so as it will not diminish but increase the wonder of a believing soul. It is ignorance that magnifies other mysteries, for ignorance vilifies thorough knowledge; but it is the true knowledge of this mystery that makes it the more wonderful, whereas ignorance only makes it common and despicable.

There are three things then, of special consideration in the words of the text, which may declare and open unto you something of this mystery. First, what was the ground and reason, or occasion of the Son's sending into the world? Next, what the Son, being sent, did in the world. And the third, to what end and use it was, that is, what fruit we have by it.

First, the Ground and Reason of God Sending His Son

God sent His Son into the world because it was an impossibility through the law to save man, which impossibility was not the law's fault, but man's defect, by reason of the weakness and impotency of our flesh to fulfill the law. God had chosen some to life, but man, having put this obstruction and impediment in his own way, made it impossible for the law to give him life, though the law was first given out as the way of life.[2] Therefore, that God should not fail in this glorious design of saving His chosen, he chose to send His own Son, in the likeness of flesh, as the only remedy of the law's impossibility. That which Christ did, being sent into the likeness of flesh, is the condemning of sin in the flesh, by a sacrifice offered for sin, even the sacrifice of His own body upon the cross.

Second, What the Son of God Did in the World

He did not come simply in the likeness of the flesh, though He was really a man, but in the likeness of sinful flesh: though without sin, yet like a sinner. As to His outward appearance, He came as a sinner inasmuch as He was subject to all those infirmities and miseries to which sin did first open a door. Sin was the inlet of afflictions, of bodily infirmities and necessities and of death itself. When the floods of these did sweep over Christ's human nature, it was a great assumption by the world, that is, to those who look and judge according to the outward appearance, that sin was the sluice[3] opened to let in such an inundation of calamity.

Now, being thus in the likeness of a sinner—though not a sinner—He came because of sin that had entered upon man and made life impossible to him by the law. He came because of that great enemy of God which had conquered mankind, and He condemned sin in His flesh, overthrowing it in its plea and power against us. He condemned that which condemned us, overcoming it in judgment and setting us free. By sustaining the curse of it in His flesh, He cut off all its plea against us. This is the great work and business, which was worthy of so noble a

---

2. Deut. 5:33; 6:24–25; 32:46–47, et al.
3. *sluice*: floodgate.

messenger, His own Son, sent by God to conquer His greatest enemy that He hates most.

Third, the Benefits We Have through His Conquest

In the third place, you see what benefit or fruit redounds to us by it; that is, what the end and purpose of it was: "That the righteousness of the law might be fulfilled in us" (v. 4). Here is the fruit of His conquest: seeing it was impossible for us to fulfill the righteousness of the law, and that it had become impossible for the law to fulfill our reward of life, it was fulfilled by Him in our name. Thus, the righteousness of the law being fulfilled in us by Christ, the reward also of eternal life can now be fulfilled by the law on our behalf; having removed the impediment of our weakness, He has rendered it not only possible, but certain for us.

The Covenant of Works

You would consider then the reason of Christ's coming. God made at first a covenant with man, promising him life upon perfect obedience to His law; and threatening death and damnation upon the transgression thereof. You see then, what was the way of life to Adam in the state of his innocence. He was made able to satisfy the law with obedience, and the law was abundantly able to satisfy him, by giving life unto him. God's image upon man's soul instructed him sufficiently for the one, and the Lord's promise made to him was as sufficient to accomplish the other; so that there was no impossibility then in the law, by reason of the strength which God had given to man.

But it continued not long so. Sin, entering upon man, utterly disabled him; and because the strength of that covenant consisted in that mutual and joint concurrence of God's promise and man's obedience—this being broken (the one party defecting) that life and salvation becomes impossible to the promise alone to perform. It is sin that is the weakness and impotence of man. This is the disease which has consumed his strength, and concluded man under a twofold impossibility, an impossibility to satisfy the curse, and an impossibility to obey the command.

There are three things in the covenant of works: first, a command of obedience; second, a threatening of wrath and condemnation upon disobedience; and third, a promise of life upon obedience. Sin has disabled us in every way. In relation to the curse and threatening, man cannot satisfy it—no price, no ransom being found sufficient for the soul. Its precious redemption has ceased forever. That curse has infinite wrath in it, which must swallow up finite man.

Why the Law Could Not Save

Consequently, in relation to the command, by reason of the first sin there has been such a diminution of all the powers of the soul—such a corruption and defilement—that that wherein man's strength lay, namely, God's image, is cut off and spoiled, so that henceforth it has become impossible to yield any acceptable obedience to the commandment. Hence it is, from our impossibility to obey in time to come, that there is a holy and faultless impossibility upon the promise to give life unto mankind. So you see that the law cannot do it, because of our weakness.

If man, either while he was created upright had continued in obedience, or man, now fallen from uprightness, could satisfy for the fault done and walk without any blemish in time coming, then it would have been feasible for the law to give life to us. But the one was not done and the other now cannot be done, and so the impossibility of life by works has redounded[4] upon ourselves, who would not when we could, and now neither will nor can obey. Thus we may see clearly that all mankind must perish, for now there is nothing that man can do according to that first transaction of God with man.

---

4. *redounded*: to come back upon, or to backfire.

Human Helplessness and Hopelessness

There was now no hope unless, that is, some other way and device could be found, which indeed was far from the eyes of all living and beyond the reach of their invention or imagination. Yet, I believe that if all the creatures, higher or lower, which have any reason, had convened to consult regarding this business—how to repair that breach made in the creation by man's sin—they might have vexed their brains, and racked their inventions unto all eternity, and yet never have fallen upon any probable way of making up this breach. They might have taken up a lamentation, not as those who bemoaned Babylon's ruin, "we would have healed you, and you would not" (cf. Jer. 51:9)—but rather, "We would heal you, but we could not, and you would not."

This design, which here refers to repairing the breach by destroying the sin that made it, lay hidden in the depth of God's wisdom, till it pleased Himself to vent and publish it to poor, forlorn, and desperate man, who out of despair of recovery had run away to hide himself. A poor shift[5] indeed, for him to think that he could hide himself from Him to whom darkness is as light, and to flee from Him whose kingdom is over all and who is present in all the corners of His universal kingdom—in hell, in heaven, in the utmost corners of the earth. But this silly invention shows how hopeless the case was.

Men Still Attempt the Impossible—To Save Themselves

Though this be the case and condition of man by nature, yet strange it is to see every man by nature attempting his own deliverance, and fancying a probability, yea, a certainty of that which is so impossible, namely, an attaining of life by ourselves according to the law and first covenant of works. Though our strength be gone, yet like Samson men rise up and think to walk and rouse up themselves as in former times, as if their strength were still in them; many never perceive that it is gone till Satan lays hold of

---

5. *shift*: an evasion.

them according to the law's injunction, and they are bound in the chains of everlasting darkness. But then, alas, it is too late, for they cannot save themselves and the season for a Savior is gone.

No doubt this will be the accession of the bitterness and torment that damned souls shall be into, that they dreamed of attaining life by a law that now is nothing but a ministration of death. For they lost life by seeking their own righteousness and made the law more able to condemn them by their apprehending in themselves an ability to satisfy it, and by resting in a form of obedience to it (Rom. 10:3–5). There is something natural in it. Adam and all his posterity were once to be saved this way, so the terms ran at first, "do this and live" (Luke 10:28).[6] No wonder that something of that impression be retained; but that which was a virtue in Adam, while he retained integrity and fulfilled his duty, was a mighty fault and is presumptuous madness in us, who have fallen from that blessed estate. If man doing his duty expected a reward according to the promise, it was commendable, but for man to look for a reward from God, now that he has become rebellious and stubborn and come short of His glory, is damnable. For God warns continually against him on account of his rebellion and enmity.

But besides this, I think this principle of self-righteousness is much corrupted in man now, compared with what it was in Adam. I conceive, though Adam looked for life upon obedience according to the promise, yet he rested not on, nor trusted in, his obedience. I believe a holy and righteous man would be a humble man too and would rather glory in God's grace than in his own works. The sense of a free and undeserved promise would not suffer him to reflect so much upon his own obedience or put such a price upon it. But now it is conjoined with unmeasurable pride and arises only from self-love. There is no ground for men's looking to be saved by their own doings, for all that remains is the inbred pride and self-love of the heart,

---

6. On the covenant of works see Westminster Confession of Faith, 2.2.

together with the ignorance of a better righteousness. Adam hid himself among the trees, and covered his nakedness with leaves, and truly the shift of the most part is no better.

In Vain Men Seek to Cover Their Nakedness
How vain and empty things do men trust unto, and from them conclude an expectation of eternal life! The most part think to be safe in the midst or thick of the trees of the church. If they be in the throng of a visible church, adorned with church privileges as baptism, hearing the Word and such like, they do persuade themselves all will be well. Some have civility and a blameless conversation before men, and with such acts of righteousness, or rather wants of some gross outbreaking, do many cover their nakedness. If there be yet a larger and finer garment of profession of religion, and some outward performances of service to God and duties to men, oh then, men do enforce upon their own hearts the persuasion of heaven and think their nakedness cannot be seen through it! These are the coverings, these are the grounds of claim and title, that men have to eternal life and, in the meantime, they are ignorant of that large glorious robe of righteousness, which Christ by His obedience and sufferings did weave for naked sinners.

Man's Only Remedy Was in Christ's Incarnation
But as to the impossibility of the law saving us by reason of the weakness of the flesh, it was the ground and occasion of Christ's coming in the flesh in order to supply that defect by taking away that impossibility. Therefore, the sense and sight of this impossibility in us to satisfy and fulfill the law, and of the law to give life is the very ground and reason of a soul's coming to Jesus Christ for the supplying of this want. As the Son would not have come in the likeness of sinful flesh, unless it had been otherwise impossible by man's doing or suffering that life should be obtained, so will not a soul come to Christ, the Son of God, through the veil of his flesh (Heb. 6:19; 10:19–23), until it discern and feel that

it is otherwise impossible to satisfy the law or attain life. That was the impulsive cause (if we may say that there was any cause beside his love) why Christ came—even man's misery and remediless misery. And this is the strong motive and impulse that drives a poor sinner unto Jesus Christ—the sense and impression of his desperate and lost estate without him.

As there was first sin and then a Savior dying for sin, because nothing else could suffice, so there must be in the soul, first, the apprehension of remediless sin incurable by any created power or act, and second, a sight of a Savior coming to destroy sin and the works of the devil and destroying it by dying for it. There is no employment for this Physician upon every slight apprehension of a wound or sickness till it be found incurable, and help sought elsewhere be seen to be in vain. Indeed, upon the least apprehension of sin and misery, men ought to come to Christ.

We shall not set or prescribe any measure of conviction to exclude you, if you can but come to him indeed. According to his own word, upon the least measure of it you will not be cast out, but it is certain that men will not come to this Physician till they find no other can save them. These two things I wish were deeply and seriously thought upon: first, that you cannot satisfy God's justice for the least point of your guilt, and then second, that you cannot do anything in obedience to please God.

Self-Deception Keeps Men Far from God's Righteousness

There is a strange inconsideration, yea, I may say, ignorance among us. When you are challenged and convinced of sin (as there is no conscience so benumbed but in some measure it accuses every man of many wrongs), what then is the course upon which you fall back to pacify your conscience or to please God? Indeed, if you can get any shadow of repentance, if it were but a bare acknowledgment of the fault, you excuse yourselves in your own consciences and answer the accusation by your excuse. Either some other good works formerly done occur to you, or else some resolution for amendment in time coming. And this you think shall pacify God and satisfy justice. But alas, you are far from the righteousness of God, and you do err even in the very foundation of religion.

These are but sparks of your own kindling, and in spite of them all you shall lie down in darkness and sorrow. These are but the vain expiations and excuses of natural consciences, which are led to some sense of a deity by the law written in their heart. But consider this once—you must first satisfy the curse of the law which you are under before you can be in any capacity to please him by new obedience.

The Double Errors That Vitiate Christ's Grace
Now, if you should undertake to pay for your former breaches of the law, that will eternally ruin you; and therefore, you see the punishment is lengthened throughout eternity to them who have this to undergo alone. Go then and first suffer the eternal wrath of an infinite God, and then come and offer obedience if you can. But now, you are in a double error, both of which are damnable. One is, you think that by consideration and resolution you are able to perform some acceptable obedience to God; the other is, that performance of obedience and amending in time coming will expiate former transgressions. If either of these were true, Christ needed not to have come in the likeness of sinful flesh, because it had been possible for the law to save you. But now, the truth is that such is the utter disability and impotency of man through sin, he can neither will nor do the least good, truly good and pleasant to God. His nature and person being defiled, all he does is unclean.

And then, suppose it were possible that man could do anything in obedience to His commands, yet it being unquestionable that all have sinned, satisfaction must first be made to God's threatening, "you shall die," before obedience be acceptable, and that is impossible too.

A Final Appeal

This, then, I leave upon your consciences, beseeching you to lay to heart the impossibility with which you are encompassed on both sides: justice requiring a ransom and you have none, and justice requiring new obedience again and you can give none; old debts urging you and new duty pressing you, and you are alike disabled for both. Therefore, so finding yourselves thus environed with indigency and impossibility within, you may be constrained to flee out of yourselves unto Him that is both able and willing.

This is not a superficial business, as you make it. It is not a matter of fancy, or memory, or expression, as most make it. Believe me, it is a serious business, a soul-work, such an exercise of spirit as used to be when the soul is between despair and hope. Impossibility within, driving a soul out of itself, and the possibility, yea, certainty of help from outside ourselves, even from Christ who draws in a soul to Himself. Thus is the closure made, which is the foundation of our happiness.

SERMON 11

The Fountain of Sweetest Consolation

For what the law could not do, in that it was weak through the flesh, God sending his own Son in the likeness of sinful flesh, and for sin, condemned sin in the flesh.
—ROMANS 8:3

Men Pay No Attention to the Momentous Matter of Salvation

For what purpose do we meet thus together? Would that we knew it—then it might be to some better purpose. In all other things we are rational and do nothing of moment without some end and purpose. But, alas, in this matter of greatest moment, our going about divine ordinances, we have scarce any distinct or deliberate thought of the end and outcome of them. Sure I am, we must all confess this, that all other businesses in our life are almost impertinent[1] to the great end of the salvation of our souls, for God in a manner trysts[2] with men and comes to dwell with them. These have the nearest and most immediate connection with God's glory and our happiness. Yet so wretched and unhappy are we, that we study and endeavor to attain a kind of wisdom and diligence in other petty things, which are to perish with the using, and have no great reach[3] to make our condi-

---

1. *impertinent*: irrelevant, improper, or inappropriate.
2. *tryst*: an arranged meeting.
3. *reach*: ability or power of comprehension.

tion either better or worse; and yet we have neither wisdom, nor consideration, nor attention to this great and momentous matter—the salvation of our souls.

Is it not high time we were shaken out of our empty, vain, and unreasonable custom of going about such solemn duties when the wrath of God is already kindled and His mighty arm is shaking the earth terribly, indeed, shaking us out of all our nests of quietness and consolation which we have built into His creation? God calls for a "reasonable service" (Rom. 12:1): but I must say, the service of most is an unreasonable and brutish kind of work—little or no consideration of what we are about, little or no purpose or aim at any real soul advantage.

Consider, my beloved, what you are doing, undoing yourselves with ignorance of your own estate and unacquainted as you are with a better. Whence comes such ignorance that you live contented in your misery and have no lively stirrings after this blessed remedy? The reason why we meet together is to learn these two things, and ought always to be learning them: first, to know sensibly our own wretched misery and second, to know that blessed remedy which God has provided. It is the sum of the Scriptures, and we desire daily to lay it out before you, if at length it may please the Lord to awaken you out of your dream and give you the light of His salvation.

Our Blindness to Our State of Spiritual Deadness

You hear of a weakness of the flesh—it was weak through the flesh (Rom. 8:3); but if you would understand it aright, it is not properly and simply a weakness. That supposes always some life and strength remaining. No, the flesh's weakness is not like an infirmity that only indisposes the wonted action and vigor. Rather it is such a weakness as the apostle elsewhere calls deadness (Eph. 2:1). It is such a weakness as may be called wickedness, yea, enmity to God, as it is called in Ephesians. Our souls are not diseased properly, for that supposes there is some remnant of spiritual life, but they are dead in sins and trespasses. And so our weakness is not merely some infirmity but rather that we are smitten with the impossibility of restoration; it is such a weakness as makes life and salvation impossible by us, on account of both our utter unwillingness and extreme inability. These two concur in all mankind: we have neither strength to satisfy justice or obey the law, nor the willingness either.

There is a general practical mistake in this. Men conceive that their natures are weak toward goodness, but few apprehend the wickedness and enmity that is in them to God and all goodness. All will grant some defect and inability, admitting it is a general complaint. But to consider that this inability is an impossibility and that this defect is a destruction of all spiritual good in us, the saving knowledge of this is given to but a few, and to those only whose eyes the Spirit opens. There may be some struggling and wrestling of natural spirits to help themselves and, upon the apprehension of their own weakness, to raise themselves up by serious consideration and earnest diligence to some pitch of serving God, and therefore to some hope of heaven. But I do suspect that it proceeds in many from the want of this thorough and deep conviction of desperate wickedness.

Our Refusal to Acknowledge the Deceitfulness of Our Hearts

Few really believe that testimony which God has given of man: he is not only weak but wicked, and not only so but desperately wicked. And that is not all, the heart is deceitful, too, and to complete the account, "deceitful above all things" (Jer. 19:9). A strange character of man, given by Him who formed the spirit of man within, making it once upright, and so He knows best how far it has departed from the first pattern. Oh, who of us believes this in our hearts? But it is the deceitfulness of our hearts to cover our desperate wickedness from our own discerning, and to flatter ourselves with self-pleasing thoughts.

When once this testimony is received, that the weakness of the flesh is a desperate wickedness, such a wretched and accursed condition that there is no hope for us, no created power able to help us, making us entirely incurable and certainly lost, then, I say, the deceitfulness of the heart would be in some measure cured. Believe this desperate wickedness of your natures, and then you have deceived the deceitfulness of your hearts to your own advantage; then you have known that which none can know aright, till the Searcher of the heart and reins reveals it unto them.

God Intervenes to Help Us in Our Miserable State

Thus, man stands environed with impossibilities. His own weakness and wickedness, and consequently the law's impossibility, these shut up all access to the Tree of Life and are like a flaming sword to guard it. Our legs are cut off by sin, and the law cannot help us; nay, our life is put out, and the law cannot quicken us. It declares our duty, but gives us no ability; it teaches well, but it cannot make us learn. While we are in this posture, God Himself steps in to succor miserable and undone man; and here is how He does it: He sends His Son in the likeness of sinful flesh, and grace and truth come by Him, which do remove those impediments that stopped all access to life.

This is a high subject, but it concerns the lowest and most wretched among us; and that is indeed the wonder of it, that there should be such a mystery, such a depth in this work of redemption of poor sinners, so much business made, and such strange things done for repairing our ruins. In the consideration of this we may borrow that meditation of the psalmist: Lord, what is man that Thou shouldest thus magnify him and make him not a little lower than the angels, but far higher (Ps. 8:4–5). For he took not on him the nature of angels but took part with the poor children of flesh and blood (Heb. 2:14, 16).

The Glorious Mystery of God Sending His Son

This deserves a pause. We shall stay a little and view it more fully in the steps and degrees by which this mystery rises and ascends. But, oh, for such an ascending frame of heart as this deserves! It is a wonder it does not draw us upward beyond our own element, for it is a subject of such admiration in itself and of so much concern to us.

Every word has a weight in it, and a peculiar emphasis. There is a gradation that the mystery goes upon till it comes to the top. Every word has a degree or stop in it, whereby it rises high, and still higher. *God sent*—that is very strange; but God sent *his own Son*—that is most strange. But go on, and it is even stranger—*in the likeness of* "flesh" and that of *sinful flesh*, and so forth. In each of these degrees you see God is descending lower and lower, while the mystery ascends and goes higher and higher. The lower God comes down, the wonder of it rises up. Thus the smaller and meaner that God appears in the flesh, the greater is the mystery of godliness, God manifested in the flesh.

We Must Descend before We Can Ascend
If you would rise up to the sensible and profitable understanding of this mystery, you must first descend into the depths of your own natural wretchedness and misery, in which man was lying when it pleased God to come so low to meet him and help him. I say you must first go down that way in the consideration of it, and then you shall ascend to the use and knowledge of this mystery of godliness.

The phrase "God sending" has some weight of wonder in it at the very first apprehension of it. If you did but know who He is and what we are, you would realize what a wonder it was that He had suffered Himself to be sent on our behalf. Indeed, you would marvel that any message or correspondence should have passed between heaven and earth, after so foul a breach of peace and covenant by man on earth. Strange, that heaven was not shut up from all intercourse with that accursed earth. If God had sent out an angel to destroy man, as He sent to destroy Jerusalem (1 Chron. 21:15)—if He had sent out His armies to kill those His enemies who had renounced the yoke of His obedience, it would have been justice (Matt. 21:41; 22:7).

Yea, if He had sent a cruel messenger against man, who had now committed so horrible a rebellion, it would have been no strange thing. As He sent an angel with a flaming sword to encompass the Tree of Life, He might have enlarged that angel's commission to take vengeance on man. But the wonder is that He did not send after this manner. But what heart could this enter into? Who could imagine such a thing as this? God sending, and sending for peace, to His rebellious footstool!

God Comes First to Man

Man could not have looked for acceptance before the throne even if he had presented and first sent up to heaven supplications and humble cries. And therefore, finding himself miserable—for he was at his wit's end—in his desperation he gives it over and flies away to hide himself, certainly expecting that the first message from heaven would be to arm all the creatures against him to destroy him. But oh, what a wonderful, yet blessed surprise! God Himself comes down, and not for any such end as vengeance, though that would have been just, but to proclaim and hold forth to the man a covenant of reconciliation and peace, not only to convince him of his sin, but to comfort him with the glad tidings of a Redeemer, one to be sent in the likeness of flesh (Gen. 3:15).

It is the grandeur and majesty of kings and great men to let others come to them with their petitions; and it is accounted a rare thing if they be accessible and affable. But the Lord of Lords and King of Kings, who sits in the circle of the heavens, before whom all the inhabitants of the earth are as poor grasshoppers or crawling worms, first came to us! Around His throne are ten thousand times ten thousand glorious spirits ministering unto him, as Daniel saw Him (7:9–10). But what wonder is this that such a One should not only admit such as us to come to Him and offer our suits to His Highness, but that He Himself should first come down unto Adam, and offer peace to him, and then send His own Son?

And what were we that He should make any motion about us or make any mission to us (Rom. 5:10)? It was while we were yet "enemies" that He sent. Oh, how has His love triumphed over His justice! But did He need to fear our enmity, that He should seek peace? In no way! One glance of His angry countenance would have reduced us into nothing: "I am consumed by the blow of thy hand. For when thou with rebukes dost correct man for iniquity, thou makest his beauty to consume away like a moth" (Ps. 39:10–11). Far more—the stroke of His hand would have consumed us. But this is the wonder indeed that He sent to us while we were yet "enemies" and weak too, neither able to help ourselves, nor hurt Him in the least. We could have done nothing to allure Him, nothing to terrify Him, nothing to engage His love, nothing to make Him fear. Yet then He makes this motion and mission to us: God sending His own Son.

God sending, and then, *sending His own Son*—that is yet a step higher. Had He sent an angel, it would have been wonderful, one of those ministering spirits about the throne being far more glorious than man. But "God so loved the world, that he sent his only Son." Might He not have done His work by others? But He had a higher project; and verily, there is more mystery in the end and manner of our redemption, than difficulty in the thing itself. No question, He might have enabled by His almighty power whatever creature He sent to have destroyed the works of the devil, and so He might have delivered captive man some other way. He needed not, for any necessity lying upon Him, to go such a round as the Father giving the Son, and the Son receiving the commission, that is, as God to send and the Son to be sent.

"Behold, What Manner of Love the Father Has Bestowed on Us"

Nay, He might have spared all pains, and without any messenger immediately pardoned men's sin and adopted them to the place of sons. Thus He could have done the business, without His Son's, or any other's travail and labor in blood and suffering. But this profound mystery, in the manner of it, declares the highness and excellency of the end God proposed, and that is the manifestation of his love: "Behold, what manner of love the Father has bestowed on us" (1 John 3:1). And "in this was manifested the love of God toward us, that God sent his only begotten Son into the world" (1 John 4:9). And truly for such a design and purpose, all the world could not have contrived such a suitable and excellent means as this. Nothing besides this could have declared such love. There is no expression of love imaginable to this—to give His Son, His one and only begotten Son for us.

It would have been enough, out of mere compassion to have saved us, however it had been done. But if He had given all and done all besides this, He had not so manifested the infinite fullness of love. There is no gift so suitable to the greatness and magnificence of His majesty as this, one that thought it no robbery to be equal with Himself (Phil. 2:6). Any gift had been infinitely above us, because from Him; but this is not only infinitely above us but equal to Himself, and fittest to declare Himself.

Jesus Emptied Himself

But then there is yet an even higher rise of the mystery, or an even lower descent of God; for it is all one, "God descending" is the wonder ascending—He sent His Son. Man's admiration is already exhausted in that. But if there were anything further to be said, this which follows would consume it—*in the flesh*. If He had sent His own Son, might He not have sent Him in an estate and condition suitable to His glory, as it became the prince and heir of all things, Him by whom all things were created and do subsist? Nay, but He is sent, and that in a state of humiliation and condescendence, infinitely below His own dignity. That ever He was made a creature, that the Maker of all should be sent in the form of anything He had made—oh, what a disparagement!

There is no such distance between the highest prince on the throne and the basest beggar on the dunghill, as there is between the only begotten of the Father, who is the brightness of His glory, and the most glorious angel that ever was made. And yet, it would be a wonder to the world if a king should send His Son in the habit and state of a beggar, to call the poor, lame, and blind into the fellowship of His kingdom. It would have been a great mystery, then, if God had been manifested in the nature of angels, a great abasement of His majesty.

"Veiled in Flesh the Godhead See"
But oh, what must it be for God to be manifested in the flesh, in the basest, naughtiest, and most corruptible of all the creatures, even the very dregs of the creation, that have sunk down to the bottom! "All flesh is grass" and what more withering and fading, even the flower and perfection of it (Isa. 40:6)! Dust it is, and what baser (Gen. 18:27)? And corruption it is—what viler (1 Cor. 15:42–44)? And yet God sent His Son in the flesh. Is this a manifestation? Nay, rather, it is a hiding and obscuration of His glory. It is the putting on of a dark veil to eclipse His brightness. Yet manifested He is, as the intendment[4] of the work He was about required—manifested to reproach and ignominy for our sin. This is one great point of Christ's humiliation that He took not on Him the nature of angels, but the seed of Abraham (Heb. 2:16).

"He Had No Form or Comeliness"
But yet, to complete this mystery more, did the Son descend a third step lower, that the mystery may ascend so much the higher, in the likeness of flesh? Not so! He descended in *the likeness of sinful flesh*. Had He appeared in the prime flower and perfection of flesh, in the very goodliness of it, still it would have been a disparagement. If He had come down as glorious as He once went up, and now sits "at the right hand of the majesty on high" (Heb. 1:3), if He had been always in that resplendent habit that He put on in His transfiguration, that would still have been an abasement of His majesty.

---

4. *intendment*: a legal requirement or obligation.

But to come in *the likeness of sinful flesh*, though not a sinner, yet in the likeness of a sinner, so that touching His outward appearance, no eye could discern any difference! For He was compassed about with all those infirmities and necessities, which are the followers and attendants of sin in us; He was "a man of sorrows and acquainted with grief" who all His lifetime had intimate acquaintance and familiarity with grief (Isa. 53:3). Grief and He were long acquainted and never parted till death parted them.

Nay, not only was He in His outward estate subject to all those miseries and infirmities unto which sin subjects other men, but something beyond them all, for "his visage was so marred more than any man, and his form more than the sons of men" (Isa. 52:14); and therefore He was a hissing and astonishment to many. He had no form nor comeliness in Him, and no beauty to make Him desirable; and therefore His own friends were ashamed of Him and hid their faces from Him; "he is despised and rejected of men" (Isa. 53:2–3). Thus you see He comes in the most despicable and disgraceful form of flesh that can be; and an abject among men, and as He Himself speaks in Psalm 22:6, "a worm, and no man; a reproach of men, and despised of the people."

The Fountain of Sweetest Consolation

Now this, I say, is the crowning of the great mystery of godliness, which, without contradiction, is the one mystery in all the world that has in it most greatness and goodness combined together; it is the subject of the highest admiration, and the fountain of the sweetest consolation that either reason or religion can afford. The mysteries of the Trinity are so high that if any dare to reach to them, he will but catch the lower fall; it is as if a worm would attempt to touch the sun in the firmament.

This then is the mystery of God coming down to man, to be handled and seen of men (1 John 1:1), because man could not rise up to God's highness. It is God descending to our baseness, and so coming near us to save us. It is not a confounding but a saving mystery. There is the highest truth in it for the understanding to contemplate and admire; and there is the greatest good in it for the will to choose and rest upon. It is contrived for wonder and delight to men and angels. These three, which the angelic song runs upon, are the jewels of it: "glory to God, peace on earth, and good will toward men" (1 John 1:1).

SERMON 12

The Mystery of the Incarnation

For what the law could not do, in that it was weak through the flesh, God sending his own Son. —ROMANS 8:3

Of all the works of God toward man, certainly none has so much wonder in it as the sending of His Son to become man; and so it requires the most exact attention in us. Let us gather our spirits to consider of this mystery. I do not want us to pry into the secrets of it curiously, as if we had no more to do but to satisfy our understandings. Rather I want us to see what there is in this mystery that concerns us, and what instruction or advantage we may have by it, that so it may ravish our affections.

Shameful Ignorance

I believe there is in thousands of men a very palpable and gross ignorance of the very thing itself. Many who profess Jesus Christ know not His nature or His glorious person; they do not apprehend either His highness as God or His lowness as man. But truly, the thing that I do most wonder at is that among those who pretend to more knowledge of this mystery, few of them enter upon any serious consideration about it—of what use and purpose it is. This ignorance is shameful for this mystery is the foundation of our salvation, the chief ground of our faith, and the great spring of our consolation. Yet to improve the knowledge of it to any purpose of that kind is a thing so rare, even among true Christians, that it is seldom the subject of their meditation.

Acknowledgment of It Draws Us into Christ's Embrace
I think, indeed, the lively improvement of this mystery of godliness would be very effectual to make us really what we are said to be, that is, Christians. There is much substance to this purpose (1 John 4:2–3, 15; 5:1). The confessing and knowing that Jesus Christ is come in the flesh, and is the Son of God before His taking on flesh, is made a character of a spiritual man that dwells in God. Not that a bare external confession or internal opinion and assent to such a truth is of so much value, which yet is the height unto which many attain. But it is such a soul acknowledgment, such a heart approbation of this mystery, as draws along the admiration and affection after it, as fixes the heart upon this object alone for life and salvation. The devils confessed and believed, but they trembled at it (Luke 4:34, 41). The unclean devil was afraid of what he knew, whereas Peter confessed and loved what he knew and, yea, did cast his soul upon that Lord whom he confessed (Mark 8:29).

It is such an acknowledgment of Christ as draws the soul and unites it to Him by a serious and living embrace. Such a sight of Jesus Christ has both truth and goodness in it in the highest measure; thus it not only constrains the assent of the mind but is also a powerful attraction to the heart to come to Him and live in Him. I pray you consider then what moment is in this truth, that you may indeed apply your souls to the consideration of what is thus revealed in Jesus Christ, not simply to know it, but for a further improvement of it. For it is by seeking life in Him that the stamp and impression of this Savior may be set so deeply on your souls that you may express this in a real confession of Him in your words and works (Titus 1:16; Matt. 7:21). This is indeed to know and confess that Jesus Christ is come in the flesh, to fetch thence the ground of all our hope and consolation, and to draw thence the most powerful motives to walk "even as he walked" (1 John 2:6), to improve it for confidence in Him, and obedience to Him.

I shall speak then a word about these two great ends and purposes of *God sending His own Son in the likeness of sinful flesh*, first, for His own glory, and second, for man's good.

The First Great Purpose of the Incarnation—The Glory of God

The song of angels at his birth shows this: "Glory to God in the highest, and on earth peace, good will toward men" (Luke 2:14). His glory is manifested in it in an eminent manner. The glory of His wisdom that found out a remedy. What a deep contrivance was it! How infinitely beyond all creaturely inventions! Truly, there are riches of wisdom, depths of wisdom in it. I think it could never have entered the thought of men or angels (1 Peter 1:12): all men at one time to be drowned under a deluge of sin and misery and made subjects to God's righteous judgment (Gen. 6:5–7; 7:21–23), and then to find out a way how to deliver and save so many! All the wisdom that shines in the order and beauty of the world seems to be but a rude draft to this.

Justice and Mercy

Therefore herein does the glory of His mercy and grace shine most brightly: He transfers the punishment due to man's sin upon His own Son; when no ransom could be found by man, God Himself finds out how to satisfy His own justice and save us. Truly, this is the most shining jewel in the crown of God's glory—so much mercy toward so miserable sinners, so much grace toward the rebellious! If He had pardoned sin without any satisfaction, what rich grace had it been! But truly, to provide the Lamb and sacrifice Himself, to find out the ransom and to exact it of His own Son in our name, is a testimony of mercy and grace far beyond that.

But then, His justice is very conspicuous in this work. And indeed these two do illustrate one another. First, the justice of

God in taking and exacting the punishment of sin upon His own well-beloved Son most eminently heightens the mercy and grace of God toward us. Then also His grace and mercy in passing by us does most marvelously illustrate the righteousness of God in making His own Son a curse for us. What testimony can be given in the world like this of God's displeasure at sin and of his righteousness in punishing sin! There was no such testimony of love to sinners and no such demonstration of hatred at sin imaginable. That He did not punish the sin in us but transferred it over on His most beloved Son—O what love and grace! And that He punished His own Son when standing in the place of sinners—O what righteousness and justice!

This is that glorious mystery, the conjunction of these two resplendent jewels, mercy, and justice—love and displeasure, in one chain of Christ's incarnation into which the angels desire to look (1 Peter 1:12). And truly they do wonder at it, and praise from their wonder. This is it, that the praises of men and angels shall roll[1] about eternally. David (Ps. 103:20f.), foreseeing this day, foretold that angels should praise Him, and now it is fulfilled when all these glorious companies of holy, powerful spirits welcome the Son of God into the world by that heavenly harmony of praise (Luke 2:14).

What lumpishness[2] and earthliness is in us that we do not rise up above to this melody in our spirits, to join with angels in this song—we, I say, whom it most concerns! The angels wonder—they praise and wonder at this—because the glory of God shines so brightly in it as if there were many suns in one firmament, or as if the light of seven days shines in one single day. These three especially—wisdom, mercy, and grace—speak of justice and righteousness; every one of the three looks like the sun in its full strength. They are carried about in this orb of the redemption of man, to the ravishing of the hearts of all the

---

1. *roll*: to make a deep reverberating sound.
2. *lumpishness*: lifeless or sluggish.

honorable and glorious companies above, making them cheerfully and willingly contribute all their service to this work, to be ministering spirits who wait on the heirs of salvation!

Now, when the glory of the highest raises up such a melodious song above among angels, oh what should both the glory of the highest God and the highest good of man do to us! When the greatest glory of God and the chief advantage of man are linked together in this chain, what should we do but admire and adore, adore and admire, and while we are in this earth send up our consent to that harmony in heaven?

In relation to our good much might be said, but we shall briefly show you that this is the greatest confirmation of our faith and the strongest motive to humility that can be afforded. Now, if we could be composed thus to confidence and reverence, to glorify Him by believing and abasing ourselves, so that we believe in Him and walk humbly with Him, meditating upon Christ's coming in the flesh, this would make us true Christians indeed.

Powerful Persuasion
There is nothing I know more powerful than this to persuade us of the reality of God's invitations and promises to us. When we are still seeking signs and tokens of God's love, something to warrant us to come to God in Christ and to persuade us that we shall be welcome, many Christians puddle themselves in the mire of their own darkness and discouragement. They cannot find anything in themselves that can give but the least probable conjecture that He will admit and welcome them to come to Him. Nor can they accept that such precious promises and sweet invitations can belong to such sinners as they conceive themselves to be.

Truly my beloved, I think that while we exercise ourselves thus, we are seeking the sun with a candle, making that which is in itself as bright as the light to be more dark. The evidence of God's reality in offering life to you in Christ and His willingness to receive you is not outside the compass of His invitation, and yet you seek it in yourselves where it is least to be found. But indeed, His invitations in the gospel carry the evidence in their bosom, what is above all other signs and evidences, that He did even send His own Son in the flesh for this purpose. Is there anything besides this, either greater or clearer?

The Culpability of Doubt
I think we are like those who, when they had seen many signs and wonders done by Christ, which bore testimony to all the world of His divine nature, yet they would not be satisfied but sought out another sign, tempting Him. And truly, He might return this answer to us, "O wicked and adulterous generation, that seeketh after a sign, there shall no sign be given to you, but the sign of the prophet Jonas" (Matt. 16:1, 4). The greatest testimony that can be imagined is given already that the Father should send His only begotten and well-beloved Son into the state of a servant for man. If this does not satisfy, I know not what will.

I see not how any work of His Spirit in us can produce so much evidence of His reality and faithfulness in the gospel and of His willingness to welcome sinners. All the works of the creation and all the works of grace are nothing compared to this, for it so clearly manifests His love to men. Therefore, there is a singular notice upon it, "God so loved the world, that he gave his Son" (John 3:16). "And in this was manifested the love of God toward us, that he sent his only begotten Son" (1 John 4:9). If men and angels had set themselves to devise and find out a pledge or confirmation of the love of God, they would have fallen upon some revelation to do it, or some operation upon their spirits. But, alas, this is infinitely above that. "The brightness of his glory, and the express image of his person" (Heb. 1:3) is come down to bear witness of his love; nay, he who is equal with himself in glory is given as a gift to men. Is not He infinitely more than created gifts or graces, who is the very spring and fountain of them all? "God so loved the world," that truly He gave no such gift besides to testify such a love.

Therefore, when all that He has done in this kind cannot satisfy your scrupulous mind, but you still go on seeking more confirmation of His readiness to receive you, I think that is tempting of the Holy One. It may well draw such an answer from Him, "O wicked and adulterous person, there shall no sign be given you, but that which is darker than the former and which you will understand less." You may get what you seek, perhaps some more satisfaction in your own condition, but it shall plunge you down more deeply in the issue. You will always be unsettled and "unstable as water, thou shalt not excel" (Gen. 49:4).

I do confess that if we are going to speak of the manifestation of your particular interest in these promises and in particular of the evidence of the love of God to you, then there needs to be something wrought by the Holy Spirit on your soul. The general testimony of God's love to mankind must be drawn down and applied into a particular application to yourself. But that is not what I am speaking of just now, because that is the sealing of the Spirit after believing (Eph. 1:13). Rather, it is because you are always unsettled in the first and main point of fleeing unto the Son and waiting on Him for life, which is why you have so much inevidence[3] and weakness in that which follows.

The Second Great Purpose of the Incarnation— Man's Salvation

No, what I am now speaking of is if it was cordially believed and seriously considered that God sent His own Son in the flesh to save sinners, you could not readily have any doubt that your coming to Him for salvation would be welcome. You would not say that such precious invitations could not belong to sinners, or that He could not love the likes of you. Truly, I think, if this general tenet was laid to heart that God has so loved mankind that He gave such a gift to them, there is none could question any longer the reality of His promise when that gift is then

---

3. *inevidence*: lack of evidence or uncertainty.

tendered to anyone in particular. Indeed, I think it is in considering this general tenet of the evidence and manifestation of His love to the whole world that makes you so perplexed regarding the particular. Could you have so much difficulty in believing His love particularly to you, if you indeed believe the general tenet that He has loved the world—that is, so many thousands like you? Is there so much distance, I pray you, between you and another, as between Him and all? If, then, He loves so many miserable sinners could there be any impossibility that He may also love you? For what is there in other sinners that might conciliate His love? Absolutely nothing!

I will tell you why I think the right apprehension of the general truths of the gospel would be able, like the sun in its strength, to scatter all the clouds and mists of our particular interest debates. It is because I find that, if you did consider them, those very grounds upon which you call in question your own particular interest, you would realize they go an even further length to conclude against all others. Thus, either they have no strength in your case, or else they will be of equal force to batter down the confidence of all the saints and the certainty of all the promises. What is it that troubles you, except that you are sinners, and such sinners, so vile and loathsome? From whence you do conclude, not only that you have no present assurance of His love, but that He cannot love such a one as you.

No One Should Doubt God's Love
Now, I say, if this holds good in reference to you, take heed that you condemn not yourselves in that which you approve, that is, that you do not dispute against the interest of all the saints who were such as you are, and the tenth of those fundamental positions of the gospel—"God so loved the world," et cetera. And so you do not only wrong yourselves but all others; not only so, but you offer the greatest indignity to Him who out of love sent His Son, and to Him who out of love came and laid down

His life. Oh, consider how you indignify[4] and set at naught that great manifestation of God's love, "God manifested in the flesh" (1 Tim. 3:16), how you despise His love-pledge to sinners, a greater than which He could not give you, because as great as Himself! Oh, that you could see the consequence of your anxious and perplexing doubts, that they do not only an injury to your own souls, but that they are of a more bloody nature! If they held good, they would cut off the life and salvation of all believers; worse still, they would by an unavoidable consequence conclude an antichristian point, that Christ is not come in the flesh. I beseech you, unbowel your evils, that you may abhor them. To do this may strengthen your faith and minister much consolation.

Christ Is the Ladder from Heaven to Earth

There is another consideration too, that which is laid down in Hebrews 2:17 and 4:15, that Christ was partaker of our nature and in all things like unto His brethren, that so He might be a merciful High Priest, able to succor us and be touched with the feeling of our infirmities. What strong consolation may be sucked out of these breasts! When it was impossible that man could rise up to God on account of His infinite highness and holiness, behold, God has come down to man, in his lowness and baseness. He has sent down this ladder from heaven to earth that poor wretched sinners may ascend upon it. It has come down as low as our infirm, weak, and frail nature that we may have easy coming up to it and rising up upon it to heaven.

Therefore His flesh is called a "new and living way" (Heb. 10:19–20) because a poor sinner may be assured of welcome and acceptance with one of his own kind, Christ his brother ("he is not ashamed to call them brethren," Heb. 2:11), flesh of His flesh and bone of His bone. It may make boldness of access for us in that we have not God to speak to or to come to immediately; after all, He is clothed with glory and majesty as the Jews heard

---

4. *indignify*: to dishonor or treat shamefully.

Him on Mount Sinai, which is why they desired a mediator between Him and them (Ex. 20:19–21). But that great prophet promised to them has now come (Deut. 18:15–18), and we have Him between us and God, as low as we, that we may speak to Him. He came "riding upon an ass," a lowly ass, that everyone may whisper their desires in His ear. Nonetheless, He was as high as God and He is able to speak directly to God, having power with Him. Truly, this is a sweet trysting place wherein to meet God, that no sinner may have any fear to come to this treaty of peace and reconciliation.

The Son of God Became the Son of Man

Then how may this persuade us of that great privilege that we may "become the sons of God," when the Son of God is become the Son of Man (John 1:11–12)? Truly, though it be hard to be believed that such as we should become the sons of the great King, yet it is nothing so strange as this, that the eternal and only begotten Son of the great God should become the Son of wretched man. That highness will be easily believed if we consider this lowness. It will not be so hard to persuade a soul that there is a way of union and reconciliation to God, of being yet at peace with Him, if this be pondered: God has married His own nature with ours in one person, to be a pledge of that union and peace. And then how much quickening and comfort may it yield us, that He was not only a man but a miserable[5] man, and that not through any necessity other than the necessity of love and compassion.

As God, the Son of Man had enough of mercy to save us; as man, He had enough of love and compassion. But He would take upon Himself misery too in His own person, that He might be experimentally merciful to us. Certainly, the experience of misery and infirmity must superadd some tenderness to the heart of our High Priest. But though it did not help Him to

---

5. *miserable*: subject to misery and sorrows.

be more pitiful, yet it was done for us to help us to have more confidence in Him and boldness to come unto Him. What an encouragement is it for a poor man to come unto the once poor Jesus Christ, who "had not where to lay his head" (Luke 9:58)? He knows the evil of poverty for He chose to know it that He might have compassion on you.

Therefore with what boldness may poor, afflicted, and despised believers come to Him! Why? Because He had experience of all that. Because He was familiarly acquainted with grief and sorrow, therefore He can sympathize best with you. Let us speak even of the sinful infirmities you are subject to. That there might be a suitableness in Him to help you, He came as nigh as might be, in that He was willing to be tempted to sin, and so He knows the power that temptations must have over weak and frail natures. Yet sin He could not, for that would have been evil for us. Let this, then, give us boldness to come to Him.

The Absolute Necessity of Humility

I would desire to persuade you to humility from this, according to the lesson Christ gives us: "Learn of me, for I am meek and lowly" (Matt. 11:29). And the apostle makes singular use of this mystery of the abasement of His majesty, for us to abate from our high esteem of ourselves (Phil. 2:3–6). Oh, should not the same mind be in us that was in Christ? God abased, man exalted! How unsuitable are these, do you think? God lowly in condition and disposition, and man, though base in condition, yet high in his deposition and in his own estimation! What more mysterious than God humbled? And what more monstrous than man proud?

Truly, pride is the most deformed thing in any man but in a Christian it is outrageous and prodigious. If He who was so high and glorious did humble Himself out of charity and love, how should we who are so low and base humble ourselves out of necessity? And out of charity and love too, to be conformed and like unto Him! Nature may persuade the one, but Christianity teaches the other—to be lowly in mind, and esteem everyone better than ourselves (Phil. 2:3). Upon the consideration of our own baseness, emptiness, frailty, and nothingness, reason may persuade us to be meek, patient, and long-suffering. But this lesson is taught in Christ's school, not from that motive only, the force of necessity, but from a higher motive—the constraint of love to Jesus Christ who says to us, "learn of me." Suppose there were no necessity of reason in it, yet affection might be a stronger necessity to persuade conformity to Him by following His example, He who became so low and humbled Himself to the death even for us.

SERMON 13

Sin Fully and Finally Dealt With

And for sin, condemned sin in the flesh.
—ROMANS 8:3

The great and wonderful actions of great and excellent persons must needs have some great ends answerable to them. Wisdom will teach them not to do strange things, other than for some rare purposes, for it would be folly and madness to do great things to compass some small and petty end, as unsuitable as that a mountain should travail to bring forth a mouse. Truly we must conceive that it must needs be some honorable and high business, that brought down so high and honorable a person from heaven as the Son of God. It must be something proportionate to His majesty and His wisdom. And indeed so it is.

Sin Is the Great Enemy of God

There is a great capital enemy against God in the world, that is, sin. This archrebel has drawn man from his subordination to God and sown a perpetual discord and enmity between them. This has conquered all mankind and among whom is included even the elect and chosen of God, those whom God in His eternal counsel has predestined to life and salvation. Sin brings all into bondage and exercises the most perfect tyranny over them that can be imagined. It makes men to serve all its imperious lusts and then, because the wages are death, it binds them over to judgment.

Now this sedition and rebellion being arisen in the world, including some of the most noble creatures carried away in this revolt from allegiance to the divine majesty, the most holy and wise counsel of heaven concluded to send the King's Son to compesce[1] this rebellion, to reduce men again unto obedience and destroy that archtraitor sin, which His nature most abhors. And for this end the Son of the great King, Jesus Christ, came down into the world to deliver captive man and to condemn conquering sin. There is no object toward which God has so pure and perfect displeasure as sin. Therefore, to condemn sin which He hates most (and perfectly He hates it!)—He sent His Son. And the errand of His coming is expressed as to "destroy the works of the devil" (1 John 3:5, 8).

Christ's Mission Was against the Works of the Devil
Consider all the devil's wicked and hellish plots and contrivances against man, all that poison of enmity and sin that out of envy and malice he spewed out upon man and instilled into his nature. Ponder all those works of that prince of darkness in enticing man from obedience to rebellion and tyrannizing over him ever since by the imperious laws of his own lusts. In a word, think of all that work that was contrived in hell to bring poor man down to that same misery with devils. All this Christ, the only begotten Son of the great King, came for this noble business to destroy. That tower which Satan was building up against heaven, having laid the foundation of it as low as hell—this was Christ's business down here on earth among men. He came to destroy that Babylon, that tower of darkness and confusion, and to build up a tower of light and life, to which tower sinners might come and be safe, and by which they might really ascend into heaven.

The First Way to Understand the Words for Sin
By these words "for sin" some understand the occasion and reason

---

1. *compesce*: restrain, repress, or curb.

of Christ's coming was, because sin had conquered the world and subjected man to condemnation, He therefore came into the world to conquer sin and condemn it, so that we might be free from condemnation by sin; it was this that was the special cause of His taking on flesh. If sin had not entered into the world, Christ would not have come into it, and if sin had not erected a throne in man's flesh, Christ would not have taken on flesh and come "in the likeness of sinful flesh," in order that this may administer unto us abundant consolation. If this indeed was the very cause of His coming, that which drew Him down from that delightful and blessed bosom of the Father, then He will certainly do that which He came for. He cannot fail in His purpose, nor can He miss His end: He must condemn sin and save sinners.

The Amazing Love of God

Truly this is wonderful love, that He took sin only for His party, and came only on account of sin, or against sin, and not against poor sinners. He had no commission of the Father but this, as He Himself declares: "God sent not his Son into the world to condemn the world, but that the world through him might be saved" (John 3:17). As one observes well, Christ would never have hinted at such a jealousy, or suggested such a thought to men's minds, had it not been in them before. But toward this naturally we are thinking harshly of God and hardly able to be persuaded of His love, when once we are persuaded of our enmity against Him.

Indeed, the most part of the world fancy a persuasion of God's love and do not have many jealousies over it, because they do not know their own enmity against God. But let a man see himself indeed as God's enemy, and it is very hard to make him believe any other thing of God, but that He still carries a hostile mind against him. Therefore Christ, to take off this, persuades and assures us that neither the Father nor He had any design upon poor sinners, nor any ambush against them; but mainly, if not only, His purpose in sending and Christ's in coming was not against man but against sin, not to condemn sinners but to condemn sin and save sinners.

O blessed and unparalleled love, that made such a real distinction between sin and sinners, who were so really one! Shall not we be content to have that woeful and accursed union with sin dissolved? Shall we not be willing to let sin be condemned in us, and to have our own souls saved? I beseech you, beloved in the Lord, do not think to maintain always Christ's enemy, that great traitor against which He came from heaven. Wonder that He does not prosecute both as enemies. But if He will destroy the one and save the other, oh let sin be destroyed, not you—so much the more because sin will destroy you!

Renounce Your Sin
Look to Christ so iniquity shall not be your ruin but that He shall be the ruin of iniquity. But if you will not admit of such a division between you and your sins, take heed that you be not eternally undivided and that you do not have one common lot for ever, that is, condemnation. Many would be saved, but they would be saved with sin too. Alas, that will condemn you! As for sin, He has proclaimed irreconcilable enmity against it; He has no quarter to give it, He will never come in terms of composition with it, and all because it is his mortal enemy. Therefore, let sin be condemned, that you may be saved. It cannot be saved with you, but you may be condemned with it.

The Second Way to Understand "For Sin"
The words *for sin* may be taken fitly in another sense as "a sacrifice for sin," so that the meaning is that Jesus Christ came to condemn and overthrow sin in its plea against us by a sacrifice for sin, that is, by offering up His own body or flesh (Heb. 10:12). And thus you have the way and means how Christ conquered sin and accomplished the business He was sent for. It was by offering a sacrifice for sin, to expiate wrath, and so satisfy justice. "The sting" and strength "of death is sin; and the strength of sin

is the law" as the apostle says (1 Cor. 15:56). We had two great enemies against us, two great tyrants over us—sin and death. "Death passed upon all men" (Rom. 5:12). Not only the miseries of this life and temporal death had subjected all men, but the fear of an eternal death, of an everlasting separation from the blessed face of God, might have seized upon all and subjected them to bondage (Heb. 2:15). But the strength and sting of that is sin for it is sin that arms death and hell against us. Take away sin, and you take away the sting, that is the strength of death; no longer has it any force or power to hurt man.

The Power of Sin
However, death being the wages due for sin (Rom. 6:23), all the certainty and efficacy in the wages flow from this work of darkness—sin. But now "the strength of sin is the law" (1 Cor. 15:56). This puts a poisonous and destructive virtue[2] in the sting of sin, for it is the sentence of God's law, and the justice and righteousness of God, that has made the connection between sin and death so inseparable. This gives sin a destroying and killing virtue: justice arms it with power and authority to condemn man. Therefore there can be no freedom, nor releasement from that condemnation, nor eschewing that fatal sting of death, unless the sentence of God's law, which has pronounced "thou shalt surely die" (Gen. 2:17), be repealed, and the justice of God be satisfied by a ransom. And this being done, the strength of sin is quite gone, and so the sting of death removed.

Now, this had been impossible for man to do. These parties were too strong for any created power. There is a sense in which the strength of sin to condemn may be called infinite, because it flows from the unchangeable law of the infinite justice of God. Now, what power could encounter that strength, except that which has infinite strength too? Therefore, it behooved the Son of God to come for this business—to condemn sin and save the

---

2. *virtue*: a power, strength, or force.

sinner. And being come, He yoked first with the very strength of sin, for He knew where its strength did lie, and so did encounter first of all with the justice of His Father and the handwriting of ordinances that was against us (Col. 2:14); for if once He can set them aside, as either vanquished or satisfied, He has little else to do.

Now, He does not take a violent way in this either. He does it not with the strong hand, but deals wisely, and (to speak so with reverence) cunningly in it; He came "under the law, to redeem them who were under the law" (Gal. 4:4). Force will not do it, the law cannot be violated, justice cannot be compelled to forego its right. Therefore, our Lord Jesus chose, as it were, to compound[3] with the law, to submit unto it: He was "made under the law," He who was above the law, being the lawgiver on Mount Sinai (Acts 7:38; Gal. 3:19). He came under the bond and tie of it to fulfill it: "I came not to destroy the law but to fulfil it" (Matt. 5:17).

Christ Paid the Full Debt of Sin

He would not offer violence to the law, to deliver sinners contrary to its commination,[4] or without satisfaction given unto it, for that would reflect upon the wisdom and righteousness of the Father who gave the law. But He does it better in an amicable way—by submission and obedience to all its demands. Whatsoever it craved of the sinner, He fulfilled that debt. He satisfied the bond in His own person by suffering and fulfilled all the commandments by obedience. And thus, by subjection to the law, He gained power over the law, because His subjection took away all its claim and right over us. Therefore it is said that He blotted out the handwriting of ordinances which was against us by nailing it to His cross; and so took it out of the way (Col. 2:14). Having fulfilled the bond, He canceled it, and so it stands in no force either against Him or us.

---

3. *compound*: to settle a matter or come to an agreement.
4. *commination*: a threat of punishment or vengeance.

Thus, the strength of sin, which is the law, is removed; and by this means, sin is condemned in the flesh. By the suffering of His flesh, it is fallen from all its plea against sinners; for that upon which it did hang, viz. the sentence of the law, is taken out of the way, so that it has no apparent ground to fasten any accusation upon a poor sinner that flies into Jesus Christ, and no ground at all to condemn Him; it is wholly disabled in that point. For, as the Philistines found where Samson's strength lay and cut his hair, so Christ has in His wisdom found where the strength of sin's plea against man lies, and has cut off the hair of it, that is, the handwriting of ordinances which was against us.

The Old Testament Rituals Foreshadowed Christ's Work

This is that which has been shadowed out from the beginning of the world by the types of sacrifices and ceremonies. All those offerings under the law of beasts, fowls, and such like, held forth this one sacrifice that was offered in the fullness of time to be a propitiation for the sins of the world. And something of this was used even among the Gentiles before Christ's coming, certainly derived by tradition from the fathers, who have looked afar off to this day, when this sweet-smelling sacrifice should be offered up to appease heaven. And it is not without a special providence, and worthy of remarking that, since the plenary and substantial One was offered, the custom of sacrificing has ceased throughout the world. As it were, God was proclaiming to all men by this cessation of sacrifices, as well as silence of oracles, that the true atonement and propitiation is come already, and the true Prophet is come from heaven, to reveal God's mind unto the world.

Under the old covenant there were many ceremonies in sacrificing observed, to hold out unto us the perfection of our atonement and propitiation. Those who brought a beast laid their hands on it (Lev. 4:15; 16:20–22), to signify the imputation of our sins to Christ, that He who knew no sin was made sin for us, that we might be made the righteousness of God in Him (2 Cor. 5:21). And truly, it is worth the observation that even those sacrifices for sin were called sin; and so the word is used promiscuously in Leviticus, to point out unto us that Jesus Christ should make His soul sin (Isa. 53:10), that is, a sacrifice for sin, and be made sin for us, that is, a sacrifice for sin.

When the blood was poured out—because without shedding of blood there was no reconciliation (Heb. 9:22)—the priest sprinkled it seven times before the Lord (Lev. 4:16–18), to shadow out the perfection of that expiation for our sins, in the virtue and perpetuity thereof (Heb. 9:26). It was to show that Christ should appear to put away sin by the sacrifice of Himself—to put it away, as if it had never been, by taking it on Himself and bearing it. And then the high priest was to bring in some of the blood into the holy place and within the vail and sprinkle the mercy seat to show unto us that the merit and efficacy of Christ's blood should enter into the highest heavens to appease the wrath of God.

Thus our High Priest by His own blood has entered into the holy place, having obtained eternal redemption for us (Heb. 9:12). And truly this is that sacrifice which, being offered without spot to God, pacifies all (v. 14). Sin has a cry, for it cries aloud for vengeance. This blood silences it and composes all to favor and mercy. It has so sweet and fragrant a smell in God's account that it fills heaven with the perfume of it. He is that true scapegoat who, notwithstanding that He did bear all the sins of His people, yet He did escape alive (Lev. 16:22). Albeit He behooved to make His soul a sacrifice for sin, and so die for it,[5] yet by this means He has condemned sin, by being condemned for sin. By this means He has overcome death and the grave, by coming under the power of death, and so is now alive for ever, to improve His victory for our salvation. And by taking on our sins He has fully abolished the power and plea of them, as the goat that was sent to the wilderness out of all men's sight was not to be seen again.

---

5. There were two scapegoats, one was sacrificed and the other went away free.

Truly, this is the way our sins are buried in the grave of oblivion and removed as a cloud, and cast into the depths of the sea, and sent away as far as the east is from the west that they may never come into judgment against us to condemn us because Christ (Ps. 103:12), by appeasing wrath and satisfying justice by the sacrifice of Himself, has overthrown them in judgment, and buried them in the grave with His own body. You see then, my beloved, here is a solid ground of consolation against all our fears and sorrows, an answer to all the accusations of our sins. Here is one for all, one above all.

A Final Appeal to the Doubters

You want to have particular answers to satisfy your particular doubts. You are always seeking some satisfaction to your consciences besides this, but you must believe that all that can be said, besides this atonement and propitiation, is of no more virtue to purge your consciences or satisfy your perplexed souls, than were those repeated sacrifices of old. Whatsoever you can pitch upon besides this, it is insufficient, and therefore you find a necessity of seeking some other grace or qualification to appease your consciences, even as they had need to multiply sacrifices.

But now since this perfect propitiation is offered up for our sins should not all these vain expiations of your works cease? Truly, there is nothing can pacify heaven but this, and nothing can appease your conscience on earth but this too. If you find any accusation against you, consider that Christ has by a sacrifice for sin condemned sin in His own flesh. The marks of the spear, of the nails, of the buffetings of His flesh, these are the tokens and pledges that He encountered with the wrath due to your sins, and so has cut off all the right that sin has over you. If you can unfeignedly in the Lord's sight say that it is your soul's desire to be delivered from sin as well as wrath, you would gladly fly from condemnation. Then come to Him who has condemned sin, by suffering the condemnation of sin, that He might save those who desire to fly from it to Him.

SERMON 14

In Christ Justice and Mercy Embrace

> *That the righteousness of the law might be fulfilled in us.*
> —ROMANS 8:4

The Dilemma of Reconciling Mercy and Justice

Having a great design to declare to the world both His justice and mercy toward men, God found out this means most suitable and proportioned unto it, which is here spoken of in the third verse—to send "his own Son in the likeness of sinful flesh, and for sin," to bear the punishment of sin, *that the righteousness of the law might be fulfilled in us*, freely and graciously in sinners. And, indeed, it was not possible for us to imagine how He could declare both His justice and mercy in the salvation of sinners. We could not have found out a way to declare His righteousness and holiness, which would not have obscured His mercy and grace; nor could He have found a way to manifest His grace and mercy, which would not have reflected upon His holiness and justice, according to the letter of the law that was given out as the rule of life. "The man that doeth them shall live in them," and cursed is everyone that doeth them not (Gal. 3:12). What could we expect, if this be fulfilled as it would appear that God's truth and holiness require? Then we are gone, for there can be no place for mercy if justice be not fulfilled; His justice could not allow mercy to be shown in pardoning sin. For then the truth and faithfulness of God would seem to be impaired.

This is the strait[1] that all sinners would have been into, if God had not found such an enlargement as this—how to show mercy without wronging justice, and how to save sinners without impairing His faithfulness. Truly, we may wonder, what was it that could straiten His majesty so, that He must send His own Son, so beloved of Him, and bruise Him, and hide His face from Him, yea, and torment Him, and not let the cup pass from Him for any entreaties? Might He not more easily have never added such a commination to the law, "you shalt die" (Gen. 3:3), or more easily relaxed and repealed that sentence, and passed by the sinner without any more threats, rather than exacting so heavy a punishment from one that was innocent? Was it the satisfaction of His justice that straitened Him, and put a necessity of this upon Him? But truly it seems it had been no more contrary to righteousness to have passed over the sinner, without demanding satisfaction, than to require and take it of one who was not really guilty.

The Attributes of God Seal His Promises of Mercy

The truth is that it was not simply the indispensable necessity of satisfying justice that put Him upon such a hard and unpleasant work as the bruising of His own Son, for no doubt He might have as well dispensed with all satisfaction, as with the personal satisfaction of the sinner. But here the strait lay, and here was the urgency of the case: He had a purpose to declare His justice, and therefore a satisfaction must be had not simply to satisfy righteousness, but rather "to declare his righteousness" (Rom. 3:25). Now, indeed, to make these two shine together in one work of the salvation of sinners, all the world could not have found out the like—to dispense with personal satisfaction in the sinner, which the rigor of the law required, and so to admit a sweet moderation and relaxation, that the riches of His grace and mercy might be manifested. Yet, how withal to exact the same punishment of another willingly coming in the sinner's place, to

---

1. *strait*: a dilemma.

the end that all sinners may behold his righteousness and justice? And so this work of the redemption of sinners has these names of God proclaimed by Himself to Moses (Ex. 34:6–7), engraved deeply upon it, mercy and goodness spelled out at length in it, for love was the rise of all, and love did run alongside in all. Yet so, there is room to speak out His holiness, righteousness, and justice, not so much to affright sinners, as to make His mercy the more amiable and wonderful.

I know not a more pressing ground of strong consolation, nor a firmer bulwark of our confidence and salvation, than this conjunction of mercy and justice in the business. There might have been always a secret hink[2] of jealousy and suspicion in our minds, when God freely proclaims mercy and forgiveness to us. Oh, how shall the law be satisfied, and the importunity of justice and faithfulness that has pronounced a sentence of death upon us, be answered? Shall not the righteous law be a loser this way if I be saved, and shall it not be satisfied by obedience or suffering? How hard it would be to persuade a soul of free pardon, seeing such a severe sentence stands against it!

Full Assurance
But now there is no place for doubting. All is contrived for the encouragement and happiness of us poor sinners, that we may come to Him with full persuasion of His readiness and willingness to pardon. Because Jesus Christ has taken the law and justice of God off our heads, and us off their hands, and because He has reckoned with them what is due by us, and has paid it without us, now we have a clear way and ready access to pardon, and we can believe His readiness to pardon. And this is it which is held out to us here: Christ condemning sin in the flesh or punishing sin in His own flesh. Thus does He give a visible and sensible representation of the justice and righteousness of God in punishing sin, and that in His own flesh, offering up Himself

---

2. *hink*: hesitation, faltering, misgiving.

as the condemned sinner, and hanging up to the view of all the world, as an evident testimony of the justice and righteousness of God against sin. By this means He cuts off the very strength of sin in the law, by fulfilling it Himself.

Christ's Wounds Bear Witness to God's Hatred of Sin

In Christ's sufferings you may behold as in a clear mirror the hatred and displeasure of God against sin, the righteousness of God in punishing sin: "Jesus Christ, whom God hath set forth to the world to be a propitiation through faith in his blood, to declare his righteousness" (Rom. 3:24–25). In this crucified Lord, you may behold the sensible image and most lively demonstration of holiness and righteousness. Christ's flesh bore the marks of both—God's holiness in hating sin and His righteousness in punishing it. Both of these are seen in His beloved and only begotten Son's person—in His flesh—and all for this purpose that the law might be no loser by our salvation, that the righteousness of the law might be fulfilled.

This is that which Christ says, "I am come not to destroy the law...but to fulfil it" (Matt. 5:17), and which Paul seconds, "Do we then make void the law through faith? God forbid: yea, we establish the law" (Rom. 3:31). The law and justice come better to their own by our cautioner than by us. There is no such way conceivable to satisfy them fully as this, whether you look to the commandment or the curse.

The Obedience of Christ

The commandment never got such satisfaction in any person as in Christ's, for He has fulfilled it by obedience. "It becometh us," saith He, "to fulfil all righteousness" (Matt. 3:15), both moral and ceremonial, so that there was no guile found in His mouth for He knew no sin, He was holy and harmless. His Father's will was His soul's delight—"I delight to do thy will, O my God" (Ps. 40:8). It was more to Him than His necessary food, His meat and drink (John 4:34). There was so absolute a correspondence between His will and God's will, and between His way and His Father's will, that it was not possible that any difference should fall between them. His obedience had more good in it, so to speak, than Adam's disobedience had evil in it (Rom. 5:18–19). Adam's disobedience was but the sin of a finite creature, but Christ's obedience was the work of an infinite person.

I think there was more real worth in Christ's obedience to the commands, than in all the united service and obedience of men and angels. All the love, delight, fear, and obedience flowing from these—take them in one bundle as they will be extended and multiplied to all eternity—there is something in Christ's obedience that elevates it above all and puts a higher price upon it. The transcendent dignity of His person—His own Son "made under the law" (Gal. 4:4)—is of more worth than if all men and angels had also been made under it. It had been no humiliation, but rather the exaltation of an angel, to be obedient to God. That subordination to a law is the highest peak of the creature's advancement. But He was such a person, as His obedience was a humbling of Himself. "He humbled himself, and became obedient unto death" (Phil. 2:8) and, though He was the Son of God, yet He stooped to learn obedience (Heb. 5:8).

Now indeed the commandment comes more honorably by this means to have such a glorious person under it than if it had poor, naughty us under it, and that it is fulfilled by Him when otherwise it would never have been done. For I suppose that justice would have exacted of us the punishment. As we could never have ended suffering for all eternity, so we would never have begun new obedience to the command for all eternity. Thus, except Christ had taken it off us, and we off its hand, it would never have been fulfilled since it was first broken.

The Impossibility of the Sinner Paying His Debt

Next, the curse of the law could not get fuller satisfaction than in Christ. I suppose it would have fallen upon the sinner. There is not so much worth in the creature's most extreme sufferings to compensate the infinite wrongs done to the holiness and righteousness of God. Therefore, what was wanting in the intrinsic value of the creature's suffering behooved to be made up in the infinite extent of it and in the eternal continuance of it upon the creature. Thus, there could never be a determined time assigned in which the curse was fulfilled and in which justice could say, "Hold, I have enough!" It is as if a man were owing an infinite debt, and he could get nothing to defray it but poor petty sums which, being all conjoined, could not amount to the smallest proportion of it. Therefore, since he cannot get one sum in value equal to it, he must be eternally paying it in small sums, according to his capacity. And so, because the utmost farthing cannot be won at, he can never be released out of prison.

Christ the Only Security for Our Debt

But our Lord Jesus has made full satisfaction for it. He was a more substantial debtor and, because of the infinite dignity of His person, there was an intrinsic value upon His sufferings, proportioned unto the infinity of man's sin, so that He could pay all the debt in a short time which a sinner could not have done during all eternity. Now, you know that any man would rather choose such a cautioner who can solidly satisfy him in gross by paying the whole sum at once. Without such a cautioner, because of his inability, he cannot reach to any considerable satisfaction in many years. Even so it is with the law and justice of God. Those with this cautioner hold themselves better contented in him than they ever could in themselves, Christ who redeemed us "being made a curse for us" (Gal. 3:13), instead of the curse falling on us. And therefore God testifies of this to poor sinners, "Deliver him from going down into the pit: I have found a ransom" (Job 33:24)—and that is the ransom which Christ gave, "his life a ransom for many" (Matt. 20:28).

You see then how this conclusion follows: *that the righteousness of the law might be fulfilled in us*. For He has fulfilled it and satisfied it, both by obedience to the commandment and His submission to the curse. It is all one in God's account as if we had done it, because Christ was surety in our stead and a common person representing us. Therefore His paying of the debt acquits us at the hand of justice, for whatsoever He did to fulfill all righteousness is accounted ours, because we were represented in Him and judicially made one with Him. And therefore we were condemned when He was condemned, we were dead when He died. That is how the righteousness of the law, in exacting a due punishment for sin, was fulfilled for us in Him and is all one as if it had been personally accomplished in us.

"Be Reconciled to God!"
This then is laid down as the foundation of that blessed embassage or message of reconciliation to sinners, as that upon which God is in Christ reconciling and beseeching us to be reconciled (2 Cor. 5:19–21)—Him who knew no sin has been made sin for us that we might be made the righteousness of God in Him. You see the blessed exchange that He has made with us: He has laid our sins on sinless Christ, and laid Christ's righteousness on sinful us. Christ took our sins on Him that He might give us His righteousness. By virtue of this transaction and communication, as it was righteous with God to condemn sin in Christ's flesh and because our sin was upon him, so it is as just with Him to impute righteousness to us because we are in Him. And as the law made Him a curse and exacted the punishment of Him, it is as righteous with the Lord to give us life and salvation and to forgive our sin, as John speaks: "If we confess our sins, he is faithful and just to forgive us our sins" (1 John 1:9).

Now consider this, my beloved, for it is propounded unto you as the greatest persuasive to move you to come to Jesus Christ, for there is such a clear and plain way in Him to salvation. If this does not move your hearts, I do not know what will. I do not expect that your troubles in this world—the frequent lashes of judgment, the impoverishing and exhausting of you, the plucking away of those things you loved, the disquieting your peace so often—that any of these things that have the image of wrath upon them, can drive you to Him; they cannot make you forsake your way, when such a motive as this does not prevail with you.

A Final Appeal

Oh, what heart could stand against the power of this persuasion if it were but rightly apprehended? Who would not willingly fly into this city of refuge, if they did but know aright the avenger of blood that pursues them and what safety is within? You are always imagining vain satisfactions to the law of God. How great a weight does your fancy impose upon your tears, your confessions, your reformations! If you can attain anything of this kind, that is what you would give to satisfy justice, for it is this wherewith you pretend to fulfill the law. But if it could be so, wherefore should God have sent His Son to condemn sin, and purchase righteousness by Him? I beseech you, once know and consider your estate, that you may open your hearts to this Redeemer. Then you may be willing to be stripped naked of all your imaginary righteousness, to put on this which will satisfy the law fully.

Will you die in your sins because you will not come to Him to have life? Will you rather be condemned with sin than saved with Christ's righteousness? And truly, there is no other altar that will preserve you but this. Now, if any, apprehending their own misery, be hardly[3] pursued in their consciences by the law of God, I beseech you come hither and behold it satisfied and fulfilled. I beseech you in Christ's stead to be reconciled unto God, to lay down all hostile affections and come to Him, because God is in Christ reconciling the world, not imputing their sins to them, because He has imputed them already to Christ. "For he has made him to be sin for us, who knew no sin; that we might be made the righteousness of God in him" (2 Cor. 5:21). Yea, God made Him to be sin for us and He is in Christ, imputing His righteousness to sinners.

---

3. *hardly*: with severity and rigor.

SERMON 15

The Relationship between Justification and Sanctification

That the righteousness of the law might be fulfilled in us.
—ROMANS 8:4

"Think not," says our Lord and Savior Jesus Christ, "that I am come to destroy the law.... I am not come to destroy, but to fulfil" (Matt. 5:17). It was a needful caveat, and a very timely advertisement because of the natural misapprehensions in men's minds of the gospel. When free forgiveness of sins and life everlasting is preached in Jesus Christ without our works and when the mercy of God is proclaimed in its freedom and fullness, the heart of man is subject to a woeful misconceit[1] of Christ, as if by these a latitude were given, and a liberty proclaimed to men to live in sin. That which is propounded as the encouragement of poor sinners to come to God and forsake their own wicked way is miserably wrested upon a mistake that becomes an encouragement to revolt more and more.

A Misconception Regarding Justification

Righteousness and life, by faith in a Savior without the works of the law, is held out as the grand persuasion of the gospel to study obedience to the law. And yet such is the perverseness of

---

1. *misconceit*: a false notion or bad understanding.

many hearts that, either in opinion or practice, they so carry themselves as if there was an inconsistency between Christ and the law, between free justification and sanctification. They act as if Christ had come to redeem us not from sin, but to sin.

Now to prevent this, "Think not," He says, "that I am come to destroy the law." Do not fancy for yourselves a liberty to live in sin and an immunity from the obligation of a commandment because I have purchased an immunity and freedom from the curse. No, rather "I am come to fulfil it," not only in My own person but in yours also. And to this purpose Paul also says, "Do we then make void the law through faith?" (Rom. 3:31). It is so natural to our rebellious hearts to desire to be free from the yoke of obedience, therefore we fancy such a notion of faith as may not give itself to working in love, but a faith that is active in nothing but imagination. The apostle abominates this: "God forbid!" Yea, he detests it as impious and sacrilegious; whereas, "Yea, we establish the law!"

Christ Came to Redeem Us from Iniquity
So then, all returns to this: one of the great ends of Christ's coming in the flesh, and one main intention of the gospel proclaimed in His name, is not only to deliver us from wrath and redeem us from the curse (Gal. 3:13; 1 Thess. 1:10), but also, and especially, to redeem us from all iniquity, that we might be a people zealous of good works (Titus 2:14). He came to take away sin and to "destroy the works of the devil" (1 John 3:5, 8). We said something before noon, how Christ has fulfilled the law and established it in His own person by obedience and suffering—neither of which ways could it be so well contented by any other means. But there is yet a third way that He fulfills and establishes His coming in the flesh: it is in our persons, that the righteousness of the law might be fulfilled in us, who walk not after the flesh, but after the Spirit. He has obliged Himself to fulfill it, not only for believers, but in believers. Therefore, the promises run thus, "I will write my law in their hearts, and cause

them to walk in my statutes" (Jer. 31:33; Ezek. 36:27). Not only "I delight to do thy will" (Ps. 40:8; cf. John 4:34), but I will make them delight to do it also. And truly, in this respect, the law is more fulfilled and established by Christ than ever it could have been if man had been left to satisfy it alone.

Our Incapability of Obeying the Law's Demands
If we had reckoned alone with the law, we would have been taken up eternally with trying to achieve satisfaction for our breaches of it, so that there would have been no access to obedience of the command and no acceptance either. A sinner must first satisfy the curse for the fault done, before ever he can be in a capacity to perform new obedience on the terms of acceptation of it with God. Now the first would have taken up eternity, so that there could have been no place of entry to the second; therefore, if Christ had not found out a way of free pardon of the sins that are past and assurance of forgiveness for the time to come, the commandments of God would have been wholly frustrated.

Forgiveness Is Bestowed from God's Treasure of Mercies
"But there is forgiveness with thee, that thou mayest be feared" (Ps. 130:4). The word "fear" also implies "worship." Truly, my beloved, this is the foundation of all religion—free forgiveness. There would have been no religion, no worship of God, no obedience to His commands throughout all eternity, nor would there ever have been any holy fear, any love, any delight in God, any reverence and subjection to Him if He had not granted forgiveness. From His treasure of mercies is first the bestowal of forgiveness upon sinners. And this makes for access to stand and serve in His sight. The cloud of our transgressions is so thick and dark, that there never could have been any communion with God if He had not found out the way to scatter and blot it out, for His own name's sake.

First Must Come Imputed Righteousness

Religion, then, must begin at this great and inestimable free gift of imputed righteousness, that is, of accounting us what we are not in ourselves, because we are found so in another. It begins at remission of sins. But that is not all. This has a further end, and truly remission of sins is but introductive to this further end, that a soul may be made partaker of the gift of holiness within and have that image of God renewed in holiness and righteousness (Eph. 4:24). I would have you once persuaded to begin with this, to receive the free gift of another's righteousness (Rom. 5:17) and another's obedience, to find your own nakedness and loathsomeness without this covering and to know how far short all other coverings of your own works are.

O that we could once persuade you to renounce yourselves, to embrace this righteousness! Then it would be easy to prevail with you to renounce sin, and to put on holiness. I say that first you must renounce yourselves as undone in all you do, as loathsome in all that you ever loved, and you must come under the wide and broad skirt of Christ's righteousness which He did weave upon the earth in order to hide our nakedness. Before anything you do to be accepted, you must first have the righteousness of the law fulfilled perfectly by another, for only then can you have access to fulfill one jot of it yourselves. And until this foundation be laid, you do but beat the air in religion, you build on the sand.

A Step Further: Renounce the Love of Cherished Sin

Now, if once you were brought this length to renounce all confidence in yourselves and to flee into Christ's righteousness, then it would be easy to lead you a step further—to renounce the love of your most cherished sins. And the more lovely that Christ's righteousness is in your eyes, the more beauty would holiness and obedience also have in righteousness as you now see it. Then you would labor to walk after the guidance of the Spirit.

I would have the impression of this deep in your hearts that the gospel is not a doctrine of licentiousness, but a doctrine of the purest liberty and the most complete redemption. Many think it liberty to serve their lusts, and indeed it needs bonds and cords to restrain them. Because there is no man who would not be content to be saved from the wrath to come, many snatch at such sentences of the gospel, taking them lightly without consideration of what further is in it. But truly if this was all, it would not complete redemption unless there was redemption from sin too, that most absolute tyrant in this world. I think a true Christian would account the service of sin bondage, even though it was left to his own choice. He that commits sin is the servant of sin; therefore the freedom that Christ purchases is freedom from sin (John 8:36).

The Image of Christ in Us Is the Purpose of Imputed Righteousness
I will say more. We are delivered from wrath so that we may be redeemed from sin. We have the righteousness of Christ imputed to us so that the image of Christ may be renewed within us; this is the very end and purpose of redemption. I am sure anyone who discerns aright knows that sin has infinitely more of evil in it than punishment has; nay, punishment is only evil as it has a relation to sin. Although there is a beauty of justice and righteousness in punishment, there is nothing in sin but deformity and opposition to His holiness, for sin is pure evil and most purely hated of God. And if there is no more to persuade you that sin is infinitely more evil than pain, consider how our pain and punishment was really transferred upon the blessed Son of God, and that all this did not make Him a whit the worse.

Nevertheless, He was not capable of the real infusion of our sin. That would have made Christ as miserable, wretched, and impotent as any of us, and that would have disabled Him so far from helping us that He would have had as much need of a mediator as have we—all which would be highly blasphemous to imagine. Look then how much distance and difference there was between the suffering, dying Christ and wretched men living in sin. None can say but that He is infinitely better, even while in pain, than the highest prince in pleasure, so much disproportion there is between sin and pain; so much is the one worse than the other.

Second, Imputed Righteousness Also Implies Sanctification
Therefore, do not think that Christ died to purchase an indulgence for you to live in sin. Truly that would have been to take away the lesser evil, that the greater may remain; it would have been to deliver from one misery so that we may be more involved in that which is the greatest of all miseries. Nay, certainly if Christ be a Redeemer, He must redeem us from our most potent and accursed enemy—sin; He must take away the root of sin, the fountain of all misery, sin which has conceived in its womb all pains, sorrows, sicknesses, death, and hell. You have the great end of redemption expressed in Luke 1:74–75, "That we, being delivered out of the hand of our enemies might serve him without fear, in holiness and righteousness before him."

Justification Is to Make Us "Partakers of the Divine Nature"
It was this for which He made man at first, and it is this for which He has made him again, "created in Christ Jesus unto good works" (Eph. 2:10). Certainly, it was a higher design than only to deliver us from hell for which the Son of God became partaker of our nature. Without doubt it was to make us "partakers of the divine nature" (2 Peter 1:4) and this—holiness and goodness—is the very nature of God. As sin is the very nature and image of the devil, so the great breach of the creation was the breaking off of this image of God. That was the heaviest fall of man, from the top of divine excellency down into the bottom of devilish deformity. Now it is this that is the great plot for which Christ came into the world, to make up that breach and to restore man to that dignity again. Thus redemption from wrath is but a step upon which to ascend to that which is truly God's design and man's dignity—conformity with God in holiness and righteousness.

Oh, that you could be persuaded of this that Christ's business in the world was not to bring a notion of an imaginary righteousness only by mere imputation, but to bring forth a solid and real righteousness in our hearts by the operation of His Spirit! I say imputation, or accounting righteous, is but a mere imagination if this living operation does not follow. He came not only to spread His garment over our nakedness and deformity, but really and effectually to be a physician to save our souls and to cure all our inward distempers. The gospel is not only a doctrine of a righteousness without us, but of a righteousness both without, for, and within us too: that the righteousness of the law might be fulfilled in us. Christ without and happiness itself without, cannot make us happy until it enters and takes up dwelling within our souls.

An Appeal to Those Who Are Deceiving Themselves

Therefore, I declare to the most part of you who pretend to expect salvation by Jesus Christ, that you are still in your sins and as yet have no fellowship in this redemption. Do you think to walk after the course of the world and the lusts of the flesh—wallowing in the common pollution and uncleanness among men, swearing, lying, contention, railing, wrath, malice, envy, drunkenness, uncleanness, and such like—and yet be in Christ Jesus? Do not deceive yourselves, "God is not mocked" (Gal. 6:7). He that is in Christ is a new creature. His endeavor and study, his affection and desire, are toward a new walk after the Spirit.

Are not most of you carnal, all flesh: the flesh offers you laws, and you obey them? Are not your immortal souls enslaved to base lusts and to the base love of the world? Are those lusts not prone to prostitute themselves to the service of your fleshly and brutish part? Why do you then imagine that you are in Christ Jesus, partakers of His righteousness? Consider it in time, that so you may be indeed what you now are not but pretend to be. It is your opinion that you are already in Christ that keeps you out of Him.

Assurance Offered to Those Who Desire to Live in Obedience

Again, on the other hand, there is nothing here to discourage a poor soul that thinks subjection to sin the greatest slavery and who would as gladly be redeemed from the power of it as from hell. I say to such whose soul's desire is to be purged from all that "filthiness of the flesh and spirit" (2 Cor. 7:1) and whose continued aim is to walk in obedience, to you I say, though you have many failings and often fall and defile yourselves again, yet this comfort is held out here to you: there is no condemnation to you for Jesus Christ has condemned sin to save you and He has fulfilled all righteousness for you. Therefore, lay you the weight of your acceptation and consolation upon what He has done Himself, and not upon what is but yet doing in you. Do you not find, I say, that the grace of Jesus Christ revealed in the gospel is that which melts your hearts most? Is not the goodness of the Lord that which persuades you most? And do not these make you loathe yourselves and love holiness?

Encourage yourselves therefore in Him. Hold fast the righteousness that is outwith you by faith, and certainly you shall find that righteousness and holiness shall in due time be fulfilled within you. I know no soul so wretched, but it may lay hold on that perfect righteousness of Christ's and go under its covering and take heart from it, if the desire and affection of their soul be directed to a further end. That end is to have His Spirit dwelling within them for the renewing of their heart "in righteousness and true holiness" (Eph. 4:24). I do not say that this is a condition which you must perform before you venture to lay hold on Christ's righteousness imputed to you; nowise, but rather I would declare unto you the very nature of faith in Christ: it seeks in Him deliverance from wrath, not simply and only, but in order that a way may be made for redemption from sin and that there may be a participation of that divine nature, which is most of all in its eye and intention.

SERMON 16

The Spirit Versus the Flesh

Who walk not after the flesh, but after the Spirit. For they that are after the flesh. —ROMANS 8:4–5

Almost the Most Rational Thing in the World

If there were nothing else to engage our hearts to religion, I think this might do it, for there is so much reason in it. Truly it is the most rational thing in the world, except some revealed mysteries of faith, which are far above reason but not contrary to it. There is nothing in it other than what is the purest reason, including that part of it which is most difficult to man and which concerns the moderating of his lusts and affections and the regulating of his walk and carriage. There is nothing that Christianity requires in these matters but that which may be persuaded by most convincing reasons to be most suitable and comely for man, as man. You may apply this to the subject in hand, for it is appropriate here.

Nonetheless, nothing sounds harsher to men nor seems harder in religion than such a victory over the flesh, such an abstractedness[1] from sensual and earthly things. And yet, truly, there is nothing in the world that more adorns and beautifies a man, nothing that so elevates him above beasts as this. Indeed, many natural spirits that are void of this saving light have,

---

1. *abstractedness*: a withdrawal.

notwithstanding, been taken with the beauty of it, and so greatly enamored with it as to count all the world mad and brutish who follow those lower things, enslaving themselves unto them.

Ignorance of God and Ignorance of Ourselves
I take the two fountains of all the pollutions, disorders, and defilements among men to be, first, the inconsideration and ignorance of God, the eternal Spirit and Fountain-being and, second, the ignorance of our own souls, those immortal spirits within us, which are derived from that Fountain-spirit. This is the misery of men, that scarce do they once seriously reflect upon their own spirits, or think what immortal souls are within them, and what affinity these have to the fountain of all spirits. Therefore men basely throw down themselves to the satisfaction of the lusts of the flesh. Now, indeed, this is the very beginning of Christianity, to reduce men from these baser thoughts and employments to the consideration of their immortal souls within. Oh, how will a Christian blush to behold himself in that light, to see the very image of a beast upon his nature and to look on that slavery and bondage of his far better part to the worst and brutish part within him—his flesh!

Humanity's Divine Origins
Man ought wisely to consider from its first divine origins the constitution of his nature and what a thing the soul is, for it is truly and more properly himself than his body. He should study what excellency is in the soul beyond the body, and so what preeminence it advances a man unto beyond a beast, then he could not but count religion to be the very ornament and perfection of his nature. Reason will say that the spirit should rule and command the body, that the flesh is but the minister and servant of the spirit and there is nothing that is the proper and peculiar good of man, other than that which adorns and rectifies the spirit. For all those external things which men's senses are carried after with so much violence do not better a man as

man, but are common to beasts. Further, in these things a man's happiness as man does not at all consist, but in some higher and more transcending good of which beasts are not capable and which may satisfy the immortal spirit, and yet not perish in the using but live with it. The very natural frame and constitution of man convincingly persuades men of all these things.

Now then, may a soul think within itself, "Oh, how far have I departed from my origins! How far degenerated from that noble and royal dignity that God by the stamp of His image once put upon me! How is it that I am become a slave and drudge to that baser and brutish part, the flesh?" I would have you all retire into your own hearts and ask such things of them. Man being created in honor, yet not understanding it, is even like the beasts that perish. Because we do not consider that we are men and advanced by creation far above beasts, truly we have become like beasts.

The Proper Effect of Grace Is the Restoration of Humanity
This failure to reflect on the immortal, spiritual nature of our souls has in a manner transformed us into the nature of beasts, perishing beasts. As sin was the deforming of man into a beast, now Christianity is the very transforming of a beast into a man. This is the proper effect of Christianity, to restore humanity, elevate it, and purify it from all those defilements and corruptions that were engrossed and incorporated into it by the state of subjection to the flesh. Therefore, the apostle delineates the nature of it unto us and draws the difference wide between the natural man and a Christian: *For they that are after the flesh do mind the things of the flesh; but they that are after the Spirit the things of the Spirit.*

The natures of things are dark and hidden in themselves, but they come to be known to us by their operations and acting. Their inclinations and instincts are known in this way. Grace is truly a very spiritual thing, and the nature of it lies high. Yet as Christ could not be hidden in the house, neither can grace be hidden in the heart—it will be known by its outworking. Christ can be more easily hidden in a home than in the heart because, when He is in a heart, He is engaged to restore that heart and soul to its native dignity and preeminency over the flesh; for a season this cannot but cause much disturbance in the man. To change governments, I mean to cast out usurpers and to restore the lawful and righteous owner to the possession of his right, cannot be done secretly and easily. It will shake the very foundations of a kingdom to accomplish it. So it is here: the restitution of the soul to the possession of its right and dominion over the flesh—the casting down of that tyrannous and base usurper, the flesh—cannot be done without the man knowing and feeling it and, in a manner, being wounded by it.

Believers Will Be Known by Their Natures
Now, the nature of Christianity lays itself open to us in these two things especially: first in what it minds and savors, and second in how it causes us to walk. Life is known especially by affection and motion. A feeling, thinking, savoring power is a living power, so is a moving, walking power a living power, and these are being referred to here. In short, the Christian is described by his nature. He is one who is *after the Spirit* and *not after the flesh*, and by the proper characteristic operations of that nature, first, minding or savoring *the things of the Spirit*, which comprehends his inward thoughts, affections, intentions, and cogitations. All his inward senses are exercised about such objects. And then he is one who is walking *after the Spirit*, and his motions are in a course of obedience, proceeding from that inward relish or taste that he has of the things of God.

It is not without very good reason that the nature of a Christian is thus expressed—one who is "after the Spirit." It is the Spirit's character that expresses His nature unto us. Whether you look to the origin of Christianity, or to the prime subject of it, or to the chief end of it, it deserves to be called by this name: "who walk…after the Spirit." The origin of it is very high, as high as that eternal Spirit, as high as the God of the spirits of all flesh. Things are like their original source and in some way participate in the nature of their source's causes. "That which is born of the Spirit, is spirit" (John 3:6). That which is born of God, who is a Spirit, must be spirit. How royal a descent is this! How it ennobles a man's nature!

Truly, all other degrees of birth among men are vain imaginary things that have no worth at all, other than in men's fancies. They put no real excellence in men. This only is true nobility. This alone extracts a man *de faece vulgi*—"out of the dregs of the multitude." There is no intrinsic difference between bloods or natures, but what being born of God creates—this divine birth, this second birth. All other differences are but mere opinion, this is reality. It puts the image of that blessed Spirit upon a man. Truly, such a new creature is not begotten in the womb of any natural cause, neither of any human persuasion, nor enticing words of man's wisdom, nor of any external mercy or judgment. No instruction, no persuasion, no allurement, nor any affrightment can make you Christians in the Spirit. It is not until the Spirit blows when He pleases and creates you again. It must come from above—the power that alone can set your hearts aright and enable them to look straight above.

Only the Spirit and the Word Can Beget True Believers
Christ Jesus came down from heaven to the earth and took on our flesh so that the almighty Spirit might come down to transform our spirits and lift them up from the earth to the heaven. We cast the seed into the ground of men's hearts (and alas! It gets entry into but few souls for it is scattered rather on the highway side and cannot reach into the arable soil of the heart). Nevertheless, it can do nothing without the influence of heaven, for unless the Spirit beget you again by that immortal seed of the word, the heart remains infertile as stony ground. Therefore, we can cease our wondering that all the means of God's Word and works do not beget more true Christians. I do rather wonder

that any of Adam's wretched posterity should be begotten again and advanced to so high a dignity to be born of the Spirit. Oh, that Christians would be mindful of their origin and wonder at it and study to be like it!

If you believe and consider that your descent is from that uncreated Spirit, how powerful might that be to conform you more and more to Him and to transform more and more of your flesh into spirit! There is nothing will raise up the spirits of the children of princes more than to know their royal birth and dignity. How should the consideration of this make your spirits suitable to your state or fortunes, as is said regarding those born into earthly families of the nobility? You would labor to raise those born of the Spirit up to that height of their origins and so to walk worthy of that high calling. Oh that we could learn from that instruction which Paul gives: "But of him are ye in Christ Jesus," therefore, "he that glories, let him glory in the Lord" (1 Cor. 1:30–31). Truly, a soul possessed with the meditation of this royal descent from God could not possibly glory in those so-called glorious but baser things in which men glory and would not be able to restrain themselves or refrain from glorying and boasting in Him.

False Glory
The glory of many is their shame because they glory in their sin of which they should be ashamed. But suppose that in which men glory is not in itself shameful, for it pertains to lawful things of this present world, yet certainly it is a great shame for a Christian to glory in them or to esteem himself as better on account of them. If it was minded always that we are of God, born of God, what power do you think temptations or solicitations to sin would have over us? "Whosoever is born of God sinneth not; but he that is begotten of God keepeth himself, and that wicked one toucheth him not" (1 John 5:18). Truly, this consideration, imprinted in the heart, would elevate us above all these baser persuasions of the flesh. This would make sin loathsome

and despicable, as the greatest indignity we could do to our own natures.

The strength and advantage sin has over us is by causing us to forget what we are and to whom we are related, so that we drink ourselves drunk with the puddle of the world. Or else sin obsesses us with our own jealousies and suspicions that we may forget our birth and state and so be enticed to anything. If you would have wherewith to beat back all the fiery darts of the devil, take the shield of this faith and persuasion. Then how it would silence temptations! "Shall I who am a ruler flee?" said Nehemiah (Neh. 6:11). Shall I, who am born of the Spirit, shall I, who am of God in Christ, abase myself to such unworthy and base things? Shall I dishonor my Father, and disgrace myself?

Man's Royal Seat Is in the Spirit of His Mind
Then Christianity's chief residence, its royal seat, is in the spirit of a man, and so he is one after the Spirit. Be you "renewed in the spirit of your mind" (Eph. 4:23). As it is of a high descent, so it must have the highest and most honorable lodging in all the creation, that is, in the spirit of a man. Without this there is no room else fit for it or suitable for it in this lower world. "My son, give me thine heart," says Wisdom (Prov. 23:26). Wisdom cares for nothing besides, if it does not get the heart, that inmost cabinet of the imperial city of this isle of man, for "out of it are the issues of life" that flow into all the members (Prov. 4:23).

Do not think that grace will lodge one night in your outward man, that you can put Christianity upon your countenance or conversation without. Except you admit it into your souls, it can have no suitable entertainment there alone. It is of a spiritual nature, and it must have a spirit to abide in. Everything is best preserved and entertained by things suitable to its nature, such as do incorporate together and embosom one with another, whereas things keep a greater distance with other things that are different in nature. A flame will die out among cold stones, without any oily matter in which to burn. This heavenly fire that has descended into the world can have nothing earthly to feed upon. It must die out, except it get into the immortal spirit and then furnish, so to speak, perpetual nourishment to it, until at length all the spirit be set aflame and changed, as it were, into that heavenly substance, to mount up above from whence it came.

Do not think, my beloved, to superinduce true religion upon your outside, and within to be as rotten sepulchres. You must either open your hearts to Christ, or else He will not abide with you. Such a noble guest will not stay in the suburbs of the city, if you take Him not into the palace; and truly the palace of our hearts is too unworthy for such a worthy guest, it has been so defiled by sin. How vile is it? But if you would let Him enter, He would wash it and cleanse it for Himself.

The Character of a True Christian

Will you know then the character of a Christian? He is one much within. He has retired into his own spirit, to know how it goes with it; and he finds all so disordered and confused, all so unsettled, that he gets so much business to do at home he has no leisure to come much abroad again. It is the misery of men, that they are wholly abroad from their innermost chambers, carried only into external things. This is the very character of a beast that it cannot reflect inwardly upon itself but is wholly taken up with those things that are presented to its outward senses. There is nothing in which men are more assimilated to beasts than this, that we do not speak in ourselves or return into our own bosoms but are wholly occupied about the things that are outside of us. And thus it fares with us, as with the man who is busy in all other men's matters, and never thinks of his own. His estate must fall into ruin; all his affairs must be out of course.

Truly, while we are immersed and drowning in external things, our souls are perishing, our inward estate is being swept away. All our own affairs, that can only and properly be called ours, are disordered and jumbled. Therefore, Christianity first of all recalls the wandering and vain spirit of man into itself, as that exhortation says in Psalm 4:4, to "commune with your own heart and be still," in order to make a diligent search of his own affairs. And oh, how he finds all out of order: as a garden neglected, all overgrown, as a house not inhabited, all dropping through; in a word, all is wholly ruinous through intolerable negligence! It was the first turn of the prodigal to return to himself, "he came to himself" (Luke 15:17).

Sin Estranges Us from Both God and Ourselves
Truly, sin is not only an aversion from God, but it is also an estrangement from ourselves, from our souls, from our own happiness. It is a madness that takes away the use of reason and consideration of our own selves. But grace is a conversion, not only to God, but also to ourselves. It brings a man home to his heart, makes him sober again who previously was beside himself. Hence that phrase, "If they shall bethink themselves...and so return unto thee with all their own hearts" (1 Kings 8:47f).

It is the most laborious vanity, or the vainest labor, to compass heaven and earth—to be so busied abroad, as it were—to know other things, but meanwhile to know and consider nothing of that which of all things most nearly concerns us—ourselves. "What shall it profit a man, if he gains the whole world, and loses his soul?" for that is himself (Matt. 16:26; Mark 8:36). And what shall it profit to know all but not to know his soul, to be everywhere but where he ought to be?

Restoring to Its Primal Beauty the "Garden" Devoted to the Well-Beloved
Well, a Christian is one called home from vain impertinent diversions. He is one who is occupied most about his soul and spirit, how to have all the disorders he finds in himself ordered, all those distempers cured, all those defilements washed. This is the business he is about in this world—to wash his heart from wickedness (Jer. 4:14), to cleanse even vain thoughts and

shut up his own heart from that ordinary repair.² He is about the enclosing of it to be a garden devoted to the well-beloved, there to bring forth sweet fruits. He is about the renewing of it, the adorning of it with the new man, against that day of our Bridegroom's appearing and summoning him up into heaven to celebrate the marriage.

Though he be still in the flesh, yet he is most taken up with his spirit, how to have it restored to that primitive beauty and excellence, the image of God in it. He is concerned how to be clothed with humility and to put on the ornament of a meek and quiet spirit; he accounts this as his beauty. Also, he is concerned how to rule his own spirit in a manner that he reckons as the only true fortitude. And he thinks it a greater vassalage³ and victory to overcome himself rather than his enemy, and he esteems it the noblest revenge not to be like other men who wrong him. He is occupied about the highest gain and advantage, namely, to save his spirit and soul. He accounts all as loss compared to this, to bring Jesus Christ into his heart. That is the jewel for which he digs, esteeming all else as dung in comparison to it.

If you truly are Christians after the Spirit, no doubt you are busied this way about your spirits. For others, they are busied about the flesh, to make provision for its lusts; there needs no other mark by which to know them. Alas! Poor souls, to this you have never yet adverted⁴ that you have spirits, immortal beings within you, which must survive this dust, this corruptible flesh. What will you do when you cannot have flesh to care for and when your spirits can have nothing to be carried forth into but must eternally dwell within the bosom of an evil conscience? For there you will be tormented with that worm, the bitter remembrance of the neglect of your spirits and utter estrangement from them while you were in the body. Then you must be

---

2. *repair*: a meeting place or a habitual coming and going among others.
3. *vassalage*: an act of valor, bravery, or military prowess.
4. *adverted*: taken heed or paid attention.

confined within your own evil consciences, and be imprisoned there forever because, while yet there was time and season, you were always abroad and everywhere instead of being within your own hearts and consciences. Will not this be a just recompense?

Descending from the Father to Raise Us Up to the Eternal Spirit
Then again, as Christianity descends from the Father of spirits into the spirit of a man, to lodge there for a while, at length it raises up the spirit of a man and unites it to that eternal Spirit; thus, as its origins were high and divine, its end also is high. It issues out of that fountain and returns into the heart of man, there to embosom itself again. And truly, this is the great excellence of true religion above all those things you are busied about, that it elevates the spirit of a man to God and that it will never rest until it has carried it above to the Fountain-spirit. Our spirits are sparks and chips, to speak so with reverence, of that divine being; but just now they are wholly immersed and sunk by sin into the flesh and earth, until grace comes down and renews them, extracting them out of that dunghill and purifying them. Until then they are, as it were, in a state of violence, always striving to mount upward till they be embodied, or rather inspirited (so to speak) in that original Spirit, until they be wholly united to their own original element, the divine nature.

You know Christ's prayer in John 17: "That they may be one, as we are one; I in them, and you in me, that they may be made perfect in one" (vv. 22–23). When spirits have attained their perfection, then will they "rest from their labors" when they are one with Him. This is the only center of spirits in which they can rest immoveable. You find all the desires and affections of the saints are as so many breathings upward, panting after union with Him, and longing to be intimately present with the Lord. Therefore, a Christian is one after the Spirit, groaning to be all spirit, to have the earthly house of this tabernacle dissolved, and to be clothed with that house from heaven. He knows with Paul, that he is not at home, though he be at home in the body, because the body is that which separates from the Lord, which partition-wall he would willingly have taken down, that his spirit might be at home and so present with the Lord (2 Cor. 5:1ff).

At Death the Spirit within Us Will Bear Us Heavenwards
"Who knoweth (says Solomon) the spirit of a man that goeth upward, and the spirit of the beast that goeth downward to the earth?" (Eccl. 3:21). Truly, the natural motion of man's spirit should be to ascend upward to God who gave it. When this frail and broken vessel of the body is dissolved into the elements, the higher and purer nature that lodged within it should fly upward to heaven. On the other hand, the spirit of the beasts, being but the prime and finer part of the body and not different in nature from the earth, naturally falls down to the earth with the body and is dissolved into the elements. But regarding the consideration of the woeful order sin has brought into the world, I think all things in man have become so degenerated and brutish—both his affections and his conversation—that carnal and sensual lusts now have the whole dominion over men.

The Temptation to Doubt
I say, the serious and earnest view of this might make a man suspect and call into question whether or not there be any difference between men and beasts; whether or not there may be any more spirit in the one of a higher nature than in the other. Truly, it would half persuade a man that there is no immortal spirit in him, else how could he be such a beast all his time "serving divers lusts" (Titus 3:6)? Could it be possible, one might think, that there is any spirit in men that can ascend to heaven, when there is no motion thither to be observed among them?

I beseech you to consider this: the spirit must either ascend or descend when it goes out of the body, as now in affection and endeavor it ascends or descends while it is in the body. There is an indispensable connection between these. Whatsoever the spirit aims at, whichever way it turns and directs its flight, thither it shall be constrained to go eternally. Do you think, my beloved, while you are in the body, to bow down yourselves to the earth and to descend into the service of the flesh all your lives, never once seriously to rise up in the consideration of eternity, or lift up your heads above temporal and earthly things, and yet in the close to ascend unto heaven?

Do Not Deceive Yourselves, but Strive to Reach Upward to God
No, no, do not deceive yourselves! You must go forward. This life and eternity make one straight line, either of ascent or descent, of happiness or misery. And since while in the body you have always bowed down, there can be no rising up after the body is dissolved. Onward you must go and for you that is downward to that element into which you transformed your spirits, that is, the earth, or below the earth—to hell. Your spirits have most affinity with these, and down they must go as a stone to the earth. But if, when your spirits are let out of this prison of the body, you would desire to have them ascending up to heaven, take heed which way they turn now.

Therefore, bend and strive while here in the body. If your struggling be to be upward to God, if you have discovered that blessedness which is in Him and if this be the predominant longing of your spirit, the longing that carries it upward in desires and endeavor and turns it aside from the base study of satisfying the flesh and the base love of the world, if thy soul be mounting aloft on these wings of holy desires of a better life than can be found in anything below, certainly the motion of your spirit will be in a straight line upward. When you leave your dust to the earth, angels will be waiting to carry that spirit to that bosom of Christ where it longed and liked most to be. But devils do attend the souls of the most part of men to thrust them down below the earth, because they continued always to bend down to the earth.

SERMON 17

The Desires of the Flesh Are against the Spirit

> *For they that are after the flesh do mind the things of the flesh.* —ROMANS 8:5

Though sin has taken up the principal and inmost cabinet of the heart of man—though it has fixed its imperial throne in the spirit of man and makes use of all the powers and faculties in the soul to accomplish its accursed desires and fulfill its boundless lusts—yet it is not without good reason ordinarily expressed in Scripture under the name of "flesh" and a "body of death." Therefore, men dead in sins are said to be yet in the flesh. The reason is partly because his hearkening to the suggestions of his flesh against the clear light and knowledge of his spirit was the rise of man's first ruin or the chief ingredient in his first sin. The apple was beautiful to look on and sweet to the taste, and this engaged man. Thus the voluntary debasement and subjection of the spirit, which was breathed into it by God for the service of that dust which God had appointed to serve it, has turned into a necessary slavery so that the flesh being put upon the throne cannot be cast out.

Fallen Man Has Become a Slave to the Dregs of Creation

Therefore, this is the righteous judgment of God upon man, that he who would not serve so good and so high a Lord should be made a drudge and slave to the very dregs of the creation.

Partly also this judgment came because the flesh has in it the seeds of the most part of these evil fruits that abound in the world. The greater part of our corruptions either have their rise or their increase from the flesh, for part of men's evils are either conceived in the flesh or else, by the service and help of our degenerate spirits, they are brought forth by it. And truly this is it that makes our returning to God so hard and difficult a work, because we are in the flesh, which is like stubble, disposed to conceive flame upon any sparkle of a temptation. Indeed, there are so many dispositions and inclinations in the body since our fall that are as powerful to carry us to excess and inordinate lengths in affection or conversation, as the natural instincts of beasts drive them on to their own proper operations.

You know the flesh is oftentimes the greatest impediment that the spirit has because of its lumpishness and earthly quality. How willing would the spirit be, how nimble and active in the ways of obedience, if it were not retarded, dulled, and clogged with the heavy lump of our flesh! "The spirit indeed is willing, but the flesh is weak," said Christ (Matt. 26:41). Truly I think the great remissness, negligence, weakness, and fainting of Christians in their race of Christianity arise ordinarily from this weight that is carried about with them, that it must be some extraordinary impulse of a higher Spirit to drive us on without wearying.

The Flesh Is a Bosom Enemy That Betrays Us to Satan
Because of this indisposition of the flesh, we are not able to bear much of God's presence in this life. (It would certainly confound mortality, if even some of His glory as it is in heaven was to be let out upon us.) No more is a weak eye able to endure beholding the sun in its brightness. And then the flesh, as it is the greatest retardment[1] in good, is also the greatest incitement to evil for it is a bosom enemy that betrays us to Satan; it is near us and connatural to us. And this is the great advantage Satan has of

---

1. *retardment*: something that delays or hinders progress.

a Christian in that he has a friend within all Christians that betrays them often. You know the most part of temptations from without could have no such force or strength against us if there were not some predisposition in the flesh, some seeds of that evil within. When these predispositions are presented to some suitableness within our senses, being once engaged on Satan's side, they easily draw the whole man with them under a false color and pretense of friendship. Therefore they are said to "war against the soul" (1 Peter 2:11) and they are also said "easily" to "beset us" (Heb. 12:1). Truly it is no wonder that the enemy storms our city, when the outworks, yea, the very ports of the city, are possessed by traitors. No wonder Satan approaches near to the walls with his temptations when our senses, our fleshly part, are so apt to receive him and ready to entertain all objects without differentiation that are suitable to affect them.

You see then how much power the flesh has in man so that it is no wonder that every natural man has this denomination,[2] one "after the flesh," one carnal from the predominating part, though the worst part. Until a higher birth comes, every man by nature may be called all flesh, all of him fashioned and composed of the flesh and after the flesh; even his spirit and mind are fleshly and earthly, sunk into the flesh and transformed into a brutish quality or nature. Now the great purpose of the gospel is to bring a deliverer unto your spirits for the releasing and unfettering of them from the chains of fleshly lusts. This is the very work of Christianity, to give liberty to the captive souls of men "and the opening of the prison to them that are bound" (Isa. 61:1). The souls of men are chained with their own fleshly lusts and if at any time they can break these grosser chains, as some finer spirits have escaped out of the vilest dungeon of the flesh and cast off these heavier chains that bind the most part of men, yet wholly escape they cannot.

---

2. *denomination*: a name, designation, or characteristic.

Fallen Man Has Lost His Freedom and Is without True Liberty
There are higher and lower rooms of this prison, meaning that there are some more gross, some more subtle cords and bands of the flesh. Whatsoever it be that holds a man bound or in whatsoever house he be imprisoned does not much matter since in reality he is in bonds and his liberty restrained. If a chain of gold binds as fast as a chain of iron, there is no real difference except that mockery is added unto it when a man is detained in a golden prison with golden chains. Though some men, I say, escape the grosser pollutions of the flesh, yet they are fettered within some narrow, scant, and merely imaginary good things, for they cannot go beyond the compass of those. Every man is confined by nature within the circle of his own narrow bosom or if he expatiates[3] into the field of the world, yet how narrow and how limited are all created objects for the infinite desires of the soul.

How imprisoned in all that compass is a man, whether his wanderings are toward the enjoyment of other creatures or to the possession of some imaginary excellence in himself. How straitened are such wanderings! There is no true liberty to be found there. Though some may be disengaged from baser lusts and the common, vain employments of men, yet far they cannot go; they only engage themselves more with the love and estimation of themselves. Beyond that narrow compass they cannot possibly go, whether from another principle, or to another end. And oh how little bounds there are within any created breast for the immortal spirit, which in itself is so vast and expatiating in its desires to find somewhere to dwell in!

Christ's Deliverance Bestows a New Nature

But here is the perfect redemption that is in Jesus Christ. When He comes into the soul He unfetters and releases it not only of the grosser lusts of the flesh but even of those subtle invisible

---

3. *expatiate*: to wander unrestrained.

bands of self-love and self-seeking, that is, of all the scant, narrow, and particular objects. He sets the soul at liberty to expatiate in that universal good, the infinite fullness of God and the grace which is in Christ Jesus. Hence a Christian is called one *after the Spirit*, that is, one whose spirit is rid and delivered from that natural bondage and slavery to mere creatures and is espoused, at least in affection and endeavor, to the all-sufficient and self-sufficient God.

We told you that this new nature of a Christian shows itself in affection and motion, that is, in minding and in walking; both are signs of life and the proper actions of it. As the natural man is easily known by what he minds and savors and what way he walks, so is the spiritual man. Minding or savoring comprehends, no doubt, all the inward acts of the soul, all the imaginations, cogitations, thoughts, affections, desires, and purposes of the soul. To express it shortly, there is a concurrence of these two, cogitation and affection, the understanding and the will, in this business. The natural man knows not the things of the Spirit, so he cannot taste or relish them, since he does not know them (1 Cor. 2:14).

Ignorance of Christ Leaves Men in Their Dungeon of Darkness
How can they believe on Him whom they have not heard (Rom. 10:14)? But far more, how can men love and desire that which they do not know? Indeed, it is hard to convince some that they know not God nor the thing of the Spirit when they do have some form of knowledge and seem to understand. Further, though they can even discourse on religion, yet I wonder that the most part of men, whose ignorance is written in their foreheads with such palpable characters, should have so much difficulty in taking with this challenge. I am sure that many who persuade themselves of heaven are yet shut up in that dungeon of natural blindness and darkness of mind, a darkness that is so gross and thick that it is not possible to make them conceive any notion of spiritual things; indeed, the common twilight of nature is

almost extinguished, and little or nothing can be increased by their education in the visible church.

How can you prize and esteem Jesus Christ, of whom you know nothing but the bare name? How can you savor heaven when you have never admitted one serious thought of the life to come? Oh, that you could be persuaded that the grace of God is inconsistent with such gross ignorance, as is in the innate light within you. Truly grace is a light shining in the soul that opens the eyes to see this grace that surrounds us in the gospel. But will you consider, beloved, how ready you are to receive other things of no moment and how your memories can retain them, and your understandings receive other purposes very perplexed and laborious. As to the knowledge of your sin and misery or of that blessed remedy showed in the gospel, we cannot make you capable of even a few questions about them, and if you learn the words by heart (as we say) yet, alas! The matter and thing themselves are not in your heart or mind—you have nothing but mere words, as is clear.

The Persistence of So Many in Minding the Things of the Flesh
If we ask about the same matter and thing using other words and terms, they remain as dark and new to you as if you had never heard of them. I beseech you to consider whether you do not then *mind the things of the flesh* most when you are not only most capable of knowing these things that concern this life but are also most ready to entertain such thoughts. You have no difficulty in minding the world whole weeks and years, but you can never find leisure or time to mind the life to come, and yet vainly you say that you do mind it always. Therefore I beseech you, how do you mind God and the things of God when, if you will but recollect your thoughts and gather the sum of them, you will not in a whole week find one serious advised thought of Him or His matters! I confess that I wonder how so many can enforce upon themselves a persuasion that God is always in their heart. I think it is the height of delusion! I am sure He is

not in one of ten thousand thoughts that travel, walk, lodge, and dwell in the souls of men, and yet you consider that you need to bear upon yourselves that you always mind Him.

I am sure most of you cannot say that you always shut the doors of your hearts upon other vain objects in order that you might retire to secret meditation on God or conference with Him. Alas, I am equally as sure that many men have God oftener in their mouths by oaths and blasphemies and irreverent speaking by taking His holy name in vain, than in their minds, prayers, or praises or in any holy meditations of Him. Are you not as unwilling to fix your minds upon any sad, solemn thoughts of God's justice, of hell, of heaven, of sin, of misery, or of death, like boys whose heads are full of play and so are loath to go to their books? Does not your practice in this speak with those wicked men who say, "Depart from us, we desire not the knowledge of thy ways" (Job 21:14)?

"To Be Carnally Minded Is Death"

How constrained are all your thoughts of religion—they are treated in the same way as those that you would not desire to come again! But how unrestrained, how free are all other thoughts! Our minds can rove whole days about vanity, about fancies, dreams, nothings; but you neither like to admit nor retain the knowledge of God in your mind (Rom. 1:28). Do you not entertain any serious weighty thoughts of religion that may occasionally enter as firebrands, as hot coals into your bosom? How glad are you to get any diversion to other things! How willing to shun them or cast them out! But if it be any temporal thing, anything relating to this flesh, your thoughts come freely and are steady and fixed as long as you please. Then without wearying but using up precious time your minds can travel through all the ends of the earth to bring in some fancy of gain or advantage.

Now all these things considered, my beloved, are you not carnal? I speak to the most of you. Are you not those who are born of the flesh since you mind nothing seriously, resolutely, constantly, and willingly but the things of the flesh and the things of this life? Oh, it is no light matter to be born of the flesh; if you continue so, you are ordained for corruption and death, "For to be carnally minded is death" (v. 6).

Some Early Indications of Spiritual Renewal
But I am persuaded better things of some of you, that the true light of God has shined into your hearts and revealed more excellent things to you than these perishing fleshly things: viz., heavenly, substantial, and eternal things in the gospel, which you account only worthy of the fixed and continued meditation of your spirits. I am sure you perceive another beauty and excellency in these things than the world does because the Spirit has revealed them unto you. It is true that your minds are yet much darkened in their apprehension of spiritual things; they are not so willing to receive them, nor so ready to retain them as you desire. Your minds are still very unsettled and unsteady in the meditation of spiritual things, and there are innumerable thoughts of other things that pass through your hearts like common inns, uncontrolled in their pleasure.

All this is true, but I am sure it is the grief of your souls that your hearts are not so fixed and established as the excellency of these spiritual things require. I know it will be the aim and real endeavor of any spiritual heart to be shutting up all the entries and doors of the mind that vain thoughts enter not; yet enter they will, there are so many porches to enter in at, and our narrow spirits cannot set a watch at them all. Every sense will let in objects and imagination itself will be active in framing them and presenting them: but yet the endeavor of a Christian will be not to let them lodge long within (Jer. 4:14).

If they come in unawares, the Christian will endeavor to make a diversion to a better purpose so that it will still hold good that the current and course of a Christian's thoughts and cogitations are upon *the things of the Spirit*. For he will be intent on how to get his own heart washed and cleansed; how to be more holy and conformed to Christ; how to be at peace with God and keep that peace unbroken; how to walk in obedience to God and in duty toward men; how to forsake himself and withal to deny himself in all these I say, his most serious and solemn thoughts are about these things. Indeed, his resolved and advised thoughts will run most on this strain though it will also be true that—whether he wills it or not, whether vain or impertinent or not—other thoughts will pass more lightly and too frequently through his heart.

Further Indications of Spiritual Renewal
The other thing in which this spiritual life appears is the current of the affections, or that relish and taste of the sweetness of the things of the Spirit, flowing from the apprehension of them in the mind. When the light is discovered indeed (and oh, "it is a pleasant thing for the eyes to behold it," as Solomon says, Eccl. 11:7) then the Spirit has found an object suitable to its nature and so it relishes and delights in it. Therefore, the word *to mind*[4] is not simple minding or thinking, but savoring and thinking with affection upon its truths, tasting and feeding upon the knowledge of them; it is a minding of them with care and delight and also with earnestness. "O taste and see how good the Lord is" (Ps. 34:8).

Some things indeed cannot be known but by some sense. You cannot make a blind man apprehend what light is till he sees it. A deaf man cannot form a notion of sounds in his mind except he once heard them. Neither can a man understand the sweetness of honey but by tasting it. Truly spiritual things are of that nature. There is some hidden virtue and excellence in them, which is not obvious to every man that has the bare knowledge of the letter; there is a spirit and life in them that cannot be transmitted into your ears with the sound of words or infused into ink and paper. It is only the inspiration of the Almighty

---

4. Φρονειν.

that can inspire this sensible perception and real taste of spiritual things. Some powders do not smell till they are beaten; truly until these truths be well powdered and beaten small by meditation, they cannot smell so fragrantly to the spirit. As meats do not nourish until they are chewed and digested, so spiritual things do not give relish to a soul, nor can they truly feed the soul, until they are chewed and digested into the heart by serious and earnest consideration.

This is that which makes these same truths to be in some ways not the same. These very principles of religion, received and confessed by all, prove to be living in one, but dead in another. It is the living consideration of living truth—the application of truth to the heart—that makes it alive in one, whereas others keep it only beside them in a corner of their minds, or in a book, or in the corner of the house. If the same meat is laid before you all, most of you look at it, others contemplate it and exercise only their understandings about it. But there are others who taste it and find sweetness in it, who digest it by meditation and solemn avocation[5] of their hearts from the things of the world. Therefore while some are fed, some are starved.

A Challenge to Those Who Still Cling to Earthly Things
Need we enlarge much upon this subject? Is it not too palpable that many who fill up our churches are *after the flesh*, because they do mind and savor only the things of the flesh and not of the Spirit? Will you seriously search your hearts and ask what relishes most with them? Can you say that it is the kingdom of God or the righteousness thereof? Or is it not rather those other things such as food and raiment and the like that have no extent beyond this narrow span of time? I am persuaded that the hearts of many can taste no sweetness in religion, else they would fix more upon it and pursue it more earnestly. Are not the things of another world, the great things of the gospel, counted

---

5. *avocation*: a diversion or distraction.

all strange things (Hos. 8:12), as things that you have not much to do with? Do you not let the officers of Jesus Christ, bearing all the sweet invitations of the gospel, pass by as strangers and as if you were unconcerned in them? What taste have they more than the white of an egg?

How unsavory a discourse or thought to a carnal heart is it to speak of subduing the lusts of the flesh, of dying to this world and of living for the world to come? Who among you find their hearts inwardly stirred upon by the proposal of Jesus Christ? But if any matter of petty gain were proffered, oh how would men listen with both their ears! How beautiful in the eyes of the covetous mind is any gain or advantage! The sound of money is sweeter to him than this blessed sound of peace and salvation. How sweet is pleasure to the voluptuous! What suitableness and convenience is apprehended in these perishing things! But how little moment or weight is conceived and believed to be in things eternal? Oh how substantial do things visible seem to men, and how trifling other things invisible appear to be!

Consolation for Those Who Mind "The Things of the Spirit"
But for you whose eyes are opened, to you Christ is precious. To you the things of the Spirit are beautiful, and all your grief is that you cannot affect them according to their worth or love them according to their beauty. I say, some there are who do see a substance and subsistence only in things not seen (Heb. 11:1), and things that are seen and visible in this world they account shadows in comparison with things invisible. The world apprehends no realities other than in what they see. On the other hand, a Christian apprehends no solid reality in what he sees but only in what he does not see.

Therefore, as in his judgment he looks upon the one as a shadow and the other as a substance, so he labors to proportion and conform his affections to a suitable entertainment of them; this is why he gives a shadow of show of affection for the things of this life, but to the things invisible of another life he gives the marrow and substance of his heart. Thus the apostle in 1 Corinthians 7:30–31 says, "they that rejoice, as though they rejoiced not; and they that buy, as though they possessed not; and they that use this world, as not abusing it,"—half acts for half objects! If we give our whole spirits, the strength of our souls and minds to them, we are as foolish as he that strikes with all his strength at the air, or a feather. There is no solidity or reality in these things, able to bottom[6] much estimation or affection, only mind them and use them as in the by, as in passing through toward your country.

---

6. *to bottom*: serve as a basis or establish firmly.

SERMON 18

The Great Difference between Flesh and Spirit

For they that are after the flesh do mind the things of the flesh; but they that are after the Spirit the things of the Spirit. For to be carnally minded is death; but to be spiritually minded is life and peace. —ROMANS 8:5–6

There are many differences among men in this world which, as to outward appearance, are great and wide; indeed they are eagerly pursued and seriously minded by men as if they were great and momentous. You see what a strife and contention there is among men, how to be extracted out of the dregs of the multitude and set a little higher in dignity and degree than others. How men affect to be honorable above the base! How they seek to be rich and hate poverty! The thoughts of men are wholly taken up with these differences of poor and rich, high and low, noble and ignoble, learned and unlearned.

The Great Difference between Men

However, here is one great difference most in the eyes of God that is both substantial and eternal and that so infinitely surpasses all those differences upon which the minds of men most run: it is the great difference between flesh and spirit, and those who are *after the flesh,* and those who are *after the Spirit.* This is of all other differences the most considerable because it is the widest and most durable. I say, it is the widest of all, for although all other distinctions put no great difference between men as men, it reaches the peculiar excellence of a man, that is, the true and proper good of his spiritual and immortal part; they are such as befall alike to good and bad and so cannot have either much good or much evil in them.

I have seen "folly set in great dignity, and the rich sit in a low place. I have seen servants upon horses and princes walking on foot" (Eccl. 10:6–7). Then certainly such titles of honor and dignity, such places of eminence erected above the multitude, have little or nothing worth the spirit of a man in them, seeing that a fool or a wicked man is as capable of them as a wise man, or a man of a princely spirit. And so of all others they do not elevate a man, as a man, above others. A poor, unlearned, mean man may have more real excellence in him than a rich, learned, and great person.

One Difference Is Corruptible, the Other Is Incorruptible
But this draws a substantial and vast difference indeed, such as there is between flesh and spirit, such as there is between men and beasts. You know what preeminence a man has over a beast. There is no such wide distance among the sons of men as there is between the lowest, meanest man and the most preeminent of beasts. "But there is a spirit in man," said Elihu (Job 32:8), an immortal, eternal substance of a far higher nature and comprehension. You know what excellence is in the spirit beyond the flesh such as is in heaven beyond the earth, for the one is breathed from heaven, and the other is taken out of the dust of the earth; the one is corruptible—yea, corruption itself—the other incorruptible.

How swift and nimble are the motions of the spirit from the one end of heaven to the other! How they can compass the earth in a moment! Do but look and see what a huge difference there is between a beautiful living body, and the same body when it is a dead carcass, rotten and corrupted. It is the spirit dwelling within that makes the odds, that makes it active, beautiful, and comely, but in the removal of the spirit it becomes a piece of the most defiled and loathsome dust in the world.

Now, I say, there is such a vast and wide difference between a true Christian and a natural man. Even taking him in with all his common endowments and excellencies, the one is a man, the other a beast, the one is after the flesh, the other is after the Spirit. It is the ordinary compellation[1] of the Holy Ghost: "Man that is in honor, and understandeth not, is like the beasts that perish" (Ps. 49:20), "Understand, ye brutish among the people: and ye fools, when will ye be wise?" (Ps. 94:8), and "A brutish man knoweth not; neither doth a fool understand this" (Ps. 92:6), and "That they might see that they themselves are beasts" (Eccl. 3:18). Therefore you find the Lord often turning to beasts, to insensible creatures, thereby to reprove the folly and madness of men (Isa. 1:3; Jer. 8:7).

In His Spirit a Man May Rise, in His Body a Man May Fall

Man has two parts in him by which he has affinity to the two most distant natures; he stands in the middle between angels and beasts. In his spirit he rises up to an angelic dignity, and in his body he falls down to a brutish condition. Now, which of these has the preeminence that he is? If the spirit be indeed elevated above all sensual and earthly things, up to the life of angels, that is, to communion with God, then a man is one after the spirit, an angel incarnate, an angel dwelling in flesh; but if his spirit throw itself down to the service of the flesh, minding and savoring only things sensual and visible, then indeed a man puts off humanity and has associated himself with beasts to be as one of them. And indeed, a man made thus like a beast is worse than a beast, because he ought to be far better.

To mind only the flesh is no disparagement to a beast, but it is the greatest abasement of a man. It is this which draws him down from that higher station God has set him into, to the

---

1. *compellation*: way of addressing someone.

lowest station, that of beasts. Truly a Nebuchadnezzar among beasts is the greatest beast of all, far more brutish than any beast (Dan. 4:28–33). Now such is every man by nature for "that which is born of the flesh is flesh" (John 3:6).

Every man as he comes out of the womb is degenerate and fallen down into this brutish estate to mind, savor, and relish nothing but what relates to this fleshly or temporal being. The utmost sphere and comprehension of man is now of no larger extent than this visible world and this present life, for "he that lacketh these things is blind, and cannot see afar off" (2 Peter 1:9). Truly, such is every man by nature, whereas the proper native sphere of the spirit's motion and comprehension is as large as its endurance—that is, as long as eternity and as broad as to reach the infiniteness of God, the God of all spirits.

The Spirit Is Blinded by Life in the Flesh
Now the spirit, through the slavery and bondage of men to their flesh, is contracted into as narrow bounds as this poor life in the flesh. He that ought to look beyond time as far as eternity and has an immortal spirit given for that end is now half blind. For the eye of the mind is so overclouded with lusts and passions that it cannot see far off, not so far as to the morrow after death, not so far as to the entry into eternity. And truly, if you compare the context, you will find that whosoever does not give "all diligence, to add to your faith virtue; and to virtue knowledge; and to knowledge temperance; and to temperance patience; and to patience godliness; and to godliness brotherly kindness" (2 Peter 1:5–7), he that is not exercised and employed in this study does not know how to adorn his spirit with these graces. For this is how a man may have a victory over himself and the world. And in respect of these, he counts indifferent all other things beside.

Without such a victory man is blind and does not see far off. He has not gotten a sight of eternity, he has not taken up that everlasting endurance, else he could not spend his time upon provision for the lusts of the flesh, but he will be behooved to lay such a good foundation for the time to come as is here mentioned. If he saw afar off, he could not but make acquaintance with those courtiers of heaven, which will minister an entrance into that everlasting kingdom. But truly, while this is not your study, you have no purpose for heaven, you see nothing but what is just before your eyes and almost touch it, and so you savor and mind only what you see.

Is not this then a wide difference between the children of this world and the children of God? Is it not very substantial? All others are circumstantial in respect of this, for only this puts a real difference in that which is best in men, their spirits. The excellence of their renewed nature is known by their affections and motions. So here we see that the spiritual man savors spiritual things. Contrast the nature of the carnal man who can only savor carnal things. For everything sympathizes with that which is like itself and is ready to receive and incorporate into itself whatever is nourished and preserved by things like itself.

The Illustration of Swine
You see how swine embrace the dunghill, for that stink is a savory smell to them because it is suitable to their nature. But men have a more excellent taste and smell than swine and they are able to savor finer and sweeter things. Nonetheless, the carnal man's choice must be according to a nature more swinish or brutish than a swine, that it can relish and savor such filthy abominable works of the flesh as abound among some of you. "The works of the flesh are manifest" (Gal. 5:19). And indeed they are manifest among you, acted in the very day-time, outfacing the very light of the gospel—read them again yourselves and see if they be not too manifest in you.[2]

---

2. The apostle Paul listed the following in Gal. 5:19–21: "Adultery, fornication, uncleanness, lasciviousness, idolatry, witchcraft, hatred, variance, emulations,

Now, what a base nature, what abominable and brutish spirits must possess men that they apprehend a sweetness and fragrance in these corrupt and stinking works of the old man! Oh how base a scent must it be to smell and savor nothing but this present world and to find therein satisfaction for your senses! Truly your scent and smell, your relish and taste, argue your base, degenerate, and brutish natures, proving that you are on the worse side of this division—after the flesh. But alas, it is not possible to persuade you that there is neither sweetness nor fragrance in all these works of the flesh, nothing but corruption and rottenness such as comes out of sepulchres that are opened, until a new spirit be put in you and your natures changed. No eloquence can persuade a sick man, whose palate is possessed with an impaired bitter humor, that such things as are suitable to his vitiated taste are indeed bitter; neither could any man persuade a swine to believe that the dunghill is stinking and unpleasant. Truly it is likewise impossible to make the multitude of men to apprehend, relish, or savor any bitterness or loathsomeness in the ways and courses they are following, or any sweetness and fragrance in the ways of godliness, till once your tastes be rectified and your spirits be transformed and renewed.

The Renewed Spirit
And indeed, when once the spirit is renewed and dispossessed of that malignant humor of corruption and fleshly affection that did present all things contrary to what they are, then it is like a healthy and wholesome palate, that tastes all things as they truly are. Then the renewed spirit finds bitter to be bitter and sweet to be sweet, or it becomes like a sound eye that beholds things just as they are both in color, quantity, and distance. It is then that the soul savors the sweet smell of the fruit of the Spirit, "Love, joy, peace, longsuffering, gentleness, goodness, faith, meekness,

---

wrath, strife, seditions, heresies, envyings, murders, drunkenness, revellings, and such like."

temperance" (Gal. 5:22–23). These are fragrant and sweet to the soul and are as a sweet perfume, both to the person that has them and to others round about him—sweet also to God. These cast a savor that allures a soul to seek them and, being possessed of them, they cast a sweet smell abroad to all that are round about, even as high as heaven.

A soul that has these planted in it and growing out of it is as a garden enclosed to God. These fruits are both pleasant and sweet to the soul that eats them and, as the pleasantness of the apple allured man to taste it and sin, so the beauty and sweetness of these fruits of the Spirit draw the spirit of a man after them. When he has found the savor and seen the beauty and has been allured to taste them, he then invites the well-beloved to come and taste also and to eat of these fruits with him. We might instance this in many things. The Christian relishes more sweetness in temperance, in beating down his body and bringing it into subjection (1 Cor. 9:27), that is, in abstaining from fleshly lusts, than a carnal man tastes in the most exquisite pleasures that the world can afford. The Christian savors a sweetness in meekness and longsuffering, he has more delight in forgiving and forbearing and praying for them that wrong him, than a natural man has in the accomplishing of the most greedy desires of revenge.

Love, Joy, and Peace
Oh, what beauty gentleness, goodness, and patience have in his eyes! What sweetness is in the love of God to his taste! How ravishing is the joy of the Holy Ghost! How contenting is that peace that passes understanding! These are things of the Spirit that he minds and savors. Know, Christians, that it is to this you are called, to mind these things most and to seek them most. Beware lest the deceitfulness of sin entices you through the treacherous and deceitful lusts that are yet living in your members. If you indeed mind these things and, out of the apprehension of their beauty, savor the sweetness and smell of their

fragrance, would be content to quit all your corrupt lusts to be possessed of them, then you are now on that blessed and happy side of this great and fundamental division of men. You have indeed the privilege of all others who are not renewed. Whatever be your condition in the world, you are of the Spirit and this is better than to be rich, wise, great, and honorable. God has not given you such things as the world goes mad after, but envy them not, for He has given you better things, more real and substantial things, that make you far better and more excellent.

But then this difference, as it is the widest, is also the most durable. As it is substantial here, so it is perpetual hereafter. When all the other differences between men shall be abolished, this alone shall remain, and therefore you have it in the next verse, "For to be carnally minded is death: but to be spiritually minded is life and peace." This division that is begun here shall grow wider for all eternity. There shall be a greater difference after this life and a more sensible separation. Death and life, eternal death and eternal life, are the two sides of this difference, as it shall shortly be stated.

Two Very Different Outcomes in Eternity
When all other degrees and distances of men shall be blotted out and buried in eternal oblivion, no vestige or mark will remain of either wisdom or riches or honor or such like. Then as to these outward things, all men shall be leveled and equalized; then this one unseen and neglected difference in the world shall appear and shine in that day when the Lord makes up His jewels: "then he will discern between the righteous and the wicked, between him that feareth God, and him that feareth him not" (Mal. 3:18). The carnal and spiritual man have opposite affections and motions. The spirit of the one is on a journey or walk upward, *after the Spirit*, whereas the spirit of the other is on a walk downward, toward the flesh, *after the flesh*, and the further they go, the more distant they are. The one shall be taken up to the company of "the spirits of just men made perfect" and to the fellowship

of angels (Heb. 12:23), the other shall be thrown down into the fellowship and society of devils.

Truly it is no wonder the fall down is so low, for all the motions in the body were downward, to the fulfilling of the lusts of the flesh. Thus you see the difference will grow wider and more sensible than it is as yet between the godly and ungodly; in this world it does not so evidently appear as it will do afterward. As two men who leave one another and have their faces on contrary arts,[3] at the beginning the distance and difference is not so great and so sensible; but wait a little and the further they go the farther they are distant and the wider their separation is.

Even so, when a Christian begins to break off his way from the common course of the world, it does not appear to be so different from it as to convince himself and others; but if his face is toward the Jerusalem above and his heart thither-ward, certainly he will be daily moving further from the world till the distance be sensible both to himself and others; he will be more and more transformed and renewed till at length all shall be changed. No wonder then, that these two cannot meet together at the end of their course, whose courses were so opposite. Though wicked men will desire to "die the death of the righteous" (Num. 23:10), yet it is no more possible they can meet in the end than hell and heaven can reconcile together, because they walk toward two contrary points.

---

3. *contrary arts*: different directions or points of the compass.

SERMON 19

The Way of Death and the Way of Life

For to be carnally minded is death; but to be spiritually minded is life and peace. —ROMANS 8:6

Through Time into Eternity

It is true. This time is short and so short that scarce can similitudes or comparisons be had to shadow it out to us. It is a dream, a moment, a vapor, a flood, and a flower. It is whatever can be even more fading or perishing. Therefore it is not in itself very considerable, yet in another respect it is of all things the most precious and worthy of the deepest attention and most serious consideration. Why? Because it is linked unto eternity and there is an indissoluble knot between them that no power or art can break or loose. The beginning of eternity is continually united to the end of time. And you know all the infinite extension of eternity is uniform, admitting of no change in it from better to worse, or worse to better. Therefore the beginning of our eternity, whether it be happiness or misery, is but one perpetuated and eternalized moment, so to speak.

Seeing then we are in the body and sent unto the world for this end so that we may pass through into an unchangeable eternal estate, truly of all things it is most concerning and weighty as to which way we choose to this journey's end. Further, seeing the time is short in which we have to walk—and it is uncertain too—we ought, as the apostle Peter speaks, to "give all diligence" (2 Peter 1:5) and, as long as the day remains, we should drive the harder lest that eternal night overtake us. The shortness and uncertainty of time should constrain us to take the present opportunity and not to let it slip over as we do.

We Must Redeem the Time

Seeing it is not at all in our hand either what is past or what is to come, the one cannot be recalled nor is it in our power to call and bring forward the other, therefore the present moment that God has given us should be seized, held onto, and redeemed as the apostle speaks in Ephesians 5:16. We should buy it at the dearest rate of pains and expenses from all those vain, impertinent, and trifling diversions that take it up, in order that we may employ it as it becomes suitable to eternity that is posting on.[1] And therefore the fleeting brevity of our time on earth makes it the more precious and considerable, considering its end—eternity. As the scantiness of a thing increases the rate of it, so that same consideration should make all worldly things that are confined either in their being or use, within it, to be inconsiderable, as Paul shows in 1 Corinthians 7:29–31: seeing "the time is short: it remaineth, that both they that have wives be as though they have none; and they that weep, as though they wept not; and they that rejoice, as though they rejoiced not; and they that buy, as though they possessed not; and they that use this world, as not abusing it: for the fashion of this world passeth away."

Seeing all the worth of this world is to be esteemed from its final end, from eternity that never ends, then certainly whatsoever in time does not reach that end and has no connection with it, we should give it only such entertainment as the man gets who beholds a passing bird that, while it is in its flight, is pleasant to the eye. The shortness of the day should make us double our diligence and press on the harder in our walk or race that we may come in due time to our place of rest. That same

---

1. *posting on*: riding with haste or urgency.

should make the passenger give an overly[2] and passing look to all things that are by the wayside and which he must of necessity leave behind him.

Two Ways and Two Ends
Seeing these things, then, are so important, let us draw our hearts together to consider what the Lord speaks to us in this word, for in it you have two ways and two ends, opposite ways and paths that are contrary and whose ends are also contrary. These ways are walking after the flesh and walking after the Spirit; the ends to which they lead are death or life.

We have already spoken something of these ways and the wide difference that is between them and what excellence is in the one beyond the other. But truly it is hard to persuade you to leave off your accustomed ways and walks because your inward sense and the inclination of your hearts are wholly perverted and corrupted by nature. You know the motivating faculty is subordinate in its operations to the knowing, feeling, and understanding faculties. The locomotive power is given for a subsidiary and help to the apprehensive and appetitive powers because, without it, to the nature of the living creature things are convenient or inconvenient, good or evil. For it could not by mere knowledge, desire, or hatred of things either come into possession of them or eschew them. Therefore, God has given them a faculty of moving themselves to the prosecution and attainment of any apprehended good, or to the eschewing and aversion of any conceived evil. Thus it is that when beasts savor or smell food which is fit for them, their appetite stirs them up to motion after it to obtain it.

The Natural Man Is Infected with a Poisonous Humor
Now, I say, if this inward sense be corrupted then things that are destructive will be conceived to be good, because they are suitable

---

2. *overly*: superficial, cursory, or careless.

to that corrupt humor or quality that possesses the senses; thus all the motion and walk will be disordered. The truth is, my beloved, our spirits and minds are infected with a poisonous humor, fleshly passions and lusts that are naturally predominant. As in those who are in a fever, their organs being distempered[3] with a bitter unsavory humor, the pleasantest things seem unsavory because they are not suitable to that predominant humor, even so it is with you by nature. That which puts all upon motion is out of course since the first distemper of man. Your spirits and minds are fleshly and carnal; they have a strong and deep impression of all the lusts that are in the body and are accordingly affected.

This is why you cannot fitly judge what is good or evil for you, but according to these you must "call evil good, and good evil;…bitter for sweet, and sweet for bitter" (Isa. 5:20), because you are already prepossessed thus. And therefore the ways of the flesh, those paths that lead to destruction, you cannot but look on them as pleasant because they suit and please your corrupted sense or spirit; and so this disordered savor or smell of some fragrant perfume in the ways of the flesh puts you upon walking in these ways. Being thus possessed and engaged, you cannot but stop your ears to all contrary persuasions. You think it against your sense and reason to tell you that these are loathsome and unsavory and that the other ways of wisdom and spirit are pleasantness and peace. I say, you cannot believe this till your hearts and spirits lie purged and your taste be pure and uncorrupted.

The Way to Heaven Is "An Alley of Delight"
It is certainly upon this ground that our Savior puts such characters on the way to heaven and hell, to life and death. The one is straight and narrow and few walk in it; the other is broad and easy, and many walk in it (Matt. 7:13–14). Certainly, it is not simply the way in itself that admits of such a motion to speak

---

3. *distempered*: diseased or deranged.

properly, as the thing is. The way to life, by the guiding of the Spirit, is easiest, plainest, shortest, and broadest. It has all the properties of a good way for none is so pleasant and plain—how sweet and pleasant are the sights all the way! It is an alley of delight—the way of His commandments. It does not lack accommodation in it to refresh the traveler. The most delightful company is here: the Father and the Son, who sought no other company from all eternity, but were abundantly satisfied and rejoiced in one another. This fellowship the Christian has to solace himself with and he is admitted to become a partaker of that joy. There is nothing that disburdens the soul so of care and anxiety, nothing rids a man of so many perplexities and troubles as this way.

The Way to Hell Is Dogged by Grief and Travail

But the way of sin in itself is most laborious, most difficult. It has infinite byways that it leads a man into and he must turn and return and run in a circle all the day, all his time, to satisfy the infinite lusts and insatiable desires of sin. Oh how painful and laborious is it to fulfill the lusts of the flesh! How much service does it impose! How much serious attention! What perplexing cares and tormenting thoughts! How many sorrows and griefs are in every step of this way! Do you not perceive what drudges and slaves sin makes you, how much labor you have to satisfy your lusts? And you are always to begin, as near that which you seek in the end of your years, as in the beginning. How thorny, how miry is the way of covetousness! Are you not always out of one thorn into another, and cut asunder or pierced through with many sorrows (1 Tim. 6:10; Matt. 13:22)?

Is that a pleasant and easy way, I pray you, that makes all your sorrow and your travail grief and suffers not your heart to take rest in the night (Eccl. 2:22–23)? What pains of body! What plotting of mind! What labor and vexation of both must a sinner have as his constant attendant in this way! The way is intricate, deep, unpassable that leads to that satisfaction your lusts desire. Your desires are impotent and impatient, the means to carry you on are weak and lame, nowise accommodated or fit for such a journey. And this puts you always, as it were, on the rack, tormented between the impatience of your lusts and the impotency of means and impossibility to fulfill them. Desires and disappointments, hopes and fears, divide your souls between them. Such is the way after the flesh, an endless labyrinth of woes and miseries, of pains and cares, ever while here.

The Natural Man Is Blind to the Truth about Both Ways

But these ways receive such names from the common opinion and apprehension of men, because of our flesh which is predominant. The way after the flesh being suitable to it, though in itself infinitely more toilsome, seems easy and plain but the way after the Spirit seems strait, narrow, toilsome, and laborious. Though there be infinitely more room in the way to life because it leads to that immense universal good, it expatiates toward the all-fullness of God; yet to the flesh how narrow and strait is it, because it cannot admit of these inordinate lusts that have swelled so immeasurably toward narrow and scanty things! The true latitude of the way of the flesh is not great, for it is all enclosed within poor, lean, narrow, created objects. But because the imagination of men supplies what is really wanting and fancies an infinite or boundless extent of goodness in these things, therefore the sinner walks easily without straitening to his flesh—it is not pinched in this way by fleshly lusts. But alas, the spirit is woefully straitened, fettered, and imprisoned, though it be not sensibly bound.

What is the reason, then, that so many in the flesh walk in the way to death because their flesh finds no straitening, no pressure upon it? It is an easy entry into their natures because, suitable to the corruption that is in them, men walk on without consideration of what follows. It is like a descent or going down a hill and so easy to our flesh. On the other hand, the way of life after the Spirit is an ascent upward and is very difficult to our earthly and lumpish flesh. Our spirits by communion with and subjection to the flesh, are made of an earthly quality, near the element of the flesh, and so they bow naturally downward. However, if once they were purified and purged and unfettered by the Spirit of God and restored to their native purity, they would more easily and willingly move upward as does the flame. And until this be done in you we cannot expect that you will willingly and pleasantly walk in these pleasing walks after the Spirit; your walk will never be free and unconstrained in the paths of godliness.

The Contrast between False and Genuine Christians

From some external motives and impulses, you may move upward for a season in some particular duties of religion the way a stone can be set up, but as that impression is not from an inward principle so it will be neither constant nor durable. Consequently, you will fall down to your old bias in other things and move quite contrary when the external impression of fear or favor, custom or education, or such like wears out. But the true Christian has a spirit within him—the root of the matter in him. This carries him upward in the ways of obedience, after the motions and directions of God's Spirit. At the beginning, indeed, it is strait and uneasy to his flesh, but the difficulty is overcome if once he begins well; the beginning (as we used to say) is the half of the whole. Truly to be well entered is half progress; afterward the bulksome and burdensome lusts of the flesh are stripped off, at least in a greater measure and then the spirit moves easily and willingly; this walk that at first was a labor becomes a recreation. Now delight and desire are as wings to mount the soul aloft.

Now it is the good pleasure of the soul to walk to all well-pleasing. Indeed the way of this world is dirty and filthy and therefore a Christian has need to watch continually and to gird up his loins so that his thoughts and affections hang not down to the earth. Otherwise they will take up much filth and cannot but clog and burden the spirit, making it drive heavily and slowly as Pharaoh did his chariots when the wheels were off (Ex. 14:24–25). We had need to fly aloft above the ground and not to come down too low near it, thinking withal to double out our journey for we shall find, because of the remnants of flesh within us, that this world has a magnetic, attractive virtue to draw us down to it, if we be within the sphere of its activity.

It is not good coming near fire with flax, therefore we should endeavor to keep our hearts at much distance and disengage them from our lower consolations. This world is like the pestiferous lake of Sodom that kills all that fly over it and makes them fall down into it. If we fly low upon the surface of it, we cannot think but that the spiritual life will be much extinguished. But to prevent this we should take our flight straight upward after the Spirit (for that is the proper motion of the more pure and spiritual part of this world) and give no rest till we be out of the reach of that infection, till we be fully escaped of the pollutions of the world.

An Urgent Warning to the Carnally Minded

But if you cannot be persuaded to come off this way that seems so pleasant to your flesh, that way which is the very course of the world (for these are joined, Eph. 2:2), then, I beseech you, stand still and consider whither it will lead; do but stop a little and bethink yourselves sadly and seriously whither this will take you and where it shall end. And truly that is dreadful—the end of it is death, a never-ending death. I am sure, if you were walking by the way, and one came and told you gravely and seriously that that way was full of dangerous pits, that there are many robbers in it waiting to cut your throat, you would count the admonition worthy of so much notice as to halt and consider what to do.

But now when the Lord Himself—He who deserves infinitely more respect and credit than men—gives you warning once and often, day after day repeating this admonition to you and sends out many ambassadors to call you off, making this word to sound daily in your ears, "Oh! Why will you die? Such ways lead down to the chambers of death and hell" (cf. Jer. 27:13; Prov. 5:5). To be carnally minded in the issue is death, whatever you may promise to. I say, when He makes a voice to accompany us in all our walking, saying that this is not the way that leads to life, why then do you not think it worthy of so much consideration as once to stop and sist[4] your progress till you examine what will come of it? Are we so credulous toward men and shall not we believe God who is truth itself and who affirms it so constantly, and obtests[5] us so earnestly? Are we so wise and prudent in lesser things and shall we be mad, self-willed, and refractory in the greatest things that concern us eternally?

The Peril of an Empty Confession
Oh, unbelief is that which will condemn the world, the unbelief of this one thing, that the walking after and minding of the flesh is mortal and deadly! Though all men confess with their tongues this to be a truth, yet it is not really believed; the deep inconsideration and slight apprehension of this truth makes men boldly to walk, and violently to run on, to perdition. Did you indeed believe that eternal misery is before you at the end of this way and would you be so cruel to yourselves as to walk in it for any allurement that is in it? If you really believed that there is a precipice into utter darkness and everlasting death at the end of this alley, would the pleasure and sweetness of it be able to infatuate you and besot you so far as to lead you on into it, like an ox to the slaughter, and a fool to the correction of the stocks?

It is strange, indeed, though you neither will believe that death is the end of these things, nor yet can you be persuaded that you do not believe it. There is a twofold delusion that possesses the hearts of men: one is a dream and fancy of escaping death though they live in sin; another is a dream and fancy that they

---

4. *sist*: to postpone or suspend, especially used with reference to legal proceedings.
5. *obtest*: to charge solemnly; also to beg earnestly, beseech, entreat.

do believe that death is the wages of sin. We might wonder how they consist together if we did not find it by so many experiences. Your way proves that you do not believe that death is the end of it, but then your words give evidence that you do not believe that you are unbelievers of that. Oh, how desperate is the wickedness and how great is the deceitfulness of the heart! The false prophet that is in every man's bosom deceives him that it may destroy him. As Satan is a liar and a murderer and murders by lying, so the heart of man is a self-murderer and a self-destroyer, and this is done by lying and deceiving.

The Peril of Self-Deception

Although there is some lie in every sin, there is this gross, black, fundamental lie at the bottom of all sin—a conceit of immunity and freedom from death and hell, a strong imagination of escaping danger, even though such a way be chosen and walked into as of its own nature inevitably leads to destruction. And there is something of this bloody, murdering flattery even in the hearts of Christians. Therefore, this apostle gives us an antidote against it and labors often to purge it out by stirring up that knowledge they have received. "Know you not that the unrighteous shall not inherit the kingdom of God?" (1 Cor. 6:9). "Be not deceived, God is not mocked, for what a man soweth, that shall he reap, he that soweth to the flesh shall reap corruption" (Gal. 6:7–8).

Oh, that you might listen to this word, to this watchword given you, and stop your course at least for a season to consider what the latter end shall be! Know you not that such shall not inherit the kingdom? Know you not that the way to heaven lies upward? Know you not that your way lies downward toward the flesh and the earth? Are you so far demented[6] as to think to come to heaven by walking just downward in the lusts of the flesh? Truly this is the strongest and strangest enchantment

---

6. *demented*: destitute of reason.

that can be, that you think to sow one thing and reap another thing, to sow darkness and reap light, to sow corruption and reap incorruption. Is it possible in nature to sow nettle seed and think to reap barley or wheat? Be not deceived! Oh that you would undeceive your poor deluded souls and know that it is as natural for death and hell to grow out of sin and walking after the flesh as it is for every seed to yield its own fruit and herb! Do you then think to dissolve the course and order of nature?

Eternal Corruption, Death, and Destruction

Truly the flesh is mortal in itself; it is ordained for corruption. You see what it turns to after the life is out; that is an emblem of the state of the fleshly soul after death. As you did abase your spirits to the service of the flesh here and all your plowing, laboring, and sowing was about it, the seed which you did cast in the ground was fleshly lusts, earthly things for the satisfaction of your flesh. So then you shall reap of the flesh corruption, death, and destruction that shall make your immortal spirits mortal and corruptible. Thus you shall subject them to death and corruption with the body as far as they are capable. So it shall deprive them of all that which is their proper life and refreshment, separating them eternally from the fountain of blessedness, and banishing them out of heaven unto the fellowship of devils. And oh, that corruption of the incorruptible spirit is worse than the corruption of the mortal flesh: "The corruption of the best is worst of all!"[7]

A Man's Awareness of His Peril May Bring Hope of Recovery

Now, whoever of you is thus far undeceived as to believe your danger and misery and to discern that inbred delusion of your hearts, be not discouraged utterly. For there may be hope of recovery when you see your disease. I say, if you see that hell is at the end of your way, then know that He who sent that voice

---

7. corruptio optimi pessima.

to call you off that way of death does not leave you to your own wits to guide you into the right way. He follows with a voice behind you, saying, "Here is the way, walk in it, turn not out of it to the right hand or left" (cf. Isa. 30:21). And this voice sounding plainly in the word is nothing else but the sound of the gospel, that blessed sound that invites and allures you to come to Jesus Christ, "the way, the truth, and the life" (John 14:6)—the true way to the true life. All other ways, all other lives have no truth in them; they are but a cloud, a fancy that men apprehend and lay hold on. But come to this way and it will truly lead you to the true life, eternal life.

The Holy Spirit as Teacher, Guide, and Director

If you fly unto him out of the apprehension of your danger, you have a clear way to come to God and as plain a way to attain life and peace. Being in Christ, you have assurance of not falling into condemnation. He is such a way as will hold you in, and not suffer you to go out of it again to the way of death. And therefore He will give you a tutor, a guide, and director in this way to life and peace—the Holy Spirit, to lead in all truth and to guide your feet in the way of His commandments. So that in this new and living way of Christ, you shall have both light of the word to know where to walk and life of the Spirit to make you walk toward that eternal life. Thus grace and truth are come by Jesus Christ. Indeed, you must suffer the mortification of your flesh, you must endure the pain of the death of your lusts (Rom. 6:11–12), the cutting off your right hand and plucking out your right eye which would make you offend and stumble in the way (Matt. 5:29; 18:9; Mark 9:47), but let the remembrance of the life to come sweeten it all.

When men undergo the hazard of losing life for a little pleasure or for a poor petty advantage, then they will endure so much pain and trouble. Oh what should "eternal life," and such a life as the best life here is—but death to it!⁸ How should it mitigate and sweeten the bitterness of mortification! How should it fortify our spirits to much endurance and patience? A battle we must have for these lusts that we disengage from the devil and the world besides will lie in wait for us in this way. But when for such small and inconsiderable advantages men will endure all the disadvantages of war, even a long war, oh how should the expectation of this peace which encloses and comprehends all felicity, all well-being, animate and strengthen us to fight our way into the city of life and peace eternal!

---

8. The meaning of this rather obscure sentence must be understood as being explained by both the preceding and the subsequent sentences: "How should *it*..." referring to "eternal life," which is "the best life"; therefore "death to it!" means mortification of the desire for "a little pleasure" and "a poor petty advantage."

SERMON 20

The Vile Ugliness of Enmity against God and the Bitter Fruit of Rebellion against Him

Because the carnal mind is enmity against God: for it is not subject to the law of God, neither indeed can be.
—ROMANS 8:7

The Ignorance and Misery of Unbelief

Unbelief is that which condemns the world (John 3:18). It involves man in more condemnation than many other sins, not only because it is more universal but especially because it shuts up men in their misery, secluding them from the remedy that is brought to light in the gospel. By unbelief I mean, not only that careless neglect of Jesus Christ offered for salvation, but that which is the root of it—the inconsideration and ignorance of our desperate sinfulness and irremediable misery without Christ—which, not being laid to heart seriously, makes such slight and superficial entertainment of a Savior and Redeemer. Man is truly miserable and unhappy whether he knows it or not. But truly, without him realizing it, unbelief is an accession[1] to his misery, in that he neither apprehends what he is now by nature, nor what he must shortly be made by justice.

Indeed, if there were no remedy to be found, it would be a happy ignorance to be ignorant of misery for the knowledge and remembrance of it could do nothing but add unto the bitterness

---

1. *accession*: participation, adherence, or addition.

of it. If a man might bury it in eternal forgetfulness, it would be some ease. But now, when God has in His mercy so appointed it that the beginning of the belief of sin and misery shall in a manner be the end of misery and seeing (whether men know it or not) that they must shortly be made sensible of it when there is no remedy to be found, then certainly it is the height of man's misery that he knows but yet considers it not. If we would apply our hearts at length to hear what God the Lord speaks—for He only can give man an account of himself—we might have a survey of both in these words and in those preceding them. We would then learn of our desperate wickedness and of our intolerable misery. For the present, by nature we are enemies to God and shortly we must be dealt with as enemies, as rebels to the most potent and glorious King and so be punished with death, an endless living death.

Experience shows how hard a thing it is to persuade you that you are really under the sentence of death for you will not suffer your hearts to believe your danger lest it interrupt your present pleasures of sin. Nay, you will flatter yourselves with the fancied hope of immunity from this curse and account it a cruel and rigorous doctrine that so many creatures made by God should be eternally miserable or that a sentence of it should be passed on all flesh.

Enmity against God Is Rebellion

Now, because that which makes us hardly believe this is the unbelief and deep inconsideration of our sinfulness, the apostle therefore, to make way for the former adds, "Because the carnal mind is enmity against God." Do not wonder then that your ways and courses, your affections and inclinations, bring forth that ghostly and dreadful end of death, seeing all these are enmity to the greatest King who alone has the power of life and death. They have a perfect contrariety to His holy nature and righteous will. Not only is the carnal mind an enemy, but enmity itself, and therefore it is most suitable that the sovereign power of that King of Kings is stretched out to the vindication of his holiness and righteousness by taking vengeance on all ungodliness and unrighteousness of men. If rebellion in a state or monarchy against these petty mortal gods, who shall die as men, be so heinous as to deserve death, by the consent of all nations how much more shall enmity and rebellion against the immortal eternal King, who has absolute right and dominion over His creatures as the potter has over the clay (Rom. 9:18–23), have such a suitable recompense of eternal death?

Now, my beloved, if you once believed this—the enmity and opposition of your whole natures to God—then you could not but fearfully apprehend what might be the issue of it, nor could you bless yourselves as you do and put the evil day far off. Rather would you certainly be affrighted with the terror and majesty of the God with whom you have to do. For when He awakes to judgment you can neither resist nor escape nor stand against His wrath. There could be no flying from it out of His dominions. Knowing this would dispose and incline your minds in time to hearken to His treaty of peace. I speak of the peace that is held out in the gospel, whereby you must lay down the weapons of your enmity and make peace with Him in His Son, the Peace Maker.

The Wretchedness of Withdrawing from Union with the Creator

Amity and unity are the very being and beauty of the world. This universe is made up of innumerable different kinds and natures, and all these do climb and walk together by the bond of peace and concord among themselves and with that one high understanding that directs all, along with that supreme will of God that moves all. It is that link of union with God that gives and preserves being and beauty in all the creatures. As the dependence of the ray upon the sun or the stream upon the fountain makes them what they are, when interrupted they cease to be what they were: all things continue as you have ordained them for all are thy servants (Ps. 119:91). You see, then, this amity and union of subordination of the creatures to God is not dissolved to this day, but woeful and wretched man alone has withdrawn from this subordination and dissolved this sacred tie of happy friendship which at first he was lifted up unto and privileged with.

Amity and friendship, you know, consist in a union of hearts and wills and a communion of all good things. They make two one, as much as two can be, by the conspiracy of their affections in one thing, that is, the joint concurrence of their endeavors to communicate to one another what each has. They take away propriety,[2] making a community between persons. Now, how happy was that amity! How blessed that friendship between God and man! Though man's goodness could not extend to God, yet his soul was united to God by love and delight. Thus all that God had given him returned to the proper owner, acknowledging his absolute dependence on Him and claiming interest and propriety in nothing, certainly not in himself. And then, on the other hand, the love and goodwill of the infinite God placed on man from that fountain all the streams of happiness issuing forth toward man. For then the fullness of God opened up itself to him and laid out itself toward him, God so far descending, as in a manner, to become the creature's, to expose and dispose Himself and all in Him for poor man's use and comfort.

Sin Has Caused an Irreconcilable Enmity against God

How joyful was that amity! But the breaking of this bond of peace is as sad and grievous. There was a woeful interposal between God and us which has separated these chief friends ever since the beginning and that is sin—the seed of all enmity and discord that has rent asunder the bond of amity. Sin has made such a total aversion of the soul from God and imprinted such an irreconcilable enmity in the heart against the holy will of God that there is no possibility to reunite them again and restore the

---

2. *propriety*: property.

old friendship as long as the soul is not quite changed and transformed. That first creation is so marred and defaced, that there is no mending of it till a second creation comes. The carnal mind is not simply an enemy, but enmity itself; an enemy may reconcile again and accept terms of peace, but enmity cannot reconcile to amity, without the very destruction of itself. The opposition of the heart is so perfect[3] that as soon may enmity unite with amity and become one with it as a carnal natural mind can submit to God's holy will. That which was at the beginning voluntary is become necessary and turned into the nature of an inbred antipathy that no art can cure.

The fall was such a disjointing of the soul from God that no skill but infinite wisdom, no strength but almighty power, can set it right and put it in the first posture again. It is true, there are not many who will openly and expressly denounce[4] war against heaven; it is not so incident[5] that any man should have explicit plain thoughts of hatred against God. There are some common principles engraved by God in all men's minds which serve as His witnesses against men: that God should be loved, served, adored, and worshipped and that there is nothing so worthy of the desires of the soul.

Fragments of God's Marred Image in Men Can Delude Them

Now, this general acknowledgment deludes the most part for they take it for granted that they do love God with their heart because their consciences bear witness that they ought to love Him, as if it were all one to know our duty and to do it. Who is there but he entertains himself with this good opinion of himself that his heart is good and true to God? For, say you, whom should I love, if I love not God? I were not worthy to live if I love not Him. What you say is true indeed, but if you did know your

---

3. *perfect*: complete.
4. *denounce*: proclaim or announce threateningly.
5. *not so incident*: not likely to happen.

hearts you would find their faces turned backward and averted from God. Indeed, you would find that you could no more please yourselves in such a confession of the truth than the devil has reason to think himself a believer because he is convinced that Christ is the Son of God—he too confessed that. You would also find that you are no better than the son who promised to go to the garden to work and went not though he had grounds to think himself an obedient son (Matt. 21:30).

Such a confession of duty may be extorted from damned spirits and therefore you should not draw this veil over the wretched wickedness of your natures to the end that you may conceive well of yourselves. It is so far from extenuating or excusing that the very conviction of the great obligation to love and obey God is the greatest aggravation of the enmity. It is this which makes it the purest malice and most perfect hatred that, knowing the goodness of God and convinced of our bound duty to love and serve Him, yet in the very light of such a shining truth we then turn our hearts away from Him and exercise all acts of hostility against Him.

The Three Evidences of Enmity against God

That you may know, then, wherein the enmity of your hearts consists, I shall instance it in three branches or evidences. There is an enmity in the understanding, that it cannot stoop to believing of the truth. Second, then there is an enmity in the will that it cannot be subject to the obedience of God's holy commands. Third, this is extended also to a stubborn rebellion against the will of God, manifested in the dispensations of His providence. In a word, the natural and carnal mind is incapable of faith, of obedience, and of submission.

First Evidence of Enmity against God:
A Darkened Understanding
There are many things revealed in the Scripture that the natural man cannot receive or know, "for they are foolishness unto him"

(1 Cor. 2:14). There are some spirits that are lifted up above others, either by nature or education, in which this rebellion more evidently appears; reason in them contends with religion and they will believe no more than they can give a reason for. There is a wisdom in some others that despises the simplicity or the inevidence[6] of the gospel; they account it foolishness. The carnal mind will need to start out from implicit trusting of God when once it is possessed with some imagination of wisdom. Therefore, how many are the insurrections of men's spirits against God's absolute power over the creatures, against the mysteries of the holy Trinity and incarnation, against the resurrection of our bodies? In these and such like ways, the pretended wisdom of men has taken liberty to react with enmity and to dispute against God.

Men Reject the Full Truth about the Divine Judgments

But truly, men's rebellion and insubordination against the truth of God is more generally practiced, even by the multitude of men, though in an unfree, hidden way. How few do believe their own desperate wickedness though God has testified it of man? Does not everyone apprehend some good to remain in his nature and some power to do good? Is it not an impossibility to persuade you that all mankind is under the sentence of eternal condemnation and that children who have not done good or evil are involved in it also? Your hearts rise up against such doctrines as if they were bloody and cruel inventions. To tell you that "many are called, but few are chosen" (Matt. 22:14) and that the most part of them who profess the truth are walking in the way to hell and shall undoubtedly fall into it—you may hear such things, but you bless yourselves[7] from them. Neither can you be persuaded to admit them into your minds for the hearts of men will be giving the very lie to the God of truth

---

6. *inevidence*: obscurity or mystery.

7. *bless yourselves*: to guard oneself with God's help, usually by making the sign of the cross.

when he speaks these things in his word: if, God forbid, that all that be true!

We should expound the law unto you and show you that the least idle word, the lightest thoughts, the smallest inward motion of the heart all deserve eternal misery. For anger is murder in God's sight, lusting is fornication, covetousness and love of the world are idolatry. But these things you cannot know or receive. There are so many high imaginations in your minds that exalt themselves against the knowledge of God. For there are so many thoughts that are mustered and set in battle array against the holy truths of God that truly no weapons of human persuasion or instruction can be able to cast down your misapprehensions and imaginations, or reasonings of your hearts; nor is the natural man able to scatter these armies of rebellious thoughts and "bring them into captivity to the obedience of Christ" (2 Cor. 10:4–5). Man's darkened mind is a stronghold, that all the repeated and continued beatings of the word, the multiplying of "precept upon precept and line upon line" (Isa. 28:10) cannot storm it to make any true light shine into it. It is a dungeon, a pit so shut up and enclosed, neither door nor window in it so that, albeit the Son of righteousness shine upon it and round about it, there is no beam of that light can enter in the hearts of many thousands.

The generality of men is drowned as yet in a deluge of ignorance under the very light of daily preaching. It is a night of as thick darkness within men's souls as if there were no light about us. Certainly this declares the height of enmity, the strength of the opposition. Your minds are prisons, strongholds indeed that are proof against all preaching or instruction. Certainly they will hold out till an almighty power storms them and beats or batters open some entry into your souls to receive this shining light of the gospel.

Men's Minds Are Strongholds against the Truth
There is a rebellion against God's holy will revealed in His law or word; it cannot be subject to the law of God. It neither is nor

can be, for enmity and antipathy is sunk into its nature so deeply that it is the most deformed monstrous thing in the world; if the disfigured face of man's soul were visible—oh how ugly would it be! How would you loathe it! If there were a creature that could do nothing but hate itself and sought its own destruction, that disfigured face would be a hateful enough object.

But self-hatred and enmity are nothing so deformed and abominable compared to the creature's will that is set in opposition to the holy will of Him that made it. This needs not much demonstration if you had but a little more consideration. Look back upon the tenor of your ways, set them beside the will and commands of God, and what find you? Whether agreement or disagreement? Take a view of the current of your inclinations and affections and compare that with the holy will of God— and what find you? Friendship or enmity? You cannot digest the reproach of being called enemies to God. But I pray you consider if there be not as perfect contrariety in your desires, affections, inclinations, and actions to the will of God as if you did profess it.

Second Evidence of Enmity against God: Enmity in the Will

So what would you do if you professed yourselves enemies to God? Could you possibly vent your enmity any other way than in withdrawing from the yoke of His obedience, in revolting from that allegiance you owe to Him? You could wrong Him no further than by setting your hearts and ways contrary to His heart, in loving what He hates and hating what He loves. For you could not impair His own blessed being.

Now, consider if that be not acted as really as if you did profess it. Can you say that cursing, swearing, lying, railing, anger, strife, envy, revenge, and such like works of darkness are the things which His soul loves? Are these suitable to His holy will? And yet these are your inveterate customs to which your natures are so inured and habituated that you can no more forsake them than hate yourselves. Filthiness, drunkenness, Sabbath breaking, covetousness, and love of the world—are these His delight? And yet these are your delight.

God's Royal Commandments

Is it not His will that you should purge yourselves from all filthiness of flesh and spirit and strive to perfect holiness? Are not righteousness and truth in the inward parts that which He loves? Does not He look to a contrite heart and account that a savory sacrifice (Ps. 51:17)? Are not His royal statute and commandment, of which not one jot shall fail, that you should deny yourselves, love your enemies, forgive them that offend you, and sanctify His name always in your hearts; and especially on the holy Sabbath that you should watch unto prayer, be sober in the use of the world, and be much in watching for His second coming?

Satan's Hold on Men's Will and Affections

Now, what repugnance is in your hearts and ways to all these? Do not the conversations of men display a banner against the gospel and proclaim as much in reality as is said in words in Psalm 2:3, "Let us cast his cords behind us, and cut his bands." These things are unsavory unto you, you smell nothing pleasant in them, but only in the puddle of the world. For you consider it only freedom to be running at random, at your own liberty, after your own imaginations. Oh, when shall your hearts be subdued and your affections brought in captivity to the obedience of Christ? When shall you be delivered up to the truth and so made to obey from the heart that form of doctrine and sound words (Rom. 6:17)? This is the strongest hold that Satan has in man's heart—his will and affections—and this keeps out longest against Jesus Christ till He that is stronger comes and binds the strong man, casts out the enmity, and makes all captive in willing subjection to His loving obedience (2 Cor. 10:4–5).

Third Evidence of Enmity against God: Rejection of God's Works

Then, third, the enmity of the soul of man is acted in his rebellion against the will of God manifested in his works, and in his unsubjection and unsubmissive disposition toward the good pleasure of the Lord, in carving out such and such a lot in the world. It is certain, that as the will of God is the supreme rule of righteousness, so His will is the sovereign cause and fountain of all things. Therefore, how infinitely is the creature bound to be subject to Him as a Lawgiver by pleasant and willing obedience to his righteous and reasonable commands; also, to submit to Him as the absolute ruler by quiet and humble condescendence to all the dispensations of His providence!

The Mutinous Hearts of Men

Now, you know—if you know anything of yourselves—how cross and opposite these hearts of yours are to His good pleasure, how they are set just contrary. And whence flow all murmuring, grudging, discontent, grief, cares, and perplexities of men but from this fountain: the rebellion of the heart against God? There is nothing in all the creation mutinous and malcontent other than the heart of man. You see frequent examples of it in the murmurings of the people in the wilderness. It is frequently styled "a tempting of the Lord" (cf. Ex. 17:2), importing a high provocation of His holy majesty, a special incitement as it were and motive to declare His absolute power and righteousness against such. Therefore, these two are often conjoined as in Psalm 78:17–18: "They sinned yet more against him, by provoking the Most High.... And they tempted God in their heart," and it is added in verse 19, "Yea, they spake against God."

Herein you may observe a gradation of aggravations of this enmity. When men have already deserved infinite punishment at His hand and may always look within and find an answer to all the murmurings of their hearts as having sinned so often against Him, yet then to rise up against His good pleasure and, after we have so often sinned, to repine at anything coming from Him—this truly is an aggravation of enmity. This, certainly, is a high provocation of the Most High God; it puts a kind of necessity upon Him to inflict that which you indeed deserve and then this inward heart burning against God breaks out often in words against that most high and holy One. So it is recorded in verse 40, "How often did they provoke him" which is the plain expression of murmuring (in the margin[8] is rendered, "they tempted him"; also see verses 41, 56, 57). Then in verse 8, when a short account is given of them and when the character or anagram of such a people is expressed, it is set down thus, "a stubborn and rebellious generation."

The Ugliness of Discontentment against God's Providence
Therefore Paul, considering this woeful and wretched posture of the soul, set in the madness and folly of opposition to the always-blessed will of God, exhorts us, "Neither murmur you, as some of them murmured and were destroyed of the destroyer, for these things happened for examples" (1 Cor. 10:10–11). Truly, there is nothing more deformed and vile in itself nor more disquieting and tormenting to the soul nor more dangerous in the consequences of it than such a posture of spirit. It is a discontented humor against God's providence whether it be in withholding that good thing from us which we desire, or sending that which crosses our humor, whether sickness, or want, or reproach, or disrespect, whatsoever it be that the heart is naturally carried to pursue or eschew. What is a more abominable and ugly visage than the countenance of an angry and furious person? But when this is against God, it adds infinitely to the deformity and vileness of it.

"I do well to be angry," is the motto of a discontented soul. It elects an imaginary sovereignty against true sovereignty, it sets

---

8. That is, in the margin of the Geneva Bible.

up an anti-providence and establishes another divine power and wisdom. Thus it brings down the majesty, highness, and holiness of God to be trodden upon by the creature. And then it is its own tormentor, a sin that needs no punishment but itself, for the insurrection and mutiny of the heart against God's will sets all the powers of the soul out of course, vexes, pains, and disquiets all.

The Eternal Displeasure of God

There is no peace and tranquility but in the complacency of the heart with God's heart, as Ephraim was like a bullock unaccustomed with the yoke (Jer. 31:18); the more he fretted and spurned at his yoke, the more it galled him and grieved him till he was instructed and then he was eased. This fills the soul with hideous tormenting thoughts and cares; it feeds upon its own marrow and consumes it—as some have made the emblem of envy—which is a particular kind of this enmity as if you would imagine a creature that did waste and consume all its moisture and marrow and feed upon the destruction of itself.

Now this is but the prelude of what follows, this self-punishment is a messenger to tell what is coming: that the Most High God is engaged in His power against such persons and shall vent His displeasure to their eternal displeasure. That is the fruit of this enmity.

SERMON 21

The Implacable Enmity of the Carnal Mind against God

> *The carnal mind is enmity against God: for it is not subject to the law of God, neither indeed can be. So then they that are in the flesh cannot please God.* —ROMANS 8:7–8

The Wickedness of the Human Heart

It is not the least of man's evils that he knows not how evil he is, therefore the Searcher of the heart of man gives the most perfect account of it in Jeremiah 17:9: "The heart is deceitful above all things," as well as "desperately wicked." There are two things superlative and excessive in it, bordering upon an infiniteness and such as sin is capable of: wickedness and deceitfulness! And indeed, that which makes the wicked heart desperately and hopelessly so, is its deceitfulness. There are many specious coverings gotten to palliate[1] this wickedness and enmity and so many invisible and spiritual aspects of wickedness in the heart that it is no wonder they lurk and dwell without observation. Sin is either covered with some deceivable pretext of another thing or else altogether escapes the dim eyes of men because of its subtle and spiritual nature. Both are in this business: the enmity of man's heart against God is so subtle a thing in many, shrouded over as it is with some other pretenses in all, that few get the lively discovery and sense of it.

---

1. *palliate*: to alleviate a disease without curing it.

It is true, it is very gross and palpable in the most part of men—I mean visible to others though not visible to themselves. Any whose eyes are opened may behold the black visage of rebellion in the most part of the actions and courses of men as the apostle speaks in Galatians 5:19, "the works of the flesh are manifest." Truly this enmity against God is too manifest in most part, the weapons of your warfare against God being so carnal and visible, your opposition to His holy will and ways being so palpable.

"Against the Known God"
There is an enmity acted by many in the tenor of their conversation. They are without God in the world and are against Him, as appears in all their inveterate and godless customs of lying, swearing, cursing, drunkenness, railing, Sabbath breaking, neglect of prayer, and such like. These carry in their fore brow this inscription, "against the known God," the opposite of that on the Athenians' altar to the unknown god (Acts 17:23). The God whom you pretend to know and worship, His name is every day blasphemed, His word slighted, and His will disobeyed as if you had proclaimed war against Him.

But there is in some (and I fear in a great many of you) not only an acted but an affected enmity too, an enmity rising up to the maturity and ripeness of malignity and hatred of the image of God in all His children. Although some are not themselves willing to go to heaven, they do not disturb others in their journey; they can let others be religious about them and rawly[2] desire to be like them. But others there are who will neither enter into heaven themselves nor let others enter as Christ speaks of the Pharisees (Matt. 23:13). They hate the light of another's conversation because their own deeds are evil and are reproved and condemned by it. It is said in Revelation 11:10 that the two witnesses tormented them that dwelled on the earth. It

---

2. *rawly*: coldly or carelessly.

is strange what a torment it is to the world that the godly are in it! Piety is an eyesore to many and, if they could extirpate all that bears that image, they would think it sweet as bread (Ps. 14:4). This is a more open and declared enmity against the God of heaven and yet I know it lurks under the mask of some other thing. You pretend only to hate hypocrisy. Alas, what a scorn is it for profanity to hate hypocrisy?

An Irreconcilable Feud
Surely your feigned hatred is not because God's reflected image in His servants is a sin but is on account of the very shadow of piety it carries. You hate the thing itself so perfectly that you cannot endure the very picture of it. Do not deceive yourselves, the true quarrel is because they run not to the same excess of riot with you. If they will lie, cozen,[3] defraud, swear, and blaspheme as other men do, you could endure to make them companions as you do others. The principle of that is the enmity that was placed in the beginning—that mortal irreconcilable feud betwixt the two families are two seeds, one of Christ and the other of Satan.

But as I told you, this enmity acts in a more subtle and invisible way in some and it is painted over with some fair colors to hide the deformity of it. Not only the grosser corruptions of men carry this stamp but they take even the most refined piece or part in man, his mind, its excellency and eve, for the wisdom of the flesh is enmity with God as it may be read in our text, *mind*.[4] It is the very prudence and reason of a natural man which carries him to a distance from, and opposition with, the common defilements in the courses of men. Yet that natural reason has in its bosom a more exquisite and refined enmity against God and so the more spiritual and purified it be from grosser corruptions, the more active and powerful it is against God because it is, as it were, the very spirit and quintessence of enmity.

---

3. *cozen*: deceive or beguiled.
4. φρονημα.

The Folly of Worldly Wisdom

You see in 1 Corinthians 1 how the wisdom of God is foolishness to the wisdom of the world; then again how the wisdom of the world is the greatest folly to the only wise God. Men that have many natural advantages beyond others are at this great disadvantage: they are more ready to despise godliness as too base and simple a thing to adorn their natures. As Christ said of rich men it may also be said of wise men, of learned men, of civil and blameless persons who have a smooth carriage before the world, how hard it is for such to enter into the kingdom of heaven (Mark 10:25). Hard indeed! For they must be stripped naked of their accomplishments ere they can enter through this narrow gate. I refer to their opinion and conceit of any worth or excellency, for they must be diminished in their own eyes so that they may go through this needle's eye without crushing.

Love of Both the World and Self

The stream of enmity often runs underground and so hides itself under some other notion till at length it bursts forth openly. I find it commonly runs in the secret channel of amity or friendship to some other thing opposite to God. So James 4:4, "The amity of the world is enmity with God," and 1 John 2:15, "If any man loves the world, the love of the Father is not in him." There are two dark and underground conduits to convey this enmity against God: amity to the world and amity to ourselves—self-love and creature-love. We cannot denounce war openly against heaven, but the next course is to join to or associate with any party that is contrary to God; thus, under the covert of friendship to ourselves and love to the world, we war against God and destroy our own souls.

Only Christ Has the Right to Our Love

I say first, amity to the world carries enmity to God in its bosom and, if you believe not this, hear the apostle's sharp and pungent question, "Ye adulterers and adulteresses, know ye not that the amity of the world is enmity with God?" He does not speak only to persons guilty of that crime but to all natural men who are guilty of adultery or whoredom of a more spiritual nature, but just as abominable and more dangerous. There is a bond and special tie betwixt all men and God their Maker which obliges them to consecrate and devote themselves, their affections, and endeavors, to His honor especially when the covenant of the gospel is superadded unto that, in which Jesus Christ our Lord reveals Himself as having the only right to us and our affections. For He is willing to bestow Himself upon us and, notwithstanding all the distance between Him and wretched sinners, yet He fills it up with His infinite love and wonderful condescension, out of love demitting Himself to the form of a servant that so He might take us up to be His chaste spouse and adorn us with His beauty.

Here is His challenge to us: whoever hears and professes the gospel, this is your profession—if you understand it—that Jesus Christ shall be your well-beloved and you His. Therefore you shall separate yourself to Him, admitting no stranger in His place, that the choice and marrow[5] of your joy, love, and delight shall be bestowed on Him.

Foul Infidelity

Now, this bond and tie of a professed relationship to that glorious husband is foully broken by the most part by espousing their affections to this base world. Your hearts are carried away from Him unto strangers, that is, unto present perishing things whereas the intendment of the gospel is, to present you to Christ as pure virgins (2 Cor. 11:2). Truly your hearts are gone whoring after other things. The love of the world has withdrawn you or kept you in chains; these present things are as snares, nets, and bands, as a harlot's hands and heart (Eccl. 7:26). They are

---

5. *marrow*: the essential part.

powerful enchantments over you that bewitch you to a base love from an honorable and glorious love.

Oh that you would consider, my beloved, what opposition there is betwixt the love of the world and the love of the Father, betwixt amity and that which has nothing in it. Yet some do present bait to your deceitful lusts, seeking to allure you away from amity toward God, your only lawful husband! Affection is a transforming and conforming thing—"If you love the earth, you are earth."[6] Nevertheless, the love of God will purify your heart and lift it up to more similitude to Him whom you love, whereas the love of the world assimilates it unto the world, making it such a base and ignoble piece as the earth is.

Peace and Life Only through Christ

Do you think marriage affection can be parted? "My (well) beloved is mine," therefore the church is the turtle, the dove to Christ, of wonderful chastity (Song 2:12, 14, 16); it only ever joins itself to one and, after the death of its marrow, it sighs and mourns ever after and sits solitarily (Isa. 38:14). You must retire, my beloved, and disengage from the love of other things or you cannot love Christ. And if you love not Christ you cannot have peace with the Father and if you have not that peace you cannot have life. This is the chain of life: the first link begins at the divorce of all former loves and beloved idols, for the soul must be loosed in desire and delight; then that link must be fastened upon the most lovely and desirable object Christ, the desire of the nations, and this draws along with it another link of peace and life. Do not mistake it, religion would not hinder or prejudice your lawful business in this world. Oh, it would be the most compendious[7] way to advance it with more ease to your souls! Certainly it will teach you to exchange the love of these things for a better and more heart-contenting love.

---

6. Si terram amas terra es.
7. *compendious*: concise and comprehensive.

Pride of Life Is the Final Bastion of Darkness

Then amity toward ourselves is enmity to God. Truly, this is the last stronghold that holds out longest against God when all others may be beaten down or surrendered. Possibly a man may attain to this, to despise these lower things as below his natural dignity and the excellency of his spirit. Some may renounce much of that friendship with worldly and temporal things as being sordid and base. Nonetheless, the enmity gets into this strong and invisible tower of darkness—self-love and pride. Therefore the apostle John makes this the last and the chief—the pride of life! "For all that is in the world, the lust of the flesh, and the lust of the eyes, and the pride of life, is not of the Father, but is of the world" (1 John 2:16). When the lusts of the eyes and flesh are in some measure abated this pride of life is still growing, and what decreases of all other lusts, seems to accresce[8] unto this, as if self-love and pride did feed and nourish itself upon the ashes or consumption[9] of other vices.

Truly, this pride of life draws sap from graces and virtues and grows thereby until at length it kills that which nourished it. Indeed, the apostle James seems to proceed to this in 4:5–6 when he reminds us that "God resisteth the proud, but giveth grace unto the humble" and, "Do ye think the scripture saith in vain?" Is not self-amity this same enmity as the amity of the world? Therefore God opposes Himself unto it, as the very grand enmity. Self is the great lord, the archrebel, the head of all opposition, that in which all other enmities do center, so that when all the inferior soldiers are captives or killed this is last in the field; it lives first in opposition and dies last.[10]

---

8. *accresce*: increase.
9. *consumption*: wasting away.
10. primum vivens et ultimum moriens.

The Impregnable Barrier of Self-Love and Self-Admiration

Although a man can separate himself from many things, yet he may become more conjoined to himself, and so the further disjoined from God. Of all these vile rags of the old man, this is nearest the skin and is the last of all the members to be put off; self is the heart—first alive and last alive. What happens when the mind is surrounded by the light of the gospel, yet enmity against it retires into the heart? Or when a man is constrained to render up the outward members of his body in order to move them to a more smooth and fair carriage of civil behavior, and when the mind is forced to yield unto some light of truth and knowledge of the gospel? Even then that enmity retreats more deeply into the heart by self-love and self-estimation fortifying it even more strongly. As in winter the encompassing cold forces the heat to combine itself together into the bowels of the earth and by this means the springs of water are hotter than in summer, so the surrounding light of the gospel, or education, or natural honesty drive the heat and strength of enmity inwards where it fortifies itself even more. This is that accursed antiperistasis[11] that is made by the concurrence of some advantages of knowledge and civility, and such like.

Those Who Would Be Friends of Christ Must Die to Self

When it is chased for fear out of the outward man, the blood of enmity against God gets in about the heart. Therefore, the very first and fundamental principle of Christianity is, "Let a man deny himself, and so he shall be my disciple" (see Mark 8:34). He must become a fool in his own eyes, though he be wise, so that he may be wise (1 Cor. 3:18); he must become as ungodly, though godly, that he may be justified by faith (Rom. 4:5); he must forsake himself, that he may indeed find himself (Matt. 16:25). What I mean is that he must get a better self in another. He must not eat over much honey, that is not good (Prov. 25:16);

---

11. *antiperistasis*: opposition, resistance, or reaction.

it would swell him though it be pleasant, for he must not search his own glory or reflect much upon it if he would be a follower and a friend of Christ.

Therefore, consider! See how much soever esteem you engage to yourselves or desire to be esteemed of others. When you desire to reflect with complacency on yourselves, to mind your own satisfaction and estimation in what you do, so much do you disengage from Jesus Christ, for these are contrary points. I have been pointing you to a direct motion toward Christ, but this is an inverse and backward motion toward ourselves. As much as we move that way, we improve not but lose our way and are further from the true end.

Ezekiel's living creatures may be an emblem of a Christian's motion: he returns not as he goes, he makes a straight line to God, whithersoever He turns him (Ezek. 10:11, 22). But nature makes all crooked lines; they seem to go forth in obedience to God but they have a secret unseen reflection into their own bosom. And this is the greatest act of enmity, to idolize God and deify ourselves we make Him into a cipher;[12] then we sacrifice to ourselves His peculiar, incommunicable property of Alpha and Omega, that we sacrilegiously attribute to ourselves—the beginning of our notions and the end of them too. This is the crooked line that nature cannot possibly move out of, till a higher Spirit come and restore her that halted[13] and make plain her paths.

Refusing the Yoke of Obedience

That which is added as a reason explains this enmity more clearly: "for it is not subject to the law of God, neither indeed can be." Truly these two forementioned amities of the world and of ourselves do withdraw men wholly from the orderly subjection that they owe to the law of God. Order is the beauty of everything, of nature, of art, of the whole universe, and of its several

---

12. *cipher*: a monogram or a zero.
13. *halted*: limped or walked as a cripple.

parts such as kingdoms and republics. This indeed is the very beauty of the world, all things subordinate to Him that made them; only miserable man has broken this order and marred this beauty and he cannot be subject;[14] he cannot come again into that orderly station and subordination he was once into.

This is the only gap or breach of the creation. And it is some other engagements that draw him thus far out of course—the base love of the world and the inordinate love of himself. Oh these make his neck stiff that it cannot bow to the yoke of obedience; these have opposite and contrary commands and no man can serve two masters. When the commands of the great lord "self" come in opposition with the commands of God, then he cannot be subject to the law of God. For a time, in some things he may resemble a subjection when the will of self and the will of God command in one point as sometimes they do by accident, but that is neither frequent nor constant.

A Feigned Profession of Faith

Not only is he not subject, but there is worse in it, he cannot be subject to the law of God. This is certainly to throw down the natural pride of man that always apprehends some remnant ability in himself. You think still to make yourselves better and when convinced or challenged for sins to make amends and reform your lives. You used to promise these things as lightly and easily as if they were wholly in your power and as if you did only delay them for advantage. Yet truly it seems this principle of self-sufficiency is engraved on men's hearts when they procrastinate and delay repentance and earnest minding of religion to some other fitter season as if it were in their liberty to apply to it when they please. Then when you are urged and persuaded to some reformation, you take in hand even as that people who said, "According to all that the Lord our God shall say…we will

---

14. ουχ υποτασσιτα.

do" (Jer. 42:6, 20; cf. Ex. 24:3). You can strike hands[15] and engage to serve the Lord as easily as those people in Joshua 24:16–18.

But we may say, "Oh, that there was such a heart in you!" But, alas, such a heart is not in you! You cannot serve the Lord for He is holy and jealous, and you are not only weak but also wicked. I beseech you then, believe this one testimony that God has given to man that even the choicest thing in man, the very wisdom of a natural man, is not subject to God's law, neither can it be better, nor can it be subject. Resolution, industry, vows, and covenants will not effect this until the Most High breaks and bows the heart. And not only has this enmity against the old law of commandments an antipathy at them as crossing our lust, but even an antagonism against the new and living law of the Spirit of life in Christ.

The False Delusion of the Heart

Here is your misery: you cannot be subject to the law though commanded to obey it, nor can you be moved though threatened for disobedience to it, nor can you be subject to the gospel by promising to believe and receive it. The law commands, but your law countermands within. The law threatens and sentences you with condemnation, but you have some self-pleasing delusion and dream in your heads, therefore you bless yourselves in your own hearts, even though you walk in the imagination of your hearts, contrary to the law (Deut. 29). It is strange that you do not fore-apprehend and fear hell! But it is this delusion possesses the heart, "you shall not surely die" (Gen. 3:4). It was the first act of enmity, not only the transgression of the command but also unbelief of the truth of the curse: that which first encouraged man to sin now encourages you all to lie into it and continue in it—in the fancy of escaping wrath. This noise fills the heart: Satan whispers in the ear, "Go on, you shall not die." Thus it appears that the natural mind cannot be subject

---

15. *strike hands*: to clasp another's hand to make an agreement or bargain.

to the law of God and that no persuasion nor instruction can enforce this belief of your damnable condition upon you.

But then, when the enmity is beaten out of this fort and a soul is really convinced of its desperate and lost estate and when the heart is brought down to subjection to take with[16] that dreadful sentence, yet there is another tower of enmity in the heart that can still hold out against the weapons of the gospel such as Paul mentions in Romans 10:3: "Being ignorant of the righteousness of God, and going about to establish their own righteousness, have not submitted unto the righteousness of God." There is a natural pride and stiffness of heart that we cannot endure but to have something in ourselves to rest on and take pleasure into. And when a soul sees nothing it rather vexes and torments itself as grieving because it has no ornament or covering of its own, nor rejoices and delights in that righteousness of God revealed in Christ.

O That Necessity Would Constrain Lost Souls!

Oh, the difficulty to bow down so low as to put on another's righteousness over our nakedness (Rev. 3:18)! And should it be called submission? Is it not rather the elevating and exalting of the soul? Yet in respect of our natural posture of spirit, it is a matter of great difficulty to make a self-condemned sinner submit to this—to be saved freely by another's ransom without money or price. What empty, vain, and frivolous expiations and satisfactions[17] will souls invent, rather than trusting all to this! How long will poor souls wander abroad from hill to mountain, seeking some inherent qualification to commend them? How long will they ignore this garden and paradise of delights which is opened up in Christ? Souls look everywhere for help till all hands fail, and then necessity constrains them to come hither.

---

16. *take with*: to consider or deal with.
17. *satisfactions*: good works to contribute to the atonement for sinners.

Then indeed, when necessity brings in, charity and amity keep in, when once they know what entertainment there is in Christ.

As for you, who as yet have not stooped to the sentence of wrath, how will you submit to the righteousness of God? But I wonder how you imagine this to be so easy a thing to believe. You say you did always believe in Christ and that your hearts are still on Him and that you do it night and day. Now, there needs no other argument to persuade you that you do not at all believe in the gospel, you who have apprehended no more difficulty in it, nor anything contrary to your rebellious natures in it. Let this one word go home with you and convince you of your continued unbelief, the natural mind "is not subject to the law of God, neither indeed can be." How, then, do you think you can come so easily by it? Certainly it must be feigned and counterfeit!

SERMON 22

No Other Way — In Christ Alone

So then they that are in the flesh cannot please God.
—ROMANS 8:8

It is a kind of happiness to men to please them upon whom they depend and upon whose favor their well-being hangs. It is the servant's happiness to please his master, the courtier's to please his prince. So generally this pertains to whosoever they be that are joined in mutual relations and depend one upon another. For that which makes all pleasant is this, to please one another.

The Creatures' Total Dependence upon the Creator

Now certainly all the dependencies of creatures one upon another are but shadows unto the absolute dependence of creatures upon the Creator, "For in him we live, and move, and have our being" (Acts 17:28). The dependence of the ray upon the sun or of the stream upon the fountain are some of the greatest in nature. But all creatures have a more necessary connection with this Fountain-being, both in their being and well-being; they are nothing but a flux and emanation of His power and pleasure; as the psalmist expresses it, "Thou hidest thy face and they are troubled; thou takest away their breath, and they die, and return to their dust. Thou sendest forth thy Spirit, and they are created: and thou renewest the face of the earth" (Ps. 104:29–30).

You may extend this to the being and well-being, the happiness and misery of creatures; our souls which animate our bodies are but His breath which He breathed into the dust and can retract when He pleases. The life of our souls, their peace, tranquility, and satisfaction, are another breathing of His Spirit, another look of His countenance. As He pleases to withdraw it or interpose between His face and us, so we live or die, are blessed or miserable. Our being or well-being has a more indispensable dependence on Him than the image in the glass has upon the living face.

The Lord's Favor Is Only upon Those Who Seek to Please Him
If it be so, then certainly of all things in the world it concerns us nearest how to please Him and to be at peace with Him. If we be on good terms with Him in whose hands our breath is and whose are all our ways (Dan. 5:23), upon whose countenance our misery or felicity hangs, then certainly we are happy. If we please Him it matters not whom we displease; for He alone has absolute, uncontrolled, and universal power over us, as our Savior speaks, over "both soul and body" (Matt. 10:28). We may expect that His good pleasure toward us will not be satisfied but in communicating His fullness and manifesting His favor to us, especially since the goodness of God is so exundant[1] as to overflow even to the wicked world and vent itself as out of superabundance, in a river of goodness throughout the whole earth (Matt. 5:45). How much more will it run abundantly toward them whom He is well pleased with. And therefore the psalmist cries out, as being already so full in the very hope and expectation of it that he would burst if he had not the vent of admiration and praise, "O how great is his goodness...and how excellent his lovingkindness laid up for them that fear him!" (Pss. 31:19; 36:7).

---

1. *exundant*: exuberant or abundant.

The Misery of Those Who Are Unable to Please God
But, on the other hand, how incomparable is the misery of them who cannot please God—even though they did both please themselves and all others for the present. To be at odds with Him, in whom alone they can subsist and without whose favor is nothing, can be but wretchedness and misery. Oh that must be the worst and most cursed estate imaginable: to be in such a state as to do whatever they can, nevertheless they are unable to please Him whom alone to please must be man's only concern. What can be invented to that?[2]

Now, if you ask who they are that are such? These words speak it plainly, in way of inference from the former doctrine in verse 7, "So then they that are in the flesh cannot please God." Not they in whom there is flesh; for there are remnants of that in the most spiritual men in this life. We cannot attain here to angelic purity, though this should be the aim and endeavor of every Christian. But they that are in the flesh (or after the flesh), imports the predomination of that and a universal thralldom of nature unto it, which indeed is the state of all men that are but once born, until, by the Spirit of Jesus Christ, a second birth comes.

A Twofold Reason for Being Unable to Please God
The ground of this may be taken from the foregoing discourse, and it is chiefly twofold. One is, because they are not in Jesus Christ, in whom his soul is well pleased. The other is because they cannot suit and frame their carriage according to His pleasure.

The First Ground of Being Unable to Please God
Since all mankind has fallen under the displeasure of the Most High God by sinning against Him in preferring the pleasure of the flesh and the pleasure of Satan rather than the pleasure of God, there can be no atonement found to pacify Him, no sacrifice to appease Him, no ransom to satisfy His justice; there only

---

2. That is, "What can be conceived like that?"

remains that one perfect offering for sin, Jesus Christ, the propitiation for the sins of the elect world. This the Father accepts in the name of sinners. In testimony of His acceptance, He declared several times by a voice from heaven, first to a multitude (Matt. 3:17) and then to the beloved disciples (Matt. 17:5), and both times with great majesty and solemnity (as did become Him), he thus declared that this is His well-beloved Son in whom His soul is well pleased.

The Father's Favor Is Only Found in His Beloved Son
It pleased God to make the stream of His love to take another channel after man's sin and not to run immediately toward wretched man; rather He turned the current of His love another way to His own Son, whom He chose for this end: to reconcile man and bring him into favor. Now His love going about by that compass comes in the issue toward poor sinners with the greater force. He has appointed Christ to be the meeting place with sinners, the Daysman[3] to lay His hand on both; therefore He is God to lay His hand on God, and man to lay His hand on man, thus to bring both into a peaceable and amiable conjunction.

Now then, whoever are not in Jesus Christ, as is spoken, certainly they cannot please God by doing whatever they can, because God has made Christ the center in which He would have the good pleasure of sinners meeting with His good pleasure. Therefore, "without faith it is impossible to please God" (Heb. 11:6), not so much for the excellency of the act itself as for the well-pleasing object of it, Christ. The love of the Father terminates[4] in Him, His justice is satisfied in Him, His love is well pleased with the excellency of His person. God finds in Christ an object of delight which is nowhere else, and His justice is well pleased with the sufficiency and worthiness of His

---

3. *daysman*: an umpire, arbiter, or intermediary.
4. *terminates*: brought to a conclusion.

ransom; without this compass there is neither satisfaction to the one, nor to the other.

So then, whatsoever you are, how high soever your degree in the world, how sweet soever your disposition, let your natures be never so good, your carriage never so smooth, yet certainly there is nothing in all this that can please God either by an object of love or a price for justice. You are under that eternal displeasure which will fall on and crush you to pieces. Mountains will not be so heavy as it will appear in that great day of His wrath (Rev. 6:15–16).

In Christ Alone Is Immunity and Refuge
I say, you cannot come from under that imminent weight of eternal wrath unless you be found in Jesus Christ, that blessed place of immunity and refuge. Unless you have forsaken yourselves and your own natures and denied your own righteousness as dung and have been found in Him, clothed with His righteousness and satisfaction, you are still under eternal wrath. If the delight and pleasure of your soul do not coincide and fall in at one place with the delight and good pleasure of the Father, that is, upon His well-beloved Son, certainly the pleasure and goodwill of God has not as yet fallen upon you and met with you. Therefore, if you would please God, be pleased with Christ and you cannot do Him a greater pleasure than believe in Him (John 5:23); that is, you must absolutely resign yourselves unto Him for salvation and sanctification.

The Second Ground of Being Unable to Please God
The other ground is: Such as are in the flesh cannot frame their spirits, affections, and ways to God's good pleasure, for their very wisdom, the very excellency that is in them, is enmity to God and cannot be subject to His law. Therefore, they cannot please Him. I am sure you may easily reflect upon yourselves and find, not with much searching but upon all these as the prophet speaks (Jer. 2:34), that it is not the study and business you have

undertaken to please God but the bent and main of your aims and endeavors is to please yourselves or to please men. This makes many men's pains, even in religion, displeasing to God because they do not indeed mind His pleasure but only their own or another's satisfaction. What they do is but to conform to the custom of the time, or the commandments of men, or for their own humor; all this must needs be abominable to God.

Truly, that which is in great account among men is an abomination to God, as our Savior speaks in Luke 16:15 of the very righteousness and professed piety of the Pharisees; the more you please yourselves and the world, the further you are from pleasing God. The very beginning of pleasing God is when a soul falls in displeasure at itself and abhorrence of its own loathsomeness; therefore it is said that the humble and contrite spirit I will look unto, and dwell with him, and such sacrifices do please God (Isa. 66:2; Ps. 51:17). For the truth is that God never begins to be pleasant and lovely to a soul till it begins to fall out of love with itself and grows loathsome in its own eyes.

Without True Repentance Mere Outward Observances Avail Nothing
Therefore you may conclude this of yourselves: with many of you God is not well pleased, although you be all baptized unto Christ and do all eat of that same spiritual meat and drink of that same spiritual drink and though you have all church privileges—yet with many of you God is not well pleased as we find in 1 Corinthians 10:2–5. It is not only because those works of the flesh are directly opposite to His own known will, such as fornication, murmuring, grudging at God's dispensation, cursing and swearing, lying, drunkenness, anger, malice, strife, variance, and such like. These all abound as much among you as among that old people.

Indeed, even those of you that may be free from gross opposition to His holy will, your natures also have the seed of all that enmity even though you enact enmity in a more covered way. You are so well pleased with yourselves! Your chief study is to please men; you have not given yourselves to the study of conforming yourselves to the pleasure of God. Therefore know your dreadful condition: you are unable to please God even though without His favor and pleasure you can only be eternally displeased and tormented in yourselves. Certainly, though now you please yourselves, yet the day shall come that you shall be contrary to yourselves and all shall also be contrary to you, as it is spoken of as a punishment of the Jews (1 Thess. 2:15); of this there is some earnest[5] in this life. Many wicked persons are set contrary to themselves, and all are contrary to them. They are like Esau, their hand against all, and all men's hands against them,[6] yea, their own consciences continually vexing them. This is a fruit of that fundamental discord and enmity between men and God and if you find it not now you shall find it hereafter.

The True Grounds of Peace and Acceptance with God
But as for you that are in Jesus Christ who, being displeased with yourselves, to escape God's displeasure have fled unto the well-beloved in whom the Father is well pleased: I say to such, Your persons God is well pleased with in Christ and this shall make a way and place for acceptance of your weak and imperfect performances. This is the ground of your peace and acceptance and, as you take it so, it shall yield you much peace when you cannot be pleased with yourselves. But I would charge this upon you, that as you by believing are well pleased with Christ, so you would henceforth study to "walk worthy of your Lord unto all pleasing, being fruitful in every good work, and increasing in the knowledge of God" (Col. 1:10). This is that to which you are

---

5. *earnest*: a down payment as a guarantee of the full payment to be made later.

6. Binning is taking the angel's prediction regarding Ishmael and applying it to Esau: Gen. 16:12, "And he will be a wild man; his hand will be against every man, and every man's hand against him; and he shall dwell in the presence of all his brethren." Apparently, Binning finds an echo of this prediction in the description in 25:17 which tells us "Esau was a cunning hunter; a man of the field."

called, to such a work as may please Him in order to conform yourselves even to His pleasure and will. If you love Him, you cannot but fashion yourselves so as He may be pleased.

A Holy Ambition
Oh, how exact and observant is love of that which may ingratiate itself in the beloved's favor! It is the most studious thing to please and most afraid of displeasing. Enoch had as large and honorable testimony as ever was given to man that he pleased God (Heb. 11:5). I beseech you, be ambitious of this after a holy manner, labor to know His will and for this end that you may approve it, and prove it that you may do that good and acceptable will of God. Let His pleasure be your rule, your law, to which all within you may conform itself.

Though you cannot attain an exact correspondence with His pleasure but in many things you will offend, yet certainly this will be the resolved study of your hearts how to please Him, and in as far as you cannot please Him, you will be displeased with yourselves. But then, I would advise you, in as far as you are displeased with yourselves for not pleasing God, be as much well pleased with Christ, the pleasing sacrifice and atonement, and this shall please God as much as your obedience could do or your disobedience can displease Him. To Him be praise and glory.

SERMON 23

The Vivid Contrast between Those in the Spirit and Those in the Flesh

But ye are not in the flesh, but in the Spirit, if so be that the Spirit of God dwell in you. Now if any man have not the Spirit of Christ, he is none of his. —ROMANS 8:9

The Right Kind of Application

Application is the very life of the Word, at least it is a necessary condition for the living operation of it. The application of the word is to the hearts of hearers by preaching, along with the application of your own hearts again to the word by meditation; these two meeting together and striking one upon another will yield fire. Paul speaks of "rightly dividing of the word of truth" (2 Tim. 2:15). He does not mean that ordinary way of cutting it all into parcels and dismembering it by manifold divisions which I judge makes it lose much of its virtue. For its virtue consists in its union.[1]

Some, however, do have pleasure in cutting up the Word of truth, thinking it profitable. Yet I do not see that this was the apostolic way, either to preach the word to themselves or to recommend it to others. But rather the apostle means the real distribution of the food of souls unto their various conditions, just as it is the duty of a steward to be both faithful and wise in giving

---

1. See comments on Binning's departure from standard Puritan preaching in Ferguson's introduction above, ix–xxix.

everyone their own portion. Likewise, as it is the pastor's duty thus to distribute the Word of God unto you, so it is your part to apply it home to yourselves. Otherwise, the application of the division of the word aright will not feed your souls, for it cannot profit men unless they act as the pastor to their own hearts.

Now indeed the right application of the word to souls is the most difficult part of preaching and it is the hardest point of hearing, in which there needs both much affection and much direction, the affection to be serious and earnest, the direction to be wise and prudent. Without suitable affection it will not pass into the substance of the soul to feed it, no more than the stomach can digest meat that wants convenient heat; likewise, without discretion and wisdom to choose our own portion, it will not yield convenient food but will increase humors and superfluities or else distemper our spirits.

A Suitable Encouragement to Believers
That which I look at in these words is the discretion and prudence of this wise steward in God's house, after He has represented the wretched and woeful estate of them that are in the flesh. Having already shown how their natures cannot but be against God and how their end is death and destruction, he now subjoins in due season a suitable encouragement to believers, "But you are not in the flesh, but in the Spirit, if so be that the Spirit of God dwell in you." Because there is no man so sensible of that corruption that dwells within as he that is in part renewed—as pain to a healthful body is most sensible and as the abundance of light makes a larger discovery of what is disordered and defiled in the house. Therefore such, upon the hearing of the accursed estate of men in nature and of their natural rebellion against God and of God's displeasure against them, are most ready, I say, to apply such things to themselves, to the weakening of their own hands and saddening of their hearts, as the upright-hearted disciples were more ready to take with the challenge of betraying Christ than the false-hearted Judas.

Therefore, the apostle prevents such an abuse of the doctrine by making application of the better part unto the Romans, saying "for you are not in the flesh, but in the Spirit." Indeed, self-examination is necessary. It is like chewing of the meat before it be sent into the stomach; self-examination is as necessary and precedent before right application. I wish that every one of you would consider well how this living Word concerns you. It shows us the ground of all our barrenness. This Word which is spoken to all no one can bring home to himself; but truly the Lord does speak to all so that every man may speak to himself and ask in his own heart, "What is my concernment in it? What is my portion?"

The Lord Intends Christianity to Begin with Self-Examination

As for you whom the Lord has put upon this search of yourselves and has once made you to find yourselves in the black roll of perdition under the hazard of the eternal weight of God's displeasure, there He has showed unto your souls a way of making peace with God and a place of refuge in Jesus Christ. This knowledge has at times refreshed and eased your hearts; it was only able to purify your consciences and calm the storms that did arise in them if it became henceforth your study to walk to please Him. And this engagement being on your hearts—to make no peace with the flesh and the corruption that dwells in you—then, I say, the Lord calls and accounts you not carnal but spiritual, though there still be much carnality in you. Yet he denominates from the better part, not from the greatest part, for "you are not after the flesh but after the Spirit."

Though Isaac was a weak young child and Ishmael, the son of the bond woman, was a strong man, yet you are in God's account esteemed according to the promise which shall be the ground of your stability. Isaac must abide in the house forever and grow stronger and stronger, and Ishmael must be cast out and grow weaker and weaker; the latter is ordained for destruction and so is called the old man, drawing near to its grave; the former, Isaac, is ordained for life and so is a new man renewed day by day. Thus they are in God's promise, and you would learn thus to look upon it, not according to their present inequality in strength but that future inequality and difference which is wrapped up in the promise of God and the seed whereof is in you.

There Can Be a Superfluity of Hurtful Self-Examination
As there is a woeful penury and scantiness of examination in the most part of men who are wholly spent without and take no leisure to recognize their own souls, so there is a miserable excess and hurtful superfluity of examination and disputation among many of God's children. They are always in reflection and almost never in action, so much on knowing what is, that they take not much leisure to do or pursue what is not. Truly, I think when the apostle commands us to examine whether we be in the faith, and prove ourselves, he did not mean to make it our perpetual exercise, or so to press it as we should not endeavor to be in the faith until we know whether we be in it. To refuse to go on in our journey till we know what progress we have made, as the custom is for many, would not be the way to advance. But simply and plainly, I think, the apostle recognized that Christianity should begin in examination, as the first returning of a soul must needs be upon some inquiry and search of the way and come to acknowledge upon searching that our former way was wrong, and this way only is right.

We Must Hearken to the Plain Voice of the Gospel
But if this be the porch to enter at, will you sit down and dwell in it, and not go on into the palace itself? Because you must begin to search what you have learned wrong, that now you may unlearn it, will you be ever about the learning to know your condition, and by this means never attain to the knowledge of the truth? But when you have upon any inquiry found yourselves out of the way, you should not entertain that dispute long, but

hearken to the plain voice of the gospel, that sounds unto you, "This is the way, walk in it." "I am the way," says Christ, "enter at me, by believing in me" (cf. Isa. 30:21; John 10:7–9; 14:6).

Now, once having found that you are unbelievers by nature, to suspend believing till you prove whether you be in the faith is unreasonable and impossible, for certainly, having once found yourselves void of faith, you must first have it before you know that you have it, you must first apply yourself to action and afterward your examination shall become easier.

The Apostle Seeks to Provoke Believers into Godly Living

But I would tell of more profitable improvement of such representations of the sinful and miserable estate of the ungodly world than you were accustomed to make of it. In the frequent turning the eyes of saints to witness the accursed state of the world, I think the apostles intend partly for consolation and partly for some provocation to suitable walking. Things that are opposite are best known by comparison one with another, for each of them casts abroad a light to see the other by. Therefore it is that the apostles do frequently remind the converted Gentiles of the wretched estate the world ties into and themselves once were into. You see this in 1 Corinthians 6:11, "And such were some of you, but now you are washed." And again in Ephesians 2:1, "You who were dead in trespasses and sins has he quickened."

There is not anything that will more commend unto a Christian the grace of God toward him than to look abroad round about him and take a view of the whole world lying in wickedness, and then to look backward to what he himself once was and compare it with what the free grace of God has made him. Oh what a soul ravishing contemplation is that! We see it in 1 John 5:19, "And we know that we are of God and the whole world lieth in wickedness." How this heightens the price of grace, and how much it adds to a soul's inward contentment to think what it was of itself, and what it would undoubtedly have been, if not thus wonderfully surprised!

Believers Urged to Reflect on Their Former Godlessness

One used always to look to those below him that he might not envy those above him. When a Christian is grieved and disquieted because he has not attained to that desired measure of the image of God and fellowship with Him, truly it might do well for him to cast a look about him to the miserable and hopeless estate of so many thousands who have the image of Satan so visibly engraved on them and who have no inward stirring after this blessed image. Yea, it might do well for him to reflect a little backward to the hole of the pit whence he was taken and to look upon that primitive estate that grace found him in, so loathsome as described in Ezekiel 16. Would not such a double sight, think you, make him break out in admiration and be powerful to silence and compose his spirit? Oh, to think that I was once in that black roll of those excluded from the kingdom! "Such were some of you." And then consider that my name was taken out and washed by the blood of Christ to be enrolled in the register of heaven. What an astonishing thing is it! You see in nature that God has appointed contrarieties and varieties to beautify the world. Certainly, many things could not be known how good and beneficial they are except by the smart and hurt of that which is opposite in them, just as you could not imagine the good of light but by some sensible experience of the evil of darkness. Heat—you could not know the benefit of it but by the vexation of cold. Thus He makes one to commend another and both to beautify the world. It is thus in art: contrariety and variety of colors and lines make up one beauty, while diversity of sounds make a sweet harmony.

The Surprising Wisdom of God

Now, this is the art and wisdom of God. In the dispensation of His grace He sets the misery of some beside the happiness of others so that each of them may aggravate[2] another; likewise, He

---

2. *aggravate*: to add weight to, make greater, or increase.

puts light beside darkness, spirit fore-against[3] flesh, that so saints may have a double access to their admiration at the goodness and grace of God. Similarly, to the saints' delight and complacency in their own happiness, He presents the state of men out of Christ so that you may wonder how you are translated, and may be so abundantly satisfied as not to exchange your portion for the greatest monarchs.

Then, I say, this may provoke us and persuade us to more suitable walking. Does He make such a difference? Oh do not you unmake it again! Do not confound all again by your walking after the course of the world. Conformity to the world is a confusion of what God has separated. Has infinite grace translated you from that kingdom of darkness to His kingdom of light? Oh then walk in that light as children of light! Are you such? Own your stations,[4] consider your relations and make yourselves ashamed at the very thoughts of sin. He points out the deformed and ugly face of the conversation of the world so that you may fall in love with the beauty or holiness, as the Lacedemonians[5] let their children see their slaves drunk, that the brutish and abominable posture of such in that sin might imprint in the hearts of their children a detestation of such a vice.

Certainly the Lord calls you to mind often what you have been and what the world about you is, not to engage you to it but to alienate your minds from the deformity of sin and to commend to you the duty of obedience. You would learn to make this holy use and advantage of all the wickedness that the world lies in, to behold in it, as in a glass, your own image and likeness, that when you use to hate or despise others, you may rather loathe and dislike yourselves as having that same common nature, and so wonder at the goodness of God that

---

3. *fore-against*: opposite.
4. *station*: a person's position or standing.
5. *Lacedaemonians*: Spartans, as Lacedaemon was an area of ancient Greece that contained the city of Sparta and its surroundings.

makes such difference where none was. This would be the way to make gain of the most unprofitable thing in the world, that is, the sins of other men, for ordinarily seeing and speaking of them rather disposes and inclines us into more liberty to sin. Many look on such wickedness with delight, some with contempt and hatred of those that commit them. But there are few who know how to speak or look on sin itself with indignation, or on themselves with abhorrence because of the seeds of wickedness within them.

I would think if we were circumspect in this, the worse the world is, we might be the better; the worse the times are, we might spend it better; the more pride we see, it might make us more humble; the more impiety and impurity that abounds, it might provoke us to a further distance from and disconformity with the world. Thus, if we were wise, we might extract gold out of the dunghill and suck honey out of the most poisonous weed. The surrounding ignorance and wickedness of the world might cause a holy antiperistasis in a Christian by making the grace of God unite itself and work more powerfully as fire out of a cloud and shine more brightly as a torch in the darkness of the night.

A Final Appeal to Those Who Are Still Enemies of God

As for you, whose woeful estate is here described and who are yet in the flesh and enemies to God by nature, I would desire you to be stirred up at the consideration of this: truly, there are some who are delivered out of that prison for some have made peace with God and are no more enemies but friends and fellow citizens of the saints.

If the case were left wholly incurable and desperate, you had some ground to continue in your sins and security. But now when you hear a remedy is possible and some have been helped by it, I wonder that you do not bestir yourselves upon this door of hope offered that you may be those who are here excepted as the apostle writes—*but you are not in the flesh*. Since some are still *in the flesh*, why should I be? Will you awake yourselves with this alarm? If you had any desire after this estate, certainly such a hope as this would give you feet to rise up and come to Jesus Christ, for these are the legs of the souls of some who desire of a better estate and some probability of it conceived by hope.

SERMON 24

The Holy Spirit Dwells in Genuine Believers

If so be that the Spirit of God dwell in you. Now if any man have not the Spirit of Christ, he is none of his.
—ROMANS 8:9

The Wonder of God Dwelling in Man

"But will God in very deed dwell with men on the earth?" (2 Chron. 6:18). It was the wonder of one of the wisest of men and, indeed, it may be a wonder to the wisest of angels, considering God's infinite highness above the height of heavens and His immense and incomprehensible greatness that the heaven of heavens cannot contain Him. But add to that the baseness, emptiness, and worthlessness of man. And what is it, think you, that the angels desire to look into but this incomprehensible mystery of the descent of the Most High to dwell among the lowest and vilest of the creatures (1 Peter 1:12)? Yet as Solomon's temple and these visible symbols of God's presence were only shadows of things to come, the substance whereof is exhibited under the gospel, that wonder was therefore but a shadow or type of a greater and more real wonder regarding God's dwelling on the earth now.

It was the wonder—Shall God dwell with man among the rebellious sons of Adam? But behold a greater wonder since Christ came, God dwelling in man! First, personally in the man Christ, in whom the fullness of the Godhead dwelled bodily.

Then second, graciously in the seed of Christ, in man by His Spirit, and this makes men spiritual if so be the Spirit of Christ dwell in you.

Christ "In the Likeness of Sinful Flesh"
You heard of the first indwelling in verse 3: "God sending his own Son in the likeness of sinful flesh"—the inhabitation of the divine nature in our flesh, which had the likeness of sinful flesh, but without sin, for He sanctified Himself for our cause. And truly, this mysterious and wonderful inhabitation is not only a pledge of the other, God dwelling in sinful men by His Spirit, but also, in order of nature, it has some influence upon the other, without which God could not have dwelled in us. There is so much distance and disproportion between His Majesty and us that we could not be well united, but by this intervening: God first coming down a step into the holy nature of the man Christ that from thence He might go into the sinful nature of other men.

Our sinful and rebellious nature behooved to be first sanctified this way, by the personal indwelling of God in our flesh; this had made an easy passage into our sinful beings, for His Spirit to dwell in us powerfully and graciously. Therefore, the Spirit of Christ is said to dwell in us. Yea, Christ's Spirit dwelling in us, not only because He proceeds from Him as from the Father, but particularly because the inhabitation or operation of the Spirit in us is the proper result and fruit of that glorious union of our nature with Him. He took our flesh that He might send us His Spirit. And oh, what a blessed exchange was this! He came and dwelled in our nature so that He might dwell in us: He took up a shop, as it were, in our flesh, that He might work in us and make us again conformed to God.

We shall not cut this asunder into many parts.[1] You see these

---

1. See comments on Binning's departure from standard Puritan preaching in Ferguson's introduction above, ix–xxix.

words of verse 9 contain plainly the very essential definition of a spiritual man and of a Christian. You find a spiritual man and a Christian equivalent in this verse, that is to say, they are taken for one and the self-same thing and so they are reciprocal, of equal extent and restraint. Every Christian is one after the Spirit and whosoever is after the Spirit is a Christian. Being one of Christ's and one after the Spirit is one thing.

A Christian Is Indwelt by the Spirit of God

Now the definition of the Christian is taken from that which really and essentially constitutes him as such. He is one in whom the Spirit of Christ dwells, and this makes him one after the Spirit for it makes him one of Christ's because it is the Spirit of Christ. And if you define what a man is, you could not do it better than thus: he is one endowed with a reasonable soul. So the apostle gives you the very soul and form of a Christian, which differentiates you from all others. As the soul is to the body to make up a man, so the Spirit of Christ is to the soul and spirit of a man to make up a Christian. Contrarywise, the absence of the soul unmakes a man, so the absence of this Spirit unmakes a Christian. For you see He makes it reciprocal: if you are Christians, the Spirit dwells in you, but if the Spirit dwells not in you, you are not Christians.

Members of the Visible Body May Not Be Genuine Christians
A word then regarding the first of these that a Christian and a spiritual man are commensurable one to another. It is true, there are Jews who are not Jews inwardly, but only according to the letter (Rom. 2:28–29). And so there are Christians so-called, who are but so outwardly and only in the letter, who have no more of it but the name and visible standing in the church. But here we are speaking of that which is truly that which it is called, whose praise is not of men but of God. The name of a man may be extended to a picture or image on account of some outward

resemblance it has of him, but it is not a proper speech;[2] likewise, no more is it proper to extend the name of Christians to the "pictures" or "images" of Christians, such as are destitute of this inward life. You may be properly, according to the Scripture's phrase, members of the visible body, but not having that real and blessed relation to Jesus Christ the head, which shall be the source of happiness to all the living members.

I wish you would take it so and flatter yourselves no more with church titles, as if these were sufficient evidence for your salvation. You would all be called Christians, but it fears me that not many of you know the true meaning and significance of that word; the most comfortable sense of it is hid from you. The meaning of it is that a man is renewed by Christ in the spirit of his mind. As Christ and the Spirit are inseparable, so a Christian and a spiritual nature are not to be found severed. Certainly, the very sound of the name whereby you are called imports another nature and conversation than is to be found in many. You cannot say that you have a shadow of spirituality, either in your affections or actions, or that you have any real design and study that way other than to please your flesh and satisfy the customs of the world.

Why do you then usurp the name of Christianity? This is a common sacrilege, to give that which is holy unto dogs (Matt. 7:6). Others give it to you, and you take it to yourselves. But know that though you please yourselves and others in this, yet without such a renovation of your natures and such a sincere study to be inwardly and outwardly conformed to the profession and nature of Christianity, you do not have your praise from God. And those whom God praises not and allows not, He cannot bless forever.

Those Who Are in the Spirit Will Seek Their Praise from God
Nevertheless, I am persuaded there are some who are not only in the letter but also in the Spirit. Their greatest desire and design

---

2. *proper speech*: strictly speaking, an accurate use of language.

are to be indeed what they profess and as such their praise is from God. And if God praises them now, they shall be made to praise Him forever hereafter; such are allowed to take the name and honorable style of Christianity to themselves. You are Christ's, nearly interested in Him, and if you be Christ's own, He would not be happy without you. For such was His love that He would not be happy alone in heaven but came down to be miserable with us. And now that He is again happy in heaven, certainly He cannot enjoy it alone for long but He must draw up His members unto the fellowship of that glory.

The Indwelling Spirit in Genuine Believers

Now the other thing—that which gives being to a Christian—is the Spirit of Christ dwelling in him. Of this inhabitation, we shall not say so much as the comparison, being strained, will yield neither shall we expatiate into many notions about it. I wish rather we went home with some desires kindled in us, yearning after such a noble guest as the Holy Spirit is, and that we begin at once to weary of the base and unclean guests that lodge within us, to our own destruction. That which I have just said, that the Spirit is to a Christian what the soul is to a man, if well considered, might present the absolute necessity and excellency of this unto your eyes. Consider what a thing the body is without the soul, how defiled and deformed a piece of dust it is, void of all sense and life, loathsome to look upon.

Without the Spirit a Man Is in Darkness and Deadness
Truly the soul of man by nature is in no better case unless this Spirit enter. Until then it has no light in it, no life in it, it is a dark dungeon, such as is described in Ephesians 4:18, "Having the understanding darkened, being alienated from the life of God through the ignorance that is in them, because of the blindness of their heart." You have in those words, both darkness and deadness, want of that shining light of God in the mind so that it cannot discern spiritual things that make to our eternal peace.

All the plainness and evidence of the gospel, though it shines as a sun about you, cannot make you see or apprehend either your own misery or the way to help it.

"Why not?" someone may ask. Because your dungeon is within, the most part cannot form any sensible notion of spiritual things that are duly sounding unto them in the word. The eye of the mind is put out and if it be darkness, how great is that darkness! Certainly the whole man is without light and your way and walk must be in the dark. Indeed, it appears that it is dark night within many souls because if it were not dark, they would not run out all their speed among pits and snares in the way to destruction. And from this woeful defect flows the alienation of the whole soul from the life of God. For that primitive light being eclipsed, the soul is separated from the influence of heaven. Thus, as Nebuchadnezzar's soul acted only in a brutal way when driven out among beasts so the soul of man, being driven out from the presence of the Lord, may act in a way common to beasts, or else in some rational way in things that concern this life, but it is wholly spoiled of that divine life of communion with God. Such a soul cannot taste, smell, or savor such things.

The State of the Ruinous Soul

Oh, if it were visible unto us, the state of the ruinous soul, we would raise a more bitter lamentation over it than the Jews did over Jerusalem or the kings and merchants had reason to do over fallen Babylon. Truly, we might bemoan it thus, "How is the faithful city become a harlot!… righteousness lodged in it, but now murderers" (Isa. 1:21). Man was once the dwelling place of princely and divine graces and virtues, the Lord Himself was there; then how comely and beautiful was the soul! But now it is like the desolate cities in which the beasts of the desert lie and their houses are full of doleful creatures, where owls dwell and satyrs dance, where wild beasts cry and dragons in the pleasant places (Isa. 13:21–22; Jer. 50:39).

So mighty is the fall of the soul of man, as of Babylon, that it may be cried, "Babylon the great is fallen, and become the habitation of devils, and the hold of every foul spirit, and a cage of every unclean and hateful bird" (Rev. 18:2). All the beasts flock now to it, all the birds of darkness take their lodging in it since this noble guest left it and took away the light from it, for the sun has not shined on it since that day. All unclean affections, all beastly lusts, all earthly desires and all vain cogitations get lodging in this house; the Bethel is become a Bethaven,[3] the house of God become a house of vanity; by the continual repair of vain thoughts, the house of prayer is turned into a den of thieves and robbers. That which was at first created for the pure service and worship of God is now a receptacle of all the most rebellious and idolatrous thoughts and affections. The heart of every man is become a temple full of idols.

This is the state of it and it is even worse than can be told you now. Therefore judge if there be not need of a better guest than these. Oh, what absolute necessity is there of such a spirit as this: to repair and reform the ruinous spirit of man and to quicken and enlighten the darkened mind of man! Even that Spirit who made it at first a glorious palace for God, that Spirit who breathed the soul into the former clay, He must repair these breaches and create all again.

The Spirit of Christ Repairs, Reforms, and Enlightens

Now, when the Spirit of Christ enters into this vile ruinous cottage, He repairs it and reforms it, He strikes out lights in the heart and by a wonderful eye salve makes the eyes open to see; for He creates a new light within, which makes a man behold the light shining in the gospel. Then that man beholds all things are new and himself new, because now what was the most loathsome

---

3. *Bethaven*: house of nothingness. It was a place in the mountains of Benjamin, east of Bethel (Josh. 7:2; 18:12). It also came to stand for Bethel (Hosea 4:15; 5:8; 10:5) due to its idolatry.

and vile in his world is now new. For there appears nothing of vanity in the very perfection of it, because now God Himself appears new. Another majesty, glory, excellency, and beauty shines into the soul than ever it apprehended. And as the Spirit enlightens, so He enlivens this tabernacle or temple, He kindles a holy fire in this man's affections which must never go out. Indeed, if it goes out it is such as cannot be rekindled other than by the beams of the sun, as the poets fancied regarding the vestal-fire.[4]

The Spirit within the soul is a fire to consume the believer's corruption, to burn up his dross and vanity. Christ comes in like a refiner with the fire of the Spirit and purges away earthly lusts, making the love of the heart pure and clean to burn upward toward heaven (Mal. 3:3). This Spirit makes a Christian soul move willingly toward God in the ways that had seemed most unpleasant; it is an active principle within him that cannot rest till it rests in its place of eternal rest and delight in God. And then the Spirit reforms this house, by casting out all these wild beasts that lodged in it, the savage and unruly affections that domineered in man—this strong man entering in casts them out (cf. Matt. 12:29). There is much rubbish in old waste palaces (Neh. 4:2). Oh how much pains to cleanse them! Our house is like the house of those nobles of which the prophet speaks (Jer. 5:27), "As a cage is full of birds, so are their houses full of deceit," and our hearts are full of wickedness and vanity (Jer. 4:14).

The Spirit Must Enter with Blood and Water

Certainly it will be much labor to get your unclean spirits cast out, that is, the grosser and more palpable lusts that reign in you. But when these are gone forth, yet there is much wickedness and uncleanness in the heart of a more subtle nature and, by long

---

4. The fire of Vestal was an eternal flame, held to be sacred, in ancient Rome. The vestal virgins were selected by lot and served for thirty years, tending the holy fire in the temple of Vesta. If the fire happened by any accident to be put out, it was not to be lighted again from another fire, but new fire was to be gained by drawing a pure and unpolluted flame from the sunbeams.

indwelling, almost incorporated and mingled with the soul. Nor will this be gotten out with gentle sweeping, as was done (Luke 11:25). That takes away only the uppermost filth that lies loosest but this must be gotten out by much washing and cleansing, therefore the Spirit enters by blood and water.

There are idols in the heart to which the soul is much engaged; it unites and closes with them and these must be cleansed and washed out (Ezek. 36). There is much deceit in the heart, and this lies closest to it and is engrossed into it. Indeed, this will take the help of fire to separate it for that is of the most active nature to separate things of a diverse nature; by this means the Spirit must take out your dross. And all this the Spirit will not do alone but honors you with the fellowship of this work; therefore, you must lay your account that the operation and reformation of this house for so glorious a guest will be laborious in the meantime.

The Peace and Joy Given by the Holy Spirit

But oh how infinitely is that compensated! One hour's fellowship with Him alone, when all strangers are cast out, will compensate all, will make all to be forgotten and the pain of mortification will be swallowed up in the pleasure of His inhabitation. "I shall be satisfied, when I awake, with thy likeness" (Ps. 17:15). When He shall take up house fully in you, it will satisfy you to the full. In the meantime, as He takes the rule and command of your house so for the present He provides for it; the provision of the soul is incumbent on this divine guest, and oh how sweet and satisfying is it! Oh, the peace and joy of the Holy Ghost: such is the entertainment that He gives a soul where He reigns and has brought in righteousness (Rom. 14:17).

What noble train does the Spirit bring along with Him to furnish this house? Many rich and costly ornaments hang over it and adorn it to make it like the king's wife all glorious within— such as the ornament of a meek and quiet spirit (1 Peter 3:4), which is a far more precious and rich hanging than the most curious or precious contexture of corruptible things; such as the clothing of humility, simple in show but rich in substance (1 Peter 5:5). For these enrich and beautify the soul that has them more than all Solomon's glory could do his person; for "better is it to be of a humble spirit with the lowly, than divide the spoil with the proud" (Prov. 16:19).

In a word, the Spirit makes all new. He puts a new man, a new fashion, and a new image upon the soul which now suits the court of heaven, the highest in the world, and is conformed to the noblest and highest pattern, the holiness and beauty of the greatest King. And being lodged within, oh what sweet fruits is the Spirit daily bringing forth to feed and delight the soul withal (Gal. 5:22–23). Not is He only a Spirit of sanctification but of consolation too, and therefore of all the most worthy to be received into our hearts for He is a bosom Comforter (John 14:16). There are times when there is no friend nor lover without, but a soul in that posture of Heman (Ps. 88:18), and in that desolate estate of the churches (Lam. 1:12) where, among all her lovers, there is none to comfort her (verse 17), and though "Zion spreadeth forth her hands, and there is none to comfort her," and, "They have heard that I sigh: there is none to comfort me" (v. 21). In such a case to have a living and over-running spring of comfort within when all external and lower consolations, like winter brooks that dry up in summer, have dried up and disappointed your expectations, surely this would be a happy guest that could do this. Oh, that we could open our hearts to receive Him!

SERMON 25

Our Union with Christ through the Indwelling Spirit

If so be that the Spirit of God dwell in you. Now if any man have not the Spirit of Christ, he is none of his.
—ROMANS 8:9

The Mystical Union of Christ and His Church

There is a great marriage spoken of in Ephesians 5:22–33. It holds a great mystery which the apostle propounds as the sample and archetype of all marriages or rather as the substance of which all conjunctions and relations among the creatures are but the shadows. It is that marriage between Christ and His church for which, it would appear, this world was built to be a palace in which to celebrate it. The upper house, heaven, was especially made glorious for that great day where it shall be solemnized. The first in order of time was made by God Himself in paradise, certainly to represent a higher mystery, the marriage of the second Adam with His spouse, which is taken out of His bloody side, as the apostle implies in Ephesians 5:32.

Now there is the greatest inequality and disproportion between the parties, Christ and sinners; so that it would seem a desperate matter to bring two such distant and unequal natures to such a near union, as may cast a copy to all unions and relations of the creatures. But He who at first made a kind of marriage between heaven and earth in the composure[1] of man and joined together an immortal spirit in such a bond of amity with corruptible dust, has found out the way to help this and make it feasible. And truly, we may conceive the Lord was but making way for this greater mystery of the union of Christ with us when He joined the breath of heaven with the dust of the earth. In this He gave some representation of another more mysterious conjunction.

Christ Humbled Himself

Now, the way that the wisdom and love of God has found out to bring about this marriage is this: because there was such an infinite distance between the only begotten Son of God, who is the express character of His image and the brightness of His glory (Heb. 1:3) and us sinful, mortal creatures whose foundation is in the dust, therefore it pleased the Father, out of His goodwill to the match, to send His Son down among men. And it also pleased the Son, out of His love, to take on our flesh and so fill up that distance with His low condescendence, to be partaker of flesh and blood with the children. And now what the Lord spoke of man fallen, in a holy kind of irony or mock, "Behold, the man is become as one of us" (Gen. 3:22), that is what men may truly say of the Son of God, not fallen down from heaven, but come down willingly, "Lo, he is become as one of us," like us in all things except sin, which has made us unlike ourselves.

This bond of union you have in verse three: Christ so infinitely above sinners and higher than the heavens, coming down so low to be as like sinners as might be or could be profitable for us, "in the likeness of sinful flesh and for sin." But yet this bond is not near enough; that conjunction seems but general and infirm—both general and infirm—because it is in some manner common to all mankind, yet not all of whom shall be advanced to this privilege. By taking on our nature, He comes nearer to human nature, though not to some beyond others. And besides,

---

1. *composure*: composition or formation.

the distance is not filled up this way because there is a great disproportion between that nature in Christ and in us. In Him it is holy and undefiled and separated from sin; but in us it is unclean and immersed into sin; so that, albeit He be nearer us as a man, yet He is far distant and unlike us—a holy, perfect man.

Yet Was without Sin
Now, what fellowship can there be between light and darkness, as Paul speaks of the marriage of Christians with idolaters (2 Cor. 6:14)? Much greater distance and disagreement is between Christ and us. Therefore, it seems that some of us must be changed and transformed. But of Him this may not be. He cannot become more like us other than by partaking of our flesh; for if He had become a sinner indeed, He would have become so like us that He could not help either Himself or us. This would eclipse the glory and happiness of the marriage. But in that He came as near as could be without disabling Himself in order to make us happy, so He was content to come in the place of sinners, taking on their debt and answering to God's justice for it. Yea, and in His own person He submitted to be tempted to sin, though it would have been evil for us if He had been overcome by it.

Partakers of the Divine Nature through the Indwelling Spirit

Yet this brings Him a step lower and nearer to us and makes the union more hopeful. But since He can come no lower and can be made no more like us in the case we are in, then certainly—if the match holds—we must become more like Him and raised up out of our miserable estate to some suitableness to His holy nature. Therefore, the love and wisdom of God, to fill up the distance completely and effectuate this happy conjunction for which the creation groans—for the whole creation travails in pain till the redemption of our bodies be accomplished (v. 22)—has sent His blessed Spirit to dwell in us to transform our natures and make them partakers of the divine nature (2 Peter 1:4), as Christ was partaker of human nature. Thus the distance shall be removed.

When a blessed Spirit is made flesh, and a fleshly man made spirit, then they are near the day of espousal; and this indwelling of the Spirit is the last link of the chain that fastens us to Christ and makes our flesh in some measure like His holy flesh. By taking on our flesh, Christ became bone of our bone, and flesh of our flesh. But the union becomes mutual when we receive the Spirit, for then we become bone of His bone and flesh of His flesh, as it is expressed in Ephesians 5:30, in an allusion to the creation of Eve and her marriage to Adam. The ground of the marriage is that near bond of union—"for she was taken out of Man" (Gen. 2:23); and, therefore, because of his flesh and bone, she was made one flesh with him. Even so the sinner must be partaker of the Spirit of Christ, as Christ is partaker of the flesh of sinners; and these two concurring, these two knots interchanging and woven through each other, we become one flesh with Him.

This is a great mystery, indeed, to bring two who were so far asunder so near to each other. Yea, it is nearer than that too, for we are said not only to be one flesh with Christ but one spirit. "He that is joined unto the Lord is one spirit" (1 Cor. 6:17), because he is animated and quickened by one spirit—that same Spirit of Christ. And, indeed, spirits are more capable of union and more fit to embosom one with another than bodies; therefore, the nearest union conceivable is the union of spirits by affections; this makes two souls one for it transports their spirit out of the body where it lives and settles it there where it loves to be.

All Former Bonds and Engagements Must Be Broken

Now, my beloved, you see what way this great marriage, that heaven and earth are in a longing expectation after, shall be brought about. Christ did forsake His Father's house when He left that holy habitation, His Father's bosom—a place of marvelous delight (Prov. 8:30). For He descended into the lower parts of the earth (Eph. 4:9) and He came out from the Father into the world (John 16:28). This was a great journey to meet with poor sinners. But that there may be a full and entire meeting you must leave and forsake your father's house too and forget your own people (Ps. 45:10). You must give an entire renunciation to all former lovers if you would be His. All former bonds and engagements must be broken that this may be tied the faster. And, to hold to the subject in hand, you must forsake and forget the flesh and be possessed of His Holy Spirit. As He came down to our flesh, you must rise up to meet Him in the spirit. The Spirit of Christ must indeed prevent[2] you and take you out of that natural posture you are born into and bring you a great journey from yourselves that you may be joined unto Him.

The Spirit's Work Is to Engage the Soul to Love Him

This Spirit of Christ is His messenger and ambassador, sent beforehand to fit you and suit you for the day of betrothal and therefore He must have a dwelling and constant abode in you. This "indwelling" imports a special, familiar operation and the perpetuity or continuance of it. The Spirit is everywhere in His being, and He works everywhere too. But here He has a special and peculiar work in commission—to reveal the love of God in Christ. His work is to engage the soul to love Him again, to prepare all within for the great day of betrothal, to purify and purge the heart from all that is displeasing to Christ, to correspond between Christ and His spouse.

He also works between heaven and earth by making intercession for her when she cannot pray for herself, as you find here in verse 26, so sending up the news of the soul's panting and breathing after Christ, sending up her groans and sighs to her Beloved, giving intelligence of all her needs to Him who is above, in the place of an advocate and intercessor, and then bringing back from heaven light and life, direction from her Head—for the Spirit must lead into all truth—and consolation,

---

2. *prevent*: to arrive before, to act in advance of, or to anticipate.

for Christ has appointed the Spirit to supply His absence, and to comfort the soul in the meantime till He come again.

The Spirit Is the Messenger Who Carries Letters between Christ and His Bride

You have this mutual and reciprocal knot in 1 John 4:13, "Hereby we know that we dwell in him, and he in us, by the Spirit that he has given." It is much nearness to dwell one with another, but much greater to dwell one in Another. And it is reciprocal, such a wonderful interchange in it, we in Him, and He in us, for the Spirit carries the soul to heaven, and brings Christ, as it were, down to the earth. He is the messenger who carries letters between both—our prayers to Him, and His prayers for us and love tokens to us. He is the anointing that teaches us all things from our husband (1 John 2:27), and reveals to us the things of God (1 Cor. 2:12), giving us the firstfruits of that happy and glorious communion we must have with Christ in heaven. We see this in verse 23 of this chapter, and how He seals us to the day of redemption (1 Peter 1:13; 4:13), supplying us with divine power against our spiritual enemies and fetching along from heaven that strength whereby our Lord and Savior overcame all (Eph. 3:16; Gal. 5:25).

This is a presence that few have, such a familiar love-abode. But, certainly, all that are Christ's must have it in some measure. Now whosoever has it, it is perpetual: the Spirit dwells in them. It is not a sojourning for a season, not a lodging for a night, as some have fits and starts of seeking God or some transient motions of conviction or joy but then return again to the puddle; these go through them as lightning, but neither warm them nor change them. Rather, this is a constant residence; where the Spirit takes up house He will dwell: "he dwelleth with you and shall be in you" and "abide with you for ever" (John 14:16, 17). If "the Son abides for ever" in the house (John 8:35), much more the master of the house must abide.

The Spirit Must Rule in the House Where He Dwells
Now, the Spirit where He dwells has gotten the command of that house, all the power is put into His hand and resigned to Him for, where He dwells, He must rule as good reason is. He is about the greatest work that is now to do in the world, the repairing and renewing of the ruins and breaches of man's spirit, which was the first breach in the creation, and the cause of all the rest. He is about the cleansing and washing of this temple, and we may be persuaded that He who has begun this good work will perform it until the day of Christ, till we be presented blameless and without spot to our husband (Phil. 1:5–6). This is the grand consolation of believers that they have this presence assured to them by promise that the Spirit is fixed here by an irrevocable and unchangeable covenant or donation,[3] and will not wholly depart from them, though He may withdraw and leave you comfortless for a season (Isa. 59:2).

Therefore, I would shut up all in a word of exhortation to you, that since we have the promise of so noble and happy a guest, you would apply yourselves to seek Him and then keep Him, to receive Him and then retain Him. It is true that He must first prevent us, for as no man can say "that Jesus is the Christ, but by the Spirit of God," so no man can indeed pray for the Spirit, but by the Spirit's own intercession within him. Where God has bestowed anything of this Spirit, it is known by the kindly and fervent desires after more of it.

The Sweet and Affectionate Promise of the Spirit
Now we have a large and ample promise (Ezek. 36:27; Joel 2:28) of the pouring out of the Spirit in as absolute and free a manner as can be imagined and this is renewed by Christ, confirmed by His prayer to the Father for the performance of it (John 14:16–17). Then we have a sweet and affectionate promise propounded in the most moving and loving manner that can be (Luke 11:13).

---

3. *donation*: a legal term for bestowing or transferring a gift of land.

Thus Christ encourages us to pray for the Spirit from this ground: our heavenly Father, who placed that natural affection in earthly fathers toward their children whereby they cannot refuse them bread when they cry for it, He, who was the author of all natural affection, must certainly transcend them infinitely in His love to His children. It is as the psalmist argues, "Shall not he that planted the ear, hear? and he that formed the eye, see?" (Ps. 94:9).

So a poor soul may reason itself to some confidence and ask, "Shall not He who is the fountain of all natural love to men and beasts have much more love Himself? And if my father will not give me a stone when I seek bread, certainly the heavenly Father will far less offer me a stone. Therefore, 'If we, being evil, know how to give good things to our children, how much more shall our heavenly Father give His Spirit to them that ask him?'"

Do Not Ask Timidly or Coldly

Alas, that we should be in want of such a gift for not asking it! My beloved, let us enlarge our desires for this Spirit and seek more earnestly, then no doubt affection and importunity will not be sent away empty. Is it any wonder we receive not, because we ask not (James 4:2), or else we ask so coldly that we teach Him in a manner to deny us: "He who asks timidly and coldly invites a refusal."[4] Ask frequently and ask confidently and His heart cannot deny you. Oh, that we could lay this engagement on our own hearts to be more in prayer! Let us press ourselves to this, yet we need not press Him. Albeit the first grace be wholly a surprisal,[5] yet certainly He keeps this suitable method in the enlargements of grace in that, when He gives more, He enlarges the heart more to desire it. He opens the mouth wider to ask and receive, and, according to that capacity, so is His hand open to fill the heart (Ps. 81:10). Oh, why are our hearts shut when His hand is open?

---

4. *Qui timide rogat, frigide, docet negare.* The sentence is a quotation from Seneca.

5. *surprisal*: consternation or shock caused by an unexpected occurrence.

Neither Grieve Nor Quench the Holy Spirit

Again, I would exhort you in Jesus Christ to entertain the Spirit suitably and this shall keep Him. To this purpose are these exhortations: "Grieve not the Holy Spirit" (Eph. 4:30), and "Quench not the Spirit" (1 Thess. 5:19). There is nothing can grieve Him but sin, and if you entertain that, you cannot retain Him. He is a Spirit of holiness and because He is about the making of you holy, do not then mar Him in His work, but rather labor to advance this and you do Him a pleasure. If you make His holy temple an unclean cage for hateful birds, or a temple for idols, how can it but grieve Him? And if you grieve the Spirit, certainly the Spirit will grieve you, will make you repent it at the heart. Please Him by hearkening to His motions and following His direction, and He shall comfort you.

His office is to be a spring of consolation to you, but if you grieve Him by walking in the imagination of your hearts and following the suggestions of the flesh—His enemy—no doubt that spring will turn its channel another way and dry up for a season toward you. It is not every sin or infirmity that grieves Him thus, if so be that it grieves you; but the entertaining of any sin and making peace with any of His enemies, that cannot but displease Him. And oh, what loss you have by it! You displease your greatest friend in order to please your greatest enemy; you blot and bludder[6] that seal of the Spirit, that you shall not be able to read it till it be cleansed and washed again.

"Now if any man have not the Spirit of Christ, he is none of his"; that is, he is not a Christian. You who aim at nothing but the external and outward show or visible standing in the church, take this along with you. If you have not this Spirit and the seal of this Spirit found on you, Christ will not know you for His in that day of His appearing.

---

6. *bludder*: disfigure.

SERMON 26

Love Unites Christ with the Soul That Is Cleansed

And if Christ be in you, the body is dead because of sin; but the Spirit is life because of righteousness. —ROMANS 8:10

God's presence is in His working. His presence in a soul by His Spirit is His working in such a soul in some special manner, not common to all men, but peculiar to them whom He has chosen. Now His dwelling is nothing else but a continued, familiar, and endless working in a soul, till He has conformed all within to the image of His Son. The soul is the office house, or workhouse, that the Spirit has taken up to frame in it the most curious piece of the whole creation, even to restore and repair that masterpiece which came last from God's hand,[1] and so was the chiefest. I mean, the image of God, in righteousness and holiness (Eph. 4:24).

The Union between Christ and the Soul

Now, this is the bond of union between God and us: Christ is the bond of union with God, but the Spirit is the bond of union with Christ. Christ is the peace between God and us that makes of two one, but the Spirit is the link between Christ and us whereby He has immediate and actual interest in us and we in Him. I find the union between Christ and soul shadowed out

---

1. ab ultima manu.

in Scripture, by the nearest relations among creatures (for truly these are but shadows and that is the body or substance), and because a union that is mutual is nearest, it is often so expressed as it imports an interchangeable relation, a reciprocal conjunction with Christ. The knot is cast on both sides to make it strong. Christ in us, and we in Him; God dwelling in us, and we in Him, and both by this one Spirit as in 1 John 4:13: "Hereby we know that God dwelleth in us, and we in him, by his Spirit which he has given us."

You find it often in John who, being most possessed with the love of Christ and most sensible of His love, could best express it: I in them, and they in me (cf. John 17, esp. vv. 21–23). "He that keepeth his commandments dwelleth in him, and he in him" (1 John 3:24). As the names of married persons are spelled through other,[2] so he spells out this indwelling; it is not cohabitation but inhabitation: neither that alone singly, but mutual inhabitation, which amounts to a kind of penetration, the most intimate and immediate presence imaginable. Christ dwelleth in our hearts by faith; and we dwell in Christ by love (Eph. 3:17; also 1 John 4).

Love Transports the Soul out of Itself and into Christ
Death brings Him into the heart; for it is the very application of a Savior to a sinful soul; it is the very applying of His blood and sufferings to the wound that sin made in the conscience; it is the laying of that sacrifice propitiatory to the wounded conscience, that which heals it, pacifies it, and calms it. A Christian, by receiving the offer of the gospel cordially and affectionately, brings into his house Christ offered and then salvation comes with Him. Therefore believing is receiving (John 1:12), the very opening of the heart to let in an offered Savior; and then Christ, thus possessing the heart by faith, works by love and "he that dwelleth in love, dwelleth in God, and God in him" (1 John

---

2. That is, expressed through each other.

4:16). Love has this special value in it, that it transports the soul in a manner out of itself to the Beloved (Song 4:9). "The soul is where it loves, not where it animates";[3] the fixing and establishing of the heart on God is a dwelling in Him; for the constant and most continued residence of the most serious thoughts and affections will be their dwelling in their all-fullness and riches of grace in Jesus Christ.

As the Spirit dwells where He works, so the soul dwells where it delights, its complacency in God making a frequent issue or outgoing to him in desires and breathings after him. And by means of this same, God dwells in the heart, for love is the opening up of the inmost chamber of the heart to Him; it brings the Beloved into the very secrets of the soul, to lie all night betwixt His breasts as a bundle of myrrh (Song 1:13). And indeed all the sweet odors of holy duties, and all the performing of good works and edifying speeches, spring out only and are sent forth from this bundle of myrrh that lies betwixt the breasts of a Christian in the inmost of his heart from Christ dwelling in the affections of the soul.

Self-Love Causes Our Hearts to Deceive Themselves

Now, this being the bond of union betwixt Christ and us, it follows necessarily that whosoever has not the Spirit of Christ, he is none of His; and this is subjoined for prevention or removal of the misapprehensions and delusions of men in their self-judgments; because self-love blinds our eyes, and makes our hearts deceive themselves. We are given to this self-flattery: we pretend and lay claim to an interest in Jesus Christ, even though there be no more evidence for it than the external relation that we have to Christ as members of His visible body or as partakers of a common influence of His Spirit.

---

3. Anima est ubi amat, non ubi animat.

Loose, Unsure Knots That Are Easy to Untie
There are some external bonds and ties to Christ which are like a knot that may easily be loosed if anything gets hold of the end of it, as by our relations to Christ by baptism and hearing the Word—your outward covenanting to be His people. All these are loose, unsure knots; it is as easy to untie them as to tie them, yea, even more easy! And yet many have no other relation to Christ than what these make. But it is only the Spirit of Christ given to us that entitles and interests us in Him, and Him in us. It is the Spirit working in your souls mightily and continually, making your hearts temples for the offering of the sacrifice of prayer and praises. Such spiritual offerings necessitate the casting out all idols from these temples, that He alone may be adored and worshipped by the affectionate service of the heart, purging them from all filthiness of flesh and spirit. It is the Spirit, I say, thus dwelling in men that makes them living members of the true body of Christ, lively, joined to the Head, that is to Christ. This makes Him yours and you His; by virtue of this He may command you as His own, and you may use and employ Him as your own.

The Spirit of God Cannot Dwell in Unclean Habitations
Now, for want of this, in the most part of men, they also want this living saving interest in Christ. They have no real but an imaginary and notional propriety and right to the Lord Jesus; for Christ must first take possession of us by His Spirit before we have any true right to Him or can willingly resign ourselves to Him and give Him right over us. What shall it profit us, my beloved, to be called Christians, and to esteem ourselves so if, really, we be none of Christ's? Shall it not heighten our condemnation so much the more that we desire to pass for such and give out ourselves so, and yet have no inward acquaintance and interest in Him whose name we love to bear? Are we not for the most part shadows and pictures of true Christians, bodies without the soul of Christianity, that is, the Spirit of Christ, when

our hearts are treasures of wickedness and deceit and warehouses of iniquity and ignorance? It may be known what treasure fills the heart by that which is the constant and common vent of it, as our Savior speaks, "Out of the abundance of the heart the mouth speaks...an evil man out of the evil treasure bringeth forth evil things" (Matt. 12:34–35; see also 15:19). Whereas, in the case of a good man out of the good treasure of the heart the feet walk, and the hand works.

Consider, then, whether the Spirit of God dwells in such unclean habitations and dark dungeons; certainly no uncleanness or darkness of the house can hinder Him from coming in; but it is a sure argument and evidence that He is not as yet come in, because the prince of darkness is not yet cast out of many souls, nor yet the unclean spirits that lodge within; these haunt your hearts and are as familiar now as ever. Sure I am, many souls have never yet changed their guests, and it is as sure that the first guest that taketh up the soul is darkness and desperate wickedness with unparalleled deceitfulness. There is an accursed trinity instead of that blessed Trinity, the Father, the Son, and the Holy Spirit, and when this holy Trinity comes in to dwell, that other of hell must go out.

The Judgment of Christ
Now, my beloved, do you think this a light matter to be disowned by Jesus Christ? Truly, the word of Christ, which is the character for all our evidence and rights for heaven, disowns many as bastards and dead members, withered branches. Certainly, according to this word He will judge you: "the word that I have spoken...shall judge you in the last day" (John 12:48). Oh, that is a heavy word! You have the very rule and method of proceeding laid down before you now, which shall be punctually kept at that great day.

Now, why do you not read your ditty and condemnatory sentence here registered? If you do not read it now in your consciences, He will one day read it before men and angels and pronounce this: "I know you not for mine, you are none of mine." But if you would now take it to your hearts, there might be hope that it should go no further and come to no more public hearing. There would be hope that it should be repealed before that day, because the first entry of the Spirit of Christ is to convince men of sin, that they are unbelievers and without God in the world. And if this was done, then it would be easier to convince you of Christ's righteousness and persuade you to embrace it. Then this would lead into another link of the chain—the conviction of judgment to persuade you to resign yourselves to the Spirit's rule and to renounce the kingdom of Satan. This would be another trinity, a trinity upon earth, three bearing witness on the earth that you have the Spirit of God (1 John 5:8).

Christ's Consolation for Believers
All the verses in the preceding chapter seem to be purposely set down by the apostle for the comfort of Christians against the remnants of sin and corruption within them. For in those verses, Paul personates[4] the whole body of Christ militant, showing in his own example how much sin remains in the holiest people in this life. This he instances in his own person rather than another so that all may know that matter of continual sorrow and lamentation is furnished to the chief of saints. Nonetheless in this chapter he propounds the consolation of Christians more generally, that all may know that these privileges and immunities belong even to the meanest and weakest of Christians—that, as the best have reason to mourn in themselves, so the worst do not lack reason to rejoice in Jesus Christ.

This should always be minded that the amplest grounds of the strongest consolation are general to all that come indeed to Jesus Christ and are not restricted to saints of such and such a growth and stature. The common principles of the gospel are more full of this milk of consolation, if you would suck it out of

---

4. *personate*: to represent or play the part of.

them than many particular grounds which you are laying down for yourselves. God has so disposed and contrived the work of our salvation that in this life he that has gathered much, in some respect, has nothing over—that is to say, has no more reason to boast than another, but will be constrained to sit down and mourn over his own evil heart and the emptiness of it, while he that has gathered less has, in some sense, no want (2 Cor. 8:15). I mean, he is not excluded and shut out from the right to these glorious privileges which may express both glory and rejoicing from the heart.

In order that there might be an equality in the body, He makes the stronger Christian to partake with the weaker in his bitter things, and the weaker with the stronger in his sweet things, that none of them may conceive themselves either despised or alone regarded (2 Cor. 8:14). Therefore the eunuch may not have reason to say, "I am a dry tree." For, behold the Lord will give, even to such, "a place" in His house, and "a name better than of sons and daughters" (Isa. 56:3, 5). The soul that is in sincerity aiming at this walk, and whose inward desires stir after more of this Holy Spirit, He will not refuse to such that name and esteem that they dare not take to themselves because of their seen and felt unworthiness.

Further Consolation for Those Struggling against the Effects of Indwelling Sin

In this tenth verse he proceeds further to the fruits and effects of sin dwelling in us, in order also to enlarge the consolation against them both. Now, and if Christ be in you, the body is dead because of sin. Seeing the Word of God has made such a connection between sin and death, and because death is the wages of sin which is the just recompense of our enmity and rebellion against God, the poor troubled soul might be ready to conceive that if the body be adjudged[5] to death for sin, that the rest of the wages

---

5. *adjudged*: sentenced.

shall be paid. And because sin has so much dominion as to kill the body, it should therefore exerce[6] its full power to destroy all. Seeing we have a visible character of the curse of God engraved on us in the mortality of our bodies, it may look with such a visage on a soul troubled for sin, as if it were but the earnest of the full curse and weight of wrath, and that sin was not fully satisfied for, nor justice fully contented by, Christ's ransom.

Now, he opposes to this misconception the strongest ground of consolation: *if Christ be in you*—though your bodies must die for sin because sin dwells in them, yet that Spirit of life that is in you has begun eternal life in your souls. This implies that your spirits are not only immortal in being, but that eternal happiness is begun in you, in that the seeds of it are cast into your souls and shall certainly grow up to perfection of holiness and happiness. And this comes to you through the righteousness of Christ which assures that state unto you.

The comfort is that it is neither total for it is only the death of your body, nor is it perpetual for your bodies shall be raised again to life eternal (v. 11). Nor is it not only in part and for a season but it is for a blessed end and purpose: it is in order for sin to be wholly cleansed out that this tabernacle is taken down, as the leprous houses[7] were to be taken down under the law and as nowadays we cast down pest lodges, the better to cleanse them of the infection. It is not to prejudge[8] him of life, but to install him in a better life. Thus you see that it is neither total nor perpetual, but it is medicinal and profitable to the soul; it is but the death of the body for a moment, and the life of the soul forever.

---

6. *excerce*: exert.

7. These were temporary shelters put up for those who were infected with the plague.

8. *prejudge*: to cause detriment or loss; to deprive someone of benefits or advantages.

SERMON 27

The Truth about Death without Christ

And if Christ be in you, the body is dead because of sin.
—ROMANS 8:10

The Excellence of Christianity

This is the high excellence of the Christian religion: it contains the most absolute precepts for a holy life and the greatest comforts in death, for from these two, the truth and excellency of religion, is to be measured if it has the highest and most perfect rule of walking and the chiefest comfort withal. Now, the perfection of Christianity you saw in the rule: how spiritual it is, how reasonable, how divine, how free from all corrupt mixture. You also saw how it transcends all the most exquisite precepts and laws of men, deriving a holy conversation from the highest fountain, the Spirit of Christ, and conforms it to the highest pattern, the will of God.

Indeed, in the first words of this verse there is something of the excellent nature of Christianity holden out, if Christ be in you, which is the true description of a Christian—one in whom Christ is, which imports the divine principle and the spiritual subject of Christianity. The divine principle is Christ in a man—Christ by His Spirit dwelling in him. This great apostle knew this well in his own experience and therefore he can speak best in this style, "I live; yet not I, but Christ liveth in me" (Gal. 2:20), importing that Christ and His Spirit is to the soul what the soul is to the body. That is, there is a living influence from heaven that acts and moves the soul of a Christian as powerfully, yet as sweetly and pleasantly, as if it were the natural motion of the soul; and truly it is the natural motion of the soul. It is that primitive life which was most connatural to the soul of man, but which sin did deprive us of. All the powerful constraint and violence that Christ uses in drawing the souls of men to Himself, and after Him, is as kindly unto them and perfects them as much as that impulse by which the soul moves and turns the body, a sweet compulsion and blessed violence.

Now this should make Christians often to reflect upon another principle of their lives than themselves that by looking on Him, who is "the resurrection and the life," who is "the true vine," and by abiding in Him by faith, their lives may be continued and increased. It is certainly much reflection on Him who is all in all, and less upon ourselves, that maintains this life. Therefore, the most part of men being wholly strangers to this, whether in their purposes or practices (or judgments of both), unacquainted with any higher look in religion than they use in their natural and civil actions, it gives ground to assure us that they are strangers—alienated from the life of God, without God, and without Christ in the world.

Christ in the Inner Man
But then the spiritual subject of Christianity is here, *Christ in you*—not Christ without you, in ordinances, in profession, in some civil carriage—but Christ within the heart of a man: that is a Christian. It is the receiving of Christ into the soul and putting Him on upon the inner man, thus renewing him, that makes a Christian, not being externally clothed with Him or compassed about with Him in the administration of the ordinances. It fears me that the most part of us who bear the name of Christianity have no character of it within if we were looked and searched. Many are like the sepulchres Christ speaks of: without, painted and fair, but within, nothing but rottenness and dead bones (Matt. 23:27).

Many Are Still Rebels against Christ

What have many of you more of Christ than a blind man has of light? It is round about him but not within him. The light has shined in darkness but your darkness cannot comprehend it (John 1:5). You are environed with the outward appearances of Christ in His Word and ordinances and that is all; but neither within you, nor upon many of you, is there anything either of His light or life. Not even is there so much about you as any outward profession or behavior suitable to the revelation of Christ. As if you were ashamed to be Christians, you maintain gross ignorance and practice manifest rebellion against His known will in the very light of the gospel. How few have so much tincture of Christ, sufficient to color the external man or to clothe it with any blamelessness of their walking or form of religion! How few are so much as Christians in the letter! For you are not acquainted either with letter or spirit, either with knowledge or affection or practice.

But suppose that some have put on Christ on their outward man, and color over themselves with some performances of religious duties. They may even smooth themselves with civility in carriage, yet alas! How few are they who are renewed in the spirit of their mind and have put on Christ in their inward man! How few there are who have opened the secrets of their hearts and received him to "lie all night between their breasts" (Song 1:13)! How few are busied about their hearts, to have any new impression and dye upon their affections, to mold them after a new manner, to kill the love of this world and the lusts of it and to cast out the rottenness and superfluity of naughtiness (James 1:21) which abides within!

But some there are who are persuaded thus to do to give up their spirits to religion, and all their business and care is to have Christ within as well as without. Now, if the rest of you will not be persuaded to be of this number, consider of what you prejudge yourselves: of all the comfort of religion, for then religion is no religion and to no purpose if you have no benefit by it.

And certainly, except Christ be in you as a king to rule you and a prophet to teach you—to subdue your lusts and dispel your darkness—when He appears He cannot appear to your comfort and salvation. You are deprived of this great cordial against death, and death must seize upon all that is within you, soul and body, since Christ the Spirit of life is not within you. Happiness without you will not make you happy, salvation round about you will not save you.

A True Christian Has Christ Both "Without" and "Within"
If you would be saved, there must be a near and immediate union with happiness: Christ in the heart, and salvation cometh with Him. A Christian is not only Christ without, not imputing his sins to Him and clothing him with His righteousness, but Christ within too, cleansing the heart from the love of sin, "perfecting holiness in the fear of God" (2 Cor. 7:1). Do not think you have any share in Christ without you, except you receive Christ within you, because Christ is one within and without and His gifts are undivided. Therefore, true faith receives the whole Christ as a complete Savior, even as He is entirely offered, so He is undividedly received as He is, without saving us, and within sanctifying us. Christ without delivering from wrath, and Christ within redeeming from all iniquity—these cannot be parted any more than could His coat that had no seam.

It is a heavy and weighty word of this apostle: "Examine yourselves, whether you be in the faith; know ye not your own selves, how that Jesus Christ is in you, except ye be reprobates" (2 Cor. 13:5). I wish you would lay it to heart, you who have never yet returned to your hearts. If Christ be not formed in you (as Gal. 4:19), you are as yet among the refuse, dross, and that which must be burned with fire. You cannot but be cast away in the day when He makes up His jewels (cf. Mal. 3:17). Where Christ is, He is the hope of glory—He is an immortal seed of glory. How can you hope for Christ, you who have nothing of Him within you?

The Greatest of All Comforts in Both Life and Death

Now, the other touchstone of true religion is the great comfort it furnishes to the soul and, of all comforts, the greatest is that which is a cordial to the heart against the greatest fears and evils. Now, certainly the matter of greatest fears is death, not so much because of itself, but chiefly because of that eternity of unchangeable misery that naturally it transmits them unto. Now, it is only the Christian religion possessing the heart that arms a man completely against the fear either of death itself, or the consequences of it. It gives the most powerful consolation that not only overcomes the bitterness and takes out the sting of death, but changes the nature of it so far as to make it the matter of triumph and glorification.

There is something here supposed in our text, the worst that can befall a Christian: it is the death of a part of him and that the worst and most ignoble part only, *the body is dead because of sin*. Then, that which is opposed by way of comfort to counterbalance it is the life of his better and more noble part, *the Spirit is life because of righteousness*. And, besides, we have the fountains both of that death and this life—man's sin the cause of bodily death and Christ's righteousness the fountain of spiritual life.

Even Pagan Writers Were Concerned about "Dying Well"

Of death many have had sweet meditations, even among those that the light of the Word has not shined upon. Indeed, they may make us ashamed who profess Christianity. So, being without the hope of the resurrection from the dead, they have accounted it only true wisdom and sound philosophy to meditate often on death, and they have made it the very principal point of living well to be always learning to die. Also, they have applied their whole studies that way, neglecting present things that are in the by,[1] and have given themselves to search out some comfort against death or from death. Yea, some have so profited in this

---

1. *in the by*: off the path or of secondary importance.

that they have accounted death the greatest good that can befall man, and persuaded others to think so. Now, what may we think of ourselves who scarce apprehend mortality, especially considering that we have the true fountain of it revealed to us, and the true nature and consequents of it?

All Must Yield to Death's Universal Reign
All men must needs know that death is the most universal king in the world and that it reigns over all ages, sexes, conditions, nations, and times, though few be willing to entertain thoughts of it. Yet sooner or later they must be constrained to give it lodging upon their eyelids and suffer it to storm the very strongest tower, the heart, and batter it down and break the strings of it, having no way either to fly from it or resist it.

Now, the consideration of the general inundation of death over all mankind, and the certain approaching of it to every particular man's door, has made many serious thoughts among the wise men of the world. But being destitute of this heavenly light that shines to us, they could not attain to the original of it but have conceived that it was a common attribute of nature. It was, they thought, a universal law imposed upon all mankind by nature, having the same reason that other mutations and changes among the creatures here below have, and so they have thought it no more a strange thing than to see other things dissolved in their elements. Now, indeed, seeing they could apprehend no other bitter ingredient in it, it was no wonder that the wisest of them could not fear it, but rather wait and expect it as a rest from their labors and as the end of all their miseries.

The True Cause of Death
But the Lord has revealed unto us in His Word the true cause of it and so the true nature of it. The true cause of it is sin—"Sin entered into the world, and death by sin; and so death passed upon all, for that all have sinned" (Rom. 5:12). Man was created for another purpose and upon other conditions, and a law of

perpetual life and eternal happiness was passed in his favor, he abiding in the favor and obeying the will of Him that gave him life and being. Now, sin interposing and separating between man and God, loosing that blessed knot of union and communion, it was this other law that succeeded as a suitable recompense, "you shall die." It is resolved in the council of heaven that the union of man shall be dissolved, his soul and body separated, in just recompense of the breaking the bond of union with God.

This is it that has opened the sluice to let in an inundation of misery upon mankind: this was the just occasion of that righteous but terrible appointment, "It is appointed unto men once to die, but after death comes the judgment" (Heb. 9:27). Since the body had enticed the soul and suggested unto it such unnatural and rebellious motions of withdrawing from the blessed Fountain of life in order to satisfy its pleasure, the body should be under a sentence of deprivement and forfeiture of that great benefit and privilege of life it had by the soul's indwelling, and condemned to return to its first base original, "the dust." Thus the body becomes a feast for worms, to lodge in the grave and be a subject of the greatest corruption and rottenness. And this is because it became the instrument—yea, the incitement—of the soul to sin against what God had from heaven breathed a spirit into it, exalting it above all the dust or clay in the world.

Death Ought to Be a Compelling Warning to All

Now, my beloved, do we not get many remembrances of our sins? Do they not every day present to our view our primitive departure from God, our first separation from the Fountain of life by sin in such sad and woeful effects, and do they not point out the heinousness of sin? Do you not see men's bodies every day dissolved, the tabernacle of earth taken down, and the soul constrained to remove out of it? But what influence has it upon us, what do the multiplied funerals work upon us? It may be sorrow for our friends but little or no apprehension of our own mortality and base impression of sin that separates our souls from God. Who is made sadly to reflect upon his origins, or to mind seriously that statute and appointment of heaven, "In that day you shall die" (cf. Gen. 2:17)?

It is strange that all of us fear death yet few are afraid of sin that carries death in its bosom; it is strange also that we are so unwilling to reap corruption in our bodies and yet we are so earnest and laborious in sowing to the flesh. Be not deceived, for you are daily reaping what you have sown (Gal. 6:7). And oh, that it were all the harvest; but death is only the putting in of the sickle of vengeance, the first cut of it. But oh, to think on what follows would certainly restrain men and cool them in their fervent pursuits after sin!

SERMON 28

Christ Has Removed the Sting from Death

And if Christ be in you, the body is dead because of sin; but the Spirit is life because of righteousness. —ROMANS 8:10

"The sting of death is sin, and the strength of sin is the law," says our apostle (1 Cor. 15:56). These two concur to make man mortal and these two are the bitter ingredients of death. Sin procured it and the law appointed it; God has seen to the exact execution of that law in all ages—for what man lives and shall not taste of death? Two only escaped the common lot, Enoch and Elias, for they pleased God and he took them. Besides, it was for a pledge that at the last day all shall not die but be changed.

The True Cause and Nature of Death

The true cause of death is sin and its true nature is penal to be a punishment of sin: take away this relation to sin, and death wants the sting. But, in its first appointment, and as it prevails generally over men, death is stinging.[1] It has a sting that pierces deeper and wounds sorer than to merely the desolation of the body, for it goes into the innermost parts of the soul and wounds that eternally. The truth is the death of the body is neither the first death nor the last death: it is rather placed in the middle

---

1. aculeata est mors.

between two deaths and is the fruit of the first and the root of the last.

There is a death immediately that has ensued upon sin and it is the separation of the soul from God, the fountain of life and blessedness. It is this death often spoken of as in Ephesians 2:1 and 4:18–19: "You who were dead in sins and trespasses," and "being past feeling…and alienated from the life of God." Truly this is worse in itself than the death of the body simply, though not so sensible, because spiritual. The corruption of the best part in man, in all reason, is worse than the corruption of his worst part. But this death, which consists especially in the loss of that blessed communion with God and which made the soul happy, cannot be found till some new life enter, or else till the last death come which adds infinite pain to infinite loss.

Death Is an Appropriate Judgment upon Sin

Now the death of the body succeeds this soul's death and that is the separation of the soul from the body. This is most suitable, seeing the soul was turned from the Fountain-spirit to the body so that the body should by His command return to dust and be made the most defiled piece of dust. Now, this were not so grievous if it were not a step to the death to come and to a degree introductive to it. But that statute and appointment of heaven has thus linked it—"after death comes judgment" (Heb. 9:27)—because the soul in the body would not be sensible of its separation from God, but was wholly taken up with the body, neglecting and miskenning[2] that infinite loss of God's favor and face. Therefore, the Lord commands it to go out of the body that it may then be sensible of its infinite loss of God when it is separated from the body; then it may have leisure to reflect upon itself and find its own surpassing misery; then indeed—infinite pain and infinite loss conjoined—there must come

---

2. *miskenning*: not knowing or ignoring.

eternal banishment from the presence of that blessed Spirit and eternal torment within itself.

These two concurring, what posture do you think such a soul will be into? There are some who are earnest of this in this life. When God reveals His terror and sets men's sins in order before their face, oh, how intolerable is it and more insupportable than many deaths. They that have been acquainted with it have declared it. The terrors of God are like poisonous arrows sunk into Job's spirit, drinking up all its moisture. Such a spirit as is wounded with one of these darts shot from heaven, who can bear it? Not even the most patient and most magnanimous spirit that can sustain all other infirmities (Prov. 18:14).

Now, my beloved, if it be so now, while the soul is in the body drowned in it, what will be the case of the soul separated from the body when it shall be all one sense to reflect and consider itself? This is the sting of death indeed, worse than a thousand deaths to a soul that apprehends it. But the less it is apprehended, the worse it is, because it is the more certain and must shortly be found when there is no brazen serpent to heal that sting.

Christ Alone Has the Only Antidote against Death's Poison
Now, what comfort have you provided against this day? What way do you think to take out this sting? Truly, there is no balm for it, no physician for it, but one whom the Christian only is acquainted with. He in whom Christ is has this sovereign antidote against the poison of death; he has the very sting of it taken out by Christ, death itself killed and of a mortal enemy made the kindest friend. And so he may triumphantly say with the apostle, "O death, where is thy sting? O grave, where is thy victory? Thanks be to God in Jesus Christ, who giveth us the victory" (1 Cor. 15:55).

The Threefold Ground of the Believer's Triumph
The ground of his triumph, which a Christian has to oppose to all the sorrows and pains and fears of death mustered against

him, is threefold: one, that death is not real; second, that it is not total, even that which is; third, that it is not perpetual. This third ground is contained in the next verse, the second expressed in this verse—if Christ be in you, the body is dead because of sin: but the Spirit is life because of righteousness—and the first may be understood or implied in it.

The nature of death is so far changed in that instead of a punishment it is become a medicine; instead of a punishment for sin it is turned into the last purgative of the soul from sin. Thus the sting of it is taken away, that relation it did bear to the just wrath of God. And now as to the body of a Christian under appointment to die for sin, that is, for the death of sin, the eternal death of sin, Christ, having come under the power of death, has gotten power over it and despoiled it of its stinging virtue. He has taken away the poisonous ingredient of the curse so that it can no longer hurt them that are in him. Therefore it is not now vested with that piercing and wounding notion of punishment.

Though it be true that sin was the first inlet of death in that it first opened the sluice to let it enter and flow in upon mankind, nonetheless that appointment of death is renewed and bears a relation to the destruction of sin, rather than the punishment of the sinner who is forgiven in Christ. And oh, how much solid comfort is here that the great reason of mortality that a Christian is subject unto is that he may be made free of that which made him at first mortal! Sin has taken such possession in this earthly tabernacle and is so strong a poison that it has infected all the members and by no purgation here made can be fully cleansed out. But because there are many secret corners it lurks into and upon occasion vents itself, therefore it has pleased God in His infinite goodness to continue the former appointment of death. However, this continuation is under a new and living consideration, to take down this infected and defiled tabernacle, as the houses of leprosy were taken down under the law so that they might be the better cleansed, and this is the last purification of the soul from sin.

Ultimately Christ Will Purify and Effect a Universal Change
Therefore, as one of the ancients said well, "That we might not be eternally miserable, mercy has made us mortal."[3] Although justice has made the world mortal that they might be eternally miserable, Christ, to put an end to this misery, has continued our mortality, else He would have abolished death itself had He not meant to abolish sin by death. Indeed, it would appear this is the reason why the world must be consumed with fire at the last day and new heavens and earth succeed in its room, because, as the little house, the body, was infected, so the great house, the world, was also infected with this leprosy. So this leprous world was subjoined to vanity and corruption because of man's sin. Therefore, that there might be no remnant of man's corruption and no memorial of sin to interrupt his eternal joy, the Lord will purify and change all—that is, all the members that were made instruments of unrighteousness and all the creatures that were servants to man's lusts.

A new form and fashion shall be put on all, in order that the body, being restored, may be a fit dwelling place for the purified soul. Also that the world, being renewed, may be a fit house for righteous men. Thus you see that death for a Christian is not real death, for it is not the death of a Christian but the death of sin his greatest enemy. It is not a punishment, but rather is the enlargement of the soul.

The New Life Is Already Begun in Believers
Now, the next comfort concerns that which is but partial, for death is but the dissolution of the lowest part in man, his body; so far from prejudging the immortal life of his spirit it is rather the accomplishment of that. Though the body must die, yet eternal

---

3. The citation may well be adapted from Plotinius, quoted by Augustine in *City of God*: "'The Father in compassion made their bonds mortal,' that is to say, he considered it due to the Father's mercy that men, having a mortal body, should not be forever confined in the misery of this life."

life is begun already within the soul for the Spirit of Christ has brought in life—the righteousness of Christ has purchased it and the Spirit has performed it and applied it to us. Not only there is an immortal being within a Christian that must survive the dust (for that is common to all men), but there is a new life begun in him, an immortal well-being in joy and happiness, which alone deserves the name of life that never comes to its full perfection till the bodily and earthly houses are taken down.

If you consider seriously the new life a Christian is translated unto by the operation of the Holy Ghost and the ministration of the Word, it is most active and lively when the soul is most retired from the body in meditation. The new life of a Christian is most perfect in this life when it carries him the furthest distance from his bodily senses and is most abstracted from all sensible engagements, as you heard. For indeed it restores the spirit of a man to its native rule and dominion over the body so that it is then most perfect when it is most gathered within itself and disengaged from all external entanglements.

Christ Has Removed the Sting from Death

Now certain it is, since the perfection of the soul in this life consists in such a retirement from the body that when it is wholly separated from it then it is in the most absolute state of perfection and its life acts most purely and perfectly when it has no body to communicate with or to entangle it either with its lusts or necessities. The Spirit is life, it has a life now which is then best when furthest from the body, and therefore it cannot but be surpassing better when it is out of the body, and all this is purchased by Christ's righteousness. As man's disobedience made an end of his life, Christ's obedience has made our life endless. He suffered death to sting him and by this has taken the sting from it; now there is a new statute and appointment of heaven published in the gospel, "whosoever believeth in him shall not perish, but have eternal life" (John 3:16).

Now indeed, this has so entirely changed the nature of death that it has now the most lovely and desirable aspect on a Christian—it is no longer an object of fear but of desire, amicable, not terrible unto him. Since there is no way to save the passenger other than to let the vessel break, he will be content to have the body split that himself, that is his soul, may escape. For truly a man's soul is himself, the body is but an earthly tabernacle that must be taken down to let the inhabitant win out to come near his Lord. The body is the prison house that he groans to have opened, that he may enjoy that liberty of the sons of God.

Therefore now to a Christian death is not properly an object of patience but of desire rather: "I desire to be dissolved and be with Christ" (Phil. 1:23). He that has but advanced little in Christianity will be content to die, but because there is too much flesh, he will desire to live. But a Christian that is riper in knowledge and grace will rather desire to die, and only be content to live. He will exercise patience and submission about abiding here, but groanings and panting about removing hence, because he knows that there is no choice between that bondage and this liberty.

SERMON 29

Death's Terrors outside of Christ Contrasted with Death's Joys for Those in Christ

And if Christ be in you, the body is dead because of sin; but the Spirit is life because of righteousness.
—ROMANS 8:10

The Sentence of Death on Adam Was Graciously Delayed

It was the first curse and threatening wherein God thought fit to comprehend all misery, "You shalt die the death in that day you eat of it." Though the sentence was not presently executed according to the letter, yet from that day forward man was made mortal and there seemed to be much mercy and goodness of God intervening to plead a delay of death itself. And so the promise of life in the second Adam was to come to the first and his posterity that they might be delivered from the second death, though not from the first. Always we bear about the marks of sin in our bodies to this day. And in so far as the threatening takes place, this life we live in the body is become nothing else but a dying life, while the life that the ungodly shall live out of the body is a living death: either of these is worse than simple death or destruction of being.

The serious contemplation of the miseries of this life made wise Solomon to praise the dead more than the living, contrary to the custom of men who rejoice at the birth of a man-child but mourn at their death. Yea, it pressed him further to think them which have not at all been, better than both, because they have not seen the evil under the sun (Eccl. 6:3–5). This world is such a chaos, such a mass of miseries that, if men understood it before they came into it, they would be far more loath to enter it than they are now afraid to go out of it. And truly we want not remembrances and representations of our misery every day, in that children come weeping into the world, as it were bewailing their own misfortune, that they were brought forth to be sensible subjects of misery.

We Must Suffer Many "Deaths" before Death Comes
Further, what is all our lifetime but a repetition of sighs and groans, anxiety and satiety, loathing and longing, dividing our spirits and our time between them? How many deaths must we suffer before death comes? For the absence or loss of anything much desired is a separation no less grievous to the hearts of men than the parting of soul and body: for affection to temporal, perishing things unites the soul so unto them that there is no parting without pain, no dissolution of that continuity without much vexation. And yet the soul must suffer many such tortures in one day because the things are perishing in their own nature and uncertain.

What is sleep, which devours the most part of our time, but the very image and picture of death, a visible and daily representation of the long cessation of the sensitive life in the grave? And yet, truly, it is the best and most innocent part of our time, though we accuse it often. There is both less sin and less misery in it for it is almost the only lineament and refreshment we get in all our miseries. Job sought to assuage his grief and ease his body, but it was the extremity of his misery that he could not find it.

Now, my beloved, when you find that which is called life subject to so much misery that you are constrained often to desire you had never been born, you find it a valley of tears, a house of mourning from whence all true delight and solid happiness is banished. Seeing the very officers and sergeants of death are continually surrounding us and walking along with us—though unpleasant company—in our greatest contentment and are putting marks upon your doors as in the time of the plague upon houses infected, "Lord, have mercy upon us," and are continually bearing this motto to our view. They are sounding this direction to our ears, "quickly, afar, long"[1]—to get soon out of Sodom that is appointed for destruction, to fly quickly out of ourselves to the refuge appointed of God, even one that was dead and is alive and has redeemed us by His blood, and to get far off from ourselves and take up dwelling in the blessed Son of God, through whose flesh there is access to the Father.

Immortality and Life Is Offered in the Gospel
Therefore, I say, seeing all these are so, why do not we awake ourselves upon the sound of the promise of immortality and life brought to our ears in the gospel? Mortality has already seized upon our bodies, but why do you not catch hold of this opportunity of releasing your souls from the chains and fetters of eternal death? Truly, my beloved, regarding all that can be spoken of torments and miseries in this life, try to imagine all the exquisite torments invented by the most cruel tyrants since the beginning, being combined into one single form of torture. That would then stretch our imaginations beyond the single torment of death, for the torment which is composed of all imaginable torments surpasses the simplest death.

But we do not conceive or express unto you that death that is to come. Believe it, when the soul is out of the body it becomes a most pure activity in all sense and all knowledge. And seeing where the soul is dulled and dampished[2] in the body and how it is capable of so much grief or joy, pleasure or pain, we may conclude that, being loosed from these stupefying earthly chains,

---

1. cito, procul, diu.
2. *dampished*: bewildered.

it is capable of infinitely more vexation, or contentation,[3] in a higher and purer strain.

Therefore, we may conclude with the apostle, that all men by nature are miserable in life, but infinitely more miserable in death. Only the man who is in Jesus Christ, in whose spirit Christ dwells and who has made a temple of his body for offering up reasonable service in it (Rom. 12:1)—only that man is happy in life but far happier in death, happy that he was born but infinitely more happy that he was born mortal, born to die, for if the body be dead because of sin, the Spirit is life because of righteousness.

For Those in Christ Death Is an Entrance to Eternal Felicity
Men commonly make their accounts and calculate their time as if death were the end of it. Truly, it would be happiness in the generality of men if that computation was true, either that it had never begun or that it might end here. For that which is the greatest dignity and glory of a man—his immortal soul—it is truly the greatest misery of sinful men because it capacitates them for eternal misery. But if we make our accounts right and take the right period, truly death is but the beginning of our time, that is, of endless and unchangeable endurance in happiness (rather than in misery). Then this life in the body which, in the mistaken view of the short-sighted sons of men, is but a strait and narrow passage into the infinite ocean of eternity, becomes the entrance to eternal felicity. But so inconsiderable it is that, according as the spirit in this passage into eternity is fashioned and formed, so it must continue forever, for where the tree falls, there it lies. Though there may be hope that a tree will sprout again, truly there is no hope that ever the damned soul shall see a spring of joy, and no fear that ever the blessed spirits shall find they have entered a winter of grief. Such is the evenness of eternity that there is no shadow of change in it.

---

3. *contentation*: satisfaction.

O then, how happy are they in whose souls this life is already begun, which shall then come to its meridian, when the glory of the flesh falls down like withered hay into the dust! The life as well as the light of the righteous is progressive. It is shining more and more till that day come, the day of death, only worthy to be called the present day because it brings perfection as it mounts the soul in the highest point of the orb; there is no declining from that again. The spirit is now alive in some holy affections and motions, breathing upward, wrestling toward that point. The soul is now in part united to the Fountain of life, by loving attendance and obedience, and it is longing to be more closely united. The inward senses are exercised about spiritual things, but the burden of this mansion of clay does much to dull and damp them; it proves a great remora[4] to the spirit. For the body indisposes and weakens the soul much.

For the Believer Death Is Release from a Prison to Peace, Joy, and Love

It is life as in an infant, though a reasonable soul be there, yet overwhelmed with the incapacity of the organs. This body is truly a prison of restraint and confinement to the soul and often loathsome and ugly through the filthiness of sin. But when the spirit is delivered from this necessary burden and impediment, oh how lively is that life it then lives! Then the life, peace, joy, love, and delight of the soul surmounts all that is possible here, further than the highest exercise of the soul of the wisest men surpasses the brutish like apprehensions of an infant! Indeed, then the Christian comes to his full stature and is a perfect man when he ceases to be a man.

An Earnest Appeal

How will you not be persuaded, beloved in the Lord, to long after this life, to have Christ formed in your hearts? For truly the

---

4. *remora*: obstruction or hindrance.

generality have not so much as Christ fashioned in their outward habit, but within are only darkness, earthiness, and wickedness, and without are only impiety and profanity. Will you not long for this life? For now you are dead while you live, as the apostle speaks of widows that live in pleasure (1 Tim. 5:11–13). The more the soul be satisfied with earthly things, it is the deeper buried in the grave of the flesh and the further separated from God. Alas! many of you know no other life than that which you now live in the body; you neither apprehend what this new birth is, nor what the perfect stature of it shall be afterward. But truly while it is thus, you are but walking shadows, breathing clay, and no more.

A godly man used to calculate the years of his nativity from his second birth, his conversion to God in Christ; and truly, this is the true period of the right calculation of life, of that life which shall not see death. True life has but one period, that is, the beginning of it, for end it has none. Thus, I beseech you, reckon your years in this manner. Yet I fear that you reckon yourselves, many of you, yet dead in sins and trespasses. Is that life, I pray you, to eat, to drink, to sleep, to play, to walk, to work? Is there anything in all these worthy of a reasonable soul which must survive the body and so cease from such things forever? Think within yourselves, do you live any other life than this? What is your life but a tedious and wearisome repetition of such brutish actions which are only terminated on the body? Oh then, how miserable are you, if you have no other period to reckon from than the day of your birth! If there be not a second birthday before your burial, you may make your reckoning to be banished eternally from the life of God.

As for you, Christians, whom God has quickened by the Spirit of His Son, be much in the exercise of this new life and that will maintain and advance it. Let your care be about your spirits. To hearten you in this study and to beget in you the hope of eternal life, look much and lay fast hold on that life-giving Savior who, by His righteous life and accursed death, has purchased by His own blood both happiness and holiness to us. Consider what debtors you are to Him who loved not His own life and spared it not, to purchase this life to us. Let our thoughts and affections be occupied about this high purchase of our Savior's which is freely bestowed on them that will have it and will believe in Him for it. If we be not satisfied with such a low and wretched life as is in the body, He will give a higher and more enduring life and only worthy of that name.

SERMON 30

The Blessed Hope

But if the Spirit of him that raised up Jesus from the dead dwell in you, he that raised up Christ from the dead shall also quicken your mortal bodies by his Spirit that dwelleth in you. —ROMANS 8:11

It is true the soul is incomparably better than the body and he is only worthy of the name of a man and of a Christian who prefers this more excellent part and employs his study and time about it, for he regards his body as only for the noble guest that lodges within it. Therefore, it is one of the prime consolations that Christianity affords that it provides chiefly for the happy estate of this immortal piece in man which, truly, is alone sufficient to draw our souls wholly after religion. Suppose the body should never taste of the fruits of it but die and rise no more and never be awakened out of its sleep, yet it were a sufficient ground of engagement to godliness that the life and well-being of the far better part in man is secured for eternity. For such a future is infinitely more than all things beside can truly promise us or be able to perform.

Certainly, whatsoever else you give your hearts to and spend your time upon, either it will leave you in the midst of your days and at your end you shall be a fool or else, leaving it at the end of your days as you must, you will find yourselves as much disappointed. Or, to speak more precisely, because, when your time is ending and your life and being is but at its beginning,[1] you must then bid an eternal adieu to all these things whereupon your hearts are set when you are but beginning truly to be. But this is the only proper and true good of the soul—Christ being in it—most portable and easily carried about with you. Yea, it is He who makes the soul no burden to itself and helps it to carry all things easily—and then most inseparable. For when Christ is in the soul it is the spring of a never-ending life of peace, joy, and contentation in the fountain of an infinite goodness; therefore it outwears time and age as well as the immortal being of the soul. Yea, such is the strength of this consolation that then the soul is most closely united and fully possessed of that which is its peculiar and satisfying good when it leaves the body in the dust and escapes out of this prison unto that glorious liberty.

The Necessity of the Body of Flesh to Be Discarded at Death
But yet, there is besides this an additional comfort comprehended in the verse read, that the sleep of the body is not perpetual but that it shall once be awakened and raised up to the fellowship of this glory (1 Cor. 15:43), for though a man should be abundantly satisfied if he possesses his own soul, yet no man hates his own flesh. The soul has some kind of natural inclination to a body suitable unto it and in this it differs from an angel. Therefore the apostle, when he expresses his earnest groan for the intimate presence of his soul with Christ, he subjoins this correction, "not that we would be unclothed, but clothed upon" it (2 Cor. 5:1–4). If it were possible, says he, we would be glad to have the society of the body in this glory. We would not desire to cast off those clothes of flesh but rather that the garment of glory might be spread over them. That, however, would not be needed because our clothes of flesh are old and ragged and would not suit well in glory, for our earthly tabernacle is ruinous and would not be

---

1. That is, departing from this earthly life and entering beyond the grave into eternity.

fit for such a glorious guest to dwell in. Therefore, it is needful that it be taken down.

The Resurrection of the Body

Well, then, here is an overplus[2] and, as it were, a surcharge[3] of consolation that, seeing for the present it is expedient to put off the present clothing of flesh and take down the present earthly house, yet the day is coming that the same clothes, renewed, shall be put on and the same house repaired and made suitable to heaven. Indeed, it shall be built up and this mortal body shall be quickened with that same spirit that now quickens the soul and makes it live out of the body. So the sweet and beloved friends, who parted with so much pain and grief, shall meet again with so much pleasure and joy and, as they were sharers together in the miseries of this life, shall participate also in the blessedness of the next. It will be as it was with Saul and Jonathan, "lovely and pleasant in their lives" (2 Sam. 1:23); though for a time separated in death, yet not always divided. Now this is the highest top of happiness to which nothing can be added. It is comprehensive of the whole man and it is comprehensive of all that can be imagined to be the perfective good of man.

It is no wonder, then, that the apostle reckons this doctrine of the resurrection among the foundations of Christianity (Heb. 6:1–2), for truly these two—the immortality of the soul and the resurrection of the mortal body—are the two ground-stones or pillars of true religion; if they be not well settled in the hearts of men, all religion is tottering and ruinous and unable to support itself. That the soul cannot taste death or see corruption and that the body shall but taste it and, as it were, salute it and cannot always abide under the power of it, these are the prime foundations upon which all Christian persuasion is built. For without these being laid down in the lowest and deepest part of the

---

2. *overplus*: excess or additional amount.
3. *surcharge*: overload.

heart, all exhortations to a holy and righteous life are weak and ineffectual, all consolations are empty and vain. In a word, religion is but an airy speculation that has no consistence but in the imaginations of men; it is a house upon sand that can abide no blast of temptation, no wave of misery, but must straightway fall to the ground.

Why Are Men's Hearts So Incapable of Loving the Gospel?

From whence is it, I pray you, that the persuasions of the gospel have so little power upon men that the plain and plentiful publication of a Savior is of so small virtue to stir up the hearts of men to take hold on Him? How comes it to pass that the precepts and prohibitions of the Most High God, coming forth under His authority, lay so little restraint on men's corruptions? And how is it that so few will be persuaded to stop their course and come off the ways that they are accustomed to? Or why is it that men pull away the shoulder and stop the ear and make their hearts so adamant, incapable of being affected with either the authority or love of the gospel? And why do so few dance when He pipes unto us and why do so few lament when He mourns (Matt. 11:17)? Is it not because these two foundations are not laid, and men's hearts not dug deep by earnest consideration to receive these ground-stones of Christianity: the belief of their souls, eternal survival after the dust, and of the reviving and resurrection of the body, after it has slept a while in the dust?

I remember heathens have had some noble and rare conceptions about virtue, and some have labored to enamor men with the native beauty of it and to persuade them that it was a sufficient reward to itself. And truly it would far more become a Christian, who knows the high and divine pattern of holiness to be God Himself and so must needs behold a far surpassing beauty and excellency in the image of God than in all earthly things—I say, it would become him to accustom himself to a dutiful observance of religion, even without any respect to the reward of it. He would train his heart to do homage to God out of a loyal affection and respect to His majesty and from the love of the very intrinsic beauty of obedience, without borrowing always from such selfish considerations of our own happiness or misery.

Notwithstanding, such is the posture of man's spirit now that he cannot at all be engaged to the love of religion, except some seen advantage conciliate it. Therefore, the Lord makes use of such selfish principles in drawing men to Himself and keeping them still with Him. And, truly, considering man's infirmity, this is the spirit and life of all religion—immortality and resurrection—those doctrines which give a luster to all and quicken all; they make all to sink deep and are the teaching which makes a Christian steadfast and immoveable (2 Cor. 5:8).

The Quickening Power of Hope

It is certainly hope that is the key to the heart, that opens and shuts it to anything. Hence the apostle Peter (first epistle) first blesses God heartily for the new birth and, in expressing of it, makes hope the very term of that generation; so indeed it must be a substantial thing. "Blessed be God, who has begotten us again to a lively hope" (1:3). Hope has a quickening power in it. It makes all new where it comes and is full of spirit. It is the helmet and anchor of a Christian, that which bears the dent of temptation and makes him steady in religion. No man will put his plow in this ground or sows unto the Spirit but in hope, for he that sows must sow in hope, else his plow will not go deep (1 Cor. 9:10).

This then is the very spirit and life of religion—the resurrection of the dead—without which our faith would be in vain and men would continue still in their sins. Certainly it is the deep inconsideration of this never-ending endurance of our souls and restitution of our bodies to the same immortality that makes the most part of men so slight and superficial in religion. Otherwise, if that were laid to heart, it would not be possible but that men would make religion their business—and their chief business at that.

Christ the Firstfruits

We have here the two genuine causes of the resurrection of the bodies of Christians—the resurrection of Christ and the inhabitation of His Spirit. The influence that the resurrection of Christ has on ours is lively and fully holden out by this apostle in 1 Corinthians 15:17–18 against them who deny the resurrection from the dead: "If Christ be not raised, your faith is in vain; ye are yet in your sins, and they that are asleep are perished." Religion would be nothing but a number of empty words of show, preaching would be a mere vanity and imposture and faith a mere fancy, if this be not laid down as the ground-stone— Christ raised, not as a natural person, but as a common politic person,[4] as the firstfruits of them that sleep. We read that in verses 17 to 20, where he alludes to the ceremony of offering the firstfruits of their harvest (Lev. 23:10–11). For under the law they might not eat of the fruits of the land till they were sanctified. All was counted profane till they were some way consecrated to the Lord. Now, for this end the Lord appointed them to bring one sheaf for all and that was the representative of all the rest of the heap; this was waved before the Lord and lifted up from the earth.

Now, according to the apostle's argument in Romans 11:16, "If the firstfruits be holy, so is the lump," for it represents all the lump, and therefore Jesus Christ, the chief of all His brethren, was made the firstfruits from the dead. That is, He was lifted up from the grave as the representer of all the lump of His elect; so it must needs follow that they shall not continue in the grave, but must in due time partake of that benefit which He has first entered in possession of, in their name and for them. For if this firstfruits be holy, so the whole lump must be holy, and if the firstfruits be risen, so must the lump. You see then the force of the present reason, *If the Spirit that raised Christ dwell in you,*

---

4. *common politic person*: representative of a body of citizens; head of a federation.

He shall also raise you, namely, because He raised up Christ the very firstfruits of all the rest. Thus Christ's resurrection is a sure pledge and token of yours and both together are the main basis and groundwork of all our hope and salvation.

Final Appeal against Foolish Neglect
It is the neglect and inconsideration of this that makes the most part of pretended Christians to walk according to that Epicurean principle, "Let us eat and drink, for to-morrow we shall die" (1 Cor. 15:32). As if there were no life to come, they withhold nothing from their carnal minds that can satisfy or please their lusts. But for you who desire a part in this resurrection and dare scarcely believe so great a thing or entertain such a high hope because of the sight of your unworthiness, as you would be awakened by this hope to "righteousness, and to sin no more" (1 Cor. 15:34), so you may encourage yourselves to that hope by the resurrection of Christ; for it is that which has the mighty influence to beget you "unto a lively hope by the resurrection of Jesus Christ from the dead" (1 Peter 1:3).

Look upon this as the grand intent and special design of Christ's both dying and rising again that He might be the firstfruits to sanctify all the lump. Nevertheless, it is not the desert[5] of your bodies, for they are often a great impediment and retardment to the spirit. They lodge the enemy within their walls when he is chased out of the mind by the law of the Spirit of life. Nevertheless, it is the great design of God, through the whole work of redemption and the desert of Christ your head, that you may therefore entertain that hope. But take heed to walk worthy of it and that it is, "if we have this hope, let us purify ourselves" (cf. 1 John 3:3). Let us who believe that we are risen with Christ set our affections on things above, else we dishonor Him that is risen in our name and we dishonor that temple of the Holy Ghost which He will one day make so glorious.

---

5. *desert*: deserved reward or punishment.

SERMON 31

The Twofold Resurrection

But if the Spirit of him that raised up Jesus from the dead dwell in you, he that raised up Christ from the dead shall also quicken your mortal bodies by his Spirit that dwelleth in you. —ROMANS 8:11

The Twofold Resurrection
As there is a twofold death—the death of the soul, and the death of the body—so there is a double resurrection—the resurrection of the soul from the power of sin and the resurrection of the body from the grave. As the first death is that which is spiritual, then is followed by that which is bodily, so the first resurrection is of the spirit, followed by the second of the body. These two have a connection together, therefore says the apostle John, "Blessed are they who have part in the first resurrection, for on such the second death has no power, but they shall be priests of God and of Christ" (Rev. 20:6). Although death must seize on their bodies, yet the sting wherein the strength of it lies is taken away by Christ so that it has no power to hurt him whose spirit is raised out of the grave of sin.

Truly, it is hard to tell which is the greatest change or the most difficult: to raise a body out of corruption to life, or to raise a soul out of sin to grace. But both are the greatest changes that can be and are shadowed out under the similitude of the greatest in nature, for our conversion to God is a new birth, a new creation and a resurrection in Scripture style; so both require one and the same power, the almighty power of His Spirit: "You who were dead in trespasses and sins has he quickened" (Eph. 2:1). Oh, what a notable change! It makes them no longer the same men but new creatures and therefore it is the death of sin and the resurrection of the soul.

The Dire State of the Unregenerate

As long as the soul is under the chains of darkness and power of sin it is free from the dead, buried in the vilest sepulchre. Old graves, full of rottenness and dead men's bones, are nothing to express the lamentable case of such a soul, and yet such are all by nature. Whatsoever excellence or endowment men may have from their birth or education, yet certainly they are but apparitions rather than any real substance and, which is worse, their body is the sepulchre of their souls. If the corruption of a soul were sensible, we would think all the putrefactions of bodily things as but shadows of it. And therefore no sooner is there any inward life begotten in a soul, the very first exercise of it is the abhorrence of the soul upon the sight and smell of its own loathsomeness.

Now, there is no hope of any reviving. Though all the wisdom and art of men and angels were employed in this business, there is nothing able to quicken one such soul until it please the Lord to speak such a word as He did to Lazarus, "Arise, come forth," and send His Spirit to accomplish His Word and this will do it. When the Spirit comes into the soul He quickens it and this is the first resurrection. Oh, blessed are they who have part in this, whose souls are drawn out of the dungeon of darkness and ignorance and brought forth to behold this glorious light that shines in the gospel. Then they are raised out of the grave of the lusts of ignorance to live unto God henceforth, for such have their part in the second resurrection to life. For you see these are conjoined: "If the Spirit of him that raised up Jesus from the dead dwell in you, he that raised up Christ from the dead shall also quicken your mortal bodies by his Spirit that dwelleth in you" (Rom. 8:11). You see here two grounds and reasons of the resurrection of the body—Christ's rising and the Spirit's indwelling. Now I find these in the Scripture made the two fountains of all Christianity, both of the first and second resurrection.

The Pledge of the Believer's Resurrection

The resurrection of Christ is an evidence of our justification, the cause of our quickening or vivification, and the ground and pledge of our last resurrection; all these are grounds of strong consolation. The first you have in Romans 4:25: "Christ died for our sins, and rose for our justification," and the thirty-fourth verse of this chapter, "It is Christ that died, yea rather, that is risen again…who is he that shall condemn?" Here is a clear evidence that He has paid the debt wholly and satisfied justice fully. Since He was under the power of death imprisoned by justice, certainly He would not have won free had He not paid the uttermost farthing; therefore His glorious resurrection is a sure manifestation of His present satisfaction—it is a public acquittal and absolution of Him from all our debt and so, by consequence, of all He died for. For their debt was laid upon Him and now He is discharged.

Therefore the believing soul may tremblingly boast, "Who shall condemn me? For it is God that justifies." Why? Because all my sins were laid on Christ and God has in a most solemn manner acquitted and discharged him from all when He raised Him from the dead. Therefore, He and none other can sue me nor prosecute a plea against me, since my cautioner is fully exonered[1] of this undertaking, even by the great Creditor, God Himself. But then, His resurrection is a pawn[2] or pledge of the spiritual raising of the soul from sin. Just as the death of Christ is made

---

1. *exonered*: relieved from a charge, obligation, or duty.
2. *pawn*: surety or guaranty.

the pledge of our dying to sin, so His rising is the pledge of our living to God (Rom. 6:4–5).

The Believer Engrafted into the Risen Christ

These are not mere patterns and examples of spiritual things but assured pledges of the divine virtue and power which He, being raised again, should send abroad throughout the world. For, as there are coronation gifts when kings are solemnly installed in office, so there are coronation mercies, triumphal gifts. When Christ rose and ascended, He bestowed His gifts on the world (Eph. 4:8–13). And certainly these are the greatest gifts—the virtue of His death to kill the old man and the power of His resurrection to quicken the new. And by faith a believer is united and engrafted into Him as a plant into a choice stock. By virtue and sap coming from Christ's death and resurrection he is transformed into the similitude of both; he grows into the likeness of His death by dying to sin, by crucifying these inward affections and inclinations to it. Thus he grows up into the similitude of His resurrection by newness of life, or being alive to God, in holy desires and endeavors after holiness and obedience. In this way the first resurrection of the soul flows from Christ's resurrection.

But add unto this that Christ's rising is the pledge and pawn of the second resurrection, that is, of the body, for He is the head, and we are the members. Now, it is most incongruous that the head should rise and not draw up the members after Him. Certainly, He will not cease till He has drawn up all His members to Him. If the head be above water, it is a sure pledge that the body will win out of the water; likewise, if the root be alive, certainly the branches will out in springtime and shall live also. There is that connection between Christ and believers, that wonderful communication between them, that for Himself Christ did nothing, was nothing, and had nothing done to Him, but in what He did and was and suffered, He was personating[3]

---

3. *personating*: representing.

them, and all the benefit and advantage now redounds to them. He would not be considered of as a person by Himself but would rather be still taken in with the children. As for love He came down and took flesh to be like them and did take their sin and misery off them. So He was content to be looked upon by God as in the place of sinners as the chief sinner, so he is content and desirous that we should look on Him as in the place of sinners, as dying and as rising for us, as having no excellence or privilege incommunicable to us.

Nor was this hid from the church of old but was presented as the grand consolation, "Thy dead men shall live, together with my dead body they shall rise" (Isa. 26:19). Therefore, may poor souls awake and sing! Though they must dwell in the dust, yet as the dew and influence of heaven makes herbs to spring out of the earth, so the virtue of this resurrection shall make the earth and sea and air to cast out and render their dead. Upon what a sure and strong chain hangs the salvation of poor sinners! I wish Christians might salute one another with this: "Christ is risen, and so comfort one another with these words"—or rather, that everyone would apply this cordial to his own heart, "Christ is risen!" And you know what a golden chain this draws after it, that therefore we must rise and live!

Believers Become Temples of the Holy Spirit

The other cause, which is more immediate and will actively accomplish it, is the Spirit dwelling in us, for there is a suitable method here too. As the Lord first raised the head, Christ, and will then raise the members, and He that does the one cannot but do the other, so the Spirit first raises the soul from the woeful fall into sin, which killed us, and so makes it a temple, and the body too—for both are bought with a price and, therefore, the Spirit takes possession of both. But the inmost residence is in the soul while the bodily members are made servants of righteousness. This is a great honor and dignity when we consider the base employment they had once. Therefore it is most suitable that He who has thus dwelled in both repair His own dwelling-house. For here it is ruinous, and, therefore, must be cast down.

Because it was once a temple for the holy God, therefore it will be repaired and built again. For He that once honored it with His presence will not suffer corruption always to dwell in it. For what Christ purchased by His humiliation and suffering, the Spirit has this commission to perform this work of restoration. And what is it but the restitution of mankind to a happier estate in the second Adam than ever we had in the first Adam.

The Bodies of Believers Made Like Christ's Risen Body
Now since our Lord, who was pleased to take on our flesh, did not put it off again, but admits it to the fellowship of the same glory in heaven; for in that He died, He dies no more and because death has no more dominion over Him, He will never be wearied or ashamed of that human clothing of flesh. And therefore certainly, so that the children may be like the father, the followers like their captain, the members not disproportionate to the head, the branches not different and heterogeneous to the stock and—that our rising in Christ may leave no footstep of our falling, no remainder of our misery—the Spirit of Christ will also quicken the mortal bodies of believers and make them like Christ's glorious body. It will be as the apostle says in verse 17, "that we will also be glorified together" with Christ.

This must be done with divine power—and what more powerful than the Spirit? For it is the spirits or subtle parts in all creatures that cause all motions and work all effects. What then is that almighty Spirit not able to do? You have shadows and convincing evidence for this in nature: what is the spring but a resurrection of the earth? Is not the world every year renewed as it rises again out of the grave of winter, as you find elegantly expressed in Psalm 107? And do not the grains of seed die in the clods before they rise to the harvest (1 Cor. 15:35–45)? All the vicissitudes and alterations in nature give us a plain draft[4] of this great change and certainly it is one Spirit that effects all.

A Solemn Warning with an Urgent Invitation

But though there be the same power required to raise up the bodies of the godly and ungodly, yet oh, what infinite distance and difference in the nature and ends of their resurrections! There is the resurrection of life and there is the resurrection of condemnation (John 5:28). Oh, happy are they who rise to life that ever they died! But oh, miserable, thrice wretched, are all others that they may not ever be dead! The immortality of the soul will be infinite misery because it is that which eternalizes their misery. Thus, when this overplus of the incorruptibility of the body is added and the whole man made an inconsumable subject for that fire to feed upon perpetually, then what heart can conceive it without horror! And yet we hear it often without any such affection. It is a strange life that death is the only refreshment of it, and yet this may not be had: "they shall seek death, and it shall fly from them" (Rev. 9:6).

Now, my beloved, I would desire this discourse might open a way for the hearty and cordial entertainment of the gospel and that you might be persuaded to "awake unto righteousness and sin no more" (1 Cor. 15:34). Be not deceived, my brethren, "flesh and blood cannot inherit the kingdom of God" (1 Cor. 15:50). Certainly, if you have no other image than what you came into the world withal, you cannot have this hope to be conformed one day to the glorious body of Christ. What will become of you in that day, who declare now by the continued vent of your hearts that this Holy Spirit dwells not in you? Alas, how many are such? Oh, pity yourselves, your souls and bodies both. If for love to your bodies you will follow its present lusts, and care only for the things of the body, you act with the greatest enmity and hostility against your own bodies.

---

4. *draft*: sketch or plan.

Consider, I beseech you, the eternal state of both soul and body that your care and study will run in another channel. And for you who have any working of the Spirit in you, whether convincing you of sin and misery and of righteousness in Christ, or sometimes comforting you by the word applied to your hearts or teaching you another way than the world walks into, I recommend unto you the exhortation of the apostle: "Wherefore, my brethren, be steadfast, unmoveable, always abounding in the work of the Lord, knowing your labor is not in vain in the Lord" (1 Cor. 15:58).

SERMON 32

The Believer's Unlimited Eternal Debt of Love

Therefore, brethren, we are debtors, not to the flesh, to live after the flesh. —ROMANS 8:12

The Essential Unity of Interwoven Gospel Truth

All things in Christianity have a near and strait conjunction. It is so entire and absolute a piece that if one link be loose, all the chain falls to the ground, and if one be well fastened upon the heart, it brings all along with it. Some speak of all truths, even in nature, that they are knit so together that any truth may be concluded out of every truth, at least by a long circuit of deduction and reasoning. But whatsoever be of that, certainly religion is a more entire thing and all the parts of it more nearly conjoined together that they may mutually enforce one another. Precepts and promises are thus linked together that, if any soul lay hold upon any promise of grace, he draws along with it the obligation of some precept to walk suitable to such precious promises. There is no encouragement you can indeed fasten upon, but it will join you as nearly to the commandment; and no consolation in the gospel, that does not carry within its bosom an exhortation to holy walking.

Again, on the other hand, there is no precept, but it should lead you straightway to a promise; no exhortation, but it is environed before and behind with a strong consolation; thus, it pierces the deeper and goes down the sweeter. Therefore, you see how easily the apostle digresses from the one to the other—how sweetly and pertinently these are interwoven in his discourse.

Consolation as Both Firm Ground and a Fast-Flowing River
The first word of the chapter is a word of strong consolation: "There is no condemnation to them that are in Christ," and this like a flood carries all down with it—all precepts and exhortations—and the soul of a believer with them. Therefore, he subjoins an exhortation to holy and spiritual walking upon that very ground. And because commandments of this nature will not float (so to speak) unless they have much water of that kind and cannot have such a swift course except the tide of such encouragements flow fast, therefore he opens that spring again in the preceding words of verse 11, and lets the rivers of consolation flow forth, even the hope of immortality and eternal life. This certainly will raise up a soul that was on the ground and carry him above in motion of obedience. Therefore, he may well, in the next place, stir them up to their duty, and mind them of their obligation. "Therefore, brethren, we are debtors not to the flesh" (Rom. 8:12).

To make this the more effectual, he drops it in with affection, in a sweet compilation of love and equality, "therefore brethren." There is nothing so powerful in persuasion as love; it will sweeten a bitter and unpleasant reproof, making it go down more easily, though it makes less noise than threatening, severity, and authority; yet it is more forcible for it insinuates itself and, in a manner, surprises the soul and so prevents all resistance. As when the sun made the traveler part with his cloak whereas the wind and rain made him hold it faster,[1] so affection will prevail where authority and terror cannot; it will melt that which a stronger power cannot break.

---

1. Aesop's fable about the competition between the Wind and the Sun.

The Calm Voice of Love
The story of Elijah in 1 Kings 19 may give some representation of this. The Lord was not in the strong wind nor in the terrible earthquake nor yet in the fire, but in the calm, still voice. The Lord has chosen this way of publishing His grace in the gospel because the sum of it is love to sinners and goodwill toward men. He holds it forth in the calm voice of love and those who are His ambassadors should be clothed with such an affection if they intend to prevail with men and to engage their affections. Oh, that we were possessed with that brotherly love, one toward another for the salvation one of another; especially, that the preachers of the gospel might be thus kindly affectioned toward others and that you would take it thus, the calling you off the ways of sin as an act of the greatest love.

A Debt That Binds All

But then consider the equality of this obligation, for there is nothing pressed upon you but what lies as heavily upon them that press it. This debt binds all. Oh, that the ministers of the gospel could carry the impression of this on their hearts that, when they persuade others, they may withal persuade themselves and, when they speak to others, they may sit down among the hearers! If an apostle of so eminent dignity levels himself in this consideration ("Therefore, brethren, we are debtors"), how much more ought pastors and teachers to come in the same rank and degree of debt and obligation with others.

Truly this is the great obstruction of the success of the gospel that those who bind burdens on others do not themselves touch them with one of their fingers (Matt. 23:4), and while they seem serious in persuading others, yet withal declare by their carriage that they do not believe themselves what they bear upon others; consequently, that preaching seems to be an imposture, and affections in persuading of others seem to be borrowed, as it were, in one scene, to be laid down again when out of it.

Without Exception, All Are Debtors

But then again, there is a misconceit[2] among people that this holy and spiritual walking is not of common obligation, but peculiar to the preachers of the gospel. Many make their reckoning so, as if they were not called to such high aims and great endeavors. But truly, my beloved, this is a thing of common concern. The Holy Ghost has leveled us all in this point of duty as He has equally exalted all in the most substantial dignities and privileges of the gospel. This bond is upon the highest and upon the lowest. Greatness does not exempt from it, and meanness does not exclude from it. Though commonly great persons fancy an immunity from the strictness of a holy conservation because of their greatness, and often mean and low persons pretend a freedom from such a high obligation because of their lowness, yet certainly all are debt-bound this way and must one day give account.

You that are poor and unlearned and have not received great things of that nature from God, do not think yourselves free, do not absolve yourselves, for there is infinite debt besides. You will have no place for the excuse that you had not great parts,[3] were not learned and so forth. For as the obligation reaches you all, so there is as patent a way to the exercise of religion in the poorest cottage as in the highest palace. You may serve God as acceptably in little as others may do in much. There is no condition so low and abject that lays any restraint on this noble service and employment. This jewel loses not its beauty and virtue when it lies in a dunghill more than when it is set in gold.

The Creditor Is the Spirit

But let us inquire further into this debt: "we are debtors," says he, and he instances who is not the creditor—it is not the flesh by which he gives us to understand who the true creditor is. Therefore,

---

2. *misconceit*: inaccurate idea.
3. *parts*: personal qualities or talents.

if our debt is not to the flesh, to make out the just opposition,[4] the creditor must be the Spirit. "We are debtors," then, to the Spirit. And what is the debt we owe to Him? We may know it that same way; we do not owe to the flesh—"not to the flesh, to live after the flesh"—to make us live after its guidance and direction and so fulfill its lusts. Then, by due consequence, we owe it to the Spirit that we should live after the Spirit and resign ourselves wholly to Him, His guidance and direction.

There is a twofold kind of debt upon the creature, one remissible and pardonable, another irremissible and unpardonable (so to speak). I mean the debt of sin, that is, the guilt of it which is nothing else than the obligation of the sinner over to eternal condemnation by virtue of the curse of God. Every sinner comes under this debt to divine justice, the desert of eternal wrath and the actual ordination by a divine sentence to that wrath.

Christ Is Our Cautioner
Now, indeed, this debt was insoluble to us and utterly unpayable until God sent His Son to be our cautioner; He has paid the debt in His own person by bearing our curse, and so made it pardonable for sinners; thus He has obtained a relaxation from that woeful obligation to death. And this debt, you see, is wholly discharged to them that are in Christ by another sentence repealing the former curse—verse 1, "There is no condemnation to them that are in Christ."

But there is another debt which I may call a debt of duty and obedience which was antecedent to sin, even binding innocent Adam. Therefore, the obligation of the debt of sin has been so far from taking it away that it is rather increased exceedingly. This debt is unpardonable and indispensable. The more of the debt of sin be pardoned and the more the curse be dispensed with, the more the sinner owes of love and obedience to God. "She loved much, because much was forgiven" (Luke 7:43, 47)—and

---

4. *just opposition*: right or logical point to the contrary.

the more was forgiven of sin the more she owed of love, and the more debt was discharged the more she was indebted to him.

The Unlimited Eternal Debt of Love

Therefore, after this general acquittal of all believers in verse 1, here in verse 12 presses this obligation the more strongly. "Therefore, brethren, we are debtors." It is like that debt spoken of in Romans 13:8: "Owe no man anything, but to love one another." By this is not meant that it is unlawful to be debtors to men. No, whatever you owe, before all things else, pay it and you are free; then your debt ceases and your bond is canceled. However, as for the debt of love and benevolence, you must so owe that to all men as never to be discharged of it, never to be freed from it. When you have so done, this has no limitation of time or action; so it is here. When other debts are paid, men cease to be debtors and then they are free. But here in verse 12 the more he pays the more he is bound to pay—he owes, and he owes eternally. His bond is never canceled as long as he continues a creature subsisting in God and abides as a redeemed one in Christ. For as these debts continue, his obligation is eternally recent and fresh as the first day.

Nor does this at all obscure the infinite grace of God, neither does it diminish the happiness of saints that they are not freed from this debt of love and obedience. Rather it illustrates the one and increases the other. For it cannot be supposed to consist with the wisdom and holiness of God to loose His creature from that obligation of loving obedience and subjection, which is essential to it. Neither is it any less repugnant to the happiness of the creature to be free from sin and made debtors unto righteousness.

The Threefold Bond

Now, this debt of duty and obedience has a threefold bond, which because they stand in vigor uncancelled for all eternity, therefore the obligation arising from them is eternal too. The bond of creation, the bond of redemption, and the bond of sanctification—these are distinguished according to the persons of the Trinity, who appear most eminently in them.

We owe our being to the Father, in whom "we live, and move, and have our being" (Acts 17:28); "it is he that has made us, and not we ourselves" (Ps. 100:3); "and we are all the works of his hands" (Isa. 64:8). Now, the debt accruing from this is infinite. If men conceive themselves so much obliged to others for a petty courtesy as to be their servants—if they owe more to their parents, the instruments of their bringing forth into the world—Oh, how infinitely more owe we to God, of whom we are, and from whom we have all! Does the clay owe so much to the potter who does not make it but only fashions it? And what owe we to Him that made us out of nothing and fashioned us while we were yet without form! Truly, all relations, all obligations vanish when this comes forth, because all that a man has is less than himself, less than his immortal spirit and he owes that alone to God. Besides, whatsoever debt there is to other fellow creatures in anything, God is the principal creditor in that bond. All the creatures are but the servants of this King which, at His sole appointment, bring along His gifts unto us and, therefore, we owe no more to them than to the hands of the messenger that is sent.

Now, by this account nothing is our own, not ourselves, not our members, not our goods, but all are His to be used and bestowed, not at the will and arbitrament[5] of creatures, but to be absolutely and solely at His disposal who has the sole sovereign right to them. Therefore, you may take up the heinousness of sin, how monstrous and misshapen a thing it is, that breaks this inviolable law of creation, withdrawing the creature from subjection to Him, in whom alone it can subsist. Oh how disordered are the courses and lives of men! Men living to themselves, their own lusts, after their own will, as if they had made themselves. Men using their members as weapons of unrighteousness

---

5. *arbitrament*: judgment.

against God, as if their tongues, hands, and feet were their own, or the devils, and not God's.

Call to mind this obligation, "Remember now thy Creator" (Eccl. 12:1). That memento would be a strong engagement to another course than most take. How absurd would you think it to please yourselves in displeasing Him if you but minded the bond of creation! But when there are two other superadded—what we owe to the Son for coming down in the likeness of sinful flesh for us, and what we owe to the Holy Ghost for quickening our spirits and afterward for the resurrection of our bodies—whose hearts would not these overcome and lead captive to His love and obedience?

SERMON 33

The Threefold Cord and Our Souls on the Weighing Scales

Therefore, brethren, we are debtors, not to the flesh, to live after the flesh. For if ye live after the flesh, ye shall die.
—ROMANS 8:12–13

The Threefold Cord
Was that not enough to contain men in obedience to God—the very essential bond of dependence upon God as the original and fountain of His being! And yet man has cast away this cord from Him and, by transgressing His holy commandments, withdrawn from that allegiance he did owe to his Maker. But God, not willing that all should perish, has confirmed and strengthened that primitive obligation by two other cords as strong if not more so: if the Father did most eminently appear in the first, the Son is manifested in the second. This is the work of the redemption of man, no less glorious than his first creation. He made him first, and then, second, He sent His own Son in the likeness of sinful flesh, and, third, to make him again by His Spirit. And now "a threefold cord is not easily broken" (Eccl. 4:12).

It seems this should bind invincibly and constrain us not to be our own but the Lord's. Now, truly, they who are in Jesus Christ are thrice indebted wholly to God. But the two last obligations are the most special and most wonderful that God sent His Son for us to redeem us from sin and misery and, to restore man to happiness, took on a miserable and accursed habit[1]—that so glorious a person gave Himself for so base a one: that so excellent a Lord became a servant for the rebel; that He, whose the earth is and the fullness thereof, did empty Himself of all to supply us. In a word, the most wonderful exchange be made that ever the sun saw—God for men, His life a ransom for their life.

The Second Cord—Redemption by Christ and Its Implications
All the rare inventions and fancied stories of men come infinitely short of this. The light never saw majesty so abased and love so expressed as in this matter and all to this purpose: that we who had undone ourselves might be made up again and the righteousness of the law fulfilled in us. At first, He made us but it cost Him nothing but a word; now, to buy that which was taken captive by sin and at so dear a rate—"you are bought with a price" (1 Cor. 6:20), and this price more precious than the sum of heaven and earth could amount to. Suppose by some rare alchemy the earth was all converted into gold and the heavens into precious stones, yet these corruptible and material things come as far short of this ransom as a heap of dung is unproportioned to a mass of gold or heap of jewels.

Now, you that are thus bought, may you not conclude, "Therefore, brethren, we are debtors," and whereof? Of ourselves, for we, our persons, estates, and all were sold and have been bought with this price; therefore we are not our own but the Lord's and therefore we ought to "glorify God in our bodies and spirits which are God's" (1 Cor. 6:20). Should we henceforth claim an interest and propriety in ourselves? Should we have a will of our own? Should we serve ourselves with our members? Oh how monstrous and absurd were that! Certainly, a believing heart cannot but look upon that as the greatest indignity and vilest impiety that ever the sun shone upon. Ingratitude has a note of ignominy put upon it even among heathens. They esteemed the

---

1. *habit*: bodily condition or appearance.

reproach of it the compend[2] of all reproaches: "If you pronounce a man ungrateful, you say all that can be said about him."[3] And truly it has the most abominable visage of any vice, yea, it is all sins drawn through other[4] in one table.

Certainly, a godly heart cannot but account this execrable and detestable. For henceforth those with a godly heart will have a proper and peculiar will and pleasure and could not but devote themselves wholly to God's will and pleasure, for whose pleasure all were first created and who then redeemed us by the blood of His Son. I wish we could have this image of ingratitude always observant to our eyes and minds when we are enticed with our lusts to study our own satisfaction.

The Third Cord—The Indwelling Spirit

But there is a third bond superadded to this, which mightily aggravates the debt. As well as giving His Son for us, He has given us His Spirit to dwell within. And oh the marvelous and strange effects that this Spirit has in the favors of men! He truly repairs that image of God which sin broke down. He furnishes the soul and supplies it in all its necessities. He is a light and life to it—a spring of everlasting life and consolation. So that to the Spirit we owe that we are made again after His image, and the precious purchase of Christ applied unto our souls. For Him has our Savior left to execute His latter will on behalf of His children. And these things are but the firstfruits of the Spirit. Any peace or joy or love or obedience are but an earnest of that which is coming. We shall be yet more beholden to Him. When the walls of flesh are taken down He will carry forth the soul into that glorious liberty of the sons of God; not long after He shall quicken our very dust and raise it up in glory to the fellowship of that happiness.

---

2. *compend*: summary.
3. Ingratum si dixeris, omnia dixeris.
4. That is, united or interwoven.

Now, my beloved, consider what all this tends to; mark the inference you should make from it. "Therefore, brethren, we are debtors"—debtors indeed, under infinite obligations for infinite mercies. But what is the debt we owe? Truly it might be conceived to be some rare thing, equivalent to such inconceivable benefits. But mark what it is, "to live after the Spirit, and not after the flesh" (vv. 1 and 4), to conform our affections and actions and the tenor of our way and course to the direction of the Spirit; that is, to have our spirits led and enlightened by the Holy Spirit and not to follow the indictment of our flesh and carnal minds.

Now truly, it is a wonder that it is no other thing than this, for this is no other thing than what we owe to ourselves and to our own natures, so to speak. For truly there is a conformity and suitability of some things to the very nature of man that are beautiful. Some things are decent and becoming for it, other things are indecent and unbecoming, unsuitable to the very reasonable being of man in that they put a stain and blot upon it.

Indeed, there is nothing that can be conceived more agreeable to the very constitution of man's nature than this, that the far better and more excellent part should lead and command and the baser and earthly part should obey and follow. That the flesh should minister and serve the spirit, "does not even nature itself teach it?"[5] And yet no heavier yoke is put upon us than what our own nature has put upon us already which indeed is wonderful! And certainly this wonderful attempering of His laws unto the very natural exigence[6] of the spirit of man, makes the transgression of them so much the more heinous.

Now, all these three forementioned bonds do jointly bind on this law upon man. In general they oblige men strongly to

---

5. This quotation from 1 Cor. 11:14 was the apostle's comment on the shamefulness of men wearing their hair long. Binning is extrapolating it to include other self-evident ethical issues.

6. *exigence*: urgent needs.

subjection and obedience to the will of God, but particularly they have a constraining influence upon this living "after the Spirit" and not "after the flesh." Our very creation speaks this forth, when God made man after His own image, when He beautified the spirit of man with that divine similitude and likeness in that He breathed a spirit from heaven and took a body out of the dust; He then exalted that heavenly piece to some participation of His own nature.

The Vital Necessity of Keeping the Body in Subjection
Does not all this cry aloud upon us, that the order of creation is now dissolved—the beauty of it is marred, all is turned upside down—when men's passions and senses are their only guides and the principles of light in their conscience are choked and stifled? Does not all this teach us plainly that we should not "live after the flesh" because we owe not so much to this brutish part as to enthrone it and empower it over us? It would be the vilest anarchy and most intolerable confusion and usurpation to give it the power over us as most men do. Nay, can there be any order or beauty in man till the spirit be unfettered from the chains of fleshly lusts and restored to their native dignity and so keep the body in subjection? Indeed, Paul says so: "I keep under my body, and bring it into subjection" (1 Cor. 9:27): I beat it down because it is an imperious slave—an usurping slave—and will command if not beaten and kept under.

Again, Christ, has put a bond upon us to this very same. He has strengthened this obligation with a new cord in that He gave His precious life a ransom for the souls of men. This was the principal thing He paid for—the body only being an accessory and appendix to the soul—for it is said, "For the redemption of their soul is precious, and it ceaseth for ever" (Ps. 49:8), and "Or what can a man give in exchange for his soul?" (Mark 8:37). For what material thing can equalize a spirit? Many things may be had far more precious and fine than the body but all of them have no proportion to a spiritual being.

Man's Soul on the Weighing Scales

Now then, in that so dear a ransom and so infinite a price must be given for the spirit of man, it declares the infinite worth and excellence of it above the body and above all visible things. And here is, indeed, the greatest confirmation that can be imagined. God has valued it: He has put the soul of man in the balance to find something equal in weight of dignity and worth and, when all that is in heaven and earth is put in the other scale, the soul is down-weight by far. There is such distance that there is no proportion; only the life and blood of His own Son weighs it down and is an overvalue.

Therefore, in our redemption, we have a visible demonstration, as it were, of the infinite obligation of this law not to live after that contemptible part, our *flesh*, but to follow after the motions and directions of an enlightened spirit. We are not to spend our thoughts, care, and time upon our bodies, making provision for the lusts thereof—as most men do and all by nature are now inclined to do—but rather to be taken up with the immortal precious jewel that is within. We must be concerned how to have it rubbed and cleansed from all the filth that sin and the flesh have cast upon it, and restored to that native beauty, the image of God in righteousness and holiness (Eph. 4:24).

If you, in your practice and affection, turn the scales otherwise, and make the body and things of the body, supposing even the whole world, down-weight in your affection and imagination, you have plainly contradicted the just measure of the sanctuary and, in effect, you have declared that "Christ died in vain" (cf. 1 Cor. 15:14, 17) and gave His life out of an error and mistake of the worth of the soul. You say He needed not to have given such a price for it, seeing every day you weigh it down with every trifle of momentary fleshly satisfaction.

Believers Must Be Resigned to the Holy Spirit

Last, the Spirit binds this fast upon us, for He has chosen for His habitation the soul of man and there He delights to dwell in the heart of the contrite and humble; this habitation He intends to beautify and garnish and to restore it to that primitive excellence it once had. The spirit of man is nearer His nature and more capable of being conformed unto it; therefore, the Spirit's peculiar and special work is about our spirits. First, to enlighten and convince them, then second, to reform and direct them and lead them. This forcibly binds and constrains a believer certainly to resign himself to the Spirit, to study how to order his walk after that direction, and to be more and more distracted from the satisfaction of his body; else he cannot choose but grieve the Spirit, his best friend, who alone is the fountain of joy and peace to him and, being grieved, cannot but also grieve the believer himself.

Our Only Debt to the Flesh Is Its Mortification

Now, my beloved, consider if you owe so much to the flesh, whether or not it be so steadable[7] and profitable unto you? And if you think it can give you a sufficient reward to compensate all your pains in satisfying it, go on; I believe nonetheless, that you can reckon no good office[8] that ever it did you and your expectation is less. What fruit have you of all but shame and vexation of conscience? And what can you expect but death, the last fruits of it? What then do you owe unto it? Are you debtors to its pleasure and satisfaction which has never done you good but will do you eternal hurt? Consider whether you are so much bound and obliged to it as to lose your souls for it and whether or not you be not more obliged to God the Father and His Son Jesus Christ, to "walk not after the flesh but after the Spirit" (verse 4), though for the present it should be painful to beat down your body. You are debtors indeed, but you owe nothing to the flesh but stripes and mortification.

---

7. *steadable*: helpful or advantageous.
8. *office*: service.

SERMON 34

Choose This Day Whom You Will Serve

For if ye live after the flesh, ye shall die: but if ye through the Spirit do mortify the deeds of the body, ye shall live.
—ROMANS 8:13

The Lord, out of His absolute sovereignty, might deal with man in such a way as nothing should appear but His supreme will and almighty power, He might simply command obedience and, without any more persuasions, either leave men to the frowardness[1] of their own natures or else powerfully constrain them to their duty. However, He has chosen that way that is most suitable to His own wisdom and most connatural to man's nature to lay out before him the advantages and disadvantages, and to use these as motives and persuasions of His Spirit. For since He has by His first creation implanted in man's soul such a principle as moves itself upon the presentation of good or evil, in order that this might not be in vain, He administers all the dispensations of the law and gospel in a way suitable to that by propounding such powerful motives as may incline and persuade the heart of man.

The Two Contraries—Life or Death

It is true, there's a secret drawing withal necessary—the pull of the Father's arm and the power of the Holy Ghost—yet that

---

1. *frowardness*: defiance or obstinacy.

which is visible or sensible to the soul is the framing of all things so as to engage it upon rational terms. It is set between two contraries—death and life—death which it naturally abhors and life which it naturally loves. An even balance is holden up before the light of the conscience in which obedience and sin are weighed and it is found even to the convincing of the spirit of man that there are as many disadvantages in the one as advantages in the other.

This was the way that God used first with man in paradise. You remember the terms run so, "In the day thou eatest thou shalt die" (Gen. 2:17). He hedged him in on the one side by a promise of life, on the other by a threatening of death. And these two are very rational restraints, suited to the soul of man and its inward principles which are a kind of instinct to that which is apprehended good or gainful.

The Gospel Abounds in Inducements
Now, this verse runs even so in the form of words: "If you live after the flesh you shall die" (Rom. 8:13). You see this method is not changed under the gospel for, indeed, it is natural to the spirit of man and he has now much more need of all such persuasions, because there has been a great change of man's inclination to the worst side. All within is so disordered and perverse that a thousand hedges of persuasive grounds cannot do that which one might have done at first. Then, they were added out of superabundance but now, out of necessity; then, they were set about man to preserve him in his natural frame and inclinations but now, they are needful to change and alter them quite, which is a kind of creation. Hence says David, "Create in me a new spirit" (Ps. 51:10) and therefore the gospel abounds in variety of motives and inducements, in greater variety and of far more powerful inducements than the law.

The Covenant of Works and the Covenant of Grace
Here is that great persuasion taken from the infinite gain or

loss of the soul of man which, if anything be able to prevail, this must do, seeing it is seconded with some natural inclination in the soul of man to seek its own gain. Yet there is a difference between the nature of such like promises and threats in the first covenant and in the second. In the first covenant, though life was freely promised, yet it was immediately annexed to perfect obedience as a consequent reward of it. It was first promised unto complete righteousness of men's persons. But in the second covenant, first and principally life eternal, grace, and glory are promised to Jesus Christ and His seed, antecedent to any condition or qualification upon their part. And then again, all the promises that run by way of condition as, "He that believeth shall not perish," and "If you walk after the Spirit, you shall live" (cf. John 3:16; Gal. 5:16; Rom. 8:1). These are all the consequent fruits of that absolute gracious disposition and resignation of grace and life to them whom Christ has chosen.

Therefore, their believing, walking, and obeying come in principally as parts of the grace promised and as witnesses, evidence and confirmation of that life which is already begun and will not see an end. Besides that, by virtue of these absolute promises made to the seed of Christ, and Christ's complete performance of all conditions in their name, the promises of life are made to faith principally. For faith has this peculiar virtue to carry forth the soul to another's righteousness and sufficiency and to bottom it upon another. Then, in the next place, faith carries forth the soul to holy walking, though mixed with many infirmities. But in the first covenant, the promises of righteousness and holy walking were only annexed to perfect and absolute obedience.

The Consequences of Either Serving the Flesh or Walking in the Spirit

You have already heard in verse 12 of a strong inducement taken from the bond, debt, and duty we owe to the Spirit to walk after it, and the want of all obligation to the flesh. Now, if honesty and duty will not suffice to persuade you, you know in other things how with any honest man plain equity is a sufficient bond to him. Yet, consider what the apostle subjoins from the damage and from the advantage which may of themselves be the topics of persuasion and serve to drive in the nail of debt and duty to the head. If you will not take with this debt you owe to the Spirit but still persist in thinking that there is some greater obligation lying on you, such as caring for your bodies and satisfying them then, I say, behold the end of it—what fruit you must one day reap of the flesh and service of sin: "For if ye live after the flesh, ye shall die."

But then, consider the fruit you shall reap of the Spirit and holy walking: "ye shall live." It is true the flesh may flatter you more for the present, but the end of it will lie bitter as death—the flesh embraces you that it may strangle you.[2] And so if you knew all well you would not think you owed it anything but enmity and hatred and mortification. If your duty will not move you then let the love of yourselves and your souls persuade you, for it is an irrepealable statute: "The wages of sin is death" (Rom 6:23). Every way you choose to fulfill the lusts of your flesh and make provision for it, neglecting the eternal welfare of your souls, certainly shall prove to you to be as "the tree of the knowledge of good and evil"; it shall be like that forbidden fruit which, instead of performing what was promised, will bring forth death—the eternal separation of the soul from God.

The Varnished Bait on Satan's Hook

Adam's sin was a breviary[3] or epitome of the multiplied and enlarged sins of mankind. You may see in this tragedy all your fortunes (so to speak); you may behold in it the flattering insinuations and deceitful promises of sin and Satan who is a liar and murderer from the beginning and murdered man at first by lying to him. You find the hook covered over with the varnished bait

---

2. Amplectitur ut strangulet.
3. *breviary*: summary or condensed version.

of an imaginary life and happiness, satisfaction promised to the eye, to the taste, and to the mind. And upon these enticements man, bewitched and withdrawn from his God, pursues these vain and empty shadows by which, when he catches hold upon them, he himself is caught and laid hold upon by the wrath of God; hence he has been caught by death and all the miseries before it or after it.

Now, here is the map of the world for all that is in the world is but a larger volume of that same kind: "the lust of the eyes and the lust of the flesh and the pride of life" (1 John 2:16)! Albeit these lusts have been known and found to be the most notable and grossest deceivers. And every man, after he has spent his days in pursuit and labor for them, is constrained to acknowledge at length, though too late, that all that is in the world is but an imposture, a delusion, a dream, and worse. Yet every man hearkens after these same flatteries and lies that have cast down so many wounded and made so many strong ones to fall by them. Every man trusts the world and his own flesh as if they were of good report and of known integrity.

This is men's misery that no man will learn wisdom from others' expenses, from the woeful and tragic example of so many others; instead, men go on, even after the discovery of these deceivers, as confidently now as if this were the first time they had made such promises and used such fair words to men. Have they not been these six thousand years almost deluding the world? And have we not as many testimonies of their falsehood as there have been persons in all ages before us? After Adam tasted of this tree of pleasure and found another fruit growing on it, and that was death, should the posterity be so mad as to be meddling still with the forbidden tree? And wherefore forbidden? Because this tree's fruit is destructive to ourselves.

Everlasting Destruction
Know then and consider, beloved in the Lord, that you shall reap no other thing of all your labors and endeavors after the

flesh—all your toiling and perplexing cares, all your excessive pains in the making provision for your lusts and caring for the body only—you shall reap no other harvest of all but death and corruption. Death! You think that is a common lot and you cannot eschew it however. Nay, but the death here meant is of another sort in respect of which you may call "death-life." It is the everlasting destruction of the soul from the presence of God and the glory of His power. It is the falling of that infinite weight of the wrath of the Lamb upon you, in respect of which mountains and hills will be thought light and men would rather wish to be covered with them (Rev. 6:16).

Suppose now, you could swim in a river of delights and pleasures (which yet is given to none, for truly upon a just reckoning it will be found that the anxiety, grief, and bitterness that are intermingled with all earthly delights swallow up the sweetness of them) yet it will but carry you down ere you be aware into the sea of death and destruction, as the fish that swim and sport for a while in Jordan are carried down into the Dead Sea of Sodom, where they are presently suffocated and extinguished. As a malefactor is carried through a pleasant palace to the gallows so men walk through the delights of their flesh to their own endless torment and destruction.

The Argument of Our Debt to God's Goodness

Seeing then, my beloved, that your sins and lusts, which you are inclined and accustomed to, will certainly kill you if you entertain them, then nature itself would teach you the law of self-defense—to kill ere you be killed, to kill sin ere it kill you—to mortify the deeds and lusts of the body which abound among you, or they will certainly mortify you, that is, make you die. Now, if self-love could teach you this, which the love of God cannot persuade you to, yet it is well for being once led unto God and moved to change your course upon the fear and apprehension of the infinite danger that will ensue. Certainly, if you were but a little acquainted with the sweetness of this life and the goodness of your God, you would find the power of the former argument *a debito* (from debt and duty) upon your spirit. Let this once lead you unto God, and you will not want that which will constrain you to abide and never to depart from Him.

If through the Spirit you mortify the deeds of the body, you shall live. As sin decays you increase and grow, as sins die your souls live, and this shall be a sure pledge to you of that eternal life. And though this be painful and laborious yet consider that it is but the cutting off a rotten member that would corrupt the whole body. The want of it will never maim or mutilate the body; then you shall live perfectly when sin is perfectly expired and out of life; according as sin is nearer expiring and nearer the grave then your souls are nearer that endless life. If this does not move us what can be said next? What shall the Lord do more to His vineyard?

SERMON 35

Mortification Restores Human Dignity

> *For if ye live after the flesh, ye shall die: but if ye through the Spirit do mortify the deeds of the body, ye shall live. For as many as are led by the Spirit of God, they are the sons of God.*
> —ROMANS 8:13–14

The Believer's Duty, Reward, and Dignity

The life and being of many things consist in union; but separate them and they remain not the same, or else they lose their virtue. It is much more thus in Christianity; the power and life of it consists in the union of these things that God has conjoined, so that if any man pretend to one thing of it and neglect the other he has really none of them. And to hold to the subject in hand, there are three things which, joined together in the hearts of Christians, have a great deal of force: the duty of a Christian, his reward, and his dignity. His work and labor seem hard and unpleasant when considered alone, but the reward sweetens it when it is jointly believed. His duty seems too high, and his labor too great, yet the consideration of the real dignity he is advanced unto and privilege he has received will raise up the spirit to great and high attempts, enabling him to sustain great labors. Mortification is the work and labor; life, eternal life, is the reward. Following the Spirit is the Christian's duty, but to be the son of God—that is his dignity.

Mortification

Mortification sounds very harsh at first. The hearts of men say, "It is a hard saying, who can hear it?" (John 6:60). And indeed I cannot deny but it is so to our corrupt nature and therefore so held out in Scripture. The words chosen to press it express much pain and pains, much torment and labor. It is not so easy and trivial a business to forsake sin or subdue it as many think who only consider it easy because they have never tried it. It is a circumcision of the foreskin of the heart, and you know how it disabled a whole city (Gen. 34) and how it enraged the heart of a tender mother (Exod. 4:26).

For the believer it is the excision or cutting off a member and these the most dear and precious, be it the right hand or right foot, which is a living death, as it were, even to kill a man while he is alive. It is a new birth and the pains and throes of the birth are known. Regeneration certainly has a travailing pain within it, insomuch that Paul travailed in pain till it were accomplished in these: "My little children, of whom I travail in birth until Christ be formed in you" (Gal. 4:19). Though men conceive sin in pleasure, yet they cannot be rid of that deadly burden without throes and pains; to halve this work, or to be remiss or negligent in it, is as foolish and unwise as for a child to stay long in the place of breaking forth as the Lord complains of Ephraim: "He is an unwise son, for he should not stay long in the place of the breaking forth of children" (Hos. 13:13).

So with mortification: it is one of the greatest follies not to labor by all means to be rid of the encumbrances of sin; much violence offered to it and a total resignation of ourselves to God may be great pain, but it is short pain for then the pleasure is greater and continues. But now Christians lengthen their pain and draw out their cross and vexation to a great extent because they deal negligently in the business, they suffer the Canaanites to live, and these become thorns and briars in their sides continually.

The Pain of Mortification

Then this business is called mortification, as the word is here and Colossians 3:5, which imports a higher degree of pain, for the agonies of death are terrible; and to hold it out yet more, the most painful and lingering kind of death is chosen to express it—crucifixion (Gal. 5:24). Now, indeed, that which makes the forsaking of sin so grievous to flesh and blood is the engagements of the soul to it, the oneness that is between it and our natures as they are now fallen. For you know pain arises upon the dissolution or division of anything that is continued or united; and these things that are so nearly conjoined it is hard to separate without much violence. And truly, as the kingdom of heaven suffers violence, so we must offer violence to ourselves, to our lusts and inclinations, which are almost ourselves. Therefore, if you would be truly Christians this must be your business and employment: to cut off these things that are dearest unto you; to cast out the very idols your hearts sacrifice unto; and, if there be anything more one with you than another, to endeavor to break the bond with that and to be at the furthest distance from it.

It is easy to persuade men to forsake some sins and courses that they are not much inclined to and find not much pleasure or profit by them. You may do that and yet be dead in sins. But if indeed you aim at true mortification, you must consider what are the chief idols and predominant inclinations of your heart. Then you must set yourself impartially against all known idols, particularly against your most beloved sin, because it interrupts most the communion of God and separates you from your Beloved. For the dearer it is to you, the more dangerous certainly it is.

The Spirit's Help

But to encourage and hearten you to this: I would have you look back to that former victory that Christ has gained in our name and look about to the assistance you have for the present, that is, the Spirit to help you. Truly, my beloved, this will be a dead business, if you be not animated and quickened by these considerations—that Christ died to sin and lived to God and that in this He was a public person representing you; thus you may conclude with Paul, "I am crucified with Christ" (Gal. 2:20), and again, "We are buried with him by baptism into his death" (Rom. 6:4). Consider that mystical union with Christ crucified and life shall spring out of His cross, out of His grave, to kill sin in you; for the great business is done already, and victory gained in our Head, "This is our victory, even faith" (1 John 5:4). Believe! and then you will have overcome—even before you overcome—for this will help you to overcome in your own persons.

Then, consider and look round about to the strong helper you have, the Spirit: "If ye through the Spirit do mortify...." Stronger is He that is in you than he that is in the world. Though He does not vent all His power to you, yet you may believe that there is a secret, latent virtue in the seed of grace that cannot be wholly overcome or conquered for there is one engaged in the warfare with us who will never leave us nor forsake us. Of set purpose He withdraws His help now and then to disclose our weakness to us that we may cleave the faster to Him; He never lets sin get any power or gather any strength, but out of wisdom He acts to make the final victory the more glorious.

The Need for Obedience to the Spirit

In a word, He leads us through our weaknesses, infirmities, fainting, and wrestling that His strength may be perfected in weakness—that when we are weak, then we may be strongest in Him (2 Cor. 12:9). Our duty then is to follow this Spirit wheresoever He leads us. Christ, the captain of our salvation, when He went to heaven sent the Spirit to be our guide to lead us thither where He is, and therefore we should resign and give up ourselves to His guidance and direction. The nature of a creature is dependence, so the very essence of a Christian consists in dependence and subordination to the Spirit of God. Nature itself would teach them that want wisdom to commit themselves to those who have it and not to carry the reins of their own life themselves.

Truly, not only the sense of our own imperfection, of our folly and ignorance in these things that belong to life, should make us willing to yield ourselves over to the Spirit of God, as blind men to their leader, as children to their nurses, as orphans to their tutors. But also, because the Spirit is made our tutor and leader, Christ and our Father have left us to the Spirit in His latter will. Therefore, as we have absolute necessity, so He has both willingness and ability because this is the Spirit's office. "O Lord, I know," says Jeremiah, "that the way of man is not in himself; it is not in man that walketh to direct his steps" (Jer. 10:23). Oh, it were a great point of wisdom thus to know our ignorance and folly, for this is the great qualification of Christ's disciples to be as simple as children, as little children, as void of conceit of their own wisdom (Mark 10:15).

This simplicity alone capacitates the soul to receive the impressions of wisdom; as an empty table is fittest to write upon, so a soul must be emptied of itself. On the other hand, self-conceit draws a number of foolish, senseless drafts in the mind so that it cannot receive the true image of wisdom. Thus, then, when a soul finds that it has misled itself, being misguided by the wild fire of its lusts and has hardly escaped perishing and falling headlong in the pit, this disposes the soul to a willing resignation of itself to one wiser and more powerful, the Spirit of God; and so he gives the Spirit the string of his affections and judgment to lead him by, and he walks willingly in that way to eternal life since his heart was enlarged with so much knowledge and love.

Do Not Grieve the Spirit

And now, having given up yourselves thus, you would carefully eye your leader and attend all His motions that you may conform yourself to them. Whensoever the Spirit pulls you by the heart and draws at your conscience to drive you to prayer—

or any such duty—do not resist that pull, do not quench the Spirit lest He leaves you alone and does not call you or speak to you. If you fall out thus with your leader, then you must guide yourselves and truly you will guide yourselves into the pit, if left to yourselves. Therefore, make much of all the impulses of your conscience, of all the touches and inward motions of light and affection, to entertain these and draw them forth in meditation and action. For these are nothing else but the Spirit your leader, plucking at you to follow Him. And if you sit when He rises to walk—if you neglect such warnings—then you may grieve Him and this cannot but in the end be bitterness to you.

Certainly, many Christians are guilty in this, and prejudge themselves of the present comfort and benefit of this inward anointing that teaches all things and of this bosom guide that leads into all truth. Because they are so heavy and lumpish to be led after Him, they drive slowly and take very much pressure and persuasion to any duty, whereas we should accustom ourselves to willing and ready obedience upon the least signification of his mind. Yea, and which is worse, we often resist the Holy Ghost. He draws but we hold on to beloved sins; He pulls but we pull back from the most spiritual duties. There is so much perversity and frowardness yet in our natures that there needs the almighty draft of His arm to make it straight, as there is need of infinite grace to pardon it.

Now, my beloved, those of you who have in your desires and affections resigned yourselves over to the guidance of this Spirit and this be your real and sincere endeavor to follow it, in as far as you are carried back by temptation and corruption or retarded in your motion, if this is your lamentation before the Lord I have this to say unto you: cheer your hearts and lift them up in the belief of this privilege conferred upon you—you "are the sons of God," for He gives this tutor and pedagogue to none but to his own children. As many as are led by the Spirit of God, they are the sons of God.

The Dignity of the Children of God

Suppose you cannot exactly follow His motions but are often driven out or turned back, yet has not the Spirit the hold of your heart? Are you not detained by the cord of your judgment and the law of your mind? And is there not some chain fastened about your heart which makes it outstrip the practice by desires and affections? You are the sons of God. That is truly the greatest dignity and highest privilege, in respect of which, all relations may blush and hide their faces. What are all the splendid and glistering titles among men but empty shows and vanishing sounds in respect of this? To be called the son of a gentleman, of a nobleman, of a king, how much the sons of men do pride themselves in it? But, truly, that puts no intrinsic dignity in the persons themselves—it is a miserable poverty to borrow praise from another, and truly he that boasts of his parentage praises that which is another's, not his own.[1] But this dignity is truly a dignity; it puts intrinsic worth in the person and puts a more excellent spirit in them than that which is in the world, as is said of Caleb (Num. 14:24). Besides, it entitles to the greatest happiness imaginable.

---

1. Aliena laudat non sua.

SERMON 36

The Spirit of Adoption, Part I

For as many as are led by the Spirit of God, they are the sons of God. For ye have not received the spirit of bondage again to fear; but ye have received the Spirit of adoption, whereby we cry, Abba, Father. —ROMANS 8:14–15

Like Parent, Like Child

Children do commonly resemble their parents, not only in the outward proportion and feature of their countenances, but also in the disposition and temper of their spirits. Further, generally they are inclined to imitate the customs and carriage of their parents, so that they sometimes may be accounted the very living images of such persons; hence in them men are thought to outlive themselves. Now, indeed, they that are the sons of God are known by this character that they are led by the Spirit of God. And there is the more necessity and the more reason, too, of this resemblance of God and imitation of Him in His children, because that very divine birth that they have from heaven consists in the renovation of their natures and assimilation to the divine nature. Consequently, because they are possessed with an inward principle that carries them powerfully toward a conformity with their heavenly Father, it becomes their great study and endeavor to observe all the dispositions and carriage of their heavenly Father which are so honorable and high and suitable to Himself that they at least may breathe and halt after the imitation of Him.

Therefore, our Lord exhorts us and takes a domestic example and familiar pattern to persuade us the more by: "Be you perfect, as your heavenly Father is perfect" (Matt. 5:48). And there is one perfection He especially recommends for our imitation—mercifulness and compassion toward men, as opposed to the violence, fury, and implacableness, the oppression, revenge, and hatred that abounds among men (Luke 6:36). Generally, in all His ways of holiness and purity, goodness and mercy, we ought to be followers of Him as dear children, who are not only obliged by the common law of sympathy between parents and children, but moreover are engaged by the tender affection that he carries to us (Eph. 5:1).

The Spirit's Direction

Now, because God is high as heaven and His ways, thoughts, and dispositions are infinitely above us, the pattern seems to be so far out of sight that it is given over as desperate by many to attempt any conformity to it. Therefore, it has pleased the Lord to put His own Spirit within His own children to be a bosom pattern and example and it is our duty to resign ourselves to His leading and direction. The Spirit brings the copy near to us, and though we cannot attain, yet we should follow after. Though we cannot make out the lesson, yet we should be scribbling at it, for the more we exercise ourselves this way, setting the Spirit's direction before our eyes, the more perfect shall we be.

It is high time, indeed, to pretend to this—to be a son or a daughter of God. It is a higher word than if a man could deduce his genealogy from an uninterrupted line of a thousand kings and princes. There is more honor, true honor, in it and profit too. It is that which enriches the poorest and ennobles the basest, inconceivably beyond all the imaginary degrees of men. Now, my beloved, this is the great design of the gospel, to bestow this incomparable privilege upon you, "to become the sons of God" (John 1:12). But it is sad to think how many souls scarce think upon it and how many delude themselves in it. But consider, that as many as are the sons of God are led by the Spirit of God—they have gotten a new leader and guide other than their own fancy or humor which once they followed in the ignorance of their hearts. It is lamentable to conceive how the most part of us is acted and driven and carried headlong, rather than gently led, by our own carnal and corrupt inclinations. There are men pretending to Christianity yet hurried away with every self-pleasing object as if they were not master of themselves, furiously agitated by violent lusts, miscarried continually against the very dictates of their own reason and conscience. And I fear there is too much of these even in those who have more reason to assume this honorable title of sonship.

I know not how we are exceedingly addicted to self-pleasing in everything. Whatsoever our fancy or inclination suggests to us, that we must do without more bands if it be not directly sinful. Whatsoever we apprehend, that we must vent and speak it out, though to little or no edification. Like that of Solomon, we deny our hearts nothing they desire except the grossness of it restrain us (Eccl. 1–2). Now, certainly if we knew what we are called to, who are the sons of God, we could not but disengage more with ourselves even in lawful things and give over the conduct of our hearts and ways to the Spirit of our Father, whom we may be persuaded of that He will lead us in the ways of pleasantness and peace.

The Spirit Brings Confidence, Not Fear
Now, the special and peculiar operations of the Spirit are expressed in the following words. There are some workings of the Spirit of God that are but introductory and subservient to more excellent works and, therefore, they are transient, not appointed to continue long for they are not His great intendment. Of this kind are those terrible representations of sin and wrath, of the justice of God which put the soul in a fear, a trembling fear and, while such a soul is kept within the apprehension of sin and judgment, it is shut up, as it were, in bondage.

Though it be true that in the conversion of a sinner there is always something of this in more or less degrees, nevertheless it is not the great design of the gospel to put men in fear but rather to give them confidence. Neither is it the great intendment of God in the dispensation of the law to bring a soul in bondage under terror but rather by the gospel to free them from that bondage. Therefore, the apostle has reason to express it thus: You have not received the spirit of bondage again to fear.

The Spirit of Adoption
But there are other operations of the Spirit which are chiefly intended and principally bestowed as the great gift of our Father to express His bounty and goodness toward us; from these He is called the Spirit of adoption and the Spirit of intercession. He is the Spirit of adoption, not only in regard of that witness-bearing and testification to our consciences of God's love and favor and our interest in it as in verse 16, but also in regard of that childlike disposition of reverence, love, and respect that He begets in our hearts toward God as our Father. From both of these flows this next work, crying, "Abba, Father," aiding and assisting us in presenting our necessities to our Father, making this the continued vent of the heart in all extremities, to pour out all that burdens us in our Father's bosom. And this gives marvelous ease to the heart, releasing it from the bondage of care and anxiety which it may be subject to, after the soul is delivered from the fear and bondage of wrath.

The Spirit's Seasonable Work of Fear
Let us speak, then, to these in order. The first working of the Spirit is *to put a man in fear of himself*, and in such a fear as mightily straitens and embondages the soul of man. In itself this *fear* can neither be so pleasant nor excellent as to make it come under the notion of any gift from God, for it rather has the nature of a torment and punishment, having some sparkle of hell already kindled in the conscience. Yet it has become beautiful and

seasonable in its use and end, because the Spirit makes it usher in the pleasant and refreshing sight of a Savior and it brings to that *man* the report of God's love to the world in Christ.

It is true, all men are in bondage to sin and Satan, shut up in the darkness of ignorance and unbelief and bound in the fetters of their own lusts, which are as the chains that are put about malefactors before they go to prison. "Whosoever commits sin is the servant of sin" (John 8:34). And to be a servant of sin is slavery under the most cruel tyrant. All these things are true, yet how few souls do apprehend them seriously or are weary of their prison! How few do groan to be delivered! Nay, the most part account it only liberty to hate true deliverance as bondage. But some there are whose eyes the Spirit of God opens and lets them see their bondage and slavery and how they are concluded under the most heavy and weighty sentence that ever was pronounced. That sentence is the curse and wrath of the ever-living God, nor is there any way to flee from it or escape it through anything they can do or know.

Now indeed, this serious discovery cannot choose but make the heart of a man to tremble as with David: "My flesh trembleth for fear of thee; and I am afraid of thy judgments" (Ps. 119:120). Such a serious representation will make the stoutest and proudest heart to fall down and faint for fear of that infinitely intolerable weight of deserved wrath. Then it is that the soul is in a sensible bondage that before was in a real, but insensible bondage; then it is environed about with bitter accusations, with dreadful challenges; then it is that the law of God arrests and confines the soul within the bounds of its own accusing conscience. And this is some previous representation of that eternal imprisonment and banishment from the presence of God.

Wanton Liberty
Albeit many of you are free from this fear and enjoy a kind of liberty to serve your own lusts and are not sensible of any thralldom of your spirits. Nonetheless, certainly the Lord will

sometime arrest you and bring you to this spiritual bondage when He shall make the iniquities of your heels encompass you about and the curses of His law surround you. When your conscience accuses you and God condemns you it may be too late and out of date.

Alas! then what will you do who now put your conscience by and will not hearken to it or be put in fear by anything which can be represented to you? We do not desire to put you in fear where no fear is, but only where there is infinite cause of fear and when it is possible that fear may introduce faith and be the forerunner of these glad tidings that will compose the soul. We desire only you may know what bondage you are really into, whether it be observed or not, that you may fear lest you be enthralled[1] in the chains of everlasting darkness, and so may be persuaded to flee from it before it be irrecoverable. To the most part of men who do not feel their bondage, what a vain and empty sound is the gospel of liberty by a Redeemer! Who believes its report, or cares much for it—because it is necessity that casts a beauty and luster upon it or takes the scales off our eyes and opens our closed ears?

The Divine Purpose Is to Unveil the Redeemer's Beauty
Now for you, who either are or have been detained in this bondage and have come under the fearful apprehension of the wrath of God and the sad remembrance of your sins, know that this is not the prime intention and grand business to torment you, as it were, before the time. There is some other more beautiful and satisfying structure to be raised upon this foundation. I would have you improve it thus: to commend the necessity—the absolute necessity—of a Redeemer and to make him beautiful in your eyes. Do not dwell upon that as if it were the ultimate or last work but know that you are called in this rational way to come out of yourselves into this glorious liberty of the sons of

---

1. *enthralled*: enslaved.

God, purchased by Christ, and revealed in the gospel. Know that you have not received the spirit of bondage only to fear but to drive you to faith in a Savior. And then you ought to walk so as not to return to that former thralldom of the fear of wrath, but to believe His love.

SERMON 37

The Unspeakable Privilege of Adoption

> For as many as are led by the Spirit of God, they are the sons of God. For ye have not received the spirit of bondage again to fear; but ye have received the Spirit of adoption, whereby we cry, Abba, Father.   —ROMANS 8:14–15

Contrary Misapprehensions Can Rob Believers of Their Joy and Peace

The life of Christianity, taking it in itself, is the most pleasant and joyful life that can be, exempted from those fears and cares, those sorrows and anxieties, that all other lives are subject to. For of necessity this must be the force and efficacy of true religion—if it be indeed true to its name—to disburden and ease the heart and fill it with all manner of consolation. Certainly, it is the richest of subjects and is most completely furnished with all variety of delights to entertain a soul that can be imagined. Yet, I must confess, while we consult with the experience and practice of Christians, this bold assertion seems to be much weakened; then too much ground is given to confirm the contrary misapprehensions of the world who take it to be a sullen, melancholic, and disconsolate life, attended with many fears and sorrows.

Alas, it is too evident that many Christians are kept in bondage almost all their lifetime through fear of eternal death. How many dismal representations of sin and wrath are in the souls of some Christians, keeping them in much thralldom? At least, who is it that is not once and often brought in bondage after conversion and made to apprehend fearfully their own estate? And who has constant uninterrupted peace and joy in the Holy Ghost or lies under such direct beams of divine favor but, alas, it is sometimes eclipsed, and their souls filled with the darkness of horror and terror? For truly, the most part of believers do not taste so much sweetness in religion as to make them incessant and unwearied in the ways of godliness.

The Word of God Does Not Deceive Us Regarding Joy and Peace
Yet, notwithstanding all of this, we must vindicate Christianity itself and not impute these things unto it which are the infirmities and faults of the followers of it who do not improve it unto such a use or use it so far as in itself it is capable. Indeed, although it is true that often we are brought to fear again, yet withal it is certain that our allowance is larger and that we have received the Spirit, not to put us in bondage again to fear, but rather to seal to our hearts that love of God which may not only expel fear but bring in joy. I wish that it were deeply considered by all of us that there is such a life as this attainable—that the Word of God does not deceive us in promising fair things which it cannot perform; would that we could realize there is a certain reality in the life of Christianity, in that peace, joy, tranquility, and serenity of mind are held out, and that some have really found it and do find it. The reason why all of us do not find it in experience is not because it is not real but because we have so little apprehension of it and diligence to seek after it.

It is strange that all men who have pursued satisfaction in the things of this life, being disappointed—one generation witnessing this to another and one person to another—notwithstanding, men are this day as fresh in the pursuit of earthly fulfillment, as big in the expectations as ever. And yet, in this business of religion and the true happiness to be found in it, though the oracles of God in all ages have testified from heaven how certain and possible it is and though many have found it in experience and left it on record to others, there is so slender belief of the reality and certainty of it and so slack pursuit of it as if we did not believe it at all. Truly, my beloved, there is a great mistake in this, and it is general too. All men apprehend other things more feasible and attainable than personal holiness and happiness in Christianity. But truly, I conceive there is nothing in the world so practicable as this—nothing made so easy, so certain to a soul that really minds it.

The Problem of Superficial Faith
Let us take it so then: the fault is not religion's that those who profess it are subject to so much fear and care and disquieted with so much sorrow. It is rather because Christianity does not sink into the hearts and souls of men but only puts a tincture on their outside; or it is because the faith of divine truths is so superficial and the consideration of them so slight that they cannot have much efficacy and influence on the heart to quiet and compose it. Is it any wonder that some souls be subject again to the bondage of fear and terror when they do not stand in awe to sin? Much liberty to sin will certainly embondage the spirit of a Christian to fear.

Suppose a believer in Jesus Christ be exempted from the hazard of condemnation, yet he is the greatest fool in the world that would on that account venture on satisfaction to his lusts. For though it be true that he be not in danger of eternal wrath, yet he may find so much present wrath in his conscience as may make him think it was a foolish bargain. He may lose so much of the sweetness of the peace and joy of God as all the pleasures of sin cannot compensate. Therefore, to the end that you, whose souls are once pacified by the blood of Christ and composed by His Word of promise, may enjoy that constant rest and tranquility as not to be enthralled again to your old fears and terrors, I would advise and recommend to you two things.

Two Recommendations
The first is that you would be much in the study of that allowance which the promises of Christ afford. Be much in the serious apprehension of the gospel, and certainly your doubts and fears would vanish at one puff of such a rooted and established meditation. Think what you are called to, not "to fear" again but rather to love and honor Him as a Father. And second, take heed to walk suitably and preserve your seal of adoption unblotted, unrusted. You would study so to walk as you may not cast dirt upon it or open any gap in the conscience for the reentry of these hellish-like fears and dreadful apprehensions of God.

Certainly, it is impossible to preserve the spirit in freedom if a man be not watchful against sin and corruption. David prays, "reestablish me with thy free Spirit" (Ps. 51:12), as if his spirit had been abased, embondaged, and enthralled by the power of that corruption. If you would have your spirits kept free from the fear of wrath, study to keep them free from the power of sin for such a freedom is but a fruit of this. Moreover, it is most suitable that the soul that cares not to be in bondage to sinful lusts should, by the righteousness of God tempered with love and wisdom, be brought under a bondage he would not desire, namely, a bondage of fear and terror—the fear of God's wrath; it is by the bitterness of this second holy bondage that the Lord makes him know how evil is the first bondage, that is, the bondage to his sinful lusts.

Come to the Redeemer to Find Rest
It is usual on such a Scripture as this to propound many questions and debate many practical cases: as to whether a soul after believing can be under legal bondage; as to wherein these differ—the bondage of a soul after believing and in its first conversion; as to how far that bondage of fear is preparatory to faith, and many such like questions. But I choose rather to hold forth the simple and naked truth for your edification, than put you upon to entertain you in such needless jangling and contentions. All I desire to say to a soul in bondage is to exhort him to come to

the Redeemer and to consider that his case calls and cries for a deliverance. Come, I say, and he shall find rest and liberty to his soul. All I would say to souls delivered from this bondage is to request and beseech them to live in a holy fear of sin and jealousy over themselves; in this way they may not be readily brought under the bondage of the fear of wrath again. Perfect love casts out the fear of hell, but perfect love brings in the fear of sin. You that love the Lord, hate ill and if you hate it you will fear it in this state of infirmity and weakness, wherein we are.

And if at any time, through negligence and carelessness of walking, you lose the comfortable evidence of the Father's love and be reduced again to your old prison of legal terror, do not despair for that. Do not think that such a thing could not befall a child of God and from that ground do not raze former foundations, for the Scripture saith not that whosoever believes once in Christ and receives the Spirit of adoption, cannot fear again; for we see it otherwise in David, in Heman,[1] in Job,[2] and all holy saints. But the Scripture saith, "You have not received the spirit of bondage" for that end, "to fear again." It is not the allowance of your Father. Your allowance is better and larger, if you knew it, and did not sit below it.

Two Gifts through the Spirit of Adoption

Now, the great gift and large allowance of our Father is expressed in the next words, "But you have received the Spirit of adoption," which Spirit of adoption is a Spirit of intercession to make us cry to God as our Father. These are two gifts of adoption, that is, the sinner under the second holy bondage and the privilege of sonship through the Spirit of adoption, revealing the love and *mercy of God* to the heart and framing it to a soul like a disposition. Compare the two states together and it is a marvelous change: a condemned rebel pardoned and then adopted to be a son of

---

1. See the ascription to Psalm 88, "Maschil of Heman the Ezrahite."
2. See Job's answer to Eliphaz the Temanite in Job 16–17.

God; a sinner under bondage—a bondslave to sin and Satan—not only freed from that intolerable bondage but advanced to this liberty to be made a son of God.

This will be the continued wonder of eternity and that whereabout the song of angels and saints will be. Accursed rebels expecting nothing but present death, sinners arraigned and sentenced before His tribunal and already tasting hell in their consciences and in fear of eternal perishing, not only to be delivered from all that but to be dignified with this privilege, to be the sons of God—to be taken from the gibbet to be crowned! That is the great mystery of wisdom and grace revealed in the gospel, the proclaiming whereof will be the joint labor of all the innumerable companies above for all eternity.

Adoption Is an Unspeakable Privilege
Now, if you ask how this estate is attainable the Spirit Himself tells us, "As many as believed (or received) him, to them he gave the privilege to be the sons of God" (John 1:12). The way is made plain and easy. Christ the Son of God, the natural and eternal Son of God, became the Son of Man. To facilitate this He has taken on the burden of man's sin, the chastisement of our peace, and so the glorious Son of God He became like the wretched and accursed sons of men. Therefore, God has proclaimed in the gospel, not only an immunity and freedom from wrath to all that in the sense of their own misery cordially receive Him as He is offered, but also the unspeakable privilege of sonship and adoption for His sake who became our elder brother (Gal. 4:4–5). Men that want children used to supply their want by adopting some beloved friend in the place of a son; this is a kind of supply of nature for the comfort of them that want.

But it is strange that God having a Son so glorious, the very character of His person, and "the brightness of his glory" (Heb. 1:3), in whom He delighted from eternity; it is strange, I say, that He should in a manner lose and give away His only begotten Son that He might by His means adopt others, poor despicable creatures, yea, rebellious, to be His sons and daughters. Certainly, this is an act infinitely transcending nature—such an act that has an unsearchable mystery in it, into which angels desire to look, and never cease looking, because they never see the bottom of it (1 Peter 1:12). It was not out of indigence He did it, not for any need He had of us, or comfort expected from us, but absolutely for our necessity and consolation that He might have sons and daughters upon whom to pour the riches of His grace.

SERMON 38

The Spirit of Adoption, Part II

But ye have received the Spirit of adoption, whereby we cry, Abba, Father. —ROMANS 8:15

"Behold what manner of love the Father has bestowed upon us, that we should be called the sons of God" (1 John 3:1). It is a wonderful expression of love to advance His own creatures to such a dignity who are not only infinitely below Himself but also fallen far below other creatures. Lord, what is man that You so magnified him! For it surpasses wonder that rebellious creatures, His enemies, should have not only their rebellions freely pardoned but this privilege of sonship bestowed upon them; that He should take enemies and make sons of them, not only sons, but heirs, coheirs with His own only begotten Son. And then, how He makes them sons is as wonderful as the thing itself, that He should make His own Son our brother, "bone of our bone and flesh of our flesh" (cf. Gen. 2:23 and Heb. 2:14–17), and make Him spring out as a branch or rod out of the dry stem of Jesse, who Himself was the root of all mankind (Isa. 11:1, 10).

The Glorious Exchange

This is the way God sent His Son, made of a woman under the law, that we might receive adoption as sons (Gal. 4:5). The house of heaven marries with the earth, with them who have their foundation in the dust, the chief heir of that heavenly family joins in kindred with our base and obscure family and by this means we are made of kin to God. "But of him are you in Christ Jesus" (1 Cor. 1:30). It behooved Christ, in a manner, to lose His own sonship as to men and to have it so veiled and darkened by the superadded interest in us and His nearness to us. He was so properly a Son of Man, subject to all human infirmities (except sin) that without eyes of faith men could not perceive that He was the Son of God. And by this wonderful exchange are we made the sons of God.

Whoever, in the apprehension of their own enmity and distance from God, receives Christ Jesus offered as the peace—the bond of union between the two families of heaven and earth that were at an infinite odds and distance—whoever (I say), believes thus in Him and flies to Him is made a child of God. But they must desire to lay down the weapons of their warfare, for their peace is not only made by that marriage which Christ made with our nature but furthermore they are blessed with this power and privilege to be the sons and daughters of the Most High. And from thence you may conclude that if God be your Father you can want nothing that is good. But the determination of what is good for you, whether in spiritual enlargements or in the things of this life, you must refer to His wisdom for His love indeed is strong as death—nothing can quench it. In the point of reality and constancy there is nothing to shadow it out among men.

The Wise Love of God
The love of women is earnest and vehement but that is nothing to it (Isa. 49:15), for they may forget but He cannot. Yet His love is not a foolish dotage, like man's that is often miscarried with fancy and lust; rather is it a rational and wise affection, administered and expressed with infinite reason and wisdom; therefore, He chooses rather to profit us than to please us in His dealings. And we who are not so fit to judge and discern our own good should commit all to His fatherly and wise providence.

Therefore, if you be tempted to anxiety and carefulness of mind either through the earthliness of your dispositions or the present straits of the time, you who have resigned yourself to Jesus Christ should call to mind that your heavenly Father cares for you. And what need for you to care too?

Why not use your lawful callings and be diligent in them? This is not to prejudge that but if you believe in God then you are obliged by that profession to abate from the superfluous tormenting thoughtfulness that is good for nothing; it will only make you more miserable than your troubles can make you, and to make you miserable before you are miserable is to anticipate your sorrows. If you say that God is your Father, you are tied to devolve yourselves over on to Him and trust in His goodwill and faithfulness, and to sit down quietly as children that have parents to provide for them.

Adoption—The Greatest Gift Imaginable

Now, the other gift is great too, the "Spirit of adoption"; and because you are sons therefore has He given you "the Spirit of his Son" says this apostle (Gal. 4:6). And so it is a kind of consectary[1] of the great privilege and blessed estate of adoption. They who adopt children usually give them some kind of token to express their love to them. But as the Lord is higher than all and this privilege to be His son or child is the greatest dignity imaginable, so this gift of His Spirit suits the greatness and glory and love of our Father. It is a father's gift indeed, a gift suitable to our heavenly Father. If a father that is tender of the education of his child and would desire nothing so much as that he might be of a virtuous and gracious disposition and good ingine,[2] I think if He were to express His love in one wish it would be this: that he might have such a Spirit in him and this he would account better than all that He could leave him.

---

1. *consectary*: corollary or consequence.
2. *ingine*: good natural intelligence or cleverness.

But if it were possible to transmit a gracious, well-disposed, and understanding spirit from one to another and if men could leave it, as they do their inheritance to their children, certainly a wise and religious parent would first make over a disposition of such a spirit to his children. As Elisha sought a double measure of Elijah's spirit (2 Kings 2:9), so a father would wish such a measure to his children and, if it were possible, give it. But that may not be. All that can be done is to wish well to them and leave them a good example for imitation.

Our Hearts Are in His Hand
But in this our heavenly Father transcends all in that He can impart His own Spirit to His adopted children and His Spirit is in a manner the very essential principle that makes them children of the Father. Their natures, their dispositions, are under His power. He can as well reform them as you can change your children's garments. He can make of us what He will. Our hearts are in His hand as the water, capable of any impression He pleases to put on it. And this is the impression He puts on His children: He puts His Spirit in their hearts and writes His law in their inward parts (Heb. 8:10), a more divine and higher work than all human persuasion can reach. This Spirit they receive as an earnest of the inheritance and, withal, to make them fit for the inheritance of the saints in light (Eph. 1:13–14; Col. 1:12).

The First Work of the Spirit of Adoption

Now, the working of this Spirit of adoption I conceive to be threefold, beside that of intercession expressed in the verse. The first work of the Spirit of adoption, that wherein a father's affection seems to break first from underground, is the revealing to the heart the love and mercy of God to sinners. I do not say it is revealed to such a soul in particular for that application is neither first nor universal. But herein the Spirit of adoption first appears from under the cloud of fear; and this is the first opening of the prison of bondage wherein a soul was shut when the plain way of reconciliation to God in Christ and delivery from the bondage of sin and wrath is holden out. When such words as these come into the soul they are received with some gladness: "God so loved the world that he gave his Son" (John 3:16), and "This is a true and faithful saying" (1 Tim. 1:15), and "Come, you that labor and are weary, and I will give rest to your souls" (Matt. 11:28). When a soul is made to hear the glad tidings of liberty preached to captives—of light to the blind, of joy to the heavy in spirit, of life to the dead—though he cannot come to such a length as to see his own particular interest, yet the very receiving affectionately and greedily such a general report as good and true gives some ease and relaxation to the heart.

To see deliverance is possible is some door of hope to a desperate sinner. But to see and espy it more than a possibility, even as a great probability though he cannot reach a certainty, that will be as the breaking open of a window of light in a dark dungeon. It will be as the taking off some of the hardest fetters and the worst chains which make a man almost to think himself at liberty.

Now this is the great office of the Spirit of the Father, to beget in us good thoughts of Him, to incline us to charitable and favorable constructions of Him and make us ready to think well of Him, to beget a good understanding in us and Him and correct our jealous misapprehensions of Him. For certainly we are naturally suspicious of God that He deals not in sad earnest with us. Whenever we see the height of our provocation, and weight of deserved indignation, we think Him like ourselves and can hardly receive without suspicion the gospel that lays open His love in Christ to the world.

The Spirit Enables Us to Understand Spiritual Truths

Now, this is the Spirit's work to make us entertain that honorable thought of God that He is most inclinable to pardon sinners; and that His mercy is infinitely above man's sin; and that it is no prejudice to His holiness or justice; and to apprehend seriously a constant reality and solid truth in the promises of the gospel; and so to convince a soul of righteousness (John 16:8), that there is a way of justifying a sinner or ungodly person without wrong to God's righteousness; and all this being well pondered in the heart and received in love, the great business is done. After that, particular application is easier, of which I shall not speak now because occasion will be given in the next verse about the Spirit's witnessing with our spirits which is another of the Spirit's working.[3]

Only I say this now—that which makes this so difficult is a defect in our grasp of the first work of the Spirit. For the common principles of the gospel are not really or seriously apprehended because many souls do not put their seal to witness to the promises and truth of it. Therefore, the Lord often denies this seal and witness to our comfort. It is certainly preposterous the way Satan puts upon souls, first, to get such a testimony from the Spirit before they labor to grasp such a testimony to Christ and so echo or answer in their hearts to His Word. This way seems shortest; for they would leap into the greater liberty at the first hand. But certainly, it is farthest about, because it is impossible for souls to leap immediately out of bondage to assurance, without some middle step. They cannot pass thus from extremes to extremes without going through the middle state of receiving Christ and laying His Word up in the heart. Therefore, it proves the way furthest about because when souls have long wearied themselves, they must at length turn in hither.

The Second Work of the Spirit of Adoption

But there is a second working of the Spirit I wish you were acquainted with. As the first work is to beget a suitable apprehension of God's mind and heart toward sinners, so the next is

---

3. Sadly, Binning never reached the next verse in his expositions for he died prematurely of consumption at age twenty-six.

to beget a suitable disposition in our hearts toward God as a Father. The first apprehends His love, the second reflects it back again with the heart of a sinner to Him. The Spirit first brings the report of the love and grace of God to us, and then we carry the love and respect of the heart up to God.

You know how God complains in Malachi 1:6, "If I then be a Father, where is my fear and honour?" For these are the only fitting qualifications of children, such a reverent, respective observance of our heavenly Father, such affectionate and humble carriage toward Him, as becomes both His majesty and His love. These are tempered one with another in Him, His love not abasing His majesty and His majesty not diminishing His love. So we ought to carry ourselves so that reverence and confidence, fear and love, may be contempered one with another, and so as we may neither forget His infinite greatness, nor doubt of His unspeakable love. And this inward disposition, engraved on the heart, will be the principle of willing and ready obedience. It will in some measure be our meat and drink to do our Father's will. For Christ gave us an example how we should carry toward Him. How humble and obedient was He, though His only begotten Son!

SERMON 39

What a Man Is on His Knees before God in Prayer, That He Is and That Alone[1]

Whereby we cry, Abba, Father.
—ROMANS 8:15

As there is a light of grace in bestowing such incomparably high dignities and excellent gifts on poor sinners such as making them the sons of God who were the children of the devil and heirs of a kingdom who were heirs of wrath, so there is a depth of wisdom in the Lord's allowance and manner of dispensing His love and grace in this life. For though the love be wonderful that we should be called the sons of God, yet, as that apostle speaks, it does not yet so clearly appear what we shall be by what we now are (1 John 3:2). Our present condition is so unlike such a state and dignity and our enjoyments so unsuitable to our rights and privileges, it would not appear by the mean, low and indigent state we are now into that we have so great and glorious a Father. How many infirmities are we compassed about with! How many wants are we pressed withal! Our necessities are infinite and our enjoyments no ways proportioned to our necessities.

His Grace Is Sufficient in Our Infirmities

Notwithstanding even in this, the love and wisdom of our heavenly Father shows itself and oftentimes more gloriously in the

---

1. Words written by Robert Murray M'Cheyne.

theater of men's weakness, infirmities, and wants than they could appear in the absolute and total exemption of His children from necessities. Strength perfected in weakness and grace sufficient in infirmities have some greater glory than strength and grace alone. Therefore, He has chosen this way as most fit for the advancing of His glory. It is a way most suitable for our comfort and edification to give us but little in hand and environ us with a crowd of continued necessities and wants within and without, in order that we may learn to cry to Him as our Father and seek our supplies from Him.

Withal, He has not been sparing but liberal in promises of hearing our cries and supplying our wants; so that this way of narrow and hard dispensation that at first seems contrary to the love and bounty and riches of our Father, in the perfect view of it appears to be the only way to perpetuate our communion with Him. Indeed, often it must renew the sense of His love and grace that would grow slack in our hearts if our needs did not every day stir up fresh longing. Thus, His returns by this means are so much the more refreshing.

There is a time of children's minority when they stand in need of continual supplies from their parents or tutors because they have not yet entered into possession of their inheritance. While they are in this state, there is nothing more beseeming them in all their wants than to address to their father and represent them to him. It is fit they should be from hand to mouth, as we say, that they may know and acknowledge their dependence on their father.

For Our Needs We Have "The Messenger of Prayer"
Truly this is our minority. Our presence in the body which, because of sin that dwells in our bodies and their own natural weakness and incapacity, keeps us at much distance from the Lord that we cannot be intimately present with Him. Now, in this condition, the most natural, most comely and becoming exercise of children is to cry to our Father to present all our grievances. Thus, to

entertain some holy correspondence with our absent Father by the messenger of prayer and supplication which cannot return empty if it be not sent away because it is too full of self-conceit. This is the most natural breathing of a child of God in this world. It is the most proper acting of his new life and the most suitable expiration of that Spirit of adoption that is inspired into him, since there is so much life as to know what we want, and our wants are infinite.

Therefore, that life cannot but beat this way in holy desires after God whose fullness can supply all wants. This is the pulse of a Christian that goes continually and there is much advantage to the continuity and incessancy of the motion, arising from the infinity and multiplicity of our needs in this life and the continual assaults that are made by necessity and temptation on the heart: But ye have received the Spirit of adoption, whereby we cry, Abba, Father. He puts in his own name, "we," in the latter part, though theirs, "ye," was in the former part.

Human Dignity Is Bestowed on All with Impartiality
When he speaks of a donation or privilege, he supplies it to the meanest to show that the lowest and most despised creature is not in any incapacity to receive the greatest gifts of God. Then, when he mentions the working of that Spirit in way of intercession, because it imports necessity and want, he cares not to commit some incongruity in the language by changing the person, that he may teach us that weakness, infirmities, and wants are common to the best and chiefest among Christians. Also, that the most eminent have continual need to cry and the lowest and obscurest believers have as good ground to believe the hearing and acceptance of their cries. Thus we see that the highest are not above the weakest and lowest ordinance, and that the lowest are not below the comfort of help and acceptation in him.

Hindrances to the Spirit of Prayer

Nay, the growth and increase of grace is so far from exempting men from, or setting them above, this duty of constant supplication that, by the contrary, this is the just measure of their growth and altitude in grace. As the degrees of the height of the waters of the Nile in its overflowing are a sure sign of the fertility or barrenness of that year, so the overflowing of the spirit of prayer in a man gives a present account how his heart is—whether barren and unfruitful in the knowledge of Jesus Christ, or fruitful and lively and vigorous in it. It is certain that contraries do discover one another and the more the one be increased that is not only the more incompatible and inconsistent with the other, it gives the most perfect discerning of it. When grace is only but as twilight in the soul and the early dawn of the day, gross darkness and uncleanness is seen; but the more it grows into the perfect day, the more sin is seen and the more its hated wants are discovered that at first did not appear. Therefore, it exercises itself the more in its opposition to sin and supplication to God.

To speak the truth, our growth here is but an advancement in the knowledge and sense of our indigency, it is but a further entry into the idolatrous temple of the heart which makes a man see daily new abominations worse than the former. And therefore, you may easily know that such repeated sights and discoveries will but press out more earnest and frequent cries from the heart. And such a growth in humility and faith in God's fullness will be but as oil to feed the flame of supplication. For what is prayer, indeed, but the ardency of the affection after God, flaming up to him in cries and requests?

To speak of this exercise of a holy heart would require more of the spirit of it than we have. But truly it is to be lamented that though there be nothing more common among Christians in the outward practice of it, yet there is nothing more extraordinary and rarer even among many that use it, than to be acquainted with the inward nature of it. Truly, the most ordinary things in religion are the greatest mysteries as to the true life of them. We are strangers to the soul and life of these things which consist in the holy behavior and deportment of our spirits before the Father of spirits.

The Spirit of Prayer Does Not Arise from Great Learning
These words give some ground to speak of some special qualifications of prayer and the chief principle of it. The chief principle and origin of prayer is the Spirit of adoption received into the heart. It is a business of a higher nature than can be taught by precepts or learned by custom and education. There is a general mistake among men that the gift of prayer is attained by learning and that it consists in the freedom and plenty of expression. But oh, how many doctors and disputers of the world are there who can defend all the articles of faith against the opposers of them; yet so unacquainted are they with this exercise that the poor, unlearned, and nothings in the world, who cannot dispute for religion, send up a more savory and acceptable sacrifice and sweet incense to God daily when they offer up their soul's desires in simplicity and sincerity!

Certainly, this is a spiritual thing, derived only from the Fountain of spirits—this grace of pouring out our souls before Him and keeping communication with Him. The variety of words and riches of expression are but the shell of it, the external shadow. All the life consists in the frame of the heart before God. And this none can put in frame but He that formed the spirit of man within him. It may be that some through custom of hearing and using it attain to a habit of expressing themselves readily in it to the satisfaction of others; but, alas, they may be strangers to the first letters and elements of the life and spirit of prayer. I would have you who want both, look up to heaven for it.

Too Few Know How to Pray
Many of you cannot be induced to pray in your families (and, I fear, little or none in secret which is indeed a more serious

work). This is because you have not been used or taught to pray or such like. Alas, beloved, this comes not through education or learning! It comes from the Spirit of adoption. Therefore, if you say you cannot pray, you have not the Spirit; and if you have not the Spirit you are not the sons of God. Know what is in the inevitable sequel of your own confessions: "Now, if any man have not the Spirit of Christ, he is none of his" (v. 9).

But I hasten on to the qualifications of this divine work—fervency, reverence, and confidence; fervency in crying, reverence and confidence in crying, *Abba, Father,* for these two suit well toward our Father. The first, fervency, I fear, we must seek elsewhere than in prayer. I find it spent on other things of less moment. Truly, all the spirit and affection of men run in another channel—in the way of contention and strife, in the way of passion and miscalled zeal. And because these things whereabout we do thus earnestly contend have some interest or coherence with religion we not only excuse but approve our vehemence. But oh, much better were that employed in supplications to God: that were a divine channel.

Again, the marrow of other men's spirits is exhausted in the pursuit of things in the world. The edge of their desires is turned that way and it must needs be blunted and dulled in spiritual things that it cannot pierce into heaven and prevail effectually. I am sure many of us who are so cold in it use this excuse that we do not warm ourselves. And how shall we think to prevail with God? Our spirits make little noise when we cry all the louder. If we can scarce hear any whisper in our hearts, then how shall He hear us? Certainly, it is not the extension of the voice that pleases Him; it is the cry of the heart that is sweet harmony in His ears.

Prayer Must Become an Inner Fire
You may easily perceive this if you but consider that He is an infinite Spirit that pierces into all the corners of our hearts and has all the darkness of it as light before Him. How can you think that such a Spirit can be pleased with lip cries? How can He

endure such deceit and falsehood (who has so perfect a contrariety with all false appearances) that your heart should lie so dead and flat before him, and the affection of it turned quite another way? There were no sacrifices without fire in the Old Testament and that fire was kept perpetually. Therefore, there can be no prayer now without some inward fire, conceived in the desires, blazing up, and growing into a flame in the presenting of them to God.

The incense that was to be offered on the altar of perfume (Ex. 3:1–8), behooved to be beaten and prepared; and truly, prayer would do well to be made out of a beaten and bruised heart and contrite spirit—a spirit truly sensible of its own unworthiness and wants. And that beating and pounding of the heart will yield a good fragrant smell as some spices do not till beaten. The incense was made of divers spices (Ex. 30:22–25), intimating to us that true prayer is not one grace alone but a compound of graces. It is the joint exercise of all a Christian's graces; seasoned with all. Every one of them gives some peculiar fragrancy to it, as humility, faith, repentance, love, and so on.

A Final Appeal
The acting of the heart in supplication is a kind of compend and result of all these graces, just as one perfume is made up of many simples. But above all, as with the incense, our prayers must be kindled by fire on the altar. There must be some heat and fervor, some warmness, conceived by the Holy Spirit in our hearts which may make our spices send forth a pleasant smell as many spices do not till they get heat. Let us lay this engagement on our hearts: to be more serious in our addresses to God the Father of spirits. Above all, let us present our inward soul before Him, before whom it is naked and open, even though we do not bring it. And certainly, frequency in prayer will much help us to fervency and to keep it when we have it.

SERMON 40

Toward Understanding the Precious Privilege of Prayer

> *Whereby we cry, Abba, Father.*
> —ROMANS 8:15

Fervency in Prayer

All that know anything of religion must know and confess that there is no exercise either more suitable to him that professes it or more needful for him than to give himself to the exercise of prayer. But that which is confessed by all and, as to the outward performance, is gone about by many, yet I fear is a mystery sealed up from us as to the true and living nature of it. There is much of it expressed here in few words, "whereby we cry, Abba, Father." The divine constitution and qualifications of this divine work are here made up of a temper of fervency, reverence, and confidence. The first, *fervency*, I spoke of before; but I fear our hearts were not well heated then or may have cooled since.

It is not the loud noise of words that is best heard in heaven or that is constructed to be crying to God. No, this is transacted in the heart more silently to men, but it strikes up into the ears of God. His ear is sharp and that voice of the soul's desires is shrill and, though it were out of the depths, they will meet together. It is true, the vehemency of affection will sometimes cause the extension of the voice; but yet it may cry as loud to heaven when it is kept silent within.

I do not press such extraordinary degrees of fervor as may affect the body, but I would rather wish we accustomed ourselves to a solid, calm seriousness and earnestness of spirit which might be more constant than such raptures can be. Then we might always gather our spirits to what we are about and advocate them from impertinent wanderings and fix them upon the present object of our worship. This is to worship Him in spirit who is a Spirit.

Reverence in Prayer
The other thing that composes the sweet temper of prayer is *reverence*. And what more suitable whether you consider Him or yourselves? "If I be your Father, where is my honour? and if I be your Master, where is my fear?" (Mal. 1:6). While we call Him Father, or Lord, we proclaim this much that we ought to know both our distance from Him and His superiority to us. And if our worship in prayer does not carry this character nor express this honorable and glorious Lord whom we serve, it wants that congruity and suitableness to Him that is the beauty of it. Is there anything more unbecoming than for children to behave themselves irreverently and irrespectively toward their fathers to whom they owe themselves? It is a monstrous thing even in nature, and to nature's light.

Oh, how much more abominable must it be to draw near to the Father of spirits who made us and not we ourselves, in whose hand is our breath and whose are all our ways! In a word, we owe not only this dust to Him, but the living spirit that animates it and was breathed from heaven; and finally, it is He "in whom we live, and move, and have our being" and well-being (Acts 17:28). How could we worship such a one and yet behave ourselves so unbecomingly and irreverently in His presence, our hearts not stricken with the apprehension of His glory but lying flat and dead before Him, having scarcely in our thoughts the One we speak to?

In conclusion, our deportments in His sight are such as could not be admitted in the presence of any person a little above ourselves—to be about to speak to them and yet to turn aside continually to everyone that comes by and entertain communication with every base creature. This, I say, in the presence of a king or nobleman would be accounted the most absurd incivility as could be committed. And yet we behave ourselves just so with the Father of spirits.

Heavenly Beings Rest neither Day nor Night in Praising God
Oh, the wanderings of the hearts of men in divine worship! While we are in communication with our Father and Lord in prayer, are our hearts fixed to a constant attendance and presence by the impression of His glorious holiness? Whose spirit does not continually gad abroad, taking notice of everything that occurs, so marring his soul's correspondence? Oh that this word (Ps. 89:7) were written with great letters on our hearts: "God is greatly to be feared in the assembly of the saints, and to be had in reverence of all those that are about him." That one word, *God*, says it all. Either we must convert Him into an idol which is nothing; or if we apprehend Him to be GOD, we must apprehend our infinite distance from Him and His unspeakable, inaccessible glory above us.

He is greatly feared and reverenced in the assemblies that are above, in the upper courts of angels. Those glorious spirits must cover their feet from us because we cannot see their glory, but they must cover their faces from Him because they cannot behold His glory. What a glorious train has He and yet how reverent are they! They wait round about the throne, above and about it, as courtiers upon their king, for they are all ministering spirits and they rest not day and night to adore and admire that holy One, crying, "Holy, holy, holy, the whole earth is full of his glory" (Isa. 6:2). Now, how much more then should He be greatly feared and had in reverence in the assembly of His saints, of poor mortal men whose foundation is in the dust and in the clay, and besides drink in iniquity like water?

Those in Heaven Are Pure but We on Earth Are Defiled

There are two points of difference and distance between God and us. He is nearer angels for angels are pure spirits, but we have flesh which is furthest removed from His nature. And then angels are holy and clean; yet even theirs is but spotted to His unspotted holiness. But we are defiled with sin which puts us farthest off from Him and which His holiness has greatest antipathy at. Let us consider this, my beloved, that we may carry the impression of the glorious holiness and majesty of God on our hearts whenever we appear before Him and so we may serve and rejoice with trembling and pray with reverence and godly fear.

If we apprehend indeed our own quality and condition—how low and base it is, how we cannot endure the very clear aspect of our own consciences—we cannot look on ourselves steadfastly without shame and confusion of face at the deformed spectacle we behold. Much less would we endure to have our souls opened and presented to the view of other men, even the basest of men. Would we not be overwhelmed with shame if they could see into our hearts? Now then, apprehend seriously what He is, how glorious in holiness; consider how infinite in wisdom He is, how the secrets of your souls are plain and open in His sight. Then I am persuaded you will be composed to a reverent, humble, and trembling behavior in His sight.

We Must Rejoice with Trembling and Have Confidence with Reverence

But withal I must add this that because He is your Father you may intermingle confidence; nay, you are commanded so to do, for this honors Him as much as reverence. For confidence in God as our Father is the best acknowledgment of the greatness and goodness of God. It declares how able and willing He is to save us and so ratifies all the promises of God made to us, setting a seal to His faithfulness. There is nothing He accounts Himself more honored by than a soul's full resigning itself to Him, relying on His power and goodwill in all necessities and casting its care upon Him as a loving Father, who cares for us.

Truly, there is much beauty and harmony in the juncture of these two, rejoicing with trembling, confidence with reverence, to ask nothing doubting and yet sensible of our infinite distance from Him and the disproportion of our requests to His highness. A childlike disposition is composed thus as also the temper and carriage of a courtier has these ingredients in it. The love of his Father and the favor of his Prince makes him take liberty and assume boldness; withal, he is not unmindful of his own distance from his Father or master. "Let us draw near with a true heart with full assurance of faith" (Heb. 10:22).

There is much in the Scripture, both exhorted, commanded, and commended, of that παρρησια, that liberty and boldness of pouring out our requests to God as One that certainly will hear us and grant that which is good. Unbelief spoils all. It is a wretched and base-spirited thing that can conceive no honorable thoughts of God, but only thinks of itself. But faith is the well-pleasing ingredient of prayer. The lower thoughts a man has of himself make him conceive the higher and more honorable of God. "My ways are not your ways, nor my thoughts as your thoughts, but as far above as the heavens above the earth" (Isa. 55:8). This is the rule of a believing soul's conceiving of God and expecting from Him. When a soul is thus placed on God by trusting and believing in Him, it is fixed: "His heart is fixed, trusting in the Lord" (Ps. 112:7).

Our Souls Are Inconstant until Anchored to God's Promises

Oh, how wavering and inconstant is a soul till it fix at this anchor, upon the ground of His immutable promises! It is tossed up and down with every wind, it is double-minded, now one way, then another, now in one mind, and shortly changed; indeed, the soul is like the sea, capable of the least or greatest commotion (James 1:6–8). I know not anything that will either fix your hearts from wandering in prayer or establish your hearts from trouble and disquiet after it, nothing that will so exoner and ease your spirits of care, as laying hold on God as all-sufficient. You must lay this constraint on your hearts: wait on Him and His pleasure, cast your souls on His promises that are so full and so free; there abide as at your anchor-hold in all the vicissitudes and changes of outward or inward things.

In spiritual things that concern your salvation—that which is absolutely necessary—you may take the boldness to be absolute in it and say as Job, "though he should slay me, yet will I trust in him" (Job 13:15), and as Jacob, "I will not let you go, except you bless me" (Gen. 32:26). But either in outward things that have some usefulness in them but are not always fittest for our highest good, or in the degrees of spiritual gifts and measures of graces, the Lord calls us without anxiety to pour out our hearts in them unto Him. But withal we would do it with submission to His pleasure because He knows best what is best for us. In these, we are not bound to be confident to receive every particular we ask, but rather our confidence should pitch upon His goodwill and favor that He will certainly deny nothing that He Himself knows is good for us. And so, in these we should absolutely cast ourselves without carefulness upon His loving and fatherly providence and resign ourselves to Him to be disposed of in them as He sees convenient.

Imposing Restrictions upon God Ends in Disappointment
There is sometimes too much limitation of God and peremptoriness used with Him in such things, in which His wisdom craves a latitude both in public and private matters, even as men's affections and interests are engaged. But it is ordinarily attended and followed with shame and disappointment in the end. And there is, on the other hand, intolerable remissness and slackness in many in pressing even the weightiest petitions of salvation,

mortification, and so on, which certainly arise from the diffidence and unbelief of the heart and the want of that rooted persuasion, both of the incomparable necessity and worth of the things themselves and of His willingness and engagement to bestow them.

The word is doubled here, "Abba, Father," the Syriac and Greek words signifying one thing, expressing the tender affection and love of God toward them that come to Him. "He that cometh to God must believe that he is, and that he is a rewarder of them that seek him diligently" (Heb. 11:6). So he that comes to God must believe that He has the bowels and compassion of a Father and will be more easily inclined with our importunate cries than the fathers of our flesh. He may suffer His children to cry long but it is not because He will not hear but rather because He would hear them longer, for He delights to hear their cry oftener. If He delays, it is His wisdom to appreciate and endear His mercies to us and to teach us to press our petitions and sue for an answer.

A Final Assurance That God Hears His People's Prayers

Besides, it is much for our comfort that, from whomsoever and whatsoever corner in the world, prayers come up to Him and they cannot want acceptance. All languages, all countries, all places are sanctified by Jesus Christ. Therefore, whosoever calls upon the name of the Lord from the ends of the earth shall be saved. And truly it is a sweet meditation to think that from the ends of the earth the cries of souls are heard; and that the end is as near heaven as the middle; and a wilderness is as near as a paradise. Though we understand not one another, yet we have one loving and living Father that understands all our meanings. And so, the different languages and dialects of the members of this body make no confusion in heaven but meet together in His heart and affection and are one perfume, one incense, sent up from the whole catholic church which here is scattered on the earth. Oh, that the Lord would persuade us to cry this way to our Father in all our necessities!